18th Annual Conference of the European Association for Machine Translation (EAMT 2015)

Antalya, Turkey
11 – 13 May 2015

Editors:

İlknur Durgar El-Kahlout
Mehmed Özkan
Felipe Sánchez-Martínez
Gema Ramírez-Sánchez
Fred Hollowood
Andy Way

ISBN: 978-1-5108-1187-4

Printed from e-media with permission by:

Curran Associates, Inc.
57 Morehouse Lane
Red Hook, NY 12571

proceedings.com

Some format issues inherent in the e-media version may also appear in this print version.

Printed by Curran Associates, Inc. (2015)

For permission requests, please contact the Association for Computational Linguistics
at the address below.

Association for Computational Linguistics
209 N. Eighth Street
Stroudsburg, Pennsylvania 18360

Phone: 1-570-476-8006
Fax: 1-570-476-0860

acl@aclweb.org

Additional copies of this publication are available from:

Curran Associates, Inc.
57 Morehouse Lane
Red Hook, NY 12571 USA
Phone: 845-758-0400
Fax: 845-758-2634
Email: curran@proceedings.com
Web: www.proceedings.com

EAMT 2015

Proceedings of the 18th Annual Conference of the European Association for Machine Translation

Antalya, Turkey

May 11 - 13, 2015 at the WOW Topkapı Palace

Edited by

İlknur Durgar El-Kahlout

Mehmed Özkan

Felipe Sánchez-Martínez

Gema Ramírez-Sánchez

Fred Hollowood

Andy Way

Organized by

Contents

Foreword

It has been a huge honour for me to serve as president of the European Association for Machine Translation (EAMT) over the past six years. As I step down from office, I am delighted that the last EAMT annual conference under my presidency is being held in the beautiful location of Antalya, Turkey. This continues the policy I started in 2009 of bringing EAMT to new regions of Europe. This began with our first visit to the Iberian peninsula (Barcelona, 2009), our first conference in France in 2010 (St. Raphaël), followed by the Benelux region in 2011 (Leuven), continuing in 2012 with our first conference hosted in Italy (Trento), followed by the 2014 meeting in Croatia (Dubrovnik). Quite coincidentally, you may have noticed that we have journeyed step-by-step from West to East, almost 4,000km in fact! Just to give you a little hint, next year's conference starts to reverse this trend, but only just! Of course, you'll have to wait until the closing session of this year's meeting before you find out the actual 2016 conference location!

The EAMT organised its first Workshop/Conference back in 1996, and now we come to our Eighteenth Annual Conference in 2015. It is fair to say that for many, our EAMT conferences are pencilled in long in advance as not-to-be missed events. As well as running successful conferences over longer periods of time with much larger numbers of attendees than in the past, in 2012 we ran the very successful MT Summit in Nice on behalf of the whole MT community. All these things provide clear evidence to me that the EAMT as an organisation is continuing to grow and thrive. As I've often noted before, since its inception in 1997, the EAMT has not raised its membership rates, and we will continue to hold the cost of membership for 2015. Joining us is great value, especially in years like this when more than one IAMT-affiliated event takes place: as well as EAMT, we will converge later in the year on Miami, for MT Summit XV. The close cooperation with the other regional associations, which started with help from Alon Lavie and Hitoshi Isahara – including mutual conference discounts for all IAMT members – continues, despite both AMTA (George Foster) and AAMT (Hiromi Nakaiwa) having elected new presidents. As this is my last conference as EAMT president, I can only hope that this partnership continues and thrives in the future.

As ever, I would like to thank my colleagues on the EAMT Committee. They work tirelessly on behalf of all of us, and we are truly fortunate to have such a strong body of colleagues representing our Association. This year, there are significant changes to your Committee, which we will announce during the General Assembly. I urge all of you to consider contributing to this service to the community. I would like to thank all those who have helped me on the Committee over the past 6 years; it is testament to them all that our Association remains strong, and in good hands for the future.

As in the recent past, I am confident that the programme that has been assembled for this 18th Conference is a strong one, which will be of great interest to you all. I would like to thank the Programme Co-Chairs Felipe Sánchez-Martínez (Research track) and Gema Ramírez-Sánchez and Fred Hollowood (User track), for their assistance in helping assemble the programme you have before you, comprising Research and User tracks, poster sessions, and a terrific Invited Speaker in Olga Beregovaya. As in recent conferences, we continue to feature a special session featuring prominent FP7/H2020 projects, which has proven very popular in the past.

Last but not least, I would especially like to thank our local organizer, İlknur Durgar El-Kahlout, who very generously volunteered to hold the meeting in Antalya. We are very grateful to İlknur and her team for their excellent organization of this event.

Finally, thanks to all of you for coming. I hope you all enjoy the conference, that you benefit from the excellent programme that has been assembled, and that you go away from here having made new friends.

Andy Way
Deputy Director of ADAPT,
School of Computing,
Dublin City University.

President of the EAMT
away@computing.dcu.ie

Preface by the Programme Chairs

It is our pleasure to welcome you to the 18th Annual Conference of the European Association for Machine Translation (EAMT) to be held in Antalya, Turkey. We really enjoyed serving as a programme committee chairs for this year edition of which has become the most important event on machine translation in Europe for developers, researchers, users, professional translators and translation/localisation managers. As in previous editions, the conference is organised in three different tracks: a research track in which unpublished research results in machine translation and related areas are reported; a user track where users of machine translation companies, language service providers, government agencies and non-government organisations report their experience on using and adapting machine translation in their organisations; and a project and product description track where products and projects on machine translation have the opportunity to reach the broad audience of the conference.

We received 46 submissions to the research track, 7 submissions to the user track and 20 project/product descriptions. All these papers come from more than 20 different countries. Each of the research and user papers were peer-reviewed by three independent reviewers from the program committee. Following the reviewers' suggestion, one of the papers submitted to the research track was redirected to the user track; of the remaining 45 papers, 24 (53\%) were accepted for their publication in the conference proceedings: 10 of them were selected for oral presentation, whereas 14 will be presented as a poster. In the user track 4 papers were accepted (57\%), three of them were selected for oral presentation and one will be presented as a poster. In the project/product description track 18 papers were selected for presentation as a poster.

We will enjoy an invited talk by Olga Beregovaya, current Vice President of Language Tools at Welocalize, who has an extense experience of over 15 years in the localisation industry. We hope all attendees, researchers and users, will find her talk highly appealing. We will also have a presentation by the winner of the EAMT Best Thesis Award. Poster presenters will have a two-slides, two-minutes presentation of their papers in a poster boaster session.
We thank all the Programme Committee members and sub-reviewers, whose names are subsequently listed, for their detailed extensive reviews and useful recommendations which where vital in helping us to decide the papers to accept. We also thank all the authors, who tried their best to incorporate the reviewers' suggestions when preparing their camera-ready papers. For those papers that were not accepted we hope that the reviewers' comments will help them to improve their papers for their submission somewhere else. Special thanks goes to Mikel L. Forcada, who took care of the project/product description track.

Finally, a big thank you goes to the local organising committee and to all the authors who made this conference both possible and successful. We hope that the resulting selection of papers represents the best of machine translation research, development and real-world usage.

Felipe Sánchez-Martínez	*Gema Ramírez-Sánchez*	*Fred Hollowood*
Universitat d'Alacant	Prompsit Language Enginnering	Fred Hollowood Consulting

EAMT 2015 Programme Committee co-chairs

Message from the Conference Chair

It is my privilege and great pleasure to welcome you in WOW Topkapı Hotels for the 18th Conference of the European Association for Machine Translation. I am very proud that the EAMT conference is organized this time in Antalya, the tourism capital and most beautiful province of Turkey on the Mediterranean coast.

This year's conference format is the same as those of the last three years, two and half days of oral and poster sessions, followed by a social programme. I hope you will enjoy the high quality papers in three different tracks – research, user and product/project – that will give an overview of current developments and trends in Machine Translation.

The conference will be held at the WOW Topkapı Hotel Osmanlı Halls. Sessions and coffee breaks will be hosted in front of the conference room. Lunches will be served in the Hünkar restaurant in a separated area for EAMT'15 participants. I hope you will enjoy the social events that we have organized: the welcome reception in the Cariye Pool and the conference banquet on the beach of WOW Kremlin Palace. On the last day of the conference, a cultural tour will be organized to Kurşunlu and Perge.

I will have to express my gratitude to the EAMT Board for providing us with the opportunity to host the 18th EAMT conference; especially Andy Way, Mikel Forcada, Viggo Hansen, and Tony Clarke who helped me whenever needed. It was a great pleasure to work with you. I would like to thank the Program Chair, Felipe Sánchez-Martínez, and User Co-chairs Gema Ramírez-Sanchez and Fred Hollowood for taking care of the large number of submissions and for preparing the programme.

This conference would not be possible without the efforts of many people involved in its organization; our organizational partner DEKON particularly Kubilay Şahin and Kübra Şenkahveci who worked hard to prepare a successful setup for the conference, local organization co-chair Mehmed Özkan and our local organization committee members Kemal Oflazer, Coşkun Mermer, Yücel Bicil, Şeniz Demir and Alper Kanak who volunteered for the organization and helped during every stage of the preparations.

Lastly, I am grateful to our sponsors for their generous contributions; gold sponsor STAR, bronze sponsors KuveytTürk, Ebay, and Universal, Welcome Reception Sponsor SesTek and lastly lunch sponsor Welocalize.

I wish you a very successful 18th EAMT conference in Antalya. Enjoy both the academic program and Antalya during your stay!

İlknur Durgar El-Kahlout
TÜBİTAK-BİLGEM
ilknur.durgar@tubitak.gov.tr

EAMT 2015 Committees

Chairs

General Chair of the Conference: Andy Way - (Dublin City University, Ireland)
Research Programme Chair: Felipe Sánchez-Martínez - (Universitat d'Alacant, Spain)
User Programme Co-chair: Gema Ramírez-Sánchez - (Prompsit Language Engineering, Spain)
User Programme Co-chair: Fred Hollowood - (Fred Hollowood Consulting, Ireland)
Local Organization Co-chair: Mehmed Özkan -(Boğaziçi University)
Local Organization Co-chair: İlknur Durgar El-Kahlout -(TÜBİTAK-BİLGEM)

Local Organizing Committee

Kemal Oflazer (CMU- Qatar)
Coşkun Mermer (TÜBİTAK-BİLGEM)
Yücel Bicil (TÜBİTAK-BİLGEM)
Şeniz Demir (TÜBİTAK-BİLGEM)
Alper Kanak (TÜBİTAK-BİLGEM)

Research Committee

Jesús Andrés-Ferrer (Nuance Communications, USA)
Eleftherios Avramidis (German Research Center for Artificial Intelligence (DFKI), Germany)
Bogdan Babych (University of Leeds, UK)
Loïc Barrault (Université du Maine, France)
Núria Bel (Universitat Pompeu Fabra, Spain)
Nicola Bertoldi (Fondazione Bruno Kessler, Italy)
Laurent Besacier (Université J. Fourier, France)
Alexandra Birch (University of Edinburgh, UK)
Arianna Bisazza (University of Amsterdam, Netherlands)
Hervé Blanchon (Laboratoire d'Informatique de Grenoble, France)
Ondřej Bojar (Charles University in Prague, Czech Republic)
Nicola Cancedda (Applied Researcher at Microsoft, UK)
Michael Carl (Copenhagen Business School, Denmark)
Francisco Casacuberta (Universitat Politècnica de València, Spain)
Helena Caseli (Universidade Federal de São Carlos, Brazil)
Mauro Cettolo (Fondazione Bruno Kessler, Italy)
David Chiang (University of Notre Dame, USA)
Marta R. Costa-Jussà (Institute For Infocomm Research, Singapore)
Adrià De Gispert (University of Cambridge, UK)
Jinhua Du (Xi'an University of Technology, China)
Nadir Durrani (University of Edinburgh, UK)
Marc Dymetman (Xerox Research Centre Europe, France)
Andreas Eisele (Directorate-General for Translation (EC), Luxembourg)
Cristina España-Bonet (Universitat Politècnica de Catalunya, Spain)
Mireia Farrús (Universitat Pompeu Fabra, Spain)
Christian Federmann (Microsoft, USA)
Mark Fishel (University of Zurich, Switzerland)
Mikel L. Forcada (Universitat d'Alacant, Spain)

George Foster (National Research Council, Canada)
Federico Gaspari (Dublin City University, Ireland)
Ulrich Germann (University of Edinburgh, UK)
Jesús Giménez (Nuance Communications, USA)
Meritxell Gonzalez (Universitat Politècnica de Catalunya, Spain)
Barry Haddow (University of Edinburgh, UK)
Christian Hardmeier (University of Uppsala, Sweden)
Yifan He (New York University, USA)
Kenneth Heafield (Bloomberg Labs, USA)
Teresa Herrmann (Karlsruhe Institute of Technology, Germany)
Hieu Hoang (University of Edinburgh, UK)
Matthias Huck (University of Edinburgh, UK)
Gonzalo Iglesias (University of Cambridge, UK)
Jie Jiang (Applied Language Solutions, UK)
Marcin Junczys-Dowmunt (Adam Mickiewicz University, Poland)
Philipp Koehn (John Hopkins University, USA)
Roland Kuhn (National Research Council, Canada)
Alon Lavie (Carnegie Mellon University, USA)
Qun Liu (Dublin City University, Ireland; Chinese Academy of Sciences, China)
Yanjun Ma (Baidu, China)
Pavel Pecina (Charles University in Prague, Czech Republic)
Juan Antonio Pérez-Ortiz (Universitat d'Alacant, Spain)
Maja Popovic (German Research Center for Artificial Intelligence (DFKI), Germany)
Stefan Riezler (Heidelberg University, Germany)
Mike Rosner (University of Malta, Malta)
Raphael Rubino (Prompsit Language Engineering, Spain)
Kepa Sarasola (Euskal Herriko Unibertsitatea, Spain)
Lane Schwartz (University of Illinois, USA)
Holger Schwenk (University of Le Mans, France)
Kashif Shah (University of Sheffield, UK)
Khalil Simaan (University of Amsterdam, Netherlands)
Michel Simard (National Research Council, Canada)
Lucia Specia (University of Sheffield, UK)
Ankit Srivastava (Dublin City University, Ireland)
Sara Stymne (Uppsala University, Sweden)
Jörg Tiedemann (Uppsala University, Sweden)
Antonio Toral (Dublin City University, Ireland)
Dan Tufis (Academia Romana, Romania)
Marco Turchi (Fondazione Bruno Kessler, Italy)
Francis M. Tyers (UiT Norgga árktalaš universitehta, Norway)
Antal van Den Bosch (Radboud University Nijmegen, Netherlands)
Josef van Genabith (German Research Center for Artificial Intelligence (DFKI), Germany)
Vincent Vandeghinste (University of Leuven, Belgium)
David Vilar (Nuance Communications, USA)
Martin Volk (University of Zurich, Switzerland)
Andy Way (Dublin City University, Ireland)

Jürgen Wedekind (University of Copenhagen, Denmark)
François Yvon (Université Paris Sud, France)

User Committee

Jeff Allen (SaP, France)
Nora Aranberri (Euskal Herriko Uni, Spain)
Diego Bartolomé (Tauyou, Spain)
Olga Beregovata (Welocalise, US)
Eric Blassin (Lionbridge, France)
Arancha Caballero (Nuadda, Spain)
James Cogley (Microsoft, Ireland)
Arnaud Daix (Euroscript, Luxembourg)
Pedro Díez (Linguaserve, Spain)
Stephen Doherty (UNSW, Australia)
Kurt Eberle (Lingenio, Germany)
Wojceich Froelich (Argos, Poland)
Tatiana Gornostay (Tilde, Latvia)
Declan Groves (Microsoft, Ireland)
Manuel Herranz (Pangeanic, Spain)
Maxim Khalilov (bmmt, Germany)
Paul Mangell (alphacrc, UK)
Jay Marciano (Lionbridge, US)
Daniel Marcu (Uni Southern Calif, US)
John Moran (CNGL, Ireland)
Hideyuki Namiki (Sony, Japan)
Antoni Oliver (UOC, Spain)
Patricia Palidini (CA, Spain)
John Papaioannou (Lexcelera, France)
Niko Papula (Multilizer, Findland)
Mirko Plitt (Modulo Language Automation, Switzerland)
Phil Ritchie (Vistatec, Ireland)
Johann Roturier (Symantec, Ireland)
Javier Sastre (Ateknea Solutions, Spain)
Indra Semite (Tilde, Latvia)
Jean Senellart (Systran, France)
Pilos Spyridon (EC, Belgium)
Ventsislav Zhechev (Autodesk, Switzerland)

Sub-Reviewers

Sariya Karimova (Heidelberg University, Germany)
Arefeh Kazemi (University of Isfahan, Iran)
Gideon Maillette de Buij Wenninger (University of Amsterdam, Netherlands)
Carolina Scarton (University of Sheffield, UK)
Maarten van Gompel (Radboud University Nijmegen, Netherlands)
Longyue Wang (University of Macau, China)

Acknowledgments

The European Association for Machine Translation acknowledges with gratitude the support and sponsoring of the following institutions ahd companies:

Gold Sponsor

STAR

Bronze Sponsors

KUVEYT TÜRK
INFORMATION TECHNOLOGIES
R&D Center

ebay

universal
Language Services and Publishing

Welcome Reception Sponsor

SESTEK

Lunch Sponsor

welocalize
doing things differently

List of papers

Invited Talk
Olga Beregovaya

What we want, what we need, what we absolutely can't do without – an enterprise user's perspective on machine translation technology and stuff around it

As the gains made by current phrase-based MT systems approach a horizontal asymptote, those of us in industry who benefit from cutting-edge research are giving serious thought to what's next. The goal of this talk is to rekindle the dialog between research and industry circles on the immediate and future needs of the user community and finding mutually beneficial and interesting avenues for collaboration.
Of course, there are too many topics to cover in an hour, but I'll try to touch on some of the most relevant...

These are the areas of utmost interest and importance for the global business community as seen by a user from a major Language Service Provider:

Translation Quality: It's clear that we've nearly hit the wall with what more we can squeeze out of phrase-based MT systems, so where do we go from here? Are factored models the way to go, or should we in industry start giving serious consideration to systems using deep learning techniques and/or deep syntactic/semantic structures?

New real-life applications: User-generated content (UGC) is rapidly becoming a huge opportunity for translation & localization. Whether we're talking about blogs, reviews, or live chat, there are challenges for the MT status quo: normalization, ungrammatical/uncommon syntax, extreme sensitivity to maintaining proper negation or sentiment.

Domain adaptation: How much can we get out of minimal amounts of data? A little more data? Lots of out-of-domain data? How can we seamlessly integrate client/user dictionaries into standard SMT workflows?

Using and interpreting metadata: We're seeing a trend where we often have as much or more metadata than actual text to translate. How can this be leveraged to improve results, and make translators'/post-editors' lives easier?

Quality evaluation, utility prediction: What do we even mean by "utility"? Let's work together on establishing a standard. Can we get robust, reliable QE from limited (or no) bilingual data? (We've got some evidence that the answer is yes...) What can we say about quality *vis à vis* functionality?

Collaboration: We want to help! We're very interested to see research that's directly applicable, and we want to find ways to facilitate academic/industry partnerships. We can work with clients to try to make large amounts of domain-specific (non-parliamentary!) data available. Please reach out to us so we know what you're working on. Better yet, let's work on finding mutually beneficial projects.

Research Papers

Exploiting portability to build an RBMT prototype for a new source language

Nora Aranberri, Gorka Labaka, Arantza Díaz de Ilarraza and Kepa Sarasola
IXA Group
University of the Basque Country
Manuel Lardizabal 1, 20018 Donostia, Spain
{nora.aranberri,gorka.labaka,a.diazdeilarraza,kepa.sarasola}@ehu.eus

Abstract

This paper presents the work done to port a deep-transfer rule-based machine translation system to translate from a different source language by maximizing the exploitation of existing resources and by limiting the development work. Specifically, we report the changes and effort required in each of the system's modules to obtain an English-Basque translator, ENEUS, starting from the Spanish-Basque Matxin system. We run a human pairwise comparison for the new prototype and two statistical systems and see that ENEUS is preferred in over 30% of the test sentences.

1 Introduction

Building a corpus-based system is undeniably quicker than building a rule-based machine translation (RBMT) system, given the availability of large quantities of parallel text. However, this is often not the case for many language pairs, which makes building a mainstream statistical system suboptimal. Usually, lesser-resourced languages opt for RBMT systems, where language-specific NLP tools and resources are crafted.

Heavy investment and long development periods have been attributed to RBMT systems but (Surcin et al., 2013) pointed out that a large part of the systems' code is reusable. They state that 80% of Systran's code belongs to the analysis module, whereas the remaining 20% is equally divided into transfer and generation. Transfer is language-pair specific, but analysis and generation are built with information about one language only and they are therefore reusable for systems that use those languages. Rapid development of new language pairs benefits from existing resources but also from modular, stable infrastructures where new pairs can be developed by modifying the linguistic data.

An example of RBMT portability attempts for lesser-resourced languages is the Apertium project (Forcada et al., 2011). Apertium is a free/open-source shallow-transfer MT platform. Researchers have been active in porting the system to different language pairs (Peradin et al., 2014; Otte and Tyers, 2011). The system specializes in translation between related languages where shallow transfer suffices to produce good quality translations.

Shallow parsing is sometimes too limited for dissimilar language pairs. Unrelated languages often require a richer and more flexible deeper transfer architecture to tackle differing linguistic features. Examples are (Gasser, 2012) and Matxin (Mayor et al., 2011). In this work we present an attempt to port the deep-transfer RBMT Matxin[1], designed to cope with dissimilar languages.

The remaining work is organized as follows: Section 2 gives a brief overview of the architecture of the Matxin system. Section 3 describes the work done in each of the system's modules. Section 4 provides the results of the new Matxin ENEUS prototype's evaluation. Finally, Section 5 presents the conclusions and future work.

2 General system features

Matxin is a modular RBMT system originally developed to translate from Spanish into Basque (Mayor et al., 2011). It follows the standard three-step architecture, consisting of separate modules

[1]Matxin: https://matxin.sourceforge.net

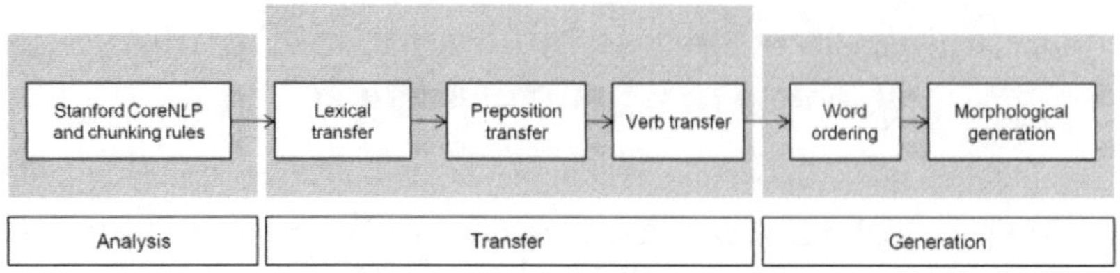

Figure 1: The general Matxin architecture.

for analysis, transfer and generation (Figure 1). It was devised to translate between dissimilar languages, that is, pairs that require deep analysis to enable translation and to do so, it works on dependency trees and chunks, and includes a module for reordering. Because it was developed with the Spanish-Basque pair in mind, the architecture can handle translation from analytic to agglutinative languages, thus dealing with rich morphology.

The portability exercise we present aims to examine the strengths and limitations of the Matxin architecture, by measuring the flexibility of the infrastructure and by specifying the language resource development needed for a new language pair. In particular, we examine the work effort required to change the source language and obtain English to Basque translations.

3 Portability exercise

Given the three-step architecture of Matxin, when modifying the system to translate from a different source language, we first need a completely new analysis module. Next, the transfer rules need to be updated to synchronize the new source with the target language. The generation module is mostly reusable and remains intact. In what follows, we describe the work done in each of the modules.

3.1 Analysis

Packages that analyze text at different levels are available, even more so for mainstream languages such as English. Therefore, what needs to be considered when selecting a package is whether it extracts the relevant information that the generation module will require. The information Matxin needs to translate into Basque is word forms, lemmas, part-of-speech categories, chunks, and dependency trees with named relations.

Note that chunks and dependency trees are different ways of representing sentence structure and both are necessary when translating into Basque. Chunks identify word groupings whereas dependency trees specify the relations between words. In Basque, postpositions are attached to the last word of the chunk they modify.[2] Therefore, chunks allow us to easily identify the word that needs to be flexed. Dependency relations provide the MT system with predicate-argument structures.

Two main contenders were found: Freeling, a rule-based analyzer developed at the Universitat Politécnica de Catalunya (Carreras et al., 2004) and the statistical analysis package developed at Stanford University (de Marneffe et al., 2006). The original architecture uses Freeling for Spanish analysis, and using their English package would make the integration easier, as tags are already known by the system. Yet we carried out a small comparison to opt for the best performing system.

We analyzed 50 sentences with both systems, 25 regular sentences and 25 news headlines. We included both simple and complex sentences showing a wide variety of features and structures. A sentence was to be correctly analyzed if all the lemmas, POS categories and the dependency tree were correctly annotated. 28% of the sentences were correctly analyzed by Freeling and 38% by Stanford. The remaining sentences show one or more errors, which would have varying impact on the translation process. Overall, the number of errors made by Freeling was higher compared to Stanford, 48 and 27 errors respectively. Freeling inserted 18 POS errors whereas Stanford inserted 17 (12 in headings). Dependency tree analyses include errors at different levels. One of the most severe error is the incorrect identification of the root (typically the main verb), which usually leads to the whole translation being wrong. Freeling failed to identify the root in 6 occasions. Stanford, in turn, did not make this type of error.

Overall, we saw that Stanford made fewer errors

[2]We include subject and object case-markers within this class because they are processed equally.

compared to Freeling. The popularity and development activity of this system at the time (Bach, 2012; Sagodkar and Damani, 2012) made us opt for the second package. The initial Spanish analysis component in Matxin was ported to English by integrating a new analysis package and by updating tag equivalences to allow for interoperability.

3.2 Transfer

The most labor-intensive component is the transfer module. In what follows, we examine the dictionaries and grammars that need to be updated in the order in which the architecture applies them.

Lexical transfer

Bilingual dictionaries are the basis for translation and these had to be compiled to include English-Basque equivalences. We used two main sources to build the new dictionaries. First, an English-Basque dictionary was made available for research purposes by Elhuyar, a Basque language technology company. We obtained 16,000 pairs and 1,047 multi-word units from this resource.

The words in the Elhuyar dictionary are probably enough to translate the most frequent English words and understand a general text. However, we decided to try to increase the coverage of Matxin ENEUS with a second resource, that is, WordNet (Miller, 1995). It is a lexical database that was initially built for English, where nouns, verbs, adjectives and adverbs are grouped around cognitive synonyms that refer to the same concept called synsets. Synsets are linked to each other through conceptual and lexical relations, making up a conceptual web of meaning-relations. Even if it was first built for English, WordNets have been developed for other languages, as is the case of Basque (Pociello et al., 2010). Words in different languages share synsets and therefore it is possible to extract equivalences, creating a bilingual pseudo-dictionary. The Basque WordNet has 33,442 synsets that are mapped to their English counterparts. We have paired the variants of each mapped synset in all possible combinations, obtaining over 82,000 pairs after discarding multiword units. These provide us with Basque equivalents for almost 32,000 English lemmas. Even if WordNet was not designed to be used as a dictionary and the equivalences have not been reviewed by an expert, we decided to include them in the system's dictionary even if priority was given to the Elhuyar data. The union of both resources accounts for around 35,000 entries.

plane + pos=[NN] → hegazkin + pos=[IZE][ARR] + num=[NUMS]
plane + pos=[NN] → plano + pos=[IZE][ARR] + num=[NUMS]
big + pos=[JJ] → handi + pos=[ADJ_IZO]
big + pos=[JJR] → handi + pos=[ADJ_IZO] + suf=[GRA][KONP]
big + pos=[JJS] → handi + pos=[ADJ_IZO] + suf=[GRA][SUP]
go + pos=[VB] → joan + pos=[ADI]
go + pos=[VBZ] → joan + pos=[ADI]
go + pos=[VBG] → joan + pos=[ADI]

Figure 2: Dummy examples of dictionary rules.

The dictionary lists the source lemma and its POS tag and points to the equivalent target lemma together with its POS and morphological information (Figure 2). The information for both languages is the same, but the tag set used is different and generator-dependent. The information in the English tag is itemized into one or more Basque tags. For example, the English *NN* tag referring to common singular nouns is broken down into three separate tags, *IZE*, *ARR* and *NUMS* referring to noun, common and singular, respectively.[3]

The dictionary lists all the possible equivalences gathered from the bilingual resources. Yet, Matxin ENEUS selects the first available equivalent regardless of the context of use. The order in which alternatives are coded in the dictionary is based on frequency in the case of the Elhuyar dictionary and therefore, this already introduces some sort of selection rule. The architecture allows creating context-specific selection rules and other word sense disambiguation (WSD) techniques can be integrated but this is out of the scope of this work.

After the information from the bilingual dictionary is collected, the selected target word is searched for in a semantic dictionary (Díaz et al., 2002) and features added if available.

Preposition transfer

English prepositions are translated into Basque mainly through postpositions. As previously mentioned, these postpositions are attached to the last word of the postpositional phrase (chunk) and the information about it must be moved to the relevant word. To allow for this, prepositions are processed differently, using a purposely-built dictionary. It consists of English prepositions and their Basque postposition equivalents, where the lemmas and morphological tags are specified.

[3]Note that verbs are handled separately, and therefore, all forms carry the same neutral target tag in the dictionary.

[4]Statistics for work in progress when only 20 prepositions have been addressed. The level of ambiguity tends to increase as detailed disambiguation work is done.

	Simple preposition	Unique equivalent	Multiple [4] equivalents	Average ambiguity
English	66	20	46	3.8
Spanish	20	7	13	3.9

Table 1: Statistics for the preposition dictionary.

We have worked with a list of 66 English simple prepositions. We have identified 20 with a unique translation. The remaining 46 have an average of 3.8 translations (ranging from 2 to 10) (Table 1).

Equivalence rule	Example
by → ergative	written by Wilde → Wilde**ek** idatzia
by → instrumental	travel by plane → hegazki**nez** bidaiatu
by → genitive	a book by Shelly → Shelly**ren** liburu bat
by → genitive + ondoan	by the door → atea**ren ondoan**
by → inessive	by candlelight → kandelaren argipe**an**
by → ablative	hold by the hand → esku**tik** heldu
by → genitive + arabera	by the barometer → barometroa**ren arabera**
by → adlative + time-location genitive	by now → hon**ezkero**
by → + bider	3 multiplied by 2 → 3 **bider** 2
by → + aurretik	drive by your house → zure etxe **aurretik**

Figure 3: Basque equivalences for *by*.

The linguistic work has to identify the different uses for the multiple equivalences, define contexts and write rules that will allow for the appropriate equivalent to be selected (Figure 3). Rules can include different types of knowledge. By default, the design of Matxin allows including elements that are in direct dependency (lemma, POS, morphological, syntactic and semantic features). At the time of write-up, 27 selection rules have been created and further effort is envisaged. If we compare the effort required for the English-Basque pair with the existing work for the Spanish-Basque system, we observe that the list includes 20 simple prepositions, that is, about a third, out of which 7 have a single translation and the ambiguous ones have an average of 3.9 translation options (ranging from 2 to 11). This reveals that the linguistic work necessary to set up the preposition transfer for the new pair is more labor-intensive. Rules are given full priority during selection, and translation equivalences which do not have a selection rule assigned to them are listed by frequency of appearance.

In addition to the equivalence table, Matxin avails of two other sources of information, which are used when no selection rules apply: lexicalized syntactic dependency triplets and verb subcategorisation, both automatically extracted from a monolingual corpus (Agirre et al., 2009).

Lexicalized triplets are groupings of verbs, lemmas and argument cases with which each verb appears in the corpus (Figure 4). In the cases where selection rules are not sufficient, the verb is identified and the lemma of the word to which the postposition needs to be attached is searched for. If the verb-lemma combination is present, the candidate argument cases from the dictionary are checked against the triplets and the first matching selected.

Verb	Lemma	Argument case
eman	unibertsitate	inessive
	Paul	ergative dative
	amore	absolutive partitive
	...	...

Figure 4: Examples of triplets for *eman* (give).

The information contained in lexicalized triplets is often too precise and restrictive. If triplets do not cover the verb-lemma combination, we turn to verb subcategorisation. This resource includes, ordered by frequency, a list of the most common argument case combinations for each verb (Figure 5). The possible postpositions for each of the prepositions that depend on a verb are collected from the dictionary and matched against the subcategorisation information until the combination that suits best is selected.

Verb	Paradigm	Subject case	Arg case	Arg case
suntsitu	subj-dObj	ergative	absolutive	-
	subj	absolutive	-	-
	subj-dObj	ergative	absolutive	instrumental
	...	...	...	...

Figure 5: Examples of verb subcategorization for *suntsitu* (destroy).

Because both Spanish and English use prepositions, the design of Matxin has been adequate for our goal. The preposition dictionary and selection rules were replaced, but verb subcategorisation and lexical triplets were reused, as they are Basque-specific and source-language-independent.

Verb transfer

Basque verbs carry considerable information, such as, person and number of the subject and objects, tense, aspect and mood. In Spanish, information about the objects is not present. In English, the verbs carry even less information: tense, aspect and mood are present, but it is only in the case of present tense third person singular that we know about the subject thanks to the *s* mark attached to the verb. No reference to the subject (exception above) or objects is made explicit in the verb.

Before applying verb transfer rules, therefore, a set of movement rules needs to collect all the relevant information for Basque verbs from the dependency tree. This difference was partially addressed during the Spanish-Basque implementation. In the case of English, movement rules were modified to include the person and number of the subject and objects, if they explicitly appeared in the text to be translated, as well as the paradigm information obtained from the preposition selection step. Thus, the developer availed of all the source text information required to work on transfer rules. Given the information of subject and objects, the rules are written to identify tense, aspect and mood information from the source verb and replacement rules gather up information to generate an equivalent Basque verb (Figure 6).

I **drive** *my car to university every morning*
input pattern to verb transfer drive[VBP]+[subj1s][dObj3s][iObj00]+[paradigm2]+gidatu
target pattern assigned by grammar gidatu{Asp}{Mod+Asp}{Aux}{Tense}{Subj}{dObj}{iObj}
transformed pattern gidatu{IMPERF}{}{edun}{A1}{subj1s}{dObj3s}
Nik nire autoa **gidatzen dut** *unibertsitatera goizero.*

Figure 6: Dummy example of verb transfer steps.

Verb transfer in the Matxin architecture is carried out using finite-state transducers (Alegria et al., 2005; Mayor et al., 2012). In short, the transducers take the source verb phrase as input, perform a number of replacements and create the final output which is ready for the syntactic and morphological generators to interpret.

We kept the three-step organization of the grammar used in the original language pair.

1. Identification of the Basque verbal schema corresponding to the source verbal chunk.

   We use 21 patterns that we then unify into 5 general schemes corresponding to simple tenses (*works, worked*), compound tenses (*have worked, will work*), continuous tenses (*is working, had been working*), simple tenses preceded by a modal (*should work*), and compound or continuous tenses preceded by a modal (*must have worked*).

2. Resolution of the values for the attributes in each of the Basque schemes.

   A total of 222 replacement rules were written to transfer verbal information into the target language in a format that is interpreted by the generators (Table 2).

3. Elimination of unnecessary information (4 rules in total).

Type	Number of rules
auxiliary verb selection	20
aspect of main verb or auxiliary	65
modal-specific	2
negation	4
paradigm selection and feature assignment	107
tense	24
Total	222

Table 2: Verb transfer rules by type.

When building the prototype, considerable effort was made to ensure wide verb coverage. Most of the tenses in the indicative have been covered, for all four paradigms in Basque (subj, subj-dObj, subj-dObj-iObj, subj-iObj) in the affirmative, negative and questions, for active and passive voices. The imperative was also included.

Work was also done for modals, even if to a more limited extent. Matxin ENEUS identifies the most common modals: ability (*can, could, would*), permission and prohibition (*must, mustnt, can, have to*), advice (*should*) and probability (*may, might, will*) for affirmative and negative cases. Depending on the context, modals acquire a slightly different meaning. At the time of writing, only one sense per modal was covered by the system.

Complex sentences

The modifications mentioned so far describe how simple sentences and their components are treated. However, complex sentences require a more intricate approach. The transfer rules that so far handled finite verbs now need to consider the varying translations of non-finite verbs as well as the permutations subordinate markers require. Also, information movements are directed by more elaborate rules. For Matxin ENEUS, we addressed, in their simplest forms, relative clauses, completives, conditionals and a number of adverbial clauses (time, place and reason).

3.3 Movements

It is the flexibility to move information along the dependency tree-nodes that provides the Matxin architecture with the capacity to tackle dissimilar languages (Mayor et al., 2011). In this first portability exercise few changes were introduced to the movement rule-sets as basic structures in Spanish and English required similar basic movements. Generally, Basque chunks (verbs aside) consist of a number of lemmas and a last word to which flexion information is attached. Therefore, the basic information movements for both Spanish and English have been (1) preposition information moved to the last word of the chunk, and (2) number and definiteness information of the source chunk moved to the last word of the target chunk.

Additionally, the movement rule-set preceding verb transfer was modified to address certain English-specific structures. For example, English *verb+to* and *verb+ing* structures, e.g. *want to eat, intend to go* and similar, require that the second verb is treated differently to how main verbs are treated. This needs to be noted before the verbs arrive in the verb transfer component. In order to do that, a special attribute needs to be passed on to the verb phrase. We tested these two cases and saw that Matxin's design can be appropriate for language-specific structures.

3.4 Generation

The generation component of an RBMT system is usually developed using target-language knowledge only to increase reuse possibilities. In Matxin, the three modules included in the generation component avail of Basque knowledge only (with the exception of the rule-set to address non-canonical source language word order). First, the sentence-level ordering rules in the generation component establish the canonical word order given the elements in the dependency tree.

Secondly, the chunk-level information stored at the chunk-level node is passed on to the word that needs to be flexed. Again, this set of rules avails of target language knowledge only. The rule-set is used as is for different source languages.

Finally, the information collected over the translation process (lemmas and corresponding tag sequences) is passed on to the word generation module, a morphological generator specifically developed for Basque, which was fully reused.

4 System evaluation

We used human evaluation as the main indicator for the prototype's performance. Also, we ran automatic metrics to compare their scores against the human evaluation even when it is known that automatic scores tend to favor SMT systems over RBMT systems because they do not consider the correctness of the output but rather compare the difference between the output and the reference translations (Callison-Burch et al., 2006). And the use of a single reference accentuates this.

To get a perspective on the overall performance, we ran the evaluation for two additional systems, an in-house statistical system, SMTs, and Google Translate, as well as Matxin ENEUS. Our SMT system was trained on a parallel corpus of 12 million Basque words and 14 million English words comprising user manuals, academic books and web data. We implemented a phrase-based system using Moses (Koehn et al., 2007). To better deal with the agglutinative nature of Basque, we trained the system on morpheme-level segmented data (Labaka, 2010). As a result, we need a generation postprocess to obtain real word forms for the decoder. We incorporated a second language model (LM) based on real word forms to be used after the morphological postprocess. We implemented the word form-based LM by using an n-best list following (Olafzer and El-Kahlout, 2007). We first generate a candidate ranking based on the segmented training. Next, these candidates are postprocessed. We then recalculate the total cost of each candidate by including the cost assigned by the new word form-based LM in the models used during decoding. Finally, the candidate list is re-ranked according to the new total cost. This revises the candidate list to promote those that are more likely to be real word form sequences. The weight for the word form-based LM was optimized with minimum error rate training together with the weights for the rest of the models.

We used the same evaluation set for both the human evaluation and the automatic metrics. It is a set of 500 sentences consisting of 250 sentences set aside from the training corpus and 250 out-of-domain sentences from online news sites and magazines. All sentences contain at least one verb, are self-contained and have 5 to 20 tokens.

4.1 Human evaluation

We performed a human evaluation for the three systems mentioned above as part of a wider evaluation campaign. We carried out a pairwise comparison evaluation with non-expert volunteer participants who accessed an evaluation platform online. They were presented with a source sentence and two machine translations. They were asked to compare the translations and decide which was better. They were given the options *1st is better, 2nd is better* and *they are both of equal quality*. Over 551 participants provided responses in the campaign which allowed us to collect over 7,500 data points for the systems we show here. We collected at least 5 evaluations per source sentence for each system-pair (2,500 evaluations per pair).

We adopted the following strategy to decide on a winning system for each evaluated sentence in each system-pair comparison: if the difference in votes between two systems is larger than 2, the system with the highest number of votes is the undisputed winner (System X++). If the difference in votes is 1 or 2, the system scoring higher is the winner (System X+). If both systems score the same amount of votes, the result is a draw (equal).

From the evaluations collected (Figure 7), we see that the output of Matxin ENEUS is considered better than its competitors 31-34% of the time, a significant proportion given the prototype's rapid development and limited coverage. This is particularly interesting for hybridization purposes. It would be invaluable to pinpoint the specific structures in which this system succeeds and its specific strengths to guide future hybridization attempts.

SMTs and Google are preferred over the prototype. When compared against each other, the difference in sentences allocated to each system is not significant, with only 8 additional sentences allocated to SMTs (229 vs 221, 50 equal).

4.2 Automatic scores

We provide BLEU and TER scores in Table 3. Low BLEU scores are common for agglutinative target languages when using word-based metrics. A unigram match in these languages can easily equate to a 3-gram match in analytic languages, i.e., a word in Basque often consists of a lemma and number, definiteness and postpositional suffixes.

The human comparison evaluation tells us which translation candidate is preferred over another but it does not capture the distance between their quality. On the other hand, BLEU tries to provide the difference in the overall quality of the systems. Our results seem to suggest that Google has a better overall quality whereas SMTs has more variability in terms of quality, and this leads to our system being preferred for over 40% of the sentences, despite having a lower BLEU score.

In the case of Matxin ENEUS, the overall quality seems to be lower, but it still surpasses the statistical systems in over 30% of the sentences, which is not captured by BLEU.

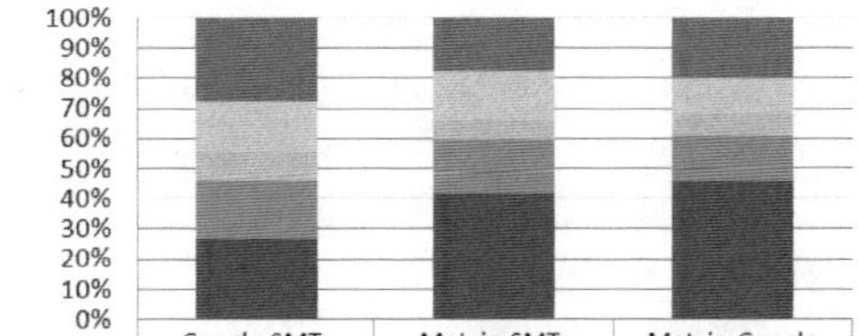

	Google-SMTs	Matxin-SMTs	Matxin-Google
System 1++	27.4	17.4	19.6
System 1+	16.8	16.4	11.8
equal	10	6.4	7.2
System 2+	19.2	17.8	15.6
System 2++	26.6	42	45.8

Figure 7: Human comparison results.

System	BLEU	TER
SMTs	8.37	75.893
Google	11.64	72.997
Matxin ENEUS	4.27	83.940

Table 3: Automatic scores.

5 Conclusions

We have ported the Matxin deep-transfer rule-based system to work with a different source language and described the requirements and effort involved in the process. More precisely, we have replaced the analysis module with an existing English package which provided us with the necessary lemma, morphological, chunk and dependency information. Most of the work was devoted to the transfer module: we compiled a new bilingual dictionary from an existing electronic version and WordNet; we wrote a preposition-specific dictionary with several disambiguation rules; we wrote the verb transfer grammar and we specified a number of information movements across the dependency tree to address complex sentences and non-finite structures. The generation module was fully reused as the target language remained the same. We estimate that this process required about 8 person month full-time work for a linguist and 1 person month full-time work for a computer scientist, although this estimates will vary depending on each professional's skills and familiarity with the architecture and linguistic work.

Overall, we have gathered evidence that, thanks to its modularity, the use of trees and the flexibility it offers to move information across tree-nodes, Matxin can be a suitable architecture to develop systems for dissimilar languages or those for which deep-transfer is necessary.

We have evaluated the new English-to-Basque prototype by a human pair-wise comparison together with two statistical systems. Although these systems are generally preferred, Matxin ENEUS surpasses statistical competitors in 30% of the cases. Apart from continuing with development work for the new language pair, we now aim to find out the characteristics of those cases, in particular, for hybridization opportunities.

Acknowledgements

The research leading to this work received funding from the People Programme (Marie Curie Actions) of the European Union's Seventh Framework Programme (FP7/2007/2013) under REA agreement 302038, FP7-ICT-2013-10-610516 (QTLeap) and Spanish MEC agreement TIN2012-38523-C02 (Tacardi) with FEDER funding.

References

Agirre, Eneko, Aitziber Atutxa, Gorka Labaka, Mikel Lersundi, Aingeru Mayor and Kepa Sarasola. 2009. Use of rich linguistic information to translate prepositions and grammar cases to Basque. *EAMT 2009*, Barcelona, Spain. 58–65.

Alegria, Iñaki, Arantza Díaz de Ilarraza, Gorka Labaka, Mikel Lersundi, Aingeru Mayor and Kepa Sarasola. 2005. An FST grammar for verb chain transfer in a Spanish-Basque MT System. *FSMNLP, Lecture Notes in Computer Science*, 4002:295–296.

Bach, Nguyen. 2012. Dependency structures for statistical machine translation. *SMNLP-2012*, Donostia, Spain. 65–69.

Callison-Burch, Chris, Miles Osborne, and Philipp Koehn. 2006. Re-evaluating the role of BLEU in machine translation research. *EACL-2006*, Trento, Italy. 249–256.

Carreras, Xavier, Isaac Chao and Lluís Padró and Muntsa Padró. 2012. FreeLing: An Open-Source Suite of Language Analyzers. *LREC-2004*, Lisbon.

Díaz de Ilarraza, Arantza, Aingeru Mayor and Kepa Sarasola. 2002. Semiautomatic labelling of semantic features. *COLING-2002*, Taipei, Taiwan.

Forcada, Mikel, Mireia Ginestí-Rosell, Jacob Nordfalk, Jim O'Regan, Sergio Ortiz-Rojas, Juan Antonio Pérez-Ortiz, Felipe Sánchez-Martnez, Gema Ramírez-Snchez and Francis Tyers. 2011. Apertium: a free/open-source platform for rule-based machine translation. *Machine Translation Journal*, 25(2):127–144.

Gasser, Michael. 2012. Toward a rule-based system for English-Amharic translation. *SALTMIL-AfLaT-2012*, Istanbul, Turkey.

Koehn, Philipp, Hieu Hoang, Alexandra Birch, Chris Callison-Burch, Marcello Federico, Nicola Bertoldi, Brooke Cowan, Wade Shen, Christine Moran, Richard Zens, Chris Dyer, Ondej Bojar, Alexandra Constantin and Evan Herbst. 2007. Moses: open source toolkit for statistical machine translation. *ACL-2007, Interactive Poster and Demonstration Sessions*, Prague, Czech Republic.

Gorka Labaka. 2010. EUSMT: Incorporating Linguistic Information into SMT for a Morphologically Rich Language. *PhD*, University of the Basque Country.

de Marneffe, Marie-Catherine, Bill MacCartney and Christopher Manning. 2006. Generating Typed Dependency Parses from Phrase Structure Parses. *LREC-2006*, Genoa, Italy.

Mayor, Aingeru, Iñaki Alegria, Arantza Diaz de Ilarraza, Gorka Labaka, Mikel Lersundi and Kepa Sarasola. 2011. Matxin, an open-source rule-based machine translation system for Basque. *Machine Translation Journal*, 25(1):53–82.

Mayor, Aingeru, Mans Hulden and Gorka Labaka. 2012. Developing an Open-Source FST Grammar for Verb Chain Transfer in a Spanish-Basque MT System. *FSMNLP-2012*, Donostia, Spain.

Miller, George. 1995. WordNet: A Lexical Database for English. *Communications of the ACM*, 38(11):39–41.

Oflazer, Kemal and Ilknur Durgar El-Kahlout. 2007. Exploring Different Representation Units in English-to-Turkish Statistical Machine Translation. *WMT-2007*, Prague, Czech Republic. 25–32.

Otte, Pim and Francis. Tyers. 2011. Rapid rule-based machine translation between Dutch and Afrikaans. *EAMT-2011*, Leuven, Belgium. 153–160.

Peradin, Hrvoje, Filip Petkovski and Francis. Tyers. 2014. Shallow-transfer rule-based machine translation for the Western group of South Slavic. *LREC-2012*, Reykjavík, Iceland. 25–30.

Pociello, Elisabete, Aitziber Atutxa and Izaskun Aldezabal. 2010. Methodology and construction of the Basque WordNet. *Language Resources and Evaluation*, 45:121–14.

Sangodkar, Amit and Om Damani. 2012. Re-ordering Source Sentences for SMT. *LREC-2012*, Istambul, Turkey. 2164–2171.

Surcin, Sylvain, Elke Lange and Jean Senellart. 2007. Rapid Development of New Language Pairs at SYSTRAN. *XI MT Summit*, Copenhagen, Denmark. 443–449.

Building hybrid machine translation systems by using an EBMT preprocessor to create partial translations

Mikel Artetxe, Gorka Labaka, Kepa Sarasola
IXA NLP Group, University of the Basque Country (UPV/EHU)
{martetxe003@ikasle., gorka.labaka@, kepa.sarasola@}ehu.eus

Abstract

This paper presents a hybrid machine translation framework based on a preprocessor that translates fragments of the input text by using example-based machine translation techniques. The preprocessor resembles a translation memory with named-entity and chunk generalization, and generates a high quality partial translation that is then completed by the main translation engine, which can be either rule-based (RBMT) or statistical (SMT). Results are reported for both RBMT and SMT hybridization as well as the preprocessor on its own, showing the effectiveness of our approach.

1 Introduction

The traditional approach to Machine Translation (MT) has been rule-based (RBMT), but it has been progressively replaced by Statistical Machine Translation (SMT) since the 1990s (Hutchins, 2007). Example-Based Machine Translation (EBMT), the other main MT paradigm, has never attracted that much attention: even though it gives excellent results with repetitive text for which accurate matches are found in the parallel corpus, its quality quickly degrades as more generalization is needed. Nevertheless, it has been argued that, along with the raise of hybrid systems that try to combine multiple paradigms, EBMT can help to overcome some of the weaknesses of the other approaches (Dandapat et al., 2011)[1].

In this paper, we propose one such system based on a multi-pass system combination: an EBMT preprocessor translates those fragments of the input text for which accurate matches are found in the parallel corpus, generating a high-quality partial translation that is then completed by the main translator, which can be either rule-based or statistical.

The function of the EBMT preprocessor is therefore similar to that of Translation Memories (TM), with the difference that previously made translations are not reused to aid human translators but a MT engine. Needless to say, if the EBMT preprocessor was only able to reuse full sentences as traditional TM systems do at the most basic level, the quality of its partial translations would match that of humans, but its contribution would be negligible in most situations. At the same time, trying to increase the coverage by generalizing too much at the expense of translation quality, as traditional EBMT systems do, would make the whole system pointless if the preprocessor is not able to outperform the main MT engine for the fragments it translates. This way, for our approach to work as intended, it is necessary to find a trade-off between coverage and translation quality. In this work, we take a preprocessor that reuses full sentences as our starting point and explore two generalization techniques similar to those used by second and third generation TM systems (Gotti et al., 2005):

- **Named-entity (NE) generalization**, giving the option to replace NEs like proper names and numerals in the parallel corpus with any other found in the text to translate.

[1]This paper refers to as hybridization to any combination of MT paradigms, no matter if they are integrated in a single engine or not. However, some authors distinguish between hybridization for systems that meet this requirement and combination for systems that do not.

- **Chunk generalization**, giving the option to reuse examples in a subsentential level.

Several other methods that combine EBMT and TM with other MT paradigms have been proposed in the literature. Koehn and Senellart (2010) use an SMT system to fill the mismatched parts from a fuzzy search in a TM. Similarly, Shirai et al. (1997) use a RBMT engine to complete the mismatched fragments from an EBMT system and smooth the resulting output using linguistic rules. On the other hand, Dandapat et al. (2012) integrate SMT phrase tables into an EBMT framework. Following the opposite approach, Groves and Way (2005) feed an SMT system with alignments obtained using EBMT techniques. Sánchez-Martínez et al. (2009) use EBMT techniques to obtain bilingual chunks that are then integrated into a RBMT system. Lastly, Alegria et al. (2008) propose a multi-engine system that selects the best translation created by a RBMT, an SMT and an EBMT engine. However, to the best of our knowledge, the use of a generic multi-pass hybridization method for EBMT that works with both SMT and RBMT has never been reported so far.

The remaining of this paper is structured as follows. The proposed method is presented in Section 2. Section 3 explains the experimental settings under which the system was tested, and the results obtained are then discussed in Section 4. Section 5 concludes the paper.

2 Method

Our method follows the so-called compiled approach to EBMT, which differs from runtime or pure EBMT in that it requires a training phase to compile translation units below the sentence level (Dandapat, 2012). Therefore, the system we propose consists of three elements: the compiling component presented in Section 2.1, which analyzes and aligns the parallel corpus to be used by the EBMT preprocessor; the EBMT preprocessor itself as presented in Section 2.2, which creates a high-quality partial translation of the input text using the data created by the previous module; and the integration with the main translator presented in Section 2.3, which completes the partial translation given by the previous module by using either a RBMT or an SMT engine.

2.1 Compiling

The compiling phase involves processing a sentence-aligned parallel corpus to be used by the EBMT preprocessor. Two steps are required for this: the analysis step, presented in Section 2.1.1, and the alignment step, presented in Section 2.1.2. The resulting data is encoded in a custom binary format based on suffix arrays (Manber and Myers, 1990) for its efficient retrieval by the EBMT preprocessor.

2.1.1 Analysis

The analysis step involves the tokenization, NE recognition and classification, lemmatization and parsing of each side of the parallel corpus. We have used Freeling (Padró and Stanilovsky, 2012) as our analyzer for Spanish, Stanford CoreNLP (Socher et al., 2013) for English and Eustagger (Ezeiza et al., 1998) for Basque, with a custom regex-based handling for numerals. The resulting constituency-based parse tree is simplified by removing inner nodes that correspond to part-of-speech tags and representing NEs as single leaves. In the case of Basque, our analyzer is only capable of shallow parsing, so we have generated a dummy tree in which chunks are the only inner nodes.

2.1.2 Alignment

The alignment step involves establishing the translation relationships among the tokens[2] and NEs of the parallel corpus. This is done separately because the latter serves as the basis for NE generalization as discussed in Section 1, so we allow the option of not aligning NEs in this level if there is not enough evidence to do so.

This way, word-alignment produces a set A_n for each nth sentence pair where $(i, j) \in A_n$ if and only if there is a translation relationship between the ith token in the source language and the jth token in the target language, as well as the lexical weightings or translation probabilities in both directions, that is, a set of $p(e|f)$ and $p(f|e)$ probabilities that express the likelihood of the f token to be translated as e and the e token to be translated as f, respectively. Our system has been integrated both with GIZA++ (Och and Ney, 2003) and Berkeley Aligner (Liang et al., 2006).

As for NE alignment, we align NEs if and only if they have the same written form, are equivalent

[2] We refer as tokens to the leaves of the parse tree obtained in the analysis phase, which implies that NEs are considered (multiword) tokens.

numerals or are found in either of the following dictionaries:

- A manually built dictionary, mostly consisting of translation relationships between proper names like countries.
- An automatically generated dictionary from Wikipedia article titles with support for redirections.
- An automatically generated dictionary from word-alignment, consisting of every NE pair $f - e$ for which $\frac{p(e|f)+p(f|e)}{2} > \theta$ and f and e appear a minimum of l times in the corpus.[3]

2.2 EBMT preprocessing

The goal of the EBMT preprocessing is to create a high-quality partial translation of the input text. As it is common in EBMT, this is done in three steps: matching, alignment and recombination, which are described in the following subsections.

2.2.1 Matching

The matching phase involves looking for fragments of the input text in the training corpus. For this purpose, the input text is first analyzed as described in Section 2.1.1, and chunks of each of the input sentences are then searched in the parallel corpus according to the following criteria:

1. The searched chunks must be syntactic units (either inner nodes or groups of consecutive inner siblings).
2. The searched chunks must contain a minimum of k tokens to avoid trivial translations that would have a negative impact on the overall translation quality. After some preliminary experiments, we have set k to 4.
3. The search process is hierarchical, that is, nodes that are closer to the root have priority over the rest in case of overlapping matches. If overlapping matches are found in the same level of the parse tree, the chunk with the biggest number of tokens has priority over the rest.
4. Full syntactic match requirement, that is, not only the leaves of the searched chunks have to match but also their corresponding subtrees.
5. The generalization of aligned NEs in the training corpus. According to this criterion, aligned NEs in the training corpus are considered to be valid matches for any NE in the input text, whereas unaligned NEs are processed as plain tokens.

2.2.2 Alignment

The next step in the EBMT preprocessing is to build a translation for each match, filtering those that are not valid. For that purpose, we first identify the translation that corresponds to each match in the parallel corpus, and we then translate the aligned NEs it contains.

For the first point, given a match of a chunk in the source language, we select the shortest sequence in the target language that satisfies the following conditions. If there is no possible translation that satisfies all these conditions for a given match, the match is rejected.

1. It must contain at least one aligned token.
2. No token in either fragment can be aligned with a token outside the other fragment.
3. The translation must be a syntactic unit as defined in Section 2.2.1, but without the requirement for the matched nodes to be inner ones (i.e. they could also be leaves).

Due to NE generalization, the translation generated this way might contain NEs that do not correspond to the searched ones. These NEs are translated as follows:

1. Identify the searched NE for each aligned NE in the translation. This is done by following the translation relationships as defined by NE alignment in the compiling phase.
2. Translate the lemma of the searched NEs. The set of dictionaries described in Section 2.1.2 is used for that purpose with a custom processing for numerals. NEs that cannot be translated by these means are left unchanged, as they would presumably correspond to proper names of persons or locations.
3. Inflect the translated lemma by applying the same morphological tags that the aligned NE had. We only apply this step for morphologically rich languages as it is the case of Basque.

[3] Based on some preliminary experiments, we set $\theta = 0.5$ and $l = 10$.

For instance, if "Putin claims victory in Russia elections" is matched with "Peña Nieto claims victory in Mexico elections", and "Peña Nietok Mexikoko hauteskundeak irabazi ditu" is selected as its translation, we would first identify that the Basque "Peña Nietok" is aligned with the English "Peña Nieto", which was matched with "Putin", and "Mexikoko" is aligned with "Mexico", which was matched with "Russia". We would then translate "Putin" as "Putin" and "Russia" as "Errusia" according to the dictionaries described in Section 2.1.2. Lastly, we would inflect these lemmas to match the lexical form of their corresponding aligned NE. In this case, "Peña Nietok" was the ergative form of "Peña Nieto", so we would inflect "Putin" in ergative giving "Putinek". Similarly, "Mexikoko" was the local-genitive form of "Mexiko", so we would inflect "Errusia" in local-genitive giving "Errusiako". This way, we would obtain the final translation "Putinek Errusiako hauteskundeak irabazi ditu".

2.2.3 Recombination

After the alignment phase, it is possible to have either zero, one, or several translation candidates for each searched chunk. Thanks to the hierarchical searching process, it is guaranteed that these translations will not overlap, so rather than combining them we try to select the best candidate for each searched chunk. For that purpose, we choose the most frequent translation in each case and, in case of a tie, the one with the highest lexical weighting.

2.3 Integration

As discussed in the previous section, the EBMT preprocessor creates a partial translation of the input text by translating chunks that are matched in the training corpus. The next and last phase involves building the full translation by completing it with the help of the main MT system. This is done differently depending on the type of system it is:

- When hybridizing with RBMT systems, the input text is translated as it is, and a postprocessor replaces translation fragments that correspond to matched chunks with the ones proposed by the EBMT preprocessor. In order to identify these fragments, the original chunks are marked with XML tags that the main MT system keeps in the translation it generates.
- When hybridizing with SMT systems, Moses' XML markup is used in its "inclusive" mode to make the translations generated by the EBMT preprocessor compete with the entries in the phrase table. It is remarkable that the "exclusive" and "constraint" modes, which force the decoder to choose the proposed translation or others that contain it, respectively, gave consistently worse results. We speculate that this could be due to the boundary friction problem, as the EBMT system translates fragments without taking their context into account, and the language model might be able to choose a better translation for the given context.

3 Experimental settings

As discussed in Section 1, it is expected that the performance of our method will greatly depend on the similarity between the input text and the examples given in the training corpus. Taking that into account, we decided to train our system in two different domains: the particularly repetitive domain of collective bargaining agreements, and the more common domain of parliamentary proceedings. For the former, we used the Spanish-Basque IVAP corpus, consisting of a total of 81 collective bargaining agreements to which we added the larger Elhuyar's administrative corpus to aid word-alignment. For the latter, we used the Spanish-English Europarl corpus as given in the shared task of the ACL 2007 workshop on statistical machine translation, consisting of proceedings of the European Parliament. Table 1 summarizes their details. As for the testing data, we used an in-domain test set for each corpus as well as an out-of-domain one for Europarl as shown in Table 2.

In order to evaluate the performance of our method we carried out the following two experiments:

- **A manual evaluation of the EBMT preprocessor** to measure both the coverage and the quality of its partial translations. For this purpose, we randomly selected 100 sentences for each in-domain test set and asked 5 volunteers to score the quality of each translated fragment in its context in a scale between 1 (incorrect translation) and 4 (correct translation).
- **An automatic evaluation of the whole system** using the Bilingual Evaluation Under-

	Language	Domain	Sentences
IVAP + Elhuyar	es-eu	collective bargaining agreements + administrative	50,824 + 4,747,332
Europarl	es-en	parliament proceedings	1,254,414

Table 1: Training corpus

	Language	Domain	In domain?	Sentences	Tokens	Tokens / sentence
IVAP	es-eu	collective bargaining agreement	yes	1,928	39,625	20.55
Europarl	es-en	parliamentary proceedings	yes	2,000	56,213	28.01
News commentary	es-en	news	no	2,007	61,341	30.67

Table 2: Test set

	Full sentences	Full sentences with NE	Chunks with NE		
			GIZA++	Berkeley (HMM)	Berkeley (synt.)
IVAP	18,284 (46.14%)	18,691 (47.17%)	23,962 (60.47%)	26,436 (66.72%)	-
Europarl	379 (0.62%)	548 (0.89%)	10,565 (17.22%)	10,986 (17.91%)	9,653 (15.74%)
News commentary	12 (0.02%)	12 (0.02%)	5,365 (9.54%)	5,566 (9.90%)	4,674 (8.31%)

Table 3: Tokens translated by the EBMT preprocessor

study (BLEU) metric (Papineni et al., 2002). For this automatic evaluation, we hybridized our system both with a RBMT and an SMT system. Our RBMT translator of choice was Matxin (Mayor et al., 2011) for Spanish-Basque and Apertium (Forcada et al., 2011) for Spanish-English, whereas we used Moses (Koehn et al., 2007) as our SMT engine for both language pairs.

4 Results and discussion

This section presents the outcomes of the experiments described in Section 3. The results for the quality and coverage experiment are discussed in Section 4.1, and the RBMT and SMT hybridization in Sections 4.2 and 4.3.

4.1 Quality and coverage of EBMT

Table 3 shows the number of tokens translated by the EBMT preprocessor according to each generalization mechanism. In the case of chunk generalization, we tried both GIZA++ and Berkeley aligner with and without syntactic tailoring (DeNero and Klein, 2007), which could presumably generate more chunk alignments that meet the restrictions of our translation process. However, contrary to our expectations syntactic tailoring gave the worst results by far both in terms of coverage and translation quality, apparently because it is still an experimental feature, and it was the default HMM mode of Berkeley Aligner which clearly outperformed the rest. We will consequently refer to the results obtained by this aligner in the remaining of this section.

As we expected, Table 3 reflects that the coverage of the EBMT preprocessing clearly depends on the similarity between the input text and the training corpus. For the domain of collective bargaining agreements, our EBMT preprocessor is able to translate around two thirds of the input tokens. Even though the results we obtain for the other test sets are poorer, the impact of our method is still very significant, as the EBMT preprocessor is able to translate 17.91% and 9.90% of the tokens in the in-domain and out-of-domain test sets for Europarl, respectively. As for the distribution of these partial translations, we observe that most of the translations in IVAP come from the traditional TM behavior of our preprocessor[4], but the relative contribution of the generalization mechanisms gets considerably higher as the distance between the input text and the training corpus increases[5].

As far as the quality of the partial translations is concerned, Tables 4 and 5 show the results of the manual evaluation we carried out for both in-domain test sets. The overall results are very positive in both cases, with an average score of 3.45 and 3.39 out of 4 for IVAP and Europarl, respectively. In spite of the average scores being similar, it is worth mentioning that there is a considerable difference in the variance of the evaluations, with Europarl obtaining much more coherent scores than IVAP (3.30-3.49 range for Europarl and 3.02-3.73 range for IVAP). We believe

[4] 69.16% of the tokens translated by the EBMT preprocessor when using all the generalization mechanisms correspond to full sentences (18,284 out of 26,436 as shown in Table 3)

[5] Only 3.45% and 0.22% of the tokens translated by the EBMT preprocessor when using all the generalization mechanisms correspond to full sentences in Europarl and News commentary, respectively (379 out of 10,986 and 12 tokens out of 5,566 as shown in Table 3)

	1	2	3	4	Average
Evaluator 1	2 (1.56%)	5 (3.91%)	19 (14.84%)	102 (79.69%)	3.73
Evaluator 2	5 (3.91%)	4 (3.13%)	18 (14.06%)	101 (78.91%)	3.68
Evaluator 3	11 (8.59%)	8 (6.25%)	9 (7.03%)	100 (78.13%)	3.55
Evaluator 4	13 (10.16%)	14 (10.94%)	25 (19.53%)	76 (59.38%)	3.28
Evaluator 5	19 (14.96%)	23 (18.11%)	21 (16.54%)	64 (50.39%)	3.02
Average	10 (7.82%)	10.8 (8.45%)	18.4 (14.4%)	88.6 (69.33%)	3.45

Table 4: Results of the manual evaluation in IVAP (es-eu)

	1	2	3	4	Average
Evaluator 1	8 (4.79%)	11 (6.59%)	40 (23.95%)	108 (64.67%)	3.49
Evaluator 2	14 (8.38%)	11 (6.59%)	28 (16.77%)	114 (68.26%)	3.45
Evaluator 3	11 (6.71%)	20 (12.2%)	25 (15.25%)	108 (65.85%)	3.40
Evaluator 4	16 (9.58%)	14 (8.38%)	38 (22.75%)	99 (59.28%)	3.32
Evaluator 5	17 (10.24%)	20 (12.05%)	25 (15.06%)	104 (62.65%)	3.30
Average	13.2 (7.94%)	15.2 (9.15%)	31.2 (18.77%)	106.6 (64.14%)	3.39

Table 5: Results of the manual evaluation in Europarl (es-en)

	RBMT baseline	RBMT + full sentences	RBMT + full sentences with NE	RBMT + chunks with NE (Berkeley HMM)
IVAP	0.0498	0.3350	0.3330	0.3168
Europarl	0.1755	0.1786	0.1790	0.1983
News commentary	0.2173	0.2173	0.2173	0.2227

Table 6: BLEU scores with RBMT hybridization

Source	Finalmente, **Señorías**, los medios de comunicacin deben **jugar también un papel importante** en esta tarea.
Baseline	Finally, **Señorías**, the media have to **play also an important paper** in this task.
System	Finally, **ladies and gentlemen**, the media have to **play an important role too** in this task.
Reference	Finally, **ladies and gentlemen**, the media must **also play an important role** in this task.

Table 7: An example of RBMT hybridization in Europarl

that the reason behind that is the unfamiliarity of some evaluators with machine translation and the register used for legal documents in Basque, which could have made them penalize minor mistakes that were sometimes even found in the reference translations too severely[6]. As a matter of fact, some full sentence translations that were equal to the reference ones got 1 and 2 scores. In any case, the reported results reflect that our EBMT preprocessor produces high-quality partial translations, with less than 20% of them obtaining a negative (1 or 2) score in average for both test sets.

4.2 RBMT hybridization

Table 6 shows the BLEU scores obtained when hybridizing with RBMT translators. As it can be seen, we obtain very good results, with our system outperforming the baseline in all the test sets. The gain in BLEU is particularly remarkable in the case of IVAP, with an improvement of 26.7 points, but still notable for the other more standard in-domain and out-of-domain test sets, with an improvement of 2.28 and 0.54 points, respectively.

As far as the contribution of each generalization step is concerned, it can be observed that, in the case of IVAP, all the improvement comes from the TM behavior of our preprocessor, and the generalization steps themselves have a negative impact. We believe that this is due to an integration problem with Matxin, as we find that it often misplaces our XML tags in its translations, yielding to senseless replacements that have a negative impact in the overall translation quality. In the case of both Apertium test sets, which do not suffer from this problem, the generalization steps work as expected and, in fact, practically all the improvement comes from them. Table 7 shows one such case, where the proposed system is able to properly translate the out-of-vocabulary word "Señorías" and the idiomatic expression "jugar un papel importante" unlike the baseline.

4.3 SMT hybridization

The BLEU scores obtained with SMT hybridization are shown in Table 8. As it can be seen, our system is not able to beat the baseline for either of the Spanish-English test sets, although there are instances in which the hybrid system gives better results as it is the case of the example in Table 9. We think that, as shown in Table 10, the reason behind

[6]Note that not all the evaluators for both test sets were the same

	SMT baseline	SMT + full sentences	SMT + full sentences with NE	SMT + chunks with NE (Berkeley HMM)
IVAP	0.3368	0.4483	0.4472	0.4593
Europarl	0.3307	0.3307	0.3304	0.3251
News commentary	0.2984	0.2982	0.2982	0.2967

Table 8: BLEU scores with SMT hybridization

Source	**De ser así, se comete un error**, ya que se trata de la credibilidad y fiabilidad que tiene la Unión Europea [...]
Baseline	**For example, we are making a mistake**, because that is the credibility and reliability of the European Union [...]
System	**If that is the case, it is a mistake**, because that is the credibility and reliability of the European Union [...]
Reference	**If it were to be the case then it is a miscalculation** because this is about the credibility and reliability of the European Union [...]

Table 9: An example of SMT hybridization in Europarl

	Full sentences	Full sentences with NE	Chunks with NE
IVAP	15.10	11.31	8.09
Europarl	7.02	9.39	5.10
News commentary	6.00	-	4.74

Table 10: Average length of the fragments translated by the EBMT preprocessor

that is that the fragments translated by the EBMT preprocessor are too short for these test sets, as the baseline SMT system would be able to properly handle this size n-grams. Increasing the minimum number of tokens k to be searched by the EBMT preprocessor as discussed in Section 2.2.1 would solve this problem, but it would also decrease its coverage, considerably reducing the impact of the whole system.

Nevertheless, we obtain very good results in IVAP, where we achieve an overall improvement of 12.25 BLEU points from which 1.1 come from the generalization steps. We therefore conclude that our system works with SMT hybridization as long as the domain is repetitive enough to reuse long text chunks that traditional SMT systems are not able to handle effectively.

5 Conclusions and future work

In summary, this paper develops a generic multi-pass hybridization method based on an EBMT preprocessor that creates partial translations making use of NE and chunk generalization. The effectiveness of the preprocessor is experimentally demonstrated both in terms of coverage and translation quality. Furthermore, our experiments show that the proposed method considerably improves the baseline with RBMT hybridization, and we also obtain very good results with SMT hybridization in repetitive enough domains.

In the future, we intend to further optimize our system by using heuristics to detect wrong alignments, improve our processing for Spanish contractions, which often led to parsing errors, and introduce a better handling for NEs with common nouns, which were incorrectly left unchanged when not found in any dictionary. In addition, we plan to improve SMT integration by increasing the minimum number of tokens to be translated by the EBMT preprocessor and optimizing the weight assigned to our partial translations. We also want to explore the possibility of selecting more than one translation for each chunk that would then compete with each other and the rest of the entries in the phrase table. Furthermore, we would like to fix the integration problems with Matxin and use a full syntactic analyzer for Basque. We also intend to try more metrics to better understand the behavior of the whole system. Lastly, we plan to release our system as an open source project.

Acknowledgments

The research leading to these results was carried out as part of the TACARDI project (Spanish Ministry of Education and Science, TIN2012-38523-C02-011, with FEDER funding) and the QTLeap project funded by the European Commission (FP7-ICT-2013.4.1-610516).

References

Alegria, Iñaki, Arantza Casillas, Arantza Díaz De Ilarraza, Jon Igartua, Gorka Labaka, Mikel Lersundi, Aingeru Mayor, Kepa Sarasola, Xabier Saralegi, and B Laskurain. 2008. Mixing Approaches to MT for Basque: Selecting the best output from RBMT, EBMT and SMT. *MATMT 2008: Mixing Approaches to Machine Translation*, pages 27–34.

Dandapat, Sandipan, Sara Morrissey, Andy Way, and Mikel L Forcada. 2011. Using example-based MT to support statistical MT when translating homogeneous data in a resource-poor setting. In *Proceedings of the 15th annual meeting of the European Association for Machine Translation (EAMT 2011)*, pages 201–208.

Dandapat, Sandipan, Sara Morrissey, Andy Way, and Joseph van Genabith. 2012. Combining EBMT, SMT, TM and IR technologies for quality and scale. In *Proceedings of the Joint Workshop on Exploiting Synergies between Information Retrieval and Machine Translation (ESIRMT) and Hybrid Approaches to Machine Translation (HyTra)*, pages 48–58. Association for Computational Linguistics.

Dandapat, Sandipan. 2012. *Mitigating the Problems of SMT using EBMT.* Ph.D. thesis, Dublin City University.

DeNero, John and Dan Klein. 2007. Tailoring Word Alignments to Syntactic Machine Translation. In *Proceedings of the 45th Annual Meeting of the Association of Computational Linguistics*, pages 17–24, Prague, Czech Republic, June. Association for Computational Linguistics.

Ezeiza, Nerea, Iñaki Alegria, Josė María Arriola, Rubén Urizar, and Itziar Aduriz. 1998. Combining stochastic and rule-based methods for disambiguation in agglutinative languages. In *Proceedings of the 36th Annual Meeting of the Association for Computational Linguistics and 17th International Conference on Computational Linguistics-Volume 1*, pages 380–384. Association for Computational Linguistics.

Forcada, Mikel L, Mireia Ginestí-Rosell, Jacob Nordfalk, Jim ORegan, Sergio Ortiz-Rojas, Juan Antonio Pérez-Ortiz, Felipe Sánchez-Martínez, Gema Ramírez-Sánchez, and Francis M Tyers. 2011. Apertium: a free/open-source platform for rule-based machine translation. *Machine Translation*, 25(2):127–144.

Gotti, Fabrizio, Philippe Langlais, Elliott Macklovitch, Didier Bourigault, Benoit Robichaud, and Claude Coulombe. 2005. 3GTM: A third-generation translation memory. In *Proceedings of the 3rd Computational Linguistics in the North-East Workshop*, pages 8–15.

Groves, Declan and Andy Way. 2005. Hybrid example-based SMT: the best of both worlds? In *Proceedings of the ACL Workshop on Building and Using Parallel Texts*, pages 183–190. Association for Computational Linguistics.

Hutchins, John. 2007. Machine translation: A concise history. *Computer aided translation: Theory and practice.*

Koehn, Philipp and Jean Senellart. 2010. Convergence of translation memory and statistical machine translation. In *Proceedings of AMTA Workshop on MT Research and the Translation Industry*, pages 21–31.

Koehn, Philipp, Hieu Hoang, Alexandra Birch, Chris Callison-Burch, Marcello Federico, Nicola Bertoldi, Brooke Cowan, Wade Shen, Christine Moran, Richard Zens, et al. 2007. Moses: Open source toolkit for statistical machine translation. In *Proceedings of the 45th Annual Meeting of the ACL on Interactive Poster and Demonstration Sessions*, pages 177–180. Association for Computational Linguistics.

Liang, Percy, Ben Taskar, and Dan Klein. 2006. Alignment by agreement. In *Proceedings of the main conference on Human Language Technology Conference of the North American Chapter of the Association of Computational Linguistics*, pages 104–111. Association for Computational Linguistics.

Manber, Udi and Gene Myers. 1990. Suffix Arrays: A New Method for On-line String Searches. In *Proceedings of the First Annual ACM-SIAM Symposium on Discrete Algorithms*, SODA '90, pages 319–327, Philadelphia, PA, USA. Society for Industrial and Applied Mathematics.

Mayor, Aingeru, Iñaki Alegria, Arantza Díaz De Ilarraza, Gorka Labaka, Mikel Lersundi, and Kepa Sarasola. 2011. Matxin, an open-source rule-based machine translation system for Basque. *Machine translation*, 25(1):53–82.

Och, Franz Josef and Hermann Ney. 2003. A systematic comparison of various statistical alignment models. *Computational linguistics*, 29(1):19–51.

Padró, Lluís and Evgeny Stanilovsky. 2012. FreeLing 3.0: Towards Wider Multilinguality. In *Proceedings of the Language Resources and Evaluation Conference (LREC 2012)*, Istanbul, Turkey, May. ELRA.

Papineni, Kishore, Salim Roukos, Todd Ward, and Wei-Jing Zhu. 2002. BLEU: a method for automatic evaluation of machine translation. In *Proceedings of the 40th annual meeting on association for computational linguistics*, pages 311–318. Association for Computational Linguistics.

Sánchez-Martınez, Felipe, Mikel L Forcada, and Andy Way. 2009. Hybrid rule-based-example-based MT: feeding Apertium with sub-sentential translation units. In *3rd International Workshop on Example-Based Machine Translation*, page 11. Citeseer.

Shirai, Satoshi, Francis Bond, and Yamato Takahashi. 1997. A hybrid rule and example-based method for machine translation. In *Proceedings of NLPRS*, volume 97, pages 49–54. Citeseer.

Socher, Richard, John Bauer, Christopher D Manning, and Andrew Y Ng. 2013. Parsing with compositional vector grammars. In *In Proceedings of the ACL conference*. Citeseer.

Using on-line available sources of bilingual information for word-level machine translation quality estimation

Miquel Esplà-Gomis **Felipe Sánchez-Martínez** **Mikel L. Forcada**
Departament de Llenguatges i Sistemes Informàtics
Universitat d'Alacant, E-03071 Alacant, Spain
{mespla,fsanchez,mlf}@dlsi.ua.es

Abstract

This paper explores the use of external sources of bilingual information available on-line for word-level machine translation quality estimation (MTQE). These sources of bilingual information are used as a *black box* to spot sub-segment correspondences between a source-language (SL) sentence S to be translated and a given translation hypothesis T in the target-language (TL). This is done by segmenting both S and T into overlapping sub-segments of variable length and translating them into the TL and the SL, respectively, using the available bilingual sources of information *on the fly*. A collection of features is then obtained from the resulting sub-segment translations, which is used by a binary classifier to determine which target words in T need to be post-edited.

Experiments are conducted based on the data sets published for the word-level MTQE task in the 2014 edition of the Workshop on Statistical Machine Translation (WMT 2014). The sources of bilingual information used are: machine translation (Apertium and Google Translate) and the bilingual concordancer Reverso Context. The results obtained confirm that, using less information and fewer features, our approach obtains results comparable to those of state-of-the-art approaches, and even outperform them in some data sets.

1 Introduction

Recent advances in the field of machine translation (MT) have led to the adoption of this technology by many companies and institutions all around the world in order to bypass the linguistic barriers and reach out to broader audiences. Unfortunately, we are still far from the point of having MT systems able to produce translations with the level of quality required for dissemination in formal scenarios, where human supervision and MT post-editing are unavoidable. It therefore becomes critical to minimise the cost of this human post-editing. This has motivated a growing interest in the field of MT quality estimation (Blatz et al., 2004; Specia et al., 2010; Specia and Soricut, 2013), which is the field that focuses on developing techniques that allow to estimate the quality of the translation hypotheses produced by an MT system.

Most efforts in MT quality estimation (MTQE) are aimed at evaluating the quality of whole translated segments, in terms of post-editing time, number of editions needed, and other related metrics (Blatz et al., 2004). Our work is focused on the sub-field of *word-level MTQE*. The main advantage of word-level MTQE is that it allows not only to estimate the effort needed to post-edit the output of an MT system, but also to guide post-editors on which words need to be post-edited.

In this paper we describe a novel method which uses black-box bilingual resources from the Internet for word-level MTQE. Namely, we combine two on-line MT systems, Apertium[1] and Google Translate,[2] and the bilingual concordancer Reverso Context[3] to spot sub-segment correspondences between a sentence S in the source language (SL) and

[1] http://www.apertium.org
[2] http://translate.google.com
[3] http://context.reverso.net/translation/

a given translation hypothesis T in the target language (TL). To do so, both S and T are segmented into overlapping sub-segments of variable length and they are translated into the TL and the SL, respectively, by means of the bilingual sources of information mentioned above. These sub-segment correspondences are used to extract a collection of features that is then used by a binary classifier to determine the words to be post-edited. Our experiments confirm that our method provides results comparable to the state of the art using considerably fewer features. In addition, given that our method uses (on-line) resources which are publicly available on the Internet, once the binary classifier is trained it can be used for word-level MTQE on the fly for new translations.

The rest of the paper is organised as follows. Section 2 briefly reviews the state of the art in word-level MTQE. Section 3 describes our binary-classification approach, the sources of information, and the collection of features used. Section 4 describes the experimental setting used for our experiments, whereas Section 5 reports and discusses the results obtained. The paper ends with some concluding remarks and the description of ongoing and possible future work.

2 Related work

Some of the early work on word-level MTQE can be found in the context of interactive MT (Gandrabur and Foster, 2003; Ueffing and Ney, 2005). Gandrabur and Foster (2003) obtain confidence scores for each word t in a given translation hypothesis T of the SL sentence S to help the interactive MT system to choose the translation suggestions to be made to the user. Ueffing and Ney (2005) extend this application to word-level MTQE also to automatically reject those target words t with low confidence scores from the translation proposals. This second approach incorporates the use of probabilistic lexicons as a source of translation information.

Blatz et al. (2003) introduce a more complex collection of features for word-level MTQE, using semantic features based on WordNet (Miller, 1995), translation probabilities from IBM model 1 (Brown et al., 1993), word posterior probabilities (Blatz et al., 2003), and alignment templates from statistical MT (SMT) models. All the features they use are combined to train a binary classifier which is used to determine the confidence scores.

Ueffing and Ney (2007) divide the features used by their approach in two types: those which are independent of the MT system used for translation (system-independent), and those which are extracted from internal data of the SMT system they use for translation (system-dependent). These features are obtained by comparing the output of an SMT system T_1 to a collection of alternative translations $\{T_i\}_{i=2}^{N_T}$ obtained by using the N-best list from the same SMT system. Several distance metrics are then used to check how often word t_j, the word in position j of T, is found in each translation alternative T_i, and how far from position j. These features rely on the assumption that a high occurrence frequency in a similar position is an evidence that t_j does not need to be post-edited. Biçici (2013) proposes a strategy for extending this kind of system-dependent features to what could be called a system-independent scenario. His approach consists in choosing parallel data from an additional parallel corpus which are close to the segment S to be translated by means of feature-decay algorithms (Biçici and Yuret, 2011). Once this parallel data are extracted, a new SMT system is trained and its internal data is used to extract these features.

The MULTILIZER approach to (sentence-level) MTQE (Bojar et al., 2014) also uses other MT systems to translate S into the TL and T into the SL. These translations are then used as a pseudo-reference and the similarity between them and the original SL and TL sentences is computed and taken as an indication of quality. This approach, as well as the one by Biçici and Yuret's (2011) are the most similar ones to our approach. One of the main differences is that they translate whole segments, whereas we translate sub-segments. As a result, we can obtain useful information about specific words in the translation. As the approach in this paper, MULTILIZER also combines several sources of bilingual information, while Biçici and Yuret (2011) only uses one MT system.[4]

Among the recent works on MTQE, it is worth mentioning the QuEst project (Specia et al., 2013), which sets a framework for MTQE, both at the sentence level and at the word level. This framework defines a large collection of features which can be divided in three groups: those measuring the complexity of the SL segment S, those measuring the confidence on the MT system, and those measuring both fluency and adequacy directly on the

[4]To the best of our knowledge, there is not any public description of the internal workings of MULTILIZIER.

translation hypothesis T. In fact, some of the most successful approaches in the word-level MTQE task in the Workshop on Statistical Machine Translation in 2014 (WMT 2014) (Bojar et al., 2014) are based on some of the features defined in that framework (Camargo de Souza et al., 2014).

The work described in this paper is aimed at being a system-independent approach that uses available on-line bilingual resources for word-level MTQE. This work is inspired by the work by Esplà-Gomis et al. (2011), in which several on-line MT systems are used for word-level quality estimation in translation-memory-based computer aided translation tasks. In the work by Esplà-Gomis et al. (2011), given a translation unit (S, T) suggested to the translator for the SL segment to be translated S', MT is used to translate sub-segments from S into the TL, and TL sub-segments from T into the SL. Sub-segment pairs obtained through MT that are found both in S and T are an evidence that they are related. The alignment between S and S', together with the sub-segment translations between S and T help to decide which words in T should be modified to get T', the desired translation of S'. Based on the same idea, we built a brand-new collection of word-level features to extend this approach to MTQE. One of the main advantages of this approach as compared to other approaches described in this section is that it uses light bilingual information extracted from any available source. Obtaining this information directly from the Internet allows us to obtain on the fly confidence estimates for the words in T without having to rely on more complex sources, such as probabilistic lexicons, part-of-speech information or word nets.

3 Word-level quality estimation using bilingual sources of information from the Internet

The approach proposed in this work for word-level MTQE uses binary classification based on features obtained through sources of bilingual information available on-line. We use these sources of bilingual information to detect connections between the original SL segment S and a given translation hypothesis T in the TL following the same method proposed by Esplà-Gomis et al. (2011): all the overlapping sub-segments of S and T, up to a given length L, are obtained and translated into the TL and the SL, respectively, using the sources of bilingual information available. The resulting collections of sub-segment translations $M_{S\to T}$ and $M_{T\to S}$ can be then used to spot sub-segment correspondences between T and S. In this section we describe a collection of features designed to identify these relations for their exploitation for word-level MTQE.

Positive features. Given a collection of sub-segment translations M (either $M_{S\to T}$ or $M_{T\to S}$), one of the most obvious features consists in computing the amount of sub-segment translations $(\sigma, \tau) \in M$ that confirm that word t_j in T should be kept in the translation of S. We consider that a sub-segment translation (σ, τ) confirms t_j if σ is a sub-segment of S, and τ is a sub-segment of T that covers position j. Based on this idea, we propose the collection of positive features Pos_n:

$$\text{Pos}_n(j, S, T, M) = \frac{|\{\tau : \tau \in \text{conf}_n(j, S, T, M)\}|}{|\{\tau : \tau \in \text{seg}_n(T) \wedge j \in \text{span}(\tau, T)\}|}$$

where $\text{seg}_n(X)$ represents the set of all possible n-word sub-segments of segment X and function $\text{span}(\tau, T)$ returns the set of word positions spanned by the sub-segment τ in the segment T.[5] Function $\text{conf}_n(j, S, T, M)$ returns the collection of sub-segment pairs (σ, τ) that confirm a given word t_j, and is defined as:

$$\text{conf}_n(j, S, T, M) = \{(\sigma, \tau) \in M : \tau \in \text{seg}_n(T) \wedge \sigma \in \text{seg}_*(S) \wedge j \in \text{span}(\tau, T)\}$$

where $\text{seg}_*(X)$ is similar to $\text{seg}_n(X)$ but without length constraints.[6]

Additionally, we propose a second collection of features, which use the information about the translation frequency between the pairs of sub-segments in M. This information is not available for MT, although it is for the bilingual concordancer we have used (see Section 4). This frequency determines how often σ is translated as τ and, therefore, how reliable this translation is. We define $\text{Pos}_n^{\text{freq}}$ to obtain these features as:

$$\text{Pos}_n^{\text{freq}}(j, S, T, M) = \sum_{\forall(\sigma,\tau)\in\text{conf}_n(j,S,T,M)} \frac{\text{occ}(\sigma, \tau, M)}{\sum_{\forall(\sigma,\tau')\in M} \text{occ}(\sigma, \tau', M)}$$

where function $\text{occ}(\sigma, \tau, M)$ returns the number of occurrences in M of the sub-segment pair (σ, τ).

[5] Note that a sub-segment τ may be found more than once in segment T: function $\text{span}(\tau, T)$ returns all the possible positions spanned.

[6] Two variants of function conf_n were tried: one applying also length constraints when segmenting S (with the consequent increment in the number of features), and one not applying length constraints at all. Preliminary results confirmed that constraining only the length of τ was the best choice.

Both positive features, $\text{Pos}(\cdot)$ and $\text{Pos}^{\text{freq}}(\cdot)$, are computed for t_j for all the values of sub-segment length n up to L. In addition, they can be computed for both $M_{S\to T}$ and $M_{T\to S}$, producing $4L$ positive features in total for each word t_j.

Negative features. Our negative features, i.e. those features that help to identify words that should be post-edited in the translation hypothesis T, are also based on sub-segment translations $(\sigma, \tau) \in M$, but they are used in a different way. Negative features use those sub-segments τ that fit two criteria: (a) they are the translation of a sub-segment σ from S but cannot be matched in T; and (b) when they are aligned to T using the Levenshtein edit distance algorithm (Levenshtein, 1966), both their first word θ_1 and last word $\theta_{|\tau|}$ can be aligned, therefore delimiting a sub-segment τ' of T. Our hypothesis is that those words t_j in τ' which cannot be aligned to τ are likely to need to be post-edited. We define our negative feature collection $\text{Neg}_{mn'}$ as:

$$\text{Neg}_{mn'}(j, S, T, M) = \sum_{\forall \tau \in \text{NegEvidence}_{mn'}(j,S,T,M)} \frac{1}{\text{alignmentsize}(\tau, T)}$$

where $\text{alignmentsize}(\tau, T)$ returns the length of the sub-segment τ' delimited by τ in T. Function $\text{NegEvidence}_{mn'}(\cdot)$ returns the set of τ sub-segments that are considered negative evidence and is defined as:

$$\begin{aligned}\text{NegEvidence}_{mn'}(j, S, T, M) = \{\tau : (\sigma, \tau) \in M \\ \wedge\, \sigma \in \text{seg}_m(S) \,\wedge\, |\tau'| = n' \,\wedge \\ \tau \notin \text{seg}_*(T) \,\wedge\, \text{IsNeg}(j, \tau, T)\}\end{aligned}$$

In this function length constraints are set so that sub-segments σ take lengths $m \in [1, L]$.[7] However, the case of the sub-segments τ is slightly different: n' does not stand for the length of the sub-segments, but the number of words in τ which are aligned to T.[8] Function $\text{IsNeg}(\cdot)$ defines the set of conditions required to consider a sub-segment τ a negative evidence for word t_j:

$$\begin{aligned}\text{IsNeg}(j, \tau, T) = \exists j', j'' \in [1, |T|] : j' < j < j'' \\ \wedge\, \text{aligned}(t_{j'}, \theta_1) \,\wedge\, \text{aligned}(t_{j''}, \theta_{|\tau|}) \,\wedge \\ \nexists \theta_k \in \text{seg}_1(\tau) : \text{aligned}(t_j, \theta_k)\end{aligned}$$

where $\text{aligned}(X, Y)$ is a binary function that checks whether words X and Y are aligned or not.

[7]In contrast to the positive features, preliminary results showed an improvement in the performance of the classifier when constraining the length of the σ sub-segments used for each feature in the set.

[8]That is, the length of longest common sub-segment of τ and T.

Negative features $\text{Neg}_{mn'}(\cdot)$ are computed for t_j for all the values of SL sub-segment lengths $m \in [1, L]$ and the number of TL words $n' \in [2, L]$ which are aligned to words θ_k in sub-segment τ. Note that the number of aligned words between T and τ cannot be lower than 2 given the constraints set by function $\text{IsNeg}(j, \tau, T)$. This results in a collection of $L \times (L - 1)$ negative features. Obviously, for these features only $M_{S\to T}$ is used, since in $M_{T\to S}$ all the sub-segments τ can be found in T.

4 Experimental setting

The experiments described in this section compare the results of our approach to those in the word-level MTQE task in WMT 2014 (Bojar et al., 2014), which are considered the state of the art in the task. In this section we describe the sources of bilingual information used for our experiments, as well as the binary classifier and the data sets used for evaluation.

4.1 Evaluation data sets

Four data sets for different language pairs were published for the word-level MTQE task in WMT 2014: English–Spanish (EN–ES), Spanish–English (ES–EN), English–German (EN–DE), and German–English (DE–EN). The data sets contain the original SL segments, and their corresponding translation hypotheses tokenised at the level of words. Each word is tagged by hand using three levels of granularity:

- **binary**: words are classified only taking into account if they need to be post-edited (class *BAD*) or not (class *OK*);
- **level 1**: extension of the binary classification which differentiates between *accuracy* errors and *fluency* errors;
- **multi-class**: fine-grained classification of errors divided in 20 categories.

In this work we focus on the binary classification, which is the base for the other classification granularities.

Four evaluation metrics were defined for this task:

- The F_1 score weighted by the rate ρ_c of instances of a given class c in the data set:

$$F_1^w = \sum_{\forall c \in C} \rho_c \frac{2 p_c r_c}{p_c + r_c}$$

where C is the collection of classes defined for a given level of granularity (OK and BAD for the binary classification) and p_c and r_c are the precision and recall for a class $c \in C$, respectively;

- The F_1 score of the less frequent class in the data set (class BAD, in the case of binary classification):

$$F_1^{\text{BAD}} = \frac{2 \times p_{\text{BAD}} \times r_{\text{BAD}}}{p_{\text{BAD}} + r_{\text{BAD}}};$$

- The Matthews correlation coefficient (MCC), which takes values in $[-1, 1]$ and is more reliable than the F_1 score for unbalanced data sets (Powers, 2011):

$$\text{MCC} = \frac{T_{\text{OK}} \times T_{\text{BAD}} - F_{\text{OK}} \times F_{\text{BAD}}}{\sqrt[2]{A_{\text{OK}} \times A_{\text{BAD}} \times P_{\text{OK}} \times P_{\text{BAD}}}}$$

  where T_{OK} and T_{BAD} stand for the number of instances correctly classified for each class, F_{OK} and F_{BAD} stand for the number of instances wrongly classified for each class, P_{OK} and P_{BAD} stand for the number of instances classified either as OK or BAD, and A_{OK} and A_{BAD} stand for the actual number of each class; and

- Total accuracy (ACC):

$$\text{ACC} = \frac{T_{\text{OK}} + T_{\text{BAD}}}{P_{\text{OK}} + P_{\text{BAD}}}$$

The comparison between the approach presented in this work and those described by Bojar et al. (2014) is based on the F_1^{BAD} score because this was the main metric used to compare the different approaches participating in WMT 2014. However, all the metrics are reported for a better analysis of the results obtained.

4.2 Sources of Bilingual Information

As already mentioned, two different sources of information were used in this work, MT and a bilingual concordancer. For our experiments we used two MT systems which are freely available on the Internet: Apertium and Google Translate. These MT systems were exploited by translating the sub-segments, for each data set, in both directions (from SL to TL and vice versa). It is worth noting that language pairs EN–DE and DE–EN are not available for Apertium. For these data sets only Google Translate was used.

The bilingual concordancer *Reverso Context* was also used for translating sub-segments. Namely, the sub-sentential translation memory of this system was used, which is a much richer source of bilingual information and provides, for a given SL sub-segment, the collection of TL translation alternatives, together with the number of occurrences of the sub-segments pair in the translation memory. Furthermore, the sub-segment translations obtained from this source of information are more reliable, since they are extracted from manually translated texts. On the other hand, its main weakness is the coverage: although Reverso Context uses a large translation memory, no translation can be obtained for those SL sub-segments which cannot be found in it. In addition, the sub-sentential translation memory contains only those sub-segment translations with a minimum number of occurrences. On the contrary, MT systems will always produce a translation, even though it may be wrong or contain untranslated out-of-vocabulary words. Our hypothesis is that combining both sources of bilingual information can lead to reasonable results for word-level MTQE.

For our experiments, we computed the features described in Section 3 separately for both sources of information. The value of the maximum sub-segment length L used was set to 5, which resulted in a collection of 40 features from the bilingual concordancer, and 30 from MT.[9]

4.3 Binary classifier

Esplà-Gomis et al. (2011) use a simple perceptron classifier for word-level quality estimation in translation-memory-based computer-aided translation. In this work, a more complex *multilayer perceptron* (Duda et al., 2000, Section 6) is used, as implemented in Weka 3.6 (Hall et al., 2009). Multilayer perceptrons (also known as *feedforward neural networks*) have a complex structure which incorporates one or more *hidden layers*, consisting of a collection of perceptrons, placed between the input of the classifier (the features) and the output perceptron. This hidden layer makes multilayer perceptrons suitable for non-linear classification problems (Duda et al., 2000, Section 6). In fact, Hornik et al. (1989) proved that neural networks with a single hidden layer containing a finite number of neurons are universal approximators and may therefore be able to perform better than a simple per-

[9]As already mentioned, the features based on translation frequency cannot be obtained for MT.

ceptron for complex problems. In our experiments, we have used a batch training strategy, which iteratively updates the weights of each perceptron in order to minimise a total error function. A subset of 10% of the training examples was extracted from the training set before starting the training process and used as a validation set. The weights were iteratively updated on the basis of the error computed in the other 90%, but the decision to stop the training (usually referred as the convergence condition) was based on this validation set. This is a usual practice whose objective is to minimise the risk of overfitting. The training process stops when the total error obtained in an iteration is worse than that obtained in the previous 20 iterations.[10]

Hyperparameter optimisation was carried out using a grid search (Bergstra et al., 2011) in a 10-fold cross-validation fashion in order to choose the hyperparameters optimising the results for the metric to be used for comparison, F_1 for class *BAD*:

- *Number of nodes in the hidden layer*: Weka (Hall et al., 2009) makes it possible to choose from among a collection of predefined network designs; the design performing best in most cases happened to have the same number of nodes in the hidden layer as the number of features.
- *Learning rate*: this parameter allows the dimension of the weight updates to be regulated by applying a factor to the error function after each iteration; the value that best performed for most of our training data sets was 0.9.
- *Momentum*: when updating the weights at the end of a training iteration, momentum smooths the training process for faster convergence by making it dependent on the previous weight value; in the case of our experiments, it was set to 0.07.

5 Results and discussion

Table 1 shows the results obtained by the baseline consisting on marking all the words as BAD, whereas Table 2 shows the reference results obtained by the best performing system according to the results published by Bojar et al. (2014). These tables are used as a reference for the results obtained with the approach described in this work.

language pair	**weighted** F_1	**BAD** F_1	**MCC**	**accuracy**
EN–ES	18.71	52.53	0.00	35.62
ES–EN	5.28	29.98	0.00	17.63
EN–ES	12.78	44.57	0.00	28.67
DE–EN	8.20	36.60	0.00	22.40

Table 1: Results of the "always BAD" baseline for the different data sets.

language pair	**weighted** F_1	**BAD** F_1	**MCC**	**accuracy**
EN–ES	62.00	48.73	18.23	61.62
ES–EN	79.54	29.14	25.47	82.98
EN–DE	71.51	45.30	28.61	72.97
DE–EN	72.41	26.13	16.08	76.14

Table 2: Results of the best performing systems for the different data sets according to the results published by Bojar et al. (2014).

Table 3 shows the results obtained when using Reverso Context as the only source of information. Using only Reverso Context leads to reasonably good results for language pairs EN–ES and EN–DE, while for the other two language pairs results are much worse, basically because no word was classified as needing to be post-edited. This situation is caused by the fact that, in both cases, the amount of examples of words to be post-edited in the training set is very small (lower than 21%). In this case, if the features are not informative enough, the strong bias leads to a classifier that always recommends to keep all words untouched. However, it is worth noting that with a small amount of features (40 features) state-of-the-art results were obtained for two data sets.[11] Namely, in the case of the EN–ES data set, the one with the largest amount of training instances, the results for the main metric (F_1 score for the less frequent class, in this case *BAD*) were better than those of the state of the art. In the case of the EN–DE data set the results are noticeably lower than the state of the art, but they are still comparable to them.

Table 4 shows the results obtained when combining the information from Reverso Context and the MT systems Apertium and Google Translate. Again, one of the best results is obtained for the EN–ES data set, which would again beat the state of the art for the F_1 score for the *BAD* class, and

[10]It is usual to set a number of additional iterations after the error stops improving, in case the function is in a local minimum, and the error starts decreasing again after a few more iterations. If the error continues to worsen after these 20 iterations, the weights used are those obtained after the iteration with the lowest error.

[11]We focus our comparison on the F_1 score for the *BAD* class because this was the metric on which the classifiers were optimised.

language pair	weighted F_1	BAD F_1	MCC	accuracy
EN–ES	60.18	49.09	16.28	59.46
ES–EN	74.41	0.00	0.00	82.37
EN–DE	65.88	41.24	17.05	65.71
DE–EN	67.82	0.00	0.00	77.60

Table 3: Results of the approach proposed in this paper for the same data sets used to obtain Table 2 using Reverso Context as the only source of bilingual information.

language pair	weighted F_1	BAD F_1	MCC	accuracy
EN–ES	61.43	49.03	17.71	60.91
ES–EN	75.87	10.44	9.61	81.82
EN–DE	66.75	43.07	19.38	78.71
DE–EN	75.00	40.33	25.85	76.03

Table 4: Results of the approach proposed in this work for the same data sets used to obtain Table 2 using both Reverso Context and both Google Translate and Apertium as the sources of bilingual information.

which obtained results still closer to those of the state of the art for the rest of metrics. In addition, the biased classification problem for data sets DE–EN and ES–EN is alleviated. Actually, the results for the DE–EN language pair are particularly good, and outperform the state of the art for all the metrics. The low F_1 score obtained for the ES–EN data set may be explained by the unbalanced amount of positive and negative instances. Actually, the ratio of negative instances is somewhat related to the results obtained: 35% for EN–ES, 17% for ES–EN, 30% for EN–DE and 21% for DE–EN. A closer analysis of the results shows that our approach is better when detecting errors in the *Terminology*, *Mistranslation*, and *Unintelligible* subclasses. The ratio of this kind of errors over the total amount of negative instances for each data set is again related to the results obtained: 73% for EN–ES, 27% for ES–EN, 47% for EN–DE and 35% for DE–EN. This information may explain the differences in the results obtained for each data set.

Again, it is worth noting that this light method using a reduced set of 70 features can obtain, for most of the data sets, results comparable to those obtained by approaches using much more features. For example, the best system for the data set EN–ES (Camargo de Souza et al., 2014) used 163 features, while the winner system for the rest of data sets (Biçici and Way, 2014; Biçici, 2013) used 511,000 features. The sources of bilingual information used in this work are rather rich; however, given that any source of bilingual information could be used on the fly, simpler sources of bilingual information could also be used. It would therefore be interesting to carry out a deeper evaluation of the impact of the type and quality of the resources used with this approach.

6 Concluding remarks

In this paper we describe a novel approach for word-level MTQE based on the use of on-line available bilingual resources. This approach is aimed at being system-independent, since it does not make any assumptions about the MT system used for producing the translation hypotheses to be evaluated. Furthermore, given that this approach can use any source of bilingual information as a black box, it can be easily used with few resources. In addition, adding new sources of information is straightforward, providing considerable room for improvement. The results described in Section 5 confirm that our approach can reach results comparable to those in the state of the art using a smaller collection of features than those used by most of the other approaches.

Although the results described in this paper are encouraging, it is worth noting that it is difficult to extract strong conclusions from the small data sets used. A wider evaluation should be done, involving larger data sets and more language pairs. As future work, we plan to extend this method by using other on-line resources to improve the on-line coverage when spotting sub-segment translations; namely, different bilingual concordancers and on-line dictionaries. Monolingual target-language information could also be obtained from the Internet to deal with fluency issues, for example, getting the frequency of a given n-gram from search engines. We will also study the combination of these features with features used in previous state-of-the-art systems (see Section 2) Finally, it would be interesting to try the new features defined here in word-level quality estimation for computer-aided translation tools, as in Esplà-Gomis et al. (2011).

Acknowledgements

Work partially funded by the Spanish Ministerio de Ciencia e Innovación through projects TIN2009-14009-C02-01 and TIN2012-32615 and by the European Commission through project PIAP-GA-2012-324414 (Abu-MaTran). We specially thank Reverso-Softissimo and Prompsit Language Engineering for providing the access to Reverso Context, and to the University Research Program for Google Translate that granted us access to the Google Translate service.

References

Bergstra, James S., Rémi Bardenet, Yoshua Bengio, and Balázs Kégl. 2011. Algorithms for hyper-parameter optimization. In Shawe-Taylor, J., R.S. Zemel, P.L. Bartlett, F. Pereira, and K.Q. Weinberger, editors, *Advances in Neural Information Processing Systems 24*, pages 2546–2554. Curran Associates, Inc.

Biçici, Ergun and Andy Way. 2014. Referential translation machines for predicting translation quality. In *Proceedings of the 9th Workshop on Statistical Machine Translation*, pages 313–321, Baltimore, USA.

Biçici, Ergun. 2013. Referential translation machines for quality estimation. In *Proceedings of the 8th Workshop on Statistical Machine Translation*, pages 343–351, Sofia, Bulgaria.

Biçici, Ergun and Deniz Yuret. 2011. Instance selection for machine translation using feature decay algorithms. In *Proceedings of the 6th Workshop on Statistical Machine Translation*, pages 272–283.

Blatz, John, Erin Fitzgerald, George Foster, Simona Gandrabur, Cyril Goutte, Alex Kulesza, Alberto Sanchis, and Nicola Ueffing. 2003. Confidence estimation for machine translation. Technical Report Final Report of the Summer Workshop, Center for Language and Speech Processing, Johns Hopkins University, Baltimore, USA.

Blatz, John, Erin Fitzgerald, George Foster, Simona Gandrabur, Cyril Goutte, Alex Kulesza, Alberto Sanchis, and Nicola Ueffing. 2004. Confidence estimation for machine translation. In *Proceedings of the 20th International Conference on Computational Linguistics*, COLING '04.

Bojar, Ondrej, Christian Buck, Christian Federmann, Barry Haddow, Philipp Koehn, Johannes Leveling, Christof Monz, Pavel Pecina, Matt Post, Herve Saint-Amand, Radu Soricut, Lucia Specia, and Aleš Tamchyna. 2014. Findings of the 2014 workshop on statistical machine translation. In *Proceedings of the 9th Workshop on Statistical Machine Translation*, pages 12–58.

Brown, Peter F., Vincent J. Della Pietra, Stephen A. Della Pietra, and Robert L. Mercer. 1993. The mathematics of statistical machine translation: Parameter estimation. *Computational Linguistics*, 19(2):263–311.

Camargo de Souza, José Guilherme, Jesús González-Rubio, Christian Buck, Marco Turchi, and Matteo Negri. 2014. FBK-UPV-UEdin participation in the wmt14 quality estimation shared-task. In *Proceedings of the 9th Workshop on Statistical Machine Translation*, pages 322–328, Baltimore, USA, June. Association for Computational Linguistics.

Duda, R. O., P. E. Hart, and D. G. Stork. 2000. *Pattern Classification*. John Wiley and Sons Inc., second edition.

Esplà-Gomis, Miquel, Felipe Sánchez-Martínez, and Mikel L. Forcada. 2011. Using machine translation in computer-aided translation to suggest the target-side words to change. In *Proceedings of the Machine Translation Summit XIII*, pages 172–179, Xiamen, China.

Gandrabur, Simona and George Foster. 2003. Confidence estimation for translation prediction. In *Proceedings of the 7th Conference on Natural Language Learning at HLT-NAACL 2003 - Volume 4*, CONLL '03, pages 95–102.

Hall, Mark, Eibe Frank, Geoffrey Holmes, Bernhard Pfahringer, Peter Reutemann, and Ian H. Witten. 2009. The WEKA Data Mining Software: an Update. *SIGKDD Explorations*, 11(1):10–18.

Hornik, K., M. Stinchcombe, and H. White. 1989. Multilayer feedforward networks are universal approximators. *Neural Networks*, 2(5):359–366, July.

Levenshtein, V.I. 1966. Binary codes capable of correcting deletions, insertions and reversals. *Soviet Physics Doklady*, 10(8):707–710.

Miller, George A. 1995. Wordnet: A lexical database for English. *Communications of the ACM*, 38(11):39–41.

Powers, David M. W. 2011. Evaluation: From precision, recall and F-measure to ROC, informedness, markedness & correlation. *Journal of Machine Learning Technologies*, 2.

Specia, Lucia and Radu Soricut. 2013. Quality estimation for machine translation: preface. *Machine Translation*, 27(3-4):167–170.

Specia, Lucia, Dhwaj Raj, and Marco Turchi. 2010. Machine translation evaluation versus quality estimation. *Machine Translation*, 24(1):39–50.

Specia, Lucia, Kashif Shah, José GC De Souza, and Trevor Cohn. 2013. QuEst-a translation quality estimation framework. In *ACL (Conference System Demonstrations)*, pages 79–84.

Ueffing, Nicola and Hermann Ney. 2005. Application of word-level confidence measures in interactive statistical machine translation. In *Proceedings of the 10th European Association for Machine Translation Conference "Practical applications of machine translation"*, pages 262–270.

Ueffing, Nicola and Hermann Ney. 2007. Word-level confidence estimation for machine translation. *Computational Linguistics*, 33(1):9–40, March.

A general framework for minimizing translation effort: towards a principled combination of translation technologies in computer-aided translation

Mikel L. Forcada **Felipe Sánchez-Martínez**
Dept. de Llenguatges i Sistemes Informàtics
Universitat d'Alacant
E-03071 Alacant (Spain)
{mlf,fsanchez}@dlsi.ua.es

Abstract

This paper motivates the need for an homogeneous way of measuring and estimating translation effort (quality) in computer-aided translation. It then defines a general framework for the measurement and estimation of translation effort so that translation technologies can be both optimized and combined in a principled manner. In this way, professional translators will benefit from the seamless integration of all the technologies at their disposal when working on a translation job.

1 Introduction

Imagine that you are a professional translator and you are given a translation job. The text to be translated comes divided in N segments, $s_1, s_2, \ldots s_N$: your job is therefore the ordered set $\{s_i\}_{i=1}^N$. You are supposed to turn this into a translation, that is, an ordered set $\{t_i\}_{i=1}^N$ with the translations of each segment, and get paid for that. Yes, this is a simplified view of your work: the translation of each sentence is treated as an independent event, which is not always the case. In any case, even in this simplified form, the job is already quite challenging.

Help coming your way? Of course, you could translate each segment s_i by hand, i.e. from scratch, into an suitable segment t_i in the target language. You are a translator and you know this is usually harder than most people think. However, there are *translation technologies* out there that are supposed to help you by reducing your translation effort; they usually come packaged as *computer-aided translation* (CAT).

Machine translation: You could, for instance, use *machine translation* (MT) to get a draft of the translation of each segment, $\mathrm{MT}(s_i)$; vendors and experts tell you that you will save effort by *post-editing* $\mathrm{MT}(s_i)$ into your desired translation t_i.[1] Machine translation output $\mathrm{MT}(s_i)$ may just be text, but it could come with annotations to help you make the most of it; for instance, words could be color-coded according to how confident the system is about them (Ueffing and Ney, 2007; Ueffing and Ney, 2005; Blatz et al., 2004), or unknown words that come out untranslated may be marked so that you spot them clearly. Machine-translated segments could even be accompanied by indicators of their estimated quality (Specia and Soricut, 2013; Specia et al., 2010; Blatz et al., 2004) which may be used to ascertain whether the output of the MT system is worth being post-edited or not. If someone measured your post-editing effort (in time, in number of keystrokes, in number of words changed, in money you would have to pay another translator to do it, etc.), when turning $\mathrm{MT}(s_i)$ into t_i, they could call that effort e_i^{MT}.

Translation memory: You could also use a *translation memory* (TM; (Somers, 2003)), where previously translated segments s are stored together with their translations t in pairs called translation units (s, t). The software searches the TM for the source segment $s_i^\star$ that best matches each one of your segments s_i, and delivers the corresponding

[1] We leave aside the debate about whether post-editors should be considered different from translators, as in the end of the day, you will be producing a translation which should be adequate for the purpose at hand, and you will be as responsible of it as if you had produced it from scratch; we will therefore call everything *translation* for the purpose of this paper.

target segment $t_i^\star$ as a proposal, but not alone: it also gives you information about how good the match was between your new segment s_i and the best *fuzzy match* $s_i^\star$ —usually as a percentage called *fuzzy match score* that accounts for the amount of text that is common to both segments[2]— and even marks for you the words in $s_i^\star$ that do not match those in s_i. Let's call all this information $\mathrm{TM}(s_i)$: your job is to use it to turn $t_i^\star$ into the final translation t_i. If the *fuzzy match* is good, you will spend less effort than if you started from scratch. Let us call e_i^{TM} the effort to turn the $t_i^\star$ provided by $\mathrm{TM}(s_i)$ into the desired translation t_i.[3]

Mixing them up: You could even have available another technology, *fuzzy-match repair* (FMR; (Ortega et al., 2014; Dandapat et al., 2011; Hewavitharana et al., 2005; Kranias and Samiotou, 2004)), that integrates the two technologies just mentioned: after a suitable fuzzy match is found, machine translation (or another source of bilingual information) is used to *repair*, i.e. edit some parts of $t_i^\star$, to take into account what changes from $s_i^\star$ to s_i to try to save even more effort; it tells you all that $\mathrm{TM}(s_i)$ tells you, but also marks the parts that have been repaired. Fuzzy-match repair is one of the technologies that TAUS, the Translation Automation User Society, calls *advanced leveraging*;[4] commercial examples of these are DeepMiner in Atril's Déjà Vu,[5] and ALTM in MultiCorpora's MultiTrans.[6] It takes an effort e_i^{FMR} to turn the output of fuzzy-match repair, $\mathrm{FMR}(s_i)$, into the desired t_i.

And many more: To summarize, each technology X you can use —where X may be MT, TM, FMR, etc.— takes each segment s_i and produces an output $X(s_i)$ that takes an effort e_i^{X} to turn into t_i. For a more general discussion, we will also consider a technology the case in which no technology is used, i.e. when the translation is performed from scratch: technologies may not be helpful at all sometimes. We will call $\mathcal{X}$ the set of all technologies X available in the CAT environment. Note that there is another simplification here: the effort e_i^{X} is assumed to depend only on s_i, but translators may vary over time, either during a job, or between jobs; they may become tired, or the effectiveness of each technology may vary.

Isn't this getting too complicated to be considered help? At this point, you are probably wondering how can you decide which technology to use for each segment s_i if the information available for each technology, such as quality indicators in the case of machine translation and fuzzy matching scores in the case of translation memories, are not directly comparable. Or even better, couldn't the decision of selecting the best technology $X_i^\star$, that is, the one that minimizes your effort for each segment s_i, be made automatically?

It is therefore clear that a framework that allows to seamlessly integrate all the translation technologies available in the CAT system is very much needed to make the most of all of them and minimize translation effort as much as possible.

Previous work on technology selection: The specific case of automatically choosing between machine translation output and translation memory fuzzy matches has received attention in the last years. Simard and Isabelle (2009) proposed a simple approach called β-combination, which simply selects machine translation when there is no translation memory proposal with a fuzzy match score above a given threshold β, which can be tuned. He et al. (2010a) and He et al. (2010b) approach this problem, which they call *translation recommendation*, by training a classifier which selects which of the two, $\mathrm{TM}(s_i)$ or $\mathrm{MT}(s_i)$, gets the lowest value for an approximate indicator of effort, called *translation error rate* (TER, (Snover et al., 2006)). Their training compares outputs to preexisting reference translations; their ideas are generalized in the approach proposed in this paper.

The next section explains two ways to minimize the effort needed to perform a translation job in a CAT environment integrating different technologies. Section 3 then describes our proposal for a general framework for training the whole CAT environment. Finally, we discuss the implications of having such a framework.

[2]The fuzzy match score is usually based on a text similarity measure like the word-level edit distance or Levenshtein distance (Levenshtein, 1966). Commercial CAT systems use trade-secret, proprietary versions of it aimed at estimating better than the edit distance the remaining effort.

[3]Interestingly enough, in contrast with the case of machine translation, even if you are actually post-editing a fuzzy-matched proposal, there does not seem to be much debate as to whether you are a translator or a *fuzzy match post-editor*.

[4]`http://www.taus.net/reports/advanced-leveraging`

[5]`http://tinyurl.com/x3dejavu`

[6]`http://multicorpora.com/resources/advanced-leveraging/`

2 Minimizing translation effort

Translation technology designers understand that translators want to minimize their total effort. To compute this total effort, the actual measurements of effort e_i^{X} need to be *extensive* magnitudes,[7] that is, magnitudes that grow with the length of the segment and make sense when added for all the segments of the job. Examples of extensive measurements have already been given: amount of words or characters changed, total amount of keystrokes, time spent in editing and total price.[8] These are magnitudes that can be compared regardless of technology and allow the total cost of a new translation job to be simply calculated as

$$E = \sum_{i=1}^{N} e_i^{X_i^\star}$$

where $e_i^{X_i^\star}$ is the effort expended in translating segment s_i using the best technology $X_i^\star$ for that segment, that is, the one that minimizes that effort.

To minimize the translation effort on a specific task, designers have to work in two main areas:

Improving each technology: One is to *improve the output of each technology* X, ideally focusing on those cases when X is going to be selected. Some such technologies have tunable parameters; for instance, *feature weights* in statistical MT (Koehn, 2010, p. 255); for other technologies, this is not usually reported, but it is not impossible to think, for instance, of fuzzy-match scores that give different weights to different kinds of edit operations. Let us call $\vec{\lambda}^X$ the vector of tunable parameters for technology X; as the output of technology X varies with these parameters, we can write its output like this: $X(s_i; \vec{\lambda}^X)$.

Learning to select the best technology: The other one is that the CAT environment needs a way to select the best technology $X_i^\star$ for each segment s_i, obviously without measuring the actual effort. To do this, CAT designers need to come up with a set of estimators $\tilde{e}^X$, one for each technology. These estimators should be trained to give the best possible estimate of the actual measured effort $e^X(X(s_i; \vec{\lambda}^X))$. If we call $\vec{\theta}^X$ the set of tunable parameters of the estimator for technology X, the output of the estimator for X can be written as $\tilde{e}^X(X(s_i; \vec{\lambda}^X); \vec{\theta}^X)$. These estimators can be used to estimate the total cost of a new translation job as

$$\tilde{E} = \sum_{i=1}^{N} \tilde{e}^{X_i^\star}(X_i^\star(s_i; \vec{\lambda}^{X_i^\star}); \vec{\theta}^{X_i^\star}),$$

where

$$X_i^\star = \operatorname*{argmin}_{X \in \mathcal{X}} \tilde{e}^X(X(s_i; \vec{\lambda}^X); \vec{\theta}^X).$$

In the case of MT, the estimators of effort (Specia and Soricut, 2013; Specia et al., 2010; Blatz et al., 2004) are based on a number of features obtained from s_i and $\mathrm{MT}(s_i; \vec{\lambda}^{\mathrm{MT}})$. The vector of parameters $\vec{\theta}^{\mathrm{MT}}$ is tuned on a development set made of bilingual segments and translation effort measurements $e^{\mathrm{MT}}(\mathrm{MT}(s_i; \vec{\lambda}^{\mathrm{MT}}))$.[9]

Getting a good estimate of effort is hard: One problem for technologists is that actual measurements of effort are expensive to collect, and they are not likely to be available for all technologies and for all segments. Therefore it is in principle not easy to determine the parameters $\vec{\theta}^X$ to get good estimates $\tilde{e}^X(X(s_i; \vec{\lambda}^X); \vec{\theta}^X)$. We will see a way to do this below.

Tuning technologies is also hard: Technologies may have tunable parameters $\vec{\lambda}^X$ which determine the output they produce. Obviously, one cannot just repetitively measure the actual effort spent by translators in editing their output for a wide variety of values of $\vec{\lambda}^X$, as this is clearly impracticable; therefore, an alternative is needed. When $X = \mathrm{MT}$, this is usually done by means of an algorithm that optimizes (Och, 2003; Chiang, 2012) *automatic evaluation measures*, such as BLEU (Papineni et al., 2002), using *reference translations* in a *development set*. Most of these automatic

[7]This concept is borrowed from physics: see, e.g., http://en.wikipedia.org/wiki/Intensive_and_extensive_properties.

[8]Examples of measurements that are not extensive, that is, *intensive*, could be the percentage of words or characters changed, the ratio of the total amount of keystrokes to the sentence length, the time spent per word, or the price per word. These are intensive properties as they are the ratio of two extensive properties.

[9]The measurements of effort that one can find in literature vary from simple scores for "perceived" post-editing effort (usually scores taking 3 or 4 values) to actual post-editing time (see, for instance, the quality estimation task in WMT 2014 (Bojar et al., 2014))

measures are measures of similarity (or dissimilarity) between raw and reference translations. Researchers hope that their use during tuning will lead to a reduction in translation effort, although this is not currently guaranteed —for instance, Denkowski and Lavie (2012) found that BLEU could not distinguish between raw and post-edited machine translation. Generally, an automatic evaluation measure for technology X may have the form $\hat{e}^X(X(s_i;\vec{\lambda}^X),\{t_{ij}\}_{j=1}^{n_i};\vec{\mu}^X)$, where $\{t_{ij}\}_{j=1}^{n_i}$ is the set of reference translations for segment s_i in the development set and $\vec{\mu}^X$ is a set of tunable parameters. Ideally, $\hat{e}^X(X(s_i;\vec{\lambda}^X),\{t_{ij}\}_{j=1}^{n_i};\vec{\mu}^X)$ should approximate $e^X(X(s_i;\vec{\lambda}^X))$, but tuning of $\vec{\mu}^X$ is surprisingly absent from current MT practice (with some exceptions, see Denkowski and Lavie (2010)). In fact, $\hat{e}^X(X(s_i;\vec{\lambda}^X),\{t_{ij}\}_{j=1}^{n_i};\vec{\mu}^X)$ can be seen as a special estimator of effort, much like $\tilde{e}^X(X(s_i;\vec{\lambda}^X);\vec{\theta}^X)$, but informed with reference translations $\{t_{ij}\}_{j=1}^{n_i}$ when they are available. This is similar to the use of pseudo-reference translations in machine translation quality estimation (Shah et al., 2013; Soricut and Narsale, 2012; Soricut et al., 2012; Soricut and Echihabi, 2010), but with actual references.

Table 1 summarizes the main concepts and the notation used along the paper.

3 A general framework for training the whole CAT environment

We describe a possible workflow to tune simultaneously the different technologies that may be used in a CAT environment and the estimators used to select them on a segment basis:

1. Design automatic evaluation measures $\hat{e}^X(X(s_i,\vec{\lambda}^X),\{t_{ij}\};\vec{\mu}^X)$ and estimators $\tilde{e}^X(X(s_i;\vec{\lambda}^X);\vec{\theta}^X)$ for each technology $X\in\mathcal{X}$, based on a series of relevant features that can easily be extracted from s_i and $X(s_i)$, and which will depend on parameters $\vec{\mu}^X$ and $\vec{\theta}^X$, respectively.

2. Give reasonable starting values to the parameters of $\tilde{e}^X(X(s_i;\vec{\lambda}^X);\vec{\theta}^X)$ for each technology X in $\mathcal{X}$, so that they can be used to preliminarily select technologies. These initial estimators $\tilde{e}_0^X(X(s_i;\vec{\lambda}^X);\vec{\theta}^X)$ could, for instance, be the ones that worked well for a related task.

3. Put together a development set $D=\{s_k\}_{k=1}^{n_D}$ having n_D segments, representative of the task at hand, and which provides reference translations $\{t_{kl}\}_{l=1}^{n_k}$ for each segment. This development set should be large enough to be used to tune the technologies in step 7; it could also be used to pre-tune the technologies (for instance, statistical machine translation could be pre-tuned using customary evaluation measures such as BLEU). Development sets of thousands of segments are common, for instance, in statistical machine translation, but the actual number may depend on the number of parameters in each $\vec{\lambda}^X$.

4. Have translators work on a representative subset $M=\{s_k\}_{k=1}^{n_M}$ of the development set D, and measure their effort when translating each segment using the best technology, selected according to the available version of estimators $\tilde{e}^X(X(s_k;\vec{\lambda}^X);\vec{\theta}^X)$. Of course, M is a small *subset* of D because translating thousands of sentences, as in a typical development set, is clearly out of the question, as this would be more like the size of a whole translation job. Note that translator work can add additional references for those segments in D which are also in M. Note also that we might be combining here measurements for a team of more than one translator. Therefore, the resulting combination of technologies may not be expected to be optimal for each individual translator, but rather *on average* for the team.

   A richer set of measurements could be obtained by having translators translate segments in M using also other technologies not selected by the estimators. This would be costly but could help mitigate the bias introduced by the initial set of estimators.

   To get evaluation measures $\hat{e}_i^X$ and estimators $\tilde{e}_i^X$ which are useful in the scenario of a new translation job, translation memories are not allowed to grow or change when translators translate the set M, and the resulting reference set is fixed after this step.

5. Use these measurements to fit all the automatic evaluation measures $\hat{e}^X(X(s_i,\vec{\lambda}^X),\{t_{ij}\};\vec{\mu}^X)$ together by varying their vectors $\vec{\mu}^X$ by means of eq. (1):

Notation	Definition
$\{s_i\}_{i=1}^N$	Translation task made up of N source segments s_i.
X	Translation technology; e.g. $X = \mathrm{MT}$, machine translation; $X = \mathrm{TM}$, translation memory; $X = \mathrm{FMR}$, fuzzy-match repair; etc.
$\mathcal{X}$	The set of all translation technologies available.
$X_i^\star$	Technology selected for the translation of the source segment s_i.
$X(s_i; \vec{\lambda}^X)$, also $X(s_i)$	Output produced by translation technology X for input segment s_i. Many provide additional information in addition to its output.
$\vec{\lambda}^X$	Optional vector of tunable parameters used by translation technology X to produce the best possible translation proposal.
$e^X(X(s_i; \vec{\lambda}^X))$, also e_i^X	Actual measured effort to produce an adequate translation starting from the proposal provided by technology X.
$\tilde{e}^X(X(s_i; \vec{\lambda}^X); \vec{\theta}^X)$, also $\tilde{e}_i^X$	Estimated effort to produce an adequate translation starting from the proposal provided by technology X.
$\vec{\theta}^X$	Optional vector of tunable parameters used in the estimator of effort $\tilde{e}^X(\cdot)$. The parameters may be tuned so that the estimated effort is as close as possible to the measured effort.
$\hat{e}^X(X(s_i; \vec{\lambda}^X), \{t_{ij}\}_{j=1}^{n_i}; \vec{\mu}^X)$, also $\hat{e}_i^X$	Estimated effort to produce an adequate translation starting from the proposal of technology X, specifically informed by a set of reference translations (sometimes called *automatic evaluation measure*).
$\{t_{ij}\}_{j=1}^{n_i}$, also $\{t_{ij}\}$	Set of *reference translations* for segment s_i.
$\vec{\mu}^X$	Optional vector of tunable parameters used in estimator $\hat{e}^X(\cdot)$. These parameters may be tuned so that the estimated effort is as close as possible to the measured effort (parameters are seldom tuned in *automatic evaluation measures*).

Table 1: A summary of the main concepts defined in the paper and the notation used.

$$\min_{\{\vec{\mu}^X\}_{X\in\mathcal{X}}} \sum_{k\in[1,n_M]} \mathcal{L}\left(\hat{e}^{X_k^\star}(X_k^\star(s_k,\vec{\lambda}^{X_k^\star}),\{t_{kl}\}_{l=1}^{n_k};\vec{\mu}^{X_k^\star}), e^{X_k^\star}(X_k^\star(s_k;\vec{\lambda}^{X_k^\star}))\right) \quad (1)$$

Here, $\mathcal{L}(x)$ is ideally a differentiable loss function (for instance $\mathcal{L}(x) = \frac{1}{2}x^2$), and $X_k^\star$ is the technology selected for s_k by using the initial estimator (if measurements had been made in step 4 for more than one technology per segment, they could be used here to get a better approximation). The result is a set of functions $\{\hat{e}^X\}$ which estimate, using reference translations, the effort needed to deal with the output of each technology X, without having to actually measure that effort.

6. **Training the technology selectors:** Use the available measurements of effort e_k^X where they are available, and the automatic evaluation measures $\hat{e}^X(X(s_k),\{t_{kl}\}_{l=1}^{n_k};\vec{\mu}^X)$ where they are not, to obtain a set of better estimators $\tilde{e}^X(X(s_k;\vec{\lambda}^X);\vec{\theta}^X)$ by varying their vectors $\vec{\theta}^X$ using the whole development set D and eq. (2):

$$\min_{\{\vec{\theta}^X\}_{X\in\mathcal{X}}} \sum_{k\in[1,n_D]} \mathcal{L}\left(\tilde{e}^{X_k^\star}(X_k^\star(s_k,\vec{\lambda}^{X_k^\star});\vec{\theta}^{X_k^\star}), \bar{e}^{X_k^\star}(X_k^\star(s_k,\vec{\lambda}^{X_k^\star}),\{t_{kl}\}_{l=1}^{n_k};\vec{\mu}^{X_k^\star})\right) \quad (2)$$

Here, $\bar{e}^X(X(s_k,\vec{\lambda}^X),\{t_{kl}\}_{l=1}^{n_k};\vec{\mu}^X)$ is the actual effort measured $e^X(X(s_k;\vec{\lambda}^X))$ if it is available, and $\hat{e}^X(X(s_k,\vec{\lambda}^{X_k^\star}),\{t_{kl}\}_{l=1}^{n_k};\vec{\mu}^X)$ otherwise, and $X_k^\star$ is the actual selection for those segments where measurements were taken, or the technology with the best $\hat{e}^X(X(s_k,\vec{\lambda}^X),\{t_{kl}\}_{l=1}^{n_k};\vec{\mu}^X)$ where they were not. The result is a set of functions $\{\tilde{e}^X\}$ which estimate, in the absence of reference translations, the effort needed to deal with the output of each technology X, without having to actually measure that effort. These functions will be used in the translator's CAT tool to automatically select the best technology for each segment.

7. **Training the technologies themselves:** The same development set, and the functions $\{\hat{e}^X\}$ may be used to train —or, as usually said in statistical machine translation, to *tune* — the technologies themselves by searching for those values of $\vec{\lambda}^X$ leading to the minimum effort for translators:

$$\min_{\{\vec{\lambda}^X\}_{X\in\mathcal{X}}} \sum_{k\in[1,n_D]} \hat{e}^{X_k^\star}(X_k^\star(s_k,\vec{\lambda}^{X_k^\star}),\{t_{kl}\}_{l=1}^{n_k};\vec{\mu}^{X_k^\star}), \quad (3)$$

where $X_k^\star$ is the translation technology with the best $\hat{e}^X(X(s_k,\vec{\lambda}^X),\{t_{kl}\}_{l=1}^{n_k};\vec{\mu}^X)$.

This training would be analogous to minimum-error-rate training (MERT) (Och, 2003), MIRA (Hasler et al., 2011), or similar iterative methods used in statistical machine translation to vary the parameters of a system and optimize the output with respect to a certain quality indicator such as BLEU (Papineni et al., 2002), but it would be applied to all sources $X \in \mathcal{X}$ and use the estimators $\hat{e}_i^X$ of extensive effort measurements tuned in step 5. Eq. (3) tunes each technology using only those segments for which it was selected. Alternatively, one may prefer to optimize all technologies on all segments as follows:

$$\min_{\{\vec{\lambda}^X\}_{X\in\mathcal{X}}} \sum_{X\in\mathcal{X}} \sum_{k\in[1,n_D]} \hat{e}^X(X(s_k,\vec{\lambda}^X),\{t_{kl}\}_{l=1}^{n_k};\vec{\mu}^X), \quad (4)$$

and run the risk of spreading optimization too thin to significantly optimize those technologies likely to be actually selected in a real translation job.

The result is a set of technologies $\mathcal{X}$ that are (approximately) optimized to reduce effort. These technologies will be used in the CAT tool to provide the best possible assistance to translators.

Note that the new estimators obtained in step 6 could have led to different technology choices, and therefore different measurement sets, if these choices had been made in step 4. This coupling between parameter sets should in principle be taken into account in an improved setting by feeding this all the way back to step 4 in some way to achieve self-consistency while keeping the need for additional effort measurements, that is, additional manual translations of segments in M, to a minimum; feasible or approximate ways of doing this should definitely be explored.

Note also that the workflow above is a *batch* workflow. *Online* workflows which improve the technologies X as translators work, would certainly be more complex, but could be devised following the rationale behind the batch workflow just described, once it is proven useful.

4 Discussion

We have introduced a unified, general framework for effort (quality) measurement, evaluation and estimation. This framework allows to simultaneously tune all the components of a computer-aided translation environment. To that end, we propose the use of estimators of remaining effort that are comparable across translation-assistance technologies.

On the one hand, tuning all the translation technologies together (which is not common in current practice), and in a way that takes into account when they are actually selected to produce a proposal for the translator, will lead to an improvement of the translation proposals these technologies produce when this improvement is relevant; that is, when the technology is actually used to propose a translation to the translator.

On the other hand, having estimators of effort whose output is comparable across technologies will allow for seamless integration of translation technologies: the CAT tool will be able to automatically select the best technology on a segment basis. In addition, if the estimations of effort are measured in time spent in editing, or in money, they could be used to accurately budget new translation jobs.

The framework proposed in this paper provides a principled way to adapt the mix of technologies to reduce total effort in a specific computer-aided translation job.

We hope that this unified framework will ease the integration of existing research being performed to actually reduce translators' effort and improve their productivity. We also hope that it will inspire new approaches and encourage best practice in computer-aided translation research and development.

Acknowledgements: We acknowledge support from the Spanish Ministry of Industry and Competitiveness through project Ayutra (TIC2012-32615) and from the European Commission through project Abu-Matran (FP7-PEOPLE-2012-IAPP, ref. 324414) and thank all three anonymous referees for very useful comments on the paper.

References

Blatz, J., E. Fitzgerald, G. Foster, S. Gandrabur, C. Goutte, A. Kulesza, A. Sanchis, and N. Ueffing. 2004. Confidence estimation for machine translation. In *Proceedings of the 20th International Conference on Computational Linguistics*, pages 315–321, Geneva, Switzerland.

Bojar, O., C. Buck, C. Federmann, B. Haddow, P. Koehn, J. Leveling, C. Monz, P. Pecina, M. Post, H. Saint-Amand, R. Soricut, L. Specia, and A. Tamchyna. 2014. Findings of the 2014 workshop on statistical machine translation. In *Proceedings of the Ninth Workshop on Statistical Machine Translation*, pages 12–58, Baltimore, Maryland, USA.

Chiang, D. 2012. Hope and fear for discriminative training of statistical translation models. *Journal of Machine Learning Research*, 13:1159–1187.

Dandapat, S., S. Morrissey, A. Way, and M. L. Forcada. 2011. Using example-based MT to support statistical MT when translating homogeneous data in a resource-poor setting. In *Proceedings of the 15th conference of the European Association for Machine Translation*, pages 201–208. Leuven, Belgium.

Denkowski, M. and A. Lavie. 2010. METEOR-NEXT and the METEOR paraphrase tables: Improved evaluation support for five target languages. In *Proceedings of the Joint 5th Workshop on Statistical Machine Translation and MetricsMATR (Uppsala, Sweden)*, page 339–342.

Denkowski, M. and A. Lavie. 2012. Challenges in predicting machine translation utility for human post-editors. In *Proceedings of The Tenth Biennial Conference of the Association for Machine Translation in the Americas*, San Diego, CA, USA.

Hasler, Eva, Barry Haddow, and Philipp Koehn. 2011. Margin infused relaxed algorithm for moses. *The Prague Bulletin of Mathematical Linguistics*, 96:69–78.

He, Y., Y. Ma, J. van Genabith, and A. Way. 2010a. Bridging SMT and TM with translation recommendation. In *Proceedings of the 48th Annual Meeting of the Association for Computational Linguistics*, pages 622–630, Uppsala, Sweden.

He, Yifan, Yanjun Ma, Johann Roturier, Andy Way, and Josef van Genabith. 2010b. Improving the post-editing experience using translation recommendation: A user study. In *Proceedings of the Ninth Conference of the Association for Machine Translation in the Americas*.

Hewavitharana, S., S. Vogel, and A. Waibel. 2005. Augmenting a statistical translation system with a translation memory. In *Proceedings of the 10th conference of the European Association for Machine Translation*, pages 126–132, Budapest, Hungary.

Koehn, P. 2010. *Statistical Machine Translation*. Cambridge University Press.

Kranias, L. and A. Samiotou. 2004. Automatic translation memory fuzzy match post-editing: a step beyond traditional TM/MT integration. In *Proceedings of the Fourth International Conference on Language Resources and Evaluation*, pages 331–334, Lisbon, Portugal.

Levenshtein, V.I. 1966. Binary codes capable of correcting deletions, insertions and reversals. *Soviet Physics Doklady*, 10(8):707–710.

Och, F.J. 2003. Minimum error rate training in statistical machine translation. In *Proceedings of the 41st Annual Meeting on Association for Computational Linguistics*, pages 160–167, Sapporo, Japan.

Ortega, J. E., M. L. Forcada, and F. Sánchez-Martínez. 2014. Using any machine translation source for fuzzy-match repair in a computer-aided translation setting. In al Onaizan, Yaser and Michel Simard, editors, *Proceedings of the 11th Conference of the Association for Machine Translation in the Americas*, volume 1: MT Researchers, pages 42–53, Vancouver, BC, Canada.

Papineni, K., S. Roukos, T. Ward, and W. J. Zhu. 2002. BLEU: a method for automatic evaluation of machine translation. In *Proceedings of the 40th Annual Meeting of the Association for Computational Linguistics*, pages 311–318, Philadelphia, PA, USA.

Shah, K., T. Cohn, and L. Specia. 2013. An investigation on the effectiveness of features for translation quality estimation. In *Proceedings of the XIV Machine Translation Summit*, pages 167–174, Nice, France.

Simard, M. and P. Isabelle. 2009. Phrase-based machine translation in a computer-assisted translation environment. In *Proceedings of the 12th Machine Translation Summit*, pages 120–127, Ottawa, Canada.

Snover, M., B. Dorr, R. Schwartz, L. Micciulla, and J. Makhoul. 2006. A study of translation edit rate with targeted human annotation. In *Proceedings of Association for Machine Translation in the Americas Conference*, pages 223–231, August.

Somers, H., 2003. *Computers and translation: a translator's guide*, chapter Translation memory systems, pages 31–48. John Benjamins Publishing, Amsterdam, Netherlands.

Soricut, R. and A. Echihabi. 2010. Trustrank: Inducing trust in automatic translations via ranking. In *In Proceedings of the 48th Annual Meeting of the Association for Computational Linguistics*, pages 612–621, Uppsala, Sweden.

Soricut, R. and S. Narsale. 2012. Combining quality prediction and system selection for improved automatic translation output. In *Proceedings of the Seventh Workshop on Statistical Machine Translation*, pages 163–170, Montreal, Canada.

Soricut, R., N. Bach, and Z. Wang. 2012. The SDL Language Weaver systems in the WMT12 quality estimation shared task. In *Proceedings of the Seventh Workshop on Statistical Machine Translation*, pages 145–151, Montreal, Canada.

Specia, L. and R. Soricut. 2013. Quality estimation for machine translation: preface. *Machine Translation*, 27(3-4):167–170.

Specia, L., D. Raj, and M. Turchi. 2010. Machine translation evaluation versus quality estimation. *Machine Translation*, 24(1):39–50.

Ueffing, Nicola and Hermann Ney. 2005. Word-level confidence estimation for machine translation using phrase-based translation models. In *Proceedings of the Conference on Human Language Technology and Empirical Methods in Natural Language Processing*, HLT '05, pages 763–770.

Ueffing, Nicola and Hermann Ney. 2007. Word-level confidence estimation for machine translation. *Computational Linguistics*, 33(1):9–40, March.

Can Translation Memories afford not to use paraphrasing?

Rohit Gupta[1], **Constantin Orăsan**[1], **Marcos Zampieri**[2,3], **Mihaela Vela**[2], **Josef van Genabith**[2,3]
[1]Research Group in Computational Linguistics, University of Wolverhampton, UK
[2]Saarland University, Germany
[3]German Research Center for Artificial Intelligence (DFKI)
{r.gupta, c.orasan}@wlv.ac.uk
{marcos.zampieri, m.vela}@uni-saarland.de
josef.van_genabith@dfki.de

Abstract

This paper investigates to what extent the use of paraphrasing in translation memory (TM) matching and retrieval is useful for human translators. Current translation memories lack semantic knowledge like paraphrasing in matching and retrieval. Due to this, paraphrased segments are often not retrieved. Lack of semantic knowledge also results in inappropriate ranking of the retrieved segments. Gupta and Orăsan (2014) proposed an improved matching algorithm which incorporates paraphrasing. Its automatic evaluation suggested that it could be beneficial to translators. In this paper we perform an extensive human evaluation of the use of paraphrasing in the TM matching and retrieval process. We measure post-editing time, keystrokes, two subjective evaluations, and HTER and HMETEOR to assess the impact on human performance. Our results show that paraphrasing improves TM matching and retrieval, resulting in translation performance increases when translators use paraphrase enhanced TMs.

1 Introduction

One of the core features of a TM system is the retrieval of previously translated similar segments for post-editing in order to avoid translation from scratch when an exact match is not available. However, this retrieval process is still limited to edit-distance based measures operating on surface form (or sometimes stem) matching. Most of the commercial systems use edit distance (Levenshtein, 1966) or some variation of it, e.g. the open-source TM OmegaT[1] uses word-based edit distance with some extra preprocessing. Although these measures provide a strong baseline, they are not sufficient to capture semantic similarity between the segments as judged by humans.

Gupta and Orăsan (2014) proposed an edit distance measure which incorporates paraphrasing in the process. In the present paper, we perform a human-centred evaluation to investigate the use of paraphrasing in translation memory matching and retrieval. We use the same system as Gupta and Orăsan (2014) and investigate the following questions: (1) how much of an improvement can paraphrasing provide in terms of retrieval? (2) What is the quality of the retrieved segments and its impact on the work of human translators? These questions are answered using human centred evaluations.

To the best of our knowledge, this paper presents the first work on assessing the quality of any type of semantically informed TM fuzzy matches based on post-editing time or keystrokes.

2 Related Work

Several researchers have used semantic or syntactic information in TMs, but their evaluations were shallow and most of the time limited to subjective evaluation carried out by the authors. This makes it hard to judge how much a semantically informed TM matching system can benefit a translator.

Existing research (Planas and Furuse, 1999; Hodász and Pohl, 2005; Pekar and Mitkov, 2007; Mitkov, 2008) pointed out the need for similarity

[1]http://www.omegat.org

calculations in TMs beyond surface form comparisons. Both Planas and Furuse (1999) and Hodasz and Pohl (2005) proposed to use lemma and parts of speech along with surface form comparison. Hodasz and Pohl (2005) also extend the matching process to a sentence skeleton where noun phrases are either tagged by a translator or by a heuristic NP aligner developed for English-Hungarian translation. Planas and Furuse (1999) tested a prototype model on 50 sentences from the software domain and 75 sentences from a journal with TM sizes of 7,192 and 31,526 segments respectively. A fuzzy match retrieved was considered usable if less than half of the words required editing to match the input sentence. The authors concluded that the approach gives more usable results compared to Trados Workbench used as a baseline. Hodasz and Pohl (2005) claimed that their approach stores simplified patterns and hence makes it more probable to find a match in the TM. Pekar and Mitkov (2007) presented an approach based on syntactic transformation rules. On evaluation of the prototype model using a query sentence, the authors found that the syntactic rules help in retrieving better segments.

Recently, work by Utiyama et al. (2011) and Gupta and Orăsan (2014) presented approaches which use paraphrasing in TM matching and retrieval. Utiyama et al. (2011) proposed an approach using a finite state transducer. They evaluate the approach with one translator and find that paraphrasing is useful for TM both in terms of precision and recall of the retrieval process. However, their approach limits TM matching to exact matches only. Gupta and Orăsan (2014) also use paraphrasing at the fuzzy match level and they report an improvement in retrieval and quality of retrieved segments. The quality of retrieved segments was evaluated using the machine translation evaluation metric BLEU (Papineni et al., 2002). Simard and Fujita (2012) used different MT evaluation metrics for similarity calculation as well as for testing the quality of retrieval. For most of the metrics, the authors find that, the metric which is used in evaluation gives better score to itself (e.g. BLEU gives highest score to matches retrieved using BLEU as similarity measure).

Keystroke and post-editing time analysis are not new for TM and MT. Keystroke analysis has been used to judge translators' productivity (Langlais and Lapalme, 2002; Whyman and Somers, 1999). Koponen et al. (2012) suggested that post-editing time reflects the cognitive effort in post-editing the MT output. Sousa et al. (2011) evaluated different MT system performances against translating from scratch. Their study also concluded that subjective evaluations of MT system output correlate with the post-editing time needed. Zampieri and Vela (2014) used post-editing time to compare TM and MT translations.

3 Our Approach and Experiments

We have used the approach presented in Gupta and Orăsan (2014) to include paraphrasing in the TM matching and retrieval process. The approach classifies paraphrases into different types for efficient implementation based on the matching of the words between the source and corresponding paraphrase. Using this approach, the fuzzy match score between segments can be calculated in polynomial time despite the inclusion of paraphrases. The method uses dynamic programming along with greedy approximation. The method calculates fuzzy match score as if the appropriate paraphrases are applied. For example, if the translation memory used has a segment "What is the actual aim of this practice ?" and the paraphrase database has paraphrases "the actual" ⇒ "the real" and "aim of this" ⇒"goal of this", for the input sentence "What is the real goal of this mission ?", the approach will give a 89.89% fuzzy match score (only one word, "practice", needs substitution with "mission") rather than 66.66% using simple word-based edit distance.

In TM, the performance of retrieval can be measured by counting the number of segments or words retrieved. However, NLP techniques are not 100% accurate and most of the time, there is a tradeoff between the precision and recall of this retrieval process. This is also one of the reasons that TM developers shy away from using semantic matching. One cannot measure the gain unless retrieval benefits the translator.

When we use paraphrasing in the matching and retrieval process, the fuzzy match score of a paraphrased segment is increased, which results in the retrieval of more segments at a particular threshold. This increment in retrieval can be classified in two types: without changing the top rank; and by changing the top rank. For example, for a particular input segment, we have two segments A and B in the TM. Using simple edit-distance, A has a 65% and B has a 60% fuzzy score; the fuzzy score of A is better than that of B. As a result of using paraphrasing we notice two types of score changes:

1. the score of A is still better than or equal to that of B, for example, A has 85% and B has 70% fuzzy score;

2. the score of A is less than that of B, for example, A has 75% and B has 80% fuzzy score.

In the first case, paraphrasing does not supersede the existing model and just facilitates it by improving the fuzzy score so that the top segment ranked using edit distance gets retrieved. However, in the second case paraphrasing changes the ranking and now the top ranked segment is different. In this case, the paraphrasing model supersedes the existing simple edit distance model. This second case also gives a different reference to compare with. We take the top segment retrieved using simple edit distance as a reference against the top segment retrieved using paraphrasing and compare to see which is better for a human translator to work with.

To evaluate the influence of paraphrasing on matching and retrieval, we have carried out four different experiments. Section 3.1 describes the settings and measures used for post-editing evaluation, and Sections 3.2 and 3.3 describe the settings for the subjective evaluations.

3.1 Post-editing Time (PET) and Keystrokes (KS)

In this evaluation, the translators were presented with fuzzy matches and the task was to post-edit the segment in order to obtain a correct translation. The translators were presented with an input English segment, the German segment retrieved from the TM for post-editing and the English segment used for matching in TM.

In this task, we recorded post-editing time (PET) and keystrokes (KS). The post-editing time taken for the whole file is calculated by summing up the time taken on each segment. Only one segment is visible on screen. The segment is only visible after clicking and the time is recorded from when the segment becomes visible until the translator finishes post-editing and goes to the next screen. The next screen is a blank screen so that the translator can have a rest after post-editing a segment. The translators were aware that the time is being recorded. Each translator post-edited half of the segments retrieved using simple edit distance (ED) and half of the segments retrieved using paraphrasing (PP). The ED and PP matches were presented one after the other (ED at odd positions and PP at even positions or vice versa). However, the same translator did not post-edit the match retrieved using PP and ED for the same segment: instead five different translators post-edited the segment retrieved using PP and another five different translators post-edited the match retrieved using ED.

Post-editing time (PET) for each segment is the mean of the normalised time (N) taken by all translators on this segment. Normalisation is applied to account for both slow and fast translators.

$$\text{PET}_j = \frac{\sum_{i=1}^{n} N_{ij}}{n} \tag{1}$$

$$N_{ij} = T_{ij} \times \frac{\text{Avg time on this file by all translators}}{\sum_{j=1}^{m} T_{ij}} \tag{2}$$

In the equations 1 and 2 above, PET_j is the post editing time for each segment j, n is the number of translators, N_{ij} is the normalised time of translator i on segment j, m is the number of segments in the file, and T_{ij} is the actual time taken by a translator i on a segment j.

Along with the post-editing time, we also recorded all printable keystrokes, whitespace and erase keys pressed. For our analysis, we considered average keystrokes pressed by all translators for each segment.

3.2 Subjective Evaluation with Two Options (SE2)

In this evaluation, we carried out subjective evaluation with two options (SE2). We presented fuzzy matches retrieved using both paraphrasing (PP) and simple edit distance (ED) to the translators. The translators were unaware of the details (ED or PP) of how the fuzzy matches were obtained. To neutralise any bias, half of the ED matches were tagged as A and the other half as B, with the same applied to PP matches. The translator has to choose between two options: A is better; or B is better. 17 translators participated in this experiment. Finally, the decision of whether 'ED is better' or 'PP is better' is made on the basis of how many translators choose one over the other.

3.3 Subjective Evaluation with Three Options (SE3)

This evaluation is similar to Evaluation SE2 except that we provided one more option to translators. Translators can choose among three options: A is better; B is better; or both are equal. 7 translators participated in this experiment.

4 Corpus, Tool and Translators expertise

As a TM and test data, we have used English-German pairs of the Europarl V7.0 (Koehn, 2005) corpus with English as the source language and German as the target language. From this corpus we have filtered out segments of fewer than seven words and greater than 40 words, to create the TM and test datasets. Tokenization of the English data was done using the Berkeley Tokenizer (Petrov et al., 2006). We have used the lexical and phrasal paraphrases from the PPDB corpus (Ganitkevitch et al., 2013) of L size. In these experiments, we have not paraphrased any capitalised words (but we lowercase them for both baseline and paraphrasing similarities calculation). This is to avoid paraphrasing any named entities. Table 1 shows our corpus statistics. The translators involved in

	TM	Test Set
Segments	1565194	9981
Source words	37824634	240916
Target words	36267909	230620

Table 1: Corpus Statistics

our experiments were third year bachelor or masters translation students who were native speakers of German with English language level C1, in the age group of 21 to 40 years with a majority of female students. Our translators were not expert in any specific technical or legal field. For this reason we did not use such a corpus. In this way we avoid any bias from unfamiliarity or familiarity with domain specific terms.

4.1 Familiarisation with the Tool

We used the PET tool (Aziz et al., 2012) for all our human experiments. However, settings were changed depending on the experiment. To familiarise translators with the PET tool we carried out a pilot experiment before the actual experiment with the Europarl corpus. This experiment was done on a corpus (Vela et al., 2007) different from Europarl. 18 segments are used in this experiment. While the findings are not included in this paper, they informed the design of our main experiments.

5 Results and Analysis

The retrieval results are given in Table 2. The table shows the similarity threshold for TM (TH), the total number of segments retrieved using the baseline approach (EDR), the additional number of segments retrieved using the paraphrasing approach (+PPR), the percentage improvement in retrieval obtained over the baseline (Imp), the number of segments that changed their ranking and rose to the top because of paraphrasing (RC), and the number of unique paraphrases used to retrieve +PPR (NP) and RC (NPRC). Table 2 shows that when using

TH	100	[85, 100)	[70, 85)	[55, 70)
EDR	117	98	225	703
+PPR	16	30	98	311
%Imp	13.67	30.61	43.55	44.23
RC	9	14	55	202
NP	24	49	169	535
NPRC	14	24	92	356

Table 2: Results of Retrieval

paraphrasing we obtain around 13.67% increase in retrieval for exact matches and more than 30% and 43% increase in the intervals [85, 100) and [70, 85), respectively. This is a clear indication that paraphrasing significantly improves the retrieval results. We have also observed that there are different paraphrases used to bring about this improvement. In the interval [70, 85), 169 different paraphrases are used to retrieve 98 additional segments.

To check the quality of the retrieved segments human evaluations are carried out. The sets' distribution for human evaluation is given in the Table 3. The sets contain randomly selected segments from the additionally retrieved segments using paraphrasing which changed their top ranking.[2]

TH	100	[85, 100)	[70, 85)	Total
Set1	2	6	6	14
Set2	5	4	7	16
Total	7	10	13	30

Table 3: Test Sets for Human Experiments

[2]The sets are constructed so that a translator can post-edit a file in one sitting. There is no differentiation between the evaluations based on sets and all evaluations are carried out in both sets in a similar fashion with different translators.

	Post-editing				Subjective Evaluations				
	PET		KS		SE2 (2 Options)		SE3 (3 options)		
Seg #	ED	PP	ED	PP	EDB	PPB	EDB	PPB	BEQ
1	42.98	41.30↑	42.4	**0.4**↑	**1**	**16**↑	0	7↑	0
2!+	13.72	10.65↑	2.8	2.4↑	10	7↓	2	2	3
3*!	13.88	12.62↑	2.0	3.6↓	12	5↓	4	1↓	2
4	37.97	**17.64**↑	26.2	**6.2**↑	**1**	**16**↑	0	6↑	1
5!+	21.52	17.69↑	22.4	13.2↑	**13**	**4**↓	2	3↑	2
6!+	41.14	42.74↓	13.2	34.4↓	**4**	**13**↑	2	0	5
7!+	33.69	31.59↑	34.0	33.4↑	10	7↓	1	0	6
8	47.14	**23.41**↑	61.6	**6.4**↑	**0**	**17**↑	0	7↑	0
9	22.89	**14.20**↑	37.2	**2.2**↑	**0**	**17**↑	0	6↑	1
10	46.89	38.20↑	77.6	65.6↑	**1**	**16**↑	0	1	6
11	58.25	53.65↑	82.8	58.8↑	**0**	**17**↑	0	3	4
12!+	34.04	45.03↓	36.8	39.6↓	**2**	**15**↑	0	6↑	1
13	30.34	**21.12**↑	54.8	39.2↑	7	10↑	1	1	5
14!+	75.50	96.54↓	38.8	50.8↓	5	12↑	0	3	4
Set1-subtotal	520.02	466.44	532.60	356.20	66	172	12	46	40
15	24.14	**9.18**↑	24.0	**0.0**↑	5	12↑	1	5↑	1
16*+	28.30	29.20↓	23.4	15.4↑	11	6↓	2	2	3
17*!	65.64	53.49↑	6.2	22.4↓	10	7↓	2	3↑	2
18	41.91	**20.98**↑	28.0	**2.0**↑	**1**	**16**↑	0	6↑	1
19	29.81	19.71↑	23.8	**6.8**↑	7	10↑	2	3↑	2
20	41.25	**15.42**↑	39.0	**3.8**↑	**0**	**17**↑	1	5↑	1
21*!	**42.04**	65.44↓	39.4	36.0↑	7	10↑	1	2	4
22	29.28	35.87↓	17.0	33.4↓	12	5↓	5	0↓	2
23	**32.64**	49.49↓	**11.4**	50.8↓	11	6↓	2	2	3
24!+	59.35	54.54↑	79.6	79.2↑	**17**	**0**↓	5	0↓	2
25	62.51	61.30↑	71.0	54.0↑	**2**	**15**↑	0	3	4
26*!	36.82	41.06↓	55.0	**23.4**↑	**1**	**16**↑	0	6↑	1
27!+	**27.21**	44.02↓	**24.4**	48.8↓	**4**	**13**↑	1	5↑	1
28	40.99	**33.08**↑	39.6	**24.6**↑	5	12↑	3	4↑	0
29	52.01	**31.55**↑	50.6	**23.4**↑	**2**	**15**↑	0	6↑	1
30*!	43.76	38.76↑	38.2	44.6↓	**15**	**2**↓	1	1	5
Set2-subtotal	657.75	603.17	570.6	468.59	110	162	26	53	33
Total	1177.77	1069.61	1103.2	824.79	176	334	38	99	73

Table 4: Results of Human Evaluation on Set1 (1-14) and Set2 (15-30)

Results for human evaluations (PET, KS, SE2 and SE3) on both sets (Set1 and Set2) are given in Table 4. Here 'Seg #' represents the segment number, 'ED' represents the match retrieved using simple edit distance and 'PP' represents the match retrieved after incorporating paraphrasing. 'EDB', 'PPB' and 'BEQ' in Subjective Evaluations represent the number of translators who judge 'ED is better', 'PP is better' and 'Both are equal', respectively.

5.1 Results: Post-editing Time (PET) and Keystrokes (KS)

As we can see in Table 4, improvements were obtained for both sets. ↑ demonstrates cases in which PP performed better than ED and ↓ shows where ED performed better than PP. Entries in bold for PET, KS and SE2 indicate where the results are statistically significant [3].

For Set1, translators made 356.20 keystrokes and 532.60 keystrokes when editing PP and ED matches, respectively. Translators took 466.44 seconds for PP as opposed to 520.02 seconds for ED matches. This means that by using PP matches, translators edit 33.12% less (49.52% more using ED), which saves 10.3% time .

For Set2, translators made 468.59 keystrokes and 570.6 keystrokes when editing PP and ED matches respectively. Translators took 603.17 seconds for PP as opposed to 657.75 seconds for ED matches. This means that by using PP matches, translators edit 17.87% less (21.76% more using ED), which saves 8.29% time.

In total, combining both the sets, translators made 824.79 keystrokes and 1103.2 keystrokes when editing PP and ED matches, respectively. Translators took 1069.61 seconds for PP as opposed to 1177.77 seconds for ED matches. Therefore, by using PP matches, translators edit 25.23% less, which saves time by 9.18%. In other words, ED matches require 33.75% more keystrokes and 10.11% more time. We observe that the percentage improvement obtained by keystroke analysis is smaller compared to the improvement obtained by post-editing time. One of the reasons for this is that the translator spends a fair amount of time reading a segment before starting editing.

[3] $p<0.05$, one tailed Welch's t-test for PET and KS, χ^2 test for SE2. Because of the small sample size for SE3, no significance test was performed on individual segment basis.

5.2 Results: Using post-edited references

We also calculated the human-targeted translation error rate (HTER) (Snover et al., 2006) and human-targeted METEOR (HMETEOR) (Denkowski and Lavie, 2014). HTER and HMETEOR was calculated between ED and PP matches presented for post-editing and references generated by editing the corresponding ED and PP match. Table 5 lists HTER5 and HMETEOR5, which use five corresponding ED or PP references only and HTER10 and HMETEOR10, which use all ten references generated using ED and PP.

Table 5 shows improvements in both the HTER5 and HMETEOR5 scores. For Set-1, HMETEOR5 improved from 59.82 to 81.44 and HTER5 improved from 39.72 to 17.63[4]. For Set-2, HMETEOR5 improved from 69.81 to 80.60 and HTER5 improved from 27.81 to 18.71. We also observe that while ED scores of Set1 and Set2 differ substantially (59.82 vs 69.81 and 39.72 vs 27.81), PP scores are nearly the same (81.44 vs 80.60 and 17.63 vs 18.71). This suggests that paraphrasing not only brings improvement but may also improve consistency.

	Set-1		Set-2	
	ED	**PP**	**ED**	**PP**
HMETEOR5	59.82	81.44	69.81	80.60
HTER5	39.72	17.63	27.81	18.71
HMETEOR10	59.82	81.44	69.81	80.61
HTER10	36.93	18.46	27.26	18.40

Table 5: Results using human targeted references

5.3 Results: Subjective evaluations

The subjective evaluations also show significant improvements.

In subjective evaluation with two options (SE2) as given in Table 4, from a total of 510 (30×17) replies for 30 segments from both sets by 17 translators, 334 replies tagged 'PP is better' and 176 replies tagged 'ED is better' [5].

In subjective evaluation with three options (SE3), from a total of 210 (30×7) replies for 30 segments from both sets by 7 translators, 99 replies tagged 'PP is better', 73 replies tagged 'both are equal' and 38 replies tagged 'ED is better' [6].

[4] For HMETEOR, higher is better and for HTER lower is better

[5] statistically significant, χ^2 test, $p < 0.001$

[6] statistically significant, χ^2 test, $p < 0.001$

5.4 Results: Segment wise analysis

A segment wise analysis of 30 segments from both sets shows that 21 segments extracted using PP were found to be better according to PET evaluation and 20 segments using PP were found to be better according to KS evaluation. In subjective evaluations, 20 segments extracted using PP were found to be better according to SE2 evaluation whereas 27 segments extracted using PP were found to be better or equally good according to SE3 evaluation (15 segments were found to be better and 12 segments were found to be equally good).

We have also observed that not all evaluations correlate with each other on segment-by-segment basis. '!, '+ and '* next to each segment number in Table 4 indicate conflicting evaluations: '!' denotes that PET and SE2 contradict each other, '+' denotes that KS and SE2 contradict each other and '*' denotes that PET and KS contradict each other. In twelve segments where KS evaluation or PET evaluation show PP as statistically significant better, except for two cases all the evaluations also shows them better.[7] For Seg #13 SE3 shows 'Both are equal' and for Seg #26, PET is better for ED, however for these two sentences also all the other evaluations show PP as better.

In three segments (Seg #'s 21, 23, 27) KS evaluation or PET evaluation show ED as statistically significant better, but none of the segment are tagged better by all the evaluations. In Seg #21 all the evaluations with the exception of PET show PP as better. In Seg #23, SE3 shows 'both are equal'. Seg #23 is given as follows:

> **Input:** The next item is the Commission declaration on Belarus .
>
> **ED:** The next item is the Commission Statement on AIDS .//Als nächster Punkt folgt die Erklärung der Kommission zu AIDS.
>
> **PP:** The next item is the Commission statement on Haiti .//Nach der Tagesordnung folgt die Erklärung der Kommission zu Haiti.

In Seg #23, apart from "AIDS" and "Haiti" the source side does not differ but the German side differs. The reason for PP match retrieval was that "statement on" in lower case was paraphrased as "declaration on" while in the other segment "Statement" was capitalised and hence was not paraphrased. If we look at the German side of both ED and PP, "Nach der Tagesordnung" requires a broader context to accept it as a translation of "The next item" whereas "Als nächster Punkt" does not require much context.

In Seg #27, we observe contradictions between post-editing evaluations and subjective evaluations. Seg #27 is given below (EDPE and PPPE are post-edited translations of ED and PP match respectively):

> **Input:** That would be an incredibly important signal for the whole region .
>
> **ED:** That could be an important signal for the future .//Dies könnte ein wichtiges Signal für die Zukunft sein.
>
> **PP:** That really would be extremely important for the whole region .//Und das wäre wirklich für die ganze Region extrem wichtig.
>
> **EDPE:** Dies könnte ein unglaublich wichtiges Signal für die gesamte Region sein.
>
> **PPPE:** Das wäre ein unglaublich wichtiges Signal für die ganze Region.

In subjective evaluations, translators tagged PP as better than ED. But, post-editing suggests that it takes more time and keystrokes to post-edit the PP compare to ED.

There is one segment, Seg #22, on which all the evaluations show that ED is better. Seg #22 is given below:

> **Input:** I would just like to comment on one point.
>
> **ED:** I would just like to emphasise one point.//Ich möchte nur eine Sache betonen.
>
> **PP:** I would just like to concentrate on one issue.//Ich möchte mich nur auf einen Punkt konzentrieren.

In segment 22, the ED match is clearly closer to the input than the PP match. Paraphrasing "on one point" as "on one issue" does not improve the result. Also, "konzentrieren" being a long word takes more time and keystrokes in post-editing.

[7] In this section all evaluations refer to all four evaluations viz PET, KS, SE2 and SE3.

6 Conclusion

Our evaluation answers the two questions previously raised. We conclude that paraphrasing significantly improves retrieval. We observe more than 30% and 43% improvement for the threshold intervals [85, 100) and [70, 85), respectively. The quality of the retrieved segment is also significantly better, which is evident from all our human translation evaluations. On average on both sets used for evaluation, compared to paraphrasing simple edit distance takes 33.75% more keystrokes and 10.11% more time when evaluating the segments who changed their top rank and come up in the threshold intervals because of paraphrasing.

Acknowledgement

The research leading to these results has received funding from the People Programme (Marie Curie Actions) of the European Union's Seventh Framework Programme FP7/2007-2013/ under REA grant agreement no. 317471.

References

Aziz, Wilker, S Castilho, and Lucia Specia. 2012. PET: a Tool for Post-editing and Assessing Machine Translation. In *Proceedings of LREC*.

Denkowski, Michael and Alon Lavie. 2014. Meteor universal: Language specific translation evaluation for any target language. In *Proceedings of WMT-2014 Workshop*.

Ganitkevitch, Juri, Van Durme Benjamin, and Chris Callison-Burch. 2013. Ppdb: The paraphrase database. In *Proceedings of NAACL-HLT*, pages 758–764, Atlanta, Georgia.

Gupta, Rohit and Constantin Orăsan. 2014. Incorporating Paraphrasing in Translation Memory Matching and Retrieval. In *Proceedings of EAMT*.

Hodász, Gábor and Gábor Pohl. 2005. MetaMorpho TM: a linguistically enriched translation memory. In *In International Workshop, Modern Approaches in Translation Technologies*.

Koehn, Philipp. 2005. Europarl: A parallel corpus for statistical machine translation. In *MT summit*, volume 5, pages 79–86.

Koponen, Maarit, Wilker Aziz, Luciana Ramos, and Lucia Specia. 2012. Post-editing time as a measure of cognitive effort. In *Workshop on Post-Editing Technology and Practice in AMTA-2012*, pages 11–20.

Langlais, Philippe and Guy Lapalme. 2002. Trans type: Development-evaluation cycles to boost translator's productivity. *Machine Translation*, 17(2):77–98.

Levenshtein, Vladimir I. 1966. Binary codes capable of correcting deletions, insertions, and reversals. In *Soviet physics doklady*, volume 10, pages 707–710.

Mitkov, Ruslan. 2008. Improving Third Generation Translation Memory systems through identification of rhetorical predicates. In *Proceedings of LangTech2008*.

Papineni, Kishore, Salim Roukos, Todd Ward, and Wei-Jing Zhu. 2002. Bleu: a method for automatic evaluation of machine translation. In *Proceedings of the ACL*, pages 311–318.

Pekar, Viktor and Ruslan Mitkov. 2007. New Generation Translation Memory: Content-Sensivite Matching. In *Proceedings of the 40th Anniversary Congress of the Swiss Association of Translators, Terminologists and Interpreters*.

Petrov, Slav, Leon Barrett, Romain Thibaux, and Dan Klein. 2006. Learning accurate, compact, and interpretable tree annotation. In *Proceedings of the COLING/ACL*, pages 433–440.

Planas, Emmanuel and Osamu Furuse. 1999. Formalizing Translation Memories. In *Proceedings of the 7th Machine Translation Summit*, pages 331–339.

Simard, Michel and Atsushi Fujita. 2012. A Poor Man s Translation Memory Using Machine Translation Evaluation Metrics . In *Proceedings of AMTA*.

Snover, Matthew, Bonnie Dorr, Richard Schwartz, Linnea Micciulla, and John Makhoul. 2006. A study of translation edit rate with targeted human annotation. In *Proceedings of AMTA*, pages 223–231.

Sousa, Sheila C.M. de, Wilker Aziz, and Lucia Specia. 2011. Assessing the post-editing effort for automatic and semi-automatic translations of dvd subtitles. In *Proceedings of RANLP*, pages 97–103.

Utiyama, Masao, Graham Neubig, Takashi Onishi, and Eiichiro Sumita. 2011. Searching Translation Memories for Paraphrases. In *Machine Translation Summit XIII*, pages 325–331.

Vela, Mihaela, Stella Neumann, and Silvia Hansen-Schirra. 2007. Querying multi-layer annotation and alignment in translation corpora. In *Proceedings of the Corpus Linguistics Conference CL*.

Whyman, Edward K and Harold L Somers. 1999. Evaluation metrics for a translation memory system. *Software-Practice and Experience*, 29(14):1265–84.

Zampieri, Marcos and Mihaela Vela. 2014. Quantifying the influence of MT output in the translators performance: A case study in technical translation. In *Workshop on Humans and Computer-assisted Translation*.

Dependency-based Reordering Model for Constituent Pairs in Hierarchical SMT

Arefeh Kazemi[†], **Antonio Toral**[⋆], **Andy Way**[⋆], **Amirhassan Monadjemi**[†], **Mohammadali Nematbakhsh**[†]

[†] Department of Computer Engineering, University of Isfahan, Isfahan, Iran

{akazemi,monadjemi,nematbakhsh}@eng.ui.ac.ir

[⋆] ADAPT Centre, School of Computing, Dublin City University, Ireland

{atoral,away}@computing.dcu.ie

Abstract

We propose a novel dependency-based reordering model for hierarchical SMT that predicts the translation order of two types of pairs of constituents of the source tree: head-dependent and dependent-dependent. Our model uses the dependency structure of the source sentence to capture the medium- and long-distance reorderings between these pairs of constituents. We describe our reordering model in detail and then apply it to a language pair in which the languages involved follow different word order patterns, English (SVO) and Farsi (free word order being SOV the most frequent pattern). Our model outperforms a baseline (standard hierarchical SMT) by 0.78 BLEU points absolute, statistically significant at $p = 0.01$.

1 Introduction

Reordering is a fundamental problem in machine translation (MT) that significantly affects translation quality, especially between languages with major differences in word order. While a great deal of work has been carried out to address this problem, none of the existing approaches can perform all the required types of reordering operations in a principled manner.

In general, there are four main approaches to address the reordering problem in statistical machine translation (SMT): distortion models, lexical phrase-based models, hierarchical phrase-based models and syntax-based models. Despite the relative success of each of these approaches in improving the overall performance of the SMT systems, they suffer from a number of shortcomings:

- *Inability to capturing long-distance reordering.* Distortion and lexical phrase-based models assign probability only to the adjacent word or phrase pairs, so they can only perform local reordering between adjacent units and fail to capture long distance reordering. This weakness has motivated research on tree-based models, such as the hierarchical phrase-based model (HPB). Although HPB models outperform phrase-based models (PB-SMT) on medium-range reordering, they still perform weakly on handling long distance reordering due to complexity constraints.
- *Sparsity.* Most of the approaches can perform the reordering of common words or phrases, but they usually cannot be generalized to unseen patterns which have the same linguistic structure. For example, if the object follows the verb in the source language and preceeds the verb in the target language, we still need to see a particular instance of a verb and an object in the training data to be able to perform reordering between them.
- *Context insensitivity.* Lexical and hierarchical phrase-based models determine the ordering of the phrases based solely on the lexical items in those phrases. However, a phrase might have different orderings in different contexts, so it is essential to include more context in order to capture the reordering behaviour.
- *High complexity.* Compared to the other reordering models, syntax-based models have access to the necessary structural information to perform long-distance reordering. However, due to the complexity of the decoding algorithm, they have very low performance on large-scale translations.

In order to overcome some of these deficiencies,

we propose a dependency-based reordering model for HPB-SMT. Our model uses the dependency structure of the source sentence to capture the medium- and long-distance reorderings between the dependent parts of the sentence. Unlike the syntax-based models that impose harsh syntactic limits on rule extraction and require serious efforts to be optimised (Wang et al., 2010), we use syntactic information only in the reordering model and augment the HPB model with soft dependency constraints. We report experimental results on a large-scale Engish-to-Farsi translation task.

The rest of this paper is organised as follows. Section 2 reviews the related work and contextualises our work. Section 3 outlines the main reordering issues due to syntactic differences between English and Farsi. Section 4 presents our reordering model, which is then evaluated in Section 5. Finally, Section 6 concludes the paper and outlines avenues of future work.

2 Related Work

Phrase-based systems can perform local (short distance) reordering inside the phrases but they are inherently weak at non-local (medium and long distance) reordering (Birch and Osborne, 2011). Previous work to address reordering in PB-SMT can generally be categorised into two groups. Approaches in the first group perform reordering in a pre-processing step (i.e. before decoding) by applying some reordering rules to the source sentences to make them in order more similar to that of the target language (Xia and McCord, 2004; Collins et al., 2005; Genzel, 2010). Although all these approaches have reported improvements, there is a fundamental problem with separating the reordering task into a pre-processing component as every faulty decision in the pre-processing step will be passed along as a hard decision to the translation system. This also violates the main principle behind statistical modelling in SMT, i.e. to avoid any hard choices and having the ability to reverse early faulty choices.

Approaches in the second group try to handle reordering in the decoding step, as a part of the translation process. They implement a probabilistic reordering model that can be used in combination with the other models in SMT to find the best translation. These approaches range from distortion models (Koehn et al., 2003) to lexical reordering models (Tillmann, 2004).

Distortion models generally prefer monotone translation which, while may work for related languages, is not a realistic assumption for translating between languages with different grammatical structure. On top of this limitation, these models do not take the content into consideration, and thus they do not generalise well.

Lexical reordering models take content into account and condition reordering on actual phrases. They try to learn local orientations for each adjacent phrase from training data. Despite the satisfactory performance of lexical models, they have two important limitations (Birch, 2011). First, since these models are conditioned on actual phrases, they have no ability to be generalised to unseen phrases. Second, these models still fail to capture long- and even medium-distance reorderings, since they try to find suitable reorderings only between adjacent phrases. The first limitation can be alleviated by using features of the phrase pair instead of the phrase itself (Xiong et al., 2006) while the second limitation can be tackled with hierarchical phrase reordering models (Galley and Manning, 2008).

HPB models (Chiang, 2005) should lead to better reordering than PB-SMT models by allowing phrases to contain gaps. In fact, this approach outperforms PB-SMT in medium-distance reordering, but it is equally weak in long-distance reordering (Birch et al., 2009). Common approaches to reordering in HPB models include preprocessing (Xu et al., 2009) and adding syntax to translation rules. The first approach results in improvements but suffers from the same issues presented above for pre-processing reordering in PB-SMT. The second introduces additional complexities and increases data sparsity (Hanneman and Lavie, 2013).

Our work falls into the recent research line that uses an external reordering model in hierarchical SMT. These models use source syntax to improve reordering without having to annotate translation rules with source syntax. Work in this line has so far looked at predicting the translation order of different types of source elements, pairs of words (Huang et al., 2013), constituents such as head and dependent words (Gao et al., 2011) and predicate-argument structures (Xiong et al., 2012; Li et al., 2013). It is worth noting that all these approaches have been applied solely to one language pair so far, Chinese-to-English.

This paper contributes to this research line on two dimensions. First, we extend the work of (Gao et al., 2011), who studied reordering of head-dependent pairs (i.e. parent and child elements in the dependency tree), and consider also the reordering of pairs of dependents (i.e. sibling elements in the dependency tree). Second, this is the first paper in this line of work to be applied to a language pair other than Chinese-to-English. Our language pair, English-to-Farsi, is comparatively challenging because (i) the target language is free word-order and morphologically rich, and (ii) it is comparatively under-resourced.

3 Word Order Differences between English and Farsi

This section provides a brief survey of the word order differences between the two languages of our case study. The main aim of this section is to make the reader familiar with the Farsi language, and specifically, to its word order peculiarities. That said, it should be noted that despite there being works that try to find specific syntactic reordering patterns for specific language pairs, e.g. (Collins et al., 2005), we have not used the syntactic information covered in this section in the proposed model as our model is language-independent.

There are two major differences between the word order in English and Farsi. First, English sentences follow the SVO (subject-verb-object) order while Farsi sentences follow, in most cases, the SOV order (Moghaddam, 2001). Second, English has strict word order while Farsi allows for free word order. In Farsi, the preferred word order is SOV, but all of the other orders are also correct.

Table 1 provides further details on word order differences by determining the element pairs that should be reordered in the translation process. In order to categorise word order differences we use the element pairs presented by Dryer (1992). Dryer has shown that these pairs can be used to distinguish SOV and SVO languages.

4 Dependency-based Reordering Model

Our reordering model is based on the source dependency tree, an example of which is shown in Figure 1. The dependency tree of a sentence shows the grammatical relations between the head and dependent words of that sentence. For example in Figure 1, the arrow from "he" to "bought" with label "nsubj", expresses that the dependent word "he" is the subject of the head word "bought". Under the assumption that constituents move as a whole (Quirk et al., 2005), our proposed reordering model aims to predict the orientation of each dependent word with respect to its head ($head-dependent$), and also with respect to the other dependents of that head ($dependent-dependent$ orientation). For example, for the sentence in Figure 1 we try to predict the appropriate orientations between the head-dependent and dependent-dependent pairs shown in Tables 2 and 3, respectively.

Our motivation for using dependency structure as the basis of our reordering model is based on the assumption that, if it is the case that a reordering pattern is employed for one English–Farsi sentence pair with a specific dependency structure, then another sentence pair containing the same dependency structure will follow the same reordering pattern. For example, in translating from English to Farsi, all of the following English sentences have the same word order in Farsi: "he puts the book on the table", "they put the desk on the ground", "he put his hand on my shoulder". In general, almost all the English sentences following the structure "subject" put "object" on "preposition-on" follow the same word order pattern in their Farsi translations.

We generate the dependency parse tree of the source sentence and perform word alignment between the source and target words in the parallel corpus. Having obtained both the source dependency tree and the word alignments, we extract the orientation type (monotone or swap) between each dependent word with respect to its head and the other dependents of that head. With the alignment points (p_{S1}, p_{T1}) and (p_{S2}, p_{T2}) for two source words $S1$ and $S2$ and their aligned target words $T1$ and $T2$, we define orientation types (ori) as in Equation 1.

$$ori = \begin{cases} monotone, \\ \text{if } (p_{S1} - p_{S2}) \times (p_{T1} - p_{T2}) > 0 \\ swap, \\ \text{otherwise.} \end{cases} \quad (1)$$

When a source word is aligned to multiple target words, we only consider the last aligned target word in determining the orientation type. For example, given the alignments for the head word $bought$ with alignment point $(1, 7)$ and dependent word $camels$ with alignment point $(2, 2)$ in Figure

Element Pairs	Example (English)	Word Order (English)	Word Order (Farsi)
subject, object and verb	Mary gave the book to John	SVO	SOV
noun and genitive	Mary's Book	noun + genitive	genitive + noun
verb and adpositional	He slept on the ground	verb + adp.	adp. + verb
verb and manner adverb	He ran slowly	Verb + m. adverb	m. adverb + verb
copula and predicate	She is a teacher	copula + predicate	predicate + copula
noun and adjective	Green Book	adjective + Noun	Noun+ Adjective
possessive affix and noun	My book	possessive + noun	noun + possessive

Table 1: word order differences between Farsi and English

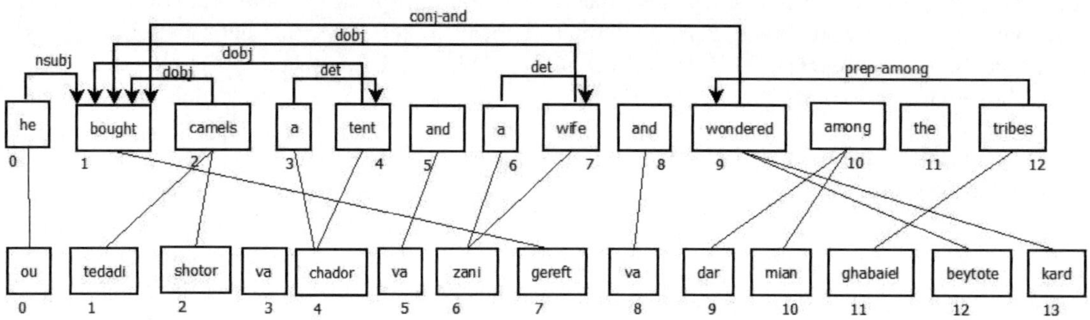

Figure 1: An example dependency tree for an English source sentence, its translation in Farsi and the word alignments

1, we consider swap orientation between *bought* and *camels* based on Equation 1.

After extracting the orientation for all the pairs in the training set, we train a Naive Bayes classifier to estimate the probability of a source dependent word being translated in a monotone or swap manner with respect to its head and the other dependent words of that head.

Making the strong independence assumption that each word is ordered in the sentence independently, the reordering probability for a sentence can be split into the reordering probability of its constitutive ($head$,$dependent$) and ($dependent$,$dependent$) pairs. Hence, we define the dependency-based reordering (DBR) feature-function score for a translation hypothesis as the sum of the log orientation probabilities for its constitutive pairs as in Equation 2, where H is the translation hypothesis and $Pairs(H)$ is the set of the pair components of H.

$$score_{DBR}(H) = \sum_{pair_i \in Pairs(H)} log(P_{DBR}(ori|pair_i)) \quad (2)$$

We implemented the reordering model P_{DBR} as a feature-function and combined it with the other feature-functions in the log-linear framework of the HPB model. This feature-function is made of four components: *monotone*, *swap*, *dependency coherence* and *unaligned pairs*. The components *monotone* and *swap* compute the sum of orientation probabilities of those pairs which are translated in monotone and swap orientation, respectively. *Dependency coherence* counts the number of translated pairs in a hypothesis and encourages concurrent translation of constituents based on the assumption that constituents move together in translation (Quirk et al., 2005). *Unaligned pairs* counts the number of pairs with at least one unaligned source word, as the other three components can not be applied to unaligned pairs.

Various features can be used to reflect the local information of each translation hypothesis H to model P_{DBR}(*orientation* |*pair*$_i$). Finally, we chose the following features to describe the translation hypothesis H for head-dependent pairs:

- The surface forms of the head word Lex(head) and the dependent word Lex(dep)
- The dependency relation of the dependent word $depRel(dep)$

we chose following features for dependent-dependent pairs:

- The surface forms of the mutual head word Lex(head), the first dependent word Lex(dep1) and the second dependent word Lex(dep2)

head	bought	bought	bought	bought	bought	wife	tent	tribes
dependent	He	camels	tent	Wife	wandered	a	a	wandered

Table 2: head-dependent pairs for the sentence in Figure 1.

dep1	He	He	He	He	camels	camels	camels	tent	tent	wife
dep2	camels	tent	wife	wandered	Tent	wife	wandered	wife	wandered	wandered

Table 3: dependent-dependent pairs for the sentence in Figure 1.

- The dependency relations of the first dependent word depRel(dep1) and the second dependent word depRel(dep2)

As an example, consider the pair $bought$ and $camels$ in our example in Figure 1. The model attempts to predict the orientation between these two words as described in Equation 3.

$$P_{DBR}(ori|lex(head), lex(dep), (depRel(dep))) \quad ori \in \{monotone, swap\} \tag{3}$$

where $lex(head)$=$bought$, $lex(dep)$=$camels$ and $depRel(dep)$=$dobj$. The orientation probabilities for $bought$ and $camels$ (0.21 and 0.79 for monotone and swap, respectively) encourage the swap orientation between them, which supports the required reordering of the object and verb, when translating from English-to-Farsi. Despite the limitations of this model, it can capture the general linguistic reordering patterns that are not available to other reordering models. For instance, it can learn that when translating between SVO and SOV languages, the object and the verb should be reordered, while the subject and the object should be translated in monotone order.

5 Experiments

5.1 Experimental Setup

We used the Mizan parallel English–Farsi corpus[1] (Supreme Council of Information and Communication Technology, 2013) which contains nearly 1 million sentence pairs. This corpus is extracted from English novel books (mostly in their classical literature domain) and their translations in Farsi. 3,000 sentence pairs were held out for development and 1,000 for testing. These sentence pairs were randomly selected from the corpus. The remaining content of the corpus is used for training. Table 4 presents the details about this dataset.

We parsed the source side (English) of the corpus using the Stanford dependency parser (Chen and Manning, 2014) and used the "collapsed representation" of the parser output to obtain direct dependencies between the words in the source sentences. We used GIZA++ (Och and Ney, 2003) to align the words in the corpus. Then we extracted 6,391,255 $head{-}dependent$ pairs and 5,247,137 $dependent{-}dependent$ pairs from train dataset and determined the orientation for each pair based on Equation 1.

	unit	**English**	**Farsi**
Train	sentences	1,016,758	1,016,758
	words	13,919,071	14,043,499
Tune	sentences	3,000	3,000
	words	40,831	41,670
Test	sentences	1,000	1,000
	words	13,165	13,444

Table 4: Mizan parallel corpus statistics

In order to measure the impact of different features on the accuracy of our reordering model (as will be described in Section 5.2), we used the Naive Bayes classifier with standard settings from the Weka machine learning toolkit (Hall et al., 2009). We trained the classifier separately for $head{-}dependent$ and $dependent{-}dependent$ pairs.

Our baseline MT system was the Moses implementation of HPM model with default settings (Hoang et al., 2009). We used a 5-gram target language model trained on the Farsi side of the training data. In all experiments, the weights of our reordering feature-function and the built-in feature-functions was tuned with MERT (Och, 2003).

5.2 Impact of different features

Since the proposed reordering model has to classify the $head{-}dependent$ and $dependent{-}dependent$ pairs into their correct monotone or swap orientation classes, its task can be seen as a binary classification task. We used the Naive Bayes algorithm to build such an orientation classifier. We then used different

[1] `http://dadegan.ir/catalog/mizan`

feature sets in each classification experiment to determine their impact on the accuracy of the model.

The features that were examined in this paper are shown in Table 5. All of these features are entirely based on the source sentence and source dependency parse, so we performed dependency parsing and feature extraction as pre-processing steps so as not to slow down the decoding phase.

Surface form of head	$Lex(head)$
Surface form of 1st dependent	$Lex(dep1)$
Surface form of 2nd dependent	$Lex(dep2)$
Dep. relation of 1st dependent	$depRel(dep1)$
Dep. relation of 2nd dependent	$depRel(dep2)$

Table 5: Features

We used 10-fold cross validation on the train data set (as described in Table 4) to evaluate the classifier. Table 6 shows the performance of the Naive Bayes classifier for monotone and swap orientation for head-dependent (rows *hd*) and dependent-dependent (rows *dd*) pairs. We use two different feature sets, with (rows ws) and without (rows wos) surface forms. The features used in each classifier are then as follows:

- hd-wos. $depRel(dep)$
- hd-ws. $Lex(head)$, $Lex(dep)$, $depRel(dep)$
- dd-wos. $depRel(dep1)$, $depRel(de2)$
- dd-ws. $Lex(head)$,[2] $Lex(dep1)$, $Lex(dep2)$, $depRel(dep1)$, $depRel(dep2)$

Features	Accuracy
hd-wos	64.75%
hd-ws	67.37%
dd-wos	70.85%
dd-ws	71.38%

Table 6: Classification results on head-dep and dep-dep relations

For both types of constituent pairs (*hd* and *dd*), the use of surface forms results in a slight improvement (2.62% and 0.53% absolute for *hd* and *dd*, respectively).

As this is the first paper that attempts to model reordering of *dd* pairs (*hd* has been attempted before (Gao et al., 2011)), we are especially interested in the results for *dd*. The fact that the classification accurary for *dd* is higher than for *hd* (71.38% vs 67.37%) motivates us to model the reordering of *dd* constituents in MT, for which we present results in the next Section.

5.3 MT Results

We build six MT systems, four according to the constituent pairs and features examined (cf. Table 6) and two additional systems that model the reordering for both types of constituent pairs (rows *all*) with (ws) and without (wos) surface forms. We compare our systems to two baselines, a standard HPB-SMT system (HPB) and a HPB-SMT system with added swap glue grammar rule (HPB_sgg) as in Equation 4. The swap glue rule allows adjacent phrases to be reversed.

$$X \rightarrow (X_1X_2, X_2X_1) \quad (4)$$

Table 7 shows the results obtained by each of the MT systems according to four automatic evaluation metrics: BLEU, NIST (Doddington, 2002), TER (Snover et al., 2006) and METEOR (Denkowski and Lavie, 2014). For each system and evaluation metric we show its relative improvement over the baseline HPB (columns diff).

The scores obtained by systems that implement our novel reordering between pairs of dependents (columns *dd*) are better than those of the baseline, both with (ws) and without (wos) surface forms, accross all the four evaluation metrics. The same is true for models that implement reordering between both pairs of constituent types (columns *all*), except for the system all_wos according to BLEU. The results for systems that perform reordering between pairs of head and dependent offer a mixed picture, with some metrics indicating improvement (e.g. BLEU) and some others deterioration (e.g. TER).

The use of surface forms leads to better results in most cases (except for *hd* systems in terms of NIST, TER and METEOR, and *dd* systems in terms of NIST and TER), confirming the trends shown in the classification experiment, cf. Table 6.

As stated earlier in the paper, Farsi is a free word-order language. When compiling the results of our experiments, we only had a single reference available against which the output from our various systems could be compared. Computing au-

[2]The mutual head between dependent word 1 and dependent word 2. For example, in Figure 1 $bought$ is the mutual head between the dependent words he and $camels$

System	BLEU	diff	NIST	diff	TER	diff	METEOR	diff
HPB	0.1083		3.7625		0.8005		0.1683	
HPB_sgg	0.1087	0.37%	3.7299	-0.87%	0.8009	0.05%	0.1665	-1.10%
dd_ws	**0.1161**‡	7.20%	3.8303†	1.80%	0.7937	-0.85%	**0.1733**	2.96%
dd_wos	0.1097	1.29%	3.8381†	2.01%	0.7929	-0.95%	0.1728	2.65%
hd_ws	0.1095	1.11%	3.6548	-2.86%	0.8155	1.88%	0.1643	-2.39%
hd_wos	0.1095	1.11%	3.7413	-0.56%	0.8061	0.70%	0.1687	0.21%
all_ws	0.1091	0.74%	**3.8614**‡	2.63%	**0.7858**	-1.84%	0.1727	2.60%
all_wos	0.1054	-2.68%	3.8374†	1.99%	0.7902	-1.29%	0.1708	1.44%

Table 7: Scores of the MT systems according to different automatic metrics. The best score according to each metric is shown in bold. Statistically significant results, calculated with paired bootstrap resampling (Koehn, 2004) for BLEU and NIST, are indicated with symbols ‡ ($p = 0.01$) and † ($p = 0.05$).

tomatic evaluation scores when translating into a free word-order language in the single-reference scenario is somewhat arbitrary. The fact that the four evaluation metrics used follow slightly different trends reflects this arbitrariness. We would expect a manual evaluation on a subset of sentences to confirm that the output translations are somewhat better than the automatic evaluation scores suggest.

6 Conclusions

This paper has proposed a dependency-based reordering model for HPB-SMT that predicts the translation order of two types of pairs of constituents of the source tree: dependent-dependent and head-dependent. Our model uses the dependency structure of the source sentence to capture the medium- and long-distance reorderings between these pairs of constituents.

It is worth mentioning that this is the first paper where a dependency-based reordering model is applied to a language pair other than Chinese-to-English. Our language pair, English-to-Farsi, is comparatively challenging because (i) the target language is free-word order and morphologically rich, and (ii) it is comparatively under-resourced.

We have evaluated our model against two baselines: standard HPB-SMT and HPB-SMT with swap glue grammar rules. Our model that reorders pairs of dependents outperforms both baselines ($>$ 0.7 absolute in terms of BLEU), with the improvement being statistically significant ($p = 0.01$ in terms of BLEU).

As for future work, several directions are worth considering. First, the use of features that hold linguistic information, such as part-of-speech tags or semantic classes. Second, an in-depth analysis of the output translations produced by our models to discern which reordering cases it succeeds at and for which other cases it fails. Third, an improved reordering model based on the findings of the previous line of work.

Acknowledgments

This research is supported by Science Foundation Ireland through the CNGL Programme (Grant 12/CE/I2267) in the ADAPT Centre (www.adaptcentre.ie) at Dublin City University, the European Union Seventh Framework Programme FP7/2007-2013 under grant agreement PIAP-GA-2012-324414 (Abu-MaTran) and by University of Isfahan.

References

Birch, Alexandra and Miles Osborne. 2011. Reordering Metrics for MT. In *Proceedings of the Association for Computational Linguistics*.

Birch, Alexandra, Phil Blunsom, and Miles Osborne. 2009. A Quantitative Analysis of Reordering Phenomena. In *Proceedings of the Fourth Workshop on Statistical Machine Translation*, pages 197–205, Athens, Greece.

Birch, Alexandra. 2011. *Reordering Metrics for Statistical Machine Translation*. Ph.D. thesis, University of Edinburgh.

Chen, Danqi and Christopher D Manning. 2014. A fast and accurate dependency parser using neural networks. In *Empirical Methods in Natural Language Processing (EMNLP)*.

Chiang, David. 2005. A hierarchical phrase-based model for statistical machine translation. In *Proceedings of the 43rd Annual Meeting on Association for Computational Linguistics*, pages 263–270.

Collins, Michael, Philipp Koehn, and Ivona Kučerová. 2005. Clause restructuring for statistical machine translation. In *Proceedings of the 43rd Annual Meeting on Association for Computational Linguistics*, pages 531–540.

Denkowski, Michael and Alon Lavie. 2014. Meteor universal: Language specific translation evaluation for any target language. In *Proceedings of the EACL 2014 Workshop on Statistical Machine Translation.*

Doddington, George. 2002. Automatic evaluation of machine translation quality using n-gram co-occurrence statistics. In *Proceedings of the Second International Conference on Human Language Technology Research*, HLT '02, pages 138–145.

Dryer, Matthew S. 1992. The Greenbergian word order correlations. *Language*, 68(1):81–138.

Galley, Michel and Christopher D. Manning. 2008. A simple and effective hierarchical phrase reordering model. In *Proceedings of the Conference on Empirical Methods in Natural Language Processing*, pages 848–856.

Gao, Yang, Philipp Koehn, and Alexandra Birch. 2011. Soft dependency constraints for reordering in hierarchical phrase-based translation. In *Proceedings of the Conference on Empirical Methods in Natural Language Processing*, pages 857–868.

Genzel, Dmitriy. 2010. Automatically learning source-side reordering rules for large scale machine translation. In *Proceedings of the 23rd International Conference on Computational Linguistics*, pages 376–384.

Hall, Mark, Eibe Frank, Geoffrey Holmes, Bernhard Pfahringer, Peter Reutemann, and Ian H. Witten. 2009. The weka data mining software: An update. *SIGKDD Explor. Newsl.*, 11(1):10–18.

Hanneman, Greg and Alon Lavie. 2013. Improving syntax-augmented machine translation by coarsening the label set. In *Proceedings of the North American Chapter of the Association of Computational Linguistics*, pages 288–297.

Hoang, Hieu, Philipp Koehn, and Adam Lopez. 2009. A unified framework for phrase-based, hierarchical, and syntax-based statistical machine translation. In *Proceedings of the International Workshop on Spoken Language Translation, IWSLT*, pages 152–159.

Huang, Zhongqiang, Jacob Devlin, and Rabih Zbib. 2013. Factored soft source syntactic constraints for hierarchical machine translation. In *Proceedings of the 2013 Conference on Empirical Methods in Natural Language Processing*, pages 556–566.

Koehn, Philipp, Franz Josef Och, and Daniel Marcu. 2003. Statistical phrase-based translation. In *Proceedings of the 2003 Conference of the North American Chapter of the Association for Computational Linguistics on Human Language Technology - Volume 1*, pages 48–54.

Koehn, Philipp. 2004. Statistical significance tests for machine translation evaluation. In *Proceedings of the 2004 Conference on Empirical Methods in Natural Language Processing*, pages 388–395.

Li, Junhui, Philip Resnik, and Hal Daumé III. 2013. Modeling syntactic and semantic structures in hierarchical phrase-based translation. In *Human Language Technologies: Conference of the North American Chapter of the Association of Computational Linguistics*, pages 540–549.

Moghaddam, Mohammad Dabir. 2001. Word order typology of iranian languages. *journal of humanities*, 8(2):17–24.

Och, Franz Josef and Hermann Ney. 2003. A systematic comparison of various statistical alignment models. *Computational Linguistics*, 29(1):19–51.

Och, Franz Josef. 2003. Minimum error rate training in statistical machine translation. In *Proceedings of the 41st Annual Meeting on Association for Computational Linguistics*, pages 160–167.

Quirk, Chris, Arul Menezes, and Colin Cherry. 2005. Dependency treelet translation: Syntactically informed phrasal smt. In *Proceedings of the 43rd Annual Meeting on Association for Computational Linguistics*, pages 271–279.

Snover, Matthew, Bonnie Dorr, Richard Schwartz, Linnea Micciulla, and Ralph Weischedel. 2006. A Study of Translation Error Rate with Targeted Human Annotation. In *Proceedings of the Association for Machine Translation in the Americas.*

Supreme Council of Information and Communication Technology. 2013. Mizan English-Persian Parallel Corpus. Tehran, I.R. Iran.

Tillmann, Christoph. 2004. A unigram orientation model for statistical machine translation. In *Proceedings of HLT-NAACL 2004: Short Papers*, pages 101–104.

Wang, Wei, Jonathan May, Kevin Knight, and Daniel Marcu. 2010. Re-structuring, re-labeling, and re-aligning for syntax-based machine translation. *Comput. Linguist.*, 36(2):247–277.

Xia, Fei and Michael McCord. 2004. Improving a statistical mt system with automatically learned rewrite patterns. In *Proceedings of the 20th International Conference on Computational Linguistics.*

Xiong, Deyi, Qun Liu, and Shouxun Lin. 2006. Maximum entropy based phrase reordering model for statistical machine translation. In *Proceedings of the 21st International Conference on Computational Linguistics and the 44th Annual Meeting of the Association for Computational Linguistics*, pages 521–528.

Xiong, Deyi, Min Zhang, and Haizhou Li. 2012. Modeling the translation of predicate-argument structure for smt. In *Proceedings of the 50th Annual Meeting of the Association for Computational Linguistics: Long Papers - Volume 1*, pages 902–911.

Xu, Peng, Jaeho Kang, Michael Ringgaard, and Franz Och. 2009. Using a dependency parser to improve smt for subject-object-verb languages. In *Proceedings of Human Language Technologies: The 2009 Annual Conference of the North American Chapter of the Association for Computational Linguistics*, pages 245–253.

The role of artificially generated negative data for quality estimation of machine translation

Varvara Logacheva
University of Sheffield
Sheffield, United Kingdom
v.logacheva@sheffield.ac.uk

Lucia Specia
University of Sheffield
Sheffield, United Kingdom
l.specia@sheffield.ac.uk

Abstract

The modelling of natural language tasks using data-driven methods is often hindered by the problem of insufficient naturally occurring examples of certain linguistic constructs. The task we address in this paper – quality estimation (QE) of machine translation – suffers from lack of negative examples at training time, i.e., examples of low quality translation. We propose various ways to artificially generate examples of translations containing errors and evaluate the influence of these examples on the performance of QE models both at sentence and word levels.

1 Introduction

The task of classifying texts as "correct" or "incorrect" often faces the problem of unbalanced training sets: examples of the "incorrect" class can be very limited or even absent. In many cases, naturally occurring instances of these examples are rare (e.g. incoherent sentences, errors in human texts). In others, the labelling of data is a non-trivial task which requires expert knowledge.

Consider the task of quality estimation (QE) of machine translation (MT) systems output. When performing binary classification of automatically translated sentences one should provide examples of both bad and good quality sentences. Good quality sentences can be taken from any parallel corpus of human translations, whereas there are very few corpora of sentences annotated as having low quality. These corpora need to be created by human translators, who post-edit automatic translations, mark errors in translations, or rate translations for quality. This process is slow and expensive. It is therefore desirable to devise automatic procedures to generate negative training data for QE model learning.

Previous work has followed the hypothesis that machine translations can be assumed to have low quality (Gamon et al., 2005). However, this is not the case nowadays: many translations can be considered flawless. Particularly for word-level QE, it is unrealistic to presume that every single word in the MT output is incorrect. Another possibility is to use automatic quality evaluation metrics based on reference translations to provide a quality score for MT data. Metrics such as BLEU (Papineni et al., 2002), TER (Snover et al., 2006) and METEOR (Banerjee and Lavie, 2005) can be used to compare the automatic and reference translations. However, these scores can be very unreliable, especially for word-level QE, as every word that differs in form or position would be annotated as bad.

Previous efforts have been made for negative data generation, including random generation of sentences from word distributions and the use of translations in low-ranked positions in n-best lists produced by statistical MT (SMT) systems. These methods are however unsuitable for QE at the word level, as they provide no information about the quality of individual words in a sentence.

In this paper we adopt a different strategy: we insert errors in otherwise correct sentences. This provides control over the proportion of errors in the negative data, as well as knowledge about the quality of individual words in the generated sentences. The goals of the research presented here are to understand the influence of artificially generated data (by various methods and in various quantities) on the performance of QE models at both sentence and word levels, and ultimately improve upon baseline models by extending the training data with suitable artificially created examples. In Section 2 we further review existing strategies for artificial data generation. We explain our generation strategies in Section 3. In Section 4 we describe our experiment and their results.

2 Previous work

2.1 Discriminative language modelling

One example of task that requires low quality examples is discriminative language modelling (DLM), i.e., the classification of sentences as "good" or "bad". It was first introduced in a monolingual context within automatic speech recognition (Collins et al., 2005), and later applied to MT. While in speech recognition negative examples can be created from system outputs that differ from the reference (Bhanuprasad and Svenson, 2008), in MT there are multiple correct outputs, so negative examples need to be defined more carefully.

In Okanohara (2007) bad sentences used as negative training instances are drawn from the distribution $P(w_i|w_{i-N+1}, ..., w_{i-1})$: first the start symbol $< s >$ is generated, then the next words are taken based on the word probability given the already generated words.

Other approaches to discriminative LMs use the n-best list of the MT system as training data (Li and Khudanpur, 2008). The translation variant which is closest to the oracle (e.g. has the highest BLEU score) is used as a positive example, while the variant with high system score and low BLEU score is used as a negative example. Such dataset allows the classifier to reduce the differences between the model score and the actual quality score of a sentence.

Li et al. (2010) simulate the generation of an n-best list using translation tables from SMT systems. By taking entries from the translation table with the same source side they create a set of alternative translations for a given target phrase. For each sentence, these are combined, generating a confusion set for this sentence.

2.2 Quality estimation for MT

QE can be modelled as a classification task where the goal is to distinguish good from bad translations, or to provide a quality score to each translation. Therefore, examples of bad sentences or words produced by the MT system are needed. To the best of our knowledge, the only previous work on adding errors to well-formed sentences is that by Raybaud et al. (2011).

In (Raybaud et al., 2011), the training data for the negative data generation process consists of a set of MT hypotheses manually post-edited by a translator. Hypotheses are aligned with the corresponding post-editions using the TERp tool (Snover et al., 2008). The alignment identifies the edit operations performed on the hypothesis in order to convert it to the post-edited version: leave word as is (no error), delete word, insert new word, substitute word with another word. Two models of generation of error strings from a well-formed sentence are proposed. Both are based on the observed frequency of errors in the post-edited corpus and do not account for any relationships between the errors and the actual words. The *bigram error model* draws errors from the bigram probabilities $P(C_i|C_{i-1})$ where C_i is an error class. The *cluster error model* generates clusters of errors based on the distribution of lengths of erroneous word sequences in the training data. Substituting words are chosen from a probability distribution defined as the product of these words' probabilities in the IBM-1 model and a 5-gram LM. A model trained only on artificial data performs slightly better than one trained on a small manually annotated corpus.

2.3 Human error correction

Another task that can benefit from artificially generated examples is language learner error correction. The input for this task is text that potentially contains errors. The goal is to find these errors, similarly to QE at the word level, and additionally correct them. While the text is written by humans, it is assumed that these are non-native speakers, who possibly translate the text from their native language. The difference is that in this task the source text is a hidden variable, whereas in MT it is observed.

The strategy of adding errors to correct sentences has also been used for this task. Human errors are more intuitive to simulate as language learners explicitly attempt to use natural language grammars. Therefore, rule-based systems can be used to model some grammar errors, particularly those affecting closed class words, e.g. determiner errors (Izumi et al., 2003) or countability errors (Brockett et al., 2006).

More recent statistical methods use the distributions of errors in corpora and small seed sets of errors. They often also concentrate on a single error type, usually with closed class words such as articles and prepositions (Rozovskaya and Roth, 2010). Felice and Yuan (2014) go beyond closed class words to evaluate how errors of different types are influenced by various linguistic parameters: text domain, learner's first language, POS tags and semantic classes of erroneous words. The approach led to the generation of high-quality artificial data for human error correction. However, it could not be used for MT error identification, as MT errors are different from human errors and usually cannot be assigned to a single type.

3 Generation of artificial data

The easiest choice for artificial data generation is to create a sentence by taking all or some of its words from a probability distribution of words in some monolingual corpus. The probability can be defined for unigrams only or conditioned on the previous words (as it was done for discriminative LMs). This however is a target language-only method that does not suit the QE task as the "quality" of a target word or sentence is dependent on the source sentence, and disregarding it will certainly lead to generation of spurious data.

Random target sentences based on a given source sentence could be generated with bilingual LMs. However another limitation of this approach is the assumption that all words in such sentences are wrong, which makes the data useless for word-level QE.

Alternatively, the artificial sentences can be generated using MT systems for back-translation. The target sentences are first fed to a target–source MT system, and then its output is passed to a source–target system. However, according to our experiments, if both systems are statistical the back-translation is too similar to the original sentence, and the majority of their differences are interchangeable paraphrases. Rule-based systems could be more effective, but the number of rule-based systems freely available would limit the work to a small number of language pairs.

3.1 A two-stage error generation method

As previously discussed, existing methods that artificially generate entire sentences have drawbacks that make them difficult or impossible to use for QE. Therefore, following Raybaud et al. (2011) and previous work on human error correction, our approach is to inject errors into otherwise correct texts. This process consists of two stages:

- labelling of a sentence with error tags,
- insertion of the errors into that sentence.

The first stage assigns an error tag to every word in a sentence. The output of this stage is the initial sentence where every word is assigned a tag denoting a type of error that needs to be incurred on this word. We use five tags corresponding to edit operations in the TERp tool: no error (**OK**), substitution (**S**), deletion (**D**), insertion (**I**) and shift (**H**). During the second stage the words in the sentence are changed according to their tag: substituted, deleted, shifted, or left in place if word has the tag **OK**. Figure 1 gives an example of the complete generation process.

3.1.1 Error tagging of sentences

We generate errors based on a corpus of post-edited machine translations. We align translations and post-editions using the TERp tool (exact matching) and extract counts on the number of shifts, substitutions, insertions and deletions. TERp does not always capture the true errors, in particular, it fails to identify phrase substitutions (e.g. *was* $\rightarrow$ *has been*). However, since editors are usually asked to minimise the number of edits, translations and post-editions are often close enough and the TERp alignment provide a good proxy to the true error distribution.

The TERp alignments can be used to collect the statistics on errors alone or to combine the frequency of errors with the words they are incurred on. We suggest three methods of generation of an error string for a sentence:

- **bigramEG**: the *bigram* error generation that uses a bigram error model regardless of the actual words (Raybaud et al., 2011).
- **wordprobEG**: the conditional probability of an error given a word.
- **crfEG**: the combination of the bigram error model and error probability conditioned on a word. This generation method can be modelled with Hidden Markov Model (HMM) or conditional random fields (CRF).

The first model has the advantage of keeping the distribution of errors as in the training data, because the probability distributions used depend

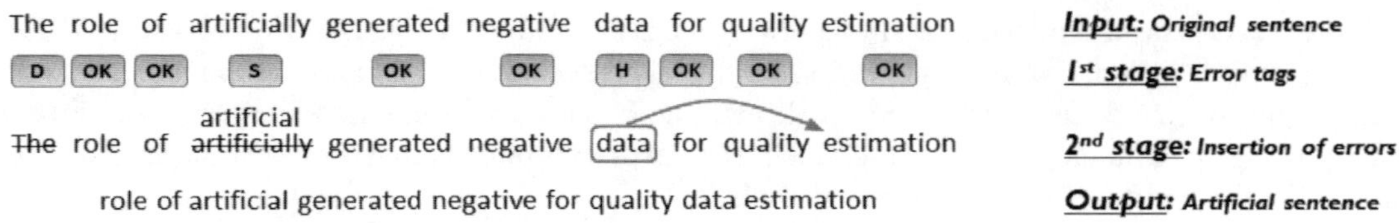

Figure 1: Example of the two-stage artificial data generation process

only on the frequency of errors themselves. The second model is more informed about which words commonly cause errors. Our implementation of the third method uses CRFs to train an error model. We use all unigrams, bigrams and trigrams that include the target word as features for training. This method is expected to produce more plausible error tags, but it can have the issue that the vocabulary we want to tag is not fully covered by the training data, so some words in the sentences to tag will be unknown to the trained model. If an unknown word needs to be tagged, it will more often be tagged with the most frequent tag, which is "Good" in our case. In order to avoid this problem we replace rare words in training set with a default string or with the word class, e.g. a POS tag.

3.1.2 Insertion of errors

We consider errors of four types: **insertion**, **deletion**, **substitution** and **shift**. Word marked with the 'deletion' error tag are simply removed. Shift errors require the distribution of shift distances which are computed based on a TERp-aligned corpus. Substitutions and insertions require word insertion (WI) and the new words need to be drawn from some probability distribution. We suggest two methods for the generation of these distributions:

- **unigramWI**: word frequencies computed based on a large monolingual corpus.
- **paraphraseWI**: distributions of words that can be used instead of the current word in the translation. This computation is performed as follows: first all possible sources of a target word are extracted from an SMT system's translation table, then all possible targets for these sources. That gives us a confusion set for each target word.

4 Experiments

We conducted a set of experiments to evaluate the performance of artificially generated data on different tasks of QE at the sentence and word levels.

4.1 Tools and datasets

The tools and resources required for our experiments are: a QE toolkit to build QE models, the training data for them, the data to extract statistics for the generation of additional examples.

The for sentence-level QE we used the QuEst toolkit (Specia et al., 2013). It trains QE models using `sklearn`[1] versions of Support Vector Machine (SVM) classifier (for ternary classification task, Section 4.4) and SVM regression (for HTER prediction, Section 4.5). The word-level version of QuEst[2] was used for word-level feature extraction. Word-level classifiers were trained with **CRFSuite**[3]. The CRF error models were trained with **CRF++**[4]. POS tagging was performed with **TreeTagger** (Schmid, 1994). Sentence-level QuEst uses 17 baseline features[5] for all tasks. Word-level QuEst reimplements the set of 30 baseline features described in (Luong et al., 2014). The QE models were built and tested based on the data provided for the WMT14 English–Spanish QE shared task (Section 4.3).

The statistics on error distributions were computed using the English–Spanish part of training data for WMT13 shared task on QE[6]. The statistics on the distributions of words, alignments and lexical probabilities were extracted from the Europarl corpus (Koehn, 2005). We trained the alignment model with **FastAlign** (Dyer et al., 2013) and extracted the lexical probabilities tables for words using scripts for phrase table building in **Moses** (Koehn et al., 2007). For all the methods, errors were injected into the News Commentary corpus[7].

[1] http://scikit-learn.org/
[2] http://github.com/ghpaetzold/quest
[3] http://www.chokkan.org/software/crfsuite/
[4] https://code.google.com/p/crfpp/
[5] http://www.quest.dcs.shef.ac.uk/quest_files/features_blackbox_baseline_17
[6] http://www.quest.dcs.shef.ac.uk/wmt13_qe.html
[7] http://statmt.org/wmt14/training-parallel-nc-v9.tgz

4.2 Generated data

Combining three methods of errors generation and two methods of errors insertion into sentences resulted in a total of six artificial datasets. Here we perform some analysis on the generated data.

The datasets differ in the percentage of errors injected into the sentences. **BigramEG** datasets have 23% of edits which matches the distribution of errors on the real data. **WordprobEG** datasets contain fewer errors — 17%.

The **crfEG** models contain the lowest number of errors — 5% of the total number of words. As it was expected, data sparsity makes the CRF model tag the majority of the words with the most frequent tag ("Good"). Replacing rare words with a default word token or with a POS tag did not improve these statistics.

Word inserters	Unigram	Paraphrase
Error generators		
Bigram	699.9	888.64
Wordprob	538.84	673.61
CRF + default word	165.36	172.97
CRF + POS tag	161.59	167.23

Table 1: Perplexities of the artificial datasets

We computed the perplexity of all datasets with respect to an LM trained on the Spanish part of the Europarl corpus (see Table 1). The figures match the error percentages in the data — the lower the number of errors, the more is kept from the original sentence, and thus the more natural it looks (lower perplexity). Note that sentences where errors were inserted from a general distribution (**unigramWI**) have lower perplexity than those generated using using paraphrases. This can be because the **unigramWI** model tends to choose high-frequency words with lower perplexity, while the constructed paraphrases contain more noise and rare words.

4.3 Experimental setup

We evaluated the performance of the artificially generated data in three tasks: the ternary classification of sentences as "good", "almost good" or "bad", the prediction of HTER (Snover et al., 2009) score for a sentence, and the classification of words in a sentence as "good" or "bad" (tasks 1.1, 1.2 and 2 of WMT14 QE shared task[8], respectively).

The goal of the experiments was to check whether it is possible to improve upon the baseline results by adding artificially generated examples to the training sets. The baseline models for all tasks were trained on the data provided for the corresponding shared tasks for the English–Spanish language pair. All models were tested on the official test sets provided for the corresponding shared tasks.

Since we know how many errors were injected into the sentences, we know the TER scores for our artificial data. The discrete labels for the ternary classification task are defined as follows: "bad" sentences have four or more non-adjacent errors (two adjacent erroneous words are considered one error), "almost good" sentences contain one erroneous phrase (possibly of several words), and "good" sentences are error-free.

The new training examples were added to the baseline datasets. We ran a number of experiments gradually increasing the number of artificially generated sentences used. At every run, the new data was chosen randomly in order to reduce the influence of outliers. In order to make the results more stable, we ran each experiment 10 times and averaged the evaluation scores.

4.4 Sentence-level ternary QE task

The original dataset for this task contains 949 "good", 2010 "almost good", and 857 "bad" sentences, whereas the test set has 600 entries: 131 "good", 333 "almost good", 136 "bad". The results were evaluated using F1-score.

The addition of new "bad" sentences leads to an improvement in quality, regardless of the sentence generation method used. Models trained on datasets generated by different strategies display the same trend: adding up to 400 sentences results in a considerable increase in quality, while further addition of data only slightly improves quality. Figure 2 shows the results of the experiments – here for clarity we included only the results for datasets generated with the **unigramWI**, although the **paraphraseWI** demonstrates a similar behaviour with slightly lower quality. The best F1-score of 0.49 is achieved by a model trained on the data generated with the **crf** error generator, which is an absolute improvement of 1.9% over the baseline.

However, adding only negative data makes the distribution of classes in the training data less

[8]http://statmt.org/wmt14/quality-estimation-task.html

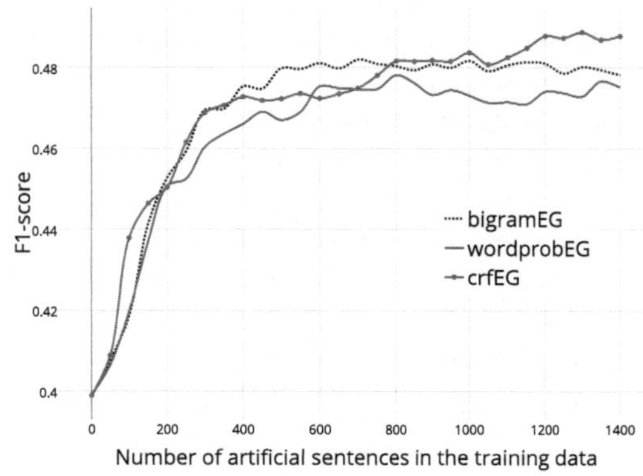

Figure 2: Ternary classification: performance of error generators

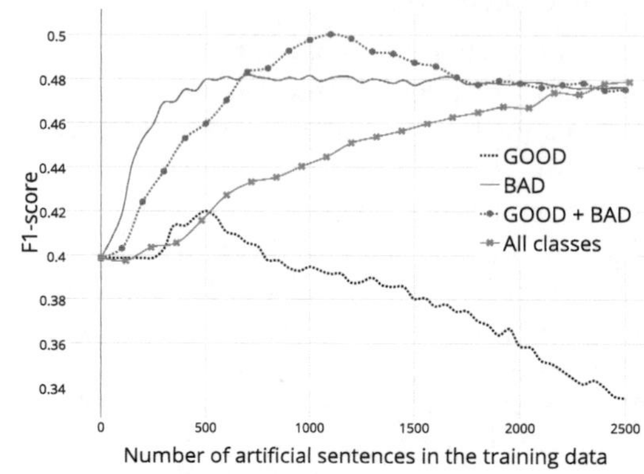

Figure 3: Ternary classification: artificial examples of different classes

similar to that of the test set, which might affect performance negatively. Therefore, we conducted other three sets of experiments: we added (i) equal amount of artificial data for the "good" and "bad" classes (ii) batches of artificial data for all classes that keep the original proportion of classes in the data (iii) artificial data for only the "good" class. The latter setting is tested in order to check whether the classifier benefits from negative instances, or just from having new data added to the training sets.

The results are shown in Figure 3. We plot only the results for the **bigramEG** + **unigramWI** setting as it achieved the best result in absolute values, but the trends are the same for all data generation techniques. The best strategy was to add both "good" and "bad" sentences: it beats the models which uses only negative examples, but after 1000 artificial sentences its performance degrades. Keeping the original distribution of classes is not beneficial for this task: it performs worse than any other tested scenario since it decreases the F1-score for the "good" class dramatically.

Overall, the additional negative training data improves the ternary sentence classification. The addition of both positive and negative examples can further improve the results, while providing additional instances of the "almost good" class did not seem to be as helpful.

4.5 Sentence-level HTER QE task

Figure 4 shows that the addition of any type of artificial data leads to substantial improvements in quality for this task. The results were evaluated in terms of Mean Absolute Error (MAE). The initial training dataset was very small – 896 sentences (200 sentences for test), which may explain the substantial improvements in prediction quality as new data is added. We also noticed that the performance of the generated datasets was primarily defined by the method of errors generation, whereas different word choice strategies did not impact the results as much. Figure 4 depicts the results for the **unigramWI** words selection method only with all error generation methods.

The addition of data from datasets generated with **crfEG** gives the largest drop in MAE (from 0.161 to 0.14). This result is achieved by a model that uses 1200 artificial sentences. Further addition of new data harms performance. The data generated by other error generators does not cause such a large improvement in quality, although it also helps reduce the error rate.

As it was described earlier, the **crfEG** model generates sentences with a small number of errors. Since the use of this dataset leads to the largest improvements, we can suggest that in the HTER prediction task, using the baseline dataset only, the majority of errors is found in sentences whose HTER score is low. However, the reason might also be that the distributions of scores in the baseline training and test sets are different: the test set has lower average score (0.26 compared to 0.31 in the training set) and lower variance (0.03 versus 0.05 in the training set). The use of artificial data with a small number of errors changes this distribution.

We also experimented with training a model using only artificial data. The results of models trained on only 100 artificial sentences for each

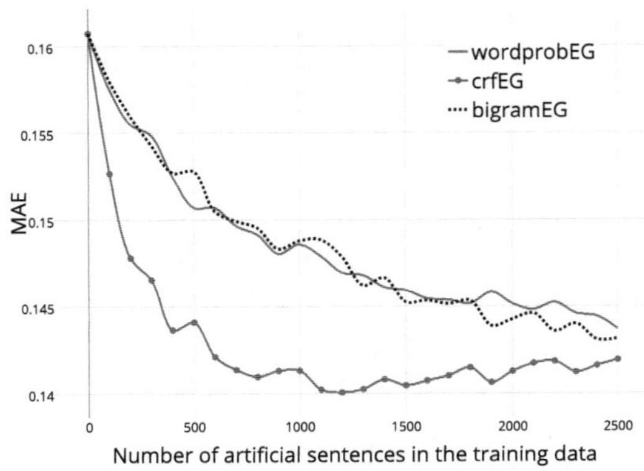

Figure 4: HTER regression results

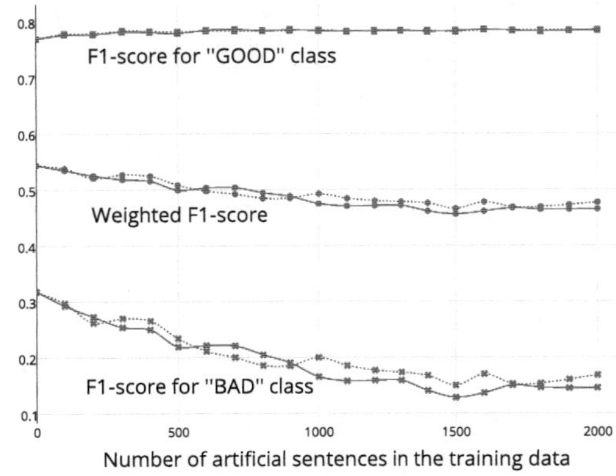

Figure 5: Word-level QE. Blue solid lines – results for **crfEG**, red dotted lines – **bigramEG**

generation method were surprisingly good: their MAE ranged from 0.149 to 0.158 (compared to the baseline result of 0.161 on the original data). However, the further addition of new artificial sentences did not lead to improvements. Thus, despite the positive impact of the artificial data on the results, the models cannot be further improved without real training examples.

4.6 Word-level QE task

Here we tested the impact of the artificial data on the task of classifying individual words as "good" or "bad". The baseline set contains 47335 words, 35% of which have the tag "bad". The test set has 9613 words with the same label distribution.

All the datasets led to similar results. Overall, the addition of artificial data harms prediction performance: the F1-score goes down until 1500 sentences are added, and then levels off. The performance for all datasets is similar. However, analogously to the previous tasks, there are differences between **crfEG** and the other two error generation techniques: the former leads to faster deterioration of F1-score. No differences were observed among the word insertion techniques tested.

Figure 5 shows the average weighted F1-score and F1-scores for both classes. Since all datasets behave similarly, we show the results for two of them that demonstrate slightly different performance: **crfEG+unigramWI** is shown with solid blue lines, while **bigramEG+unigramWI** is shown with dotted red lines. The use of data generated with CRF-based methods results in slightly faster decline in performance than the use of data generated with **bigramEG** or **wordprobEG**. One possible reason is that the CRF-generated datasets have fewer errors, hence they change the original tags distribution in the training data. Therefore, test instances are tagged as "bad" less often. That explains why the F1-score of the "bad" class decreases, whereas the F1-score of the "good" class stays at the same.

To summarise our findings for word-level QE, the strategies of data generation proposed and tested thus far do not lead to improvements. The word-level predictions are more sensitive to individual words in training sentences, so the replacement of tokens with random words may confuse the model. Therefore, the word-level task needs more elaborate methods for substituting words.

5 Conclusions and future work

We presented and experimented with a set of new methods of simulation of errors made by MT systems. Sentences with artificially added errors were used as training data in models that predict the quality of sentences or words.

The addition of artificial data can help improve the output of sentence-level QE models, with substantial improvements in HTER score prediction and some improvements in sentences classification into "good", "almost good" and "bad". However, the largest improvements are related to the fact that the additional data changes the overall distribution of scores in the training set, making it more similar to the test set. On the other hand, the fact that the artificial sentences did not decrease the quality in such cases proves that it can be used to counter-balance the large number of positive examples. Unlike sentence-level QE, the task of word-level QE did not benefit from the artificial data. That may relate to our choice of method to replace words in artificial sentences.

While thus far we analysed the usefulness of artificial data for the QE task only, it would be interesting to check if this data can also improve the performance of discriminative LMs.

Acknowledgements

This work was supported by the EXPERT (EU Marie Curie ITN No. 317471) project.

References

Banerjee, Satanjeev and Alon Lavie. 2005. METEOR: An Automatic Metric for MT Evaluation with Improved Correlation with Human Judgments. In *ACL-2005, MTSumm workshop*, pages 65–72.

Bhanuprasad, Kamadev and Mats Svenson. 2008. Errgrams A Way to Improving ASR for Highly Inflected Dravidian Languages. In *IJCNLP-2008*, pages 805–810.

Brockett, Chris, William B. Dolan, and Michael Gamon. 2006. Correcting esl errors using phrasal smt techniques. In *Coling-ACL-2006*.

Collins, Michael, Brian Roark, and Murat Saraclar. 2005. Discriminative Syntactic Language Modeling for Speech Recognition. In *ACL-2005*.

Dyer, Chris, Victor Chahuneau, and A. Noah Smith. 2013. A simple, fast, and effective reparameterization of ibm model 2. In *NAACL-HLT-2013*, pages 644–648.

Felice, Mariano and Zheng Yuan. 2014. Generating artificial errors for grammatical error correction. In *EACL-2014*, pages 116–126.

Gamon, Michael, Anthony Aue, and Martine Smets. 2005. Sentence-level MT evaluation without reference translations: beyond language modeling. In *EAMT-2005*.

Izumi, Emi, Kiyotaka Uchimoto, Toyomi Saiga, Thepchai Supnithi, and Hitoshi Isahara. 2003. Automatic error detection in the japanese learners' english spoken data. In *ACL-2003*, pages 145–148.

Koehn, Philipp, Hieu Hoang, Alexandra Birch, Chris Callison-burch, Marcello Federico, Nicola Bertoldi, Brooke Cowan, Wade Shen, Christine Moran, Richard Zens, Chris Dyer, Ondej Bojar, Alexandra Constantin, and Evan Herbst. 2007. Moses: Open Source Toolkit for Statistical Machine Translation. In *ACL-2007, Demo session*, pages 177–180.

Koehn, Philipp. 2005. Europarl: A Parallel Corpus for Statistical Machine Translation. In *MT-Summit 2005*, pages 79–86.

Li, Zhifei and Sanjeev Khudanpur. 2008. Large-scale Discriminative n -gram Language Models for Statistical Machine Translation. In *AMTA-2008*, pages 21–25.

Li, Zhifei, Ziyuan Wang, Sanjeev Khudanpur, and Jason Eisner. 2010. Unsupervised Discriminative Language Model Training for Machine Translation using Simulated Confusion Sets. In *Coling-2010*.

Luong, Ngoc Quang, Laurent Besacier, and Benjamin Lecouteux. 2014. Lig system for word level qe task at wmt14. In *WMT-2014*, pages 335–341.

Okanohara, Daisuke. 2007. A Discriminative Language Model with Pseudo-Negative Samples. In *ACL-2007*, pages 73–80.

Papineni, Kishore, Salim Roukos, Todd Ward, and Wei-jing Zhu. 2002. BLEU: a Method for Automatic Evaluation of Machine Translation. In *ACL-2002*, pages 311–318.

Raybaud, Sylvain, David Langlois, and Kamel Smaïli. 2011. This sentence is wrong. Detecting errors in machine-translated sentences. *Machine Translation*, 25(1):1–34.

Rozovskaya, Alla and Dan Roth. 2010. Generating confusion sets for context-sensitive error correction. In *EMNLP-2010*, pages 961–970.

Schmid, Helmut. 1994. Probabilistic part-of-speech tagging using decision trees. In *International Conference on New Methods in Language Processing*, pages 44–49.

Snover, Matthew, Bonnie Dorr, Richard Schwartz, Linnea Micciulla, and John Makhoul. 2006. A Study of Translation Edit Rate with Targeted Human Annotation. In *AMTA-2006*, pages 223–231.

Snover, Matthew, Nitin Madnani, Bonnie Dorr, and Richard Schwartz. 2008. TERp System Description. In *AMTA-2008, MetricsMATR workshop*.

Snover, Matthew, Nitin Madnani, Bonnie J. Dorr, and Richard Schwartz. 2009. Fluency, adequacy, or hter?: Exploring different human judgments with a tunable mt metric. In *WMT-2009*, pages 259–268.

Specia, Lucia, Kashif Shah, Jose G C de Souza, and Trevor Cohn. 2013. QuEst - A translation quality estimation framework. In *ACL-2013, Demo session*.

Document-Level Machine Translation with Word Vector Models

Eva Martínez Garcia, Cristina España-Bonet
TALP Research Center
Univesitat Politècnica de Catalunya
Jordi Girona, 1-3, 08034 Barcelona, Spain
{emartinez,cristinae}@cs.upc.edu

Lluís Màrquez
Arabic Language Technologies
Qatar Computing Research Institute
Tornado Tower, Floor 10
P.O. Box 5825, Doha, Qatar
lmarquez@qf.org.qa

Abstract

In this paper we apply distributional semantic information to document-level machine translation. We train monolingual and bilingual word vector models on large corpora and we evaluate them first in a cross-lingual lexical substitution task and then on the final translation task. For translation, we incorporate the semantic information in a statistical document-level decoder (Docent), by enforcing translation choices that are semantically similar to the context. As expected, the bilingual word vector models are more appropriate for the purpose of translation. The final document-level translator incorporating the semantic model outperforms the basic Docent (without semantics) and also performs slightly over a standard sentence-level SMT system in terms of ULC (the average of a set of standard automatic evaluation metrics for MT). Finally, we also present some manual analysis of the translations of some concrete documents.

1 Introduction

Document-level information is usually lost during the translation process when using Statistical Machine Translation (SMT) sentence-based systems (Hardmeier, 2014; Webber, 2014). Cross-sentence dependencies are totally ignored, as they translate sentence by sentence without taking into account any document context when choosing the best translation. Some simple phenomena like coreferent pronouns outside a sentence cannot be properly translated in this way, which is already important because the correct translation of pronouns in a document confers a high level of coherence to the final translation. Also, discourse connectives are valuable because they mark the flow of the discourse in a text. It is desirable to transfer them to the output translation in order to maintain the characteristics of the discourse. The evolution of the topic through a text is also an important feature to preserve.

All these aspects can be used to improve the translation quality by trying to assure coherence throughout a document. Several recent works go on that direction. Some of them present post-processing approaches making changes into a first translation according to document-level information (Martínez-Garcia et al., 2014a; Xiao et al., 2011). Others introduce the information within the decoder, by, for instance, implementing a topic-based cache approach (Gong et al., 2011; Xiong et al., 2015). The decoding methodology itself can be changed. This is the case of a document-oriented decoder, Docent (Hardmeier et al., 2013), which implements a search in the space of translations of a whole document. This framework allows us to consider features that apply at document level. One of the main goals of this paper is to take advantage of this capability to include semantic information at decoding time.

We present here the usage of a semantic representation based on word embeddings as a language model within a document-oriented decoder. To do this, we trained a word vector model (WVM) using neural networks. As a first approach, a monolingual model is used in analogy with the standard monolingual language models based on n-grams of words instead of vectors. However, to better approach translation, bilingual models are built. These models are avaluated in isolation outside the decoder by means of a cross-lingual evaluation task that resembles a translation environment. Finally, we use these models in a translation task and we observe how the semantic information enclosed in them help to improve translation quality.

The paper is organized as follows. A brief revision of the related work is done in Section 2. In Section 3, we describe our approach of using a bilingual word vector model as a language model. The model is compared to monolingual models and evaluated. We show and discuss the results of our experiments on the full translation task in Section 5. Finally, we draw the conclusions and define several lines of future work in Section 6.

2 Related Work

In the last years, approaches to document-level translation have started to emerge. The earliest ones deal with pronominal anaphora within an SMT system (Hardmeier and Federico, 2010; Nagard and Koehn, 2010). These authors develop models that, with the help of coreference resolution methods, identify links among words in a text and use them for a better translation of pronouns. More recent approaches focus on topic cohesion. (Gong et al., 2011) tackle the problem by making available to the decoder the previous translations at decoding time using a cache system. In this way, one can bias the system towards the lexicon already used. (Xiong et al., 2015) also present a topic-based coherence improvement for an SMT system by trying to preserve the continuity of sentence topics in the translation. To do that, they extract a coherence chain from the source document and, taking this coherence chain as a reference, they predict the target coherence chain by adapting a maximum entropy classifier. Document-level translation can also be seen as the post-process of an already translated document. In (Xiao et al., 2011; Martínez-Garcia et al., 2014a), they study the translation consistency of a document and retranslate source words that have been translated in different ways within a same document. The aim is to incorporate document contexts into an existing SMT system following 3 steps. First, they identify the ambiguous words; then, they obtain a set of consistent translations for each word according to the distribution of the word over the target document; and finally, generate the new translation taking into account the results of the first two steps.

These approaches report improvements in the final translations but, in most of them. the improvements can only be seen through a detailed manual evaluation. When using automatic evaluation metrics like BLEU (Papineni et al., 2002), differences are not significant.

A document-oriented SMT decoder is presented in (Hardmeier et al., 2012; Hardmeier et al., 2013). The decoder is built on top of an open-source phrase-based SMT decoder, Moses (Koehn et al., 2007). The authors present a stochastic local search decoding method for phrase-based SMT systems which allows decoding complete documents. Docent starts from an initial state (translation) given by Moses and this one is modified by the application of a hill climbing strategy to find a (local) maximum of the score function. The score function and some defined change operations are the ones encoding the document-level information. One remarkable characteristic of this decoder, besides the change of perspective in the implementation from sentence-level to document-level, is that it allows the usage of a WVM as a Semantic Space Language Model (SSLM). In this case, the decoder uses the information of the word vector model to evaluate the adequacy of a word inside a translation by calculating the distance among the current word and its context.

In the last years, several distributed word representation models have been introduced. Furthermore, distributed models have been successfully applied to several different NLP tasks. These models are able to capture and combine the semantic information of the text. An efficient implementation of the Context Bag of Words (CBOW) and the Skipgram algorithms is presented in (Mikolov et al., 2013a; Mikolov et al., 2013c; Mikolov et al., 2013d). Within this implementation WVMs are trained using a neural network. These models proved to be robust and powerful to predict semantic relations between words even across languages. They are implemented inside the *word2vec* software package. However, they are not able to handle lexical ambiguity as they conflate word senses of polysemous words into one common representation. This limitation is already discussed in (Mikolov et al., 2013b) and in (Wolf et al., 2014), in which bilingual extensions of the *word2vec* architecture are also proposed. These bilingual extensions of the models consist of a combination of two monolingual models. They combine the source vector model and the target vector model by training a new neural network. This network is able to learn the projection matrix that combines the information of both languages. A new bilingual approach is presented in (Martínez-Garcia et al., 2014b). Also, the resulting models are evaluated in a cross-lingual lexical substitution task as well as measuring their accuracy when capturing words semantic relationships.

Recently, Neural Machine Translation (NMT) has appeared as a powerful alternative to other MT techniques. Its success lies on the excellent results that deep neural networks have achieved in natural language tasks as well as in other areas. In short, NMT systems are build over a trained neural network that is able to output a translation given a source text in the input (Sutskever et al., 2014b; Sutskever et al., 2013; Bahdanau et al., 2014; Cho et al., 2014). However, these systems report some problems when translating unknown or rare words. We are aware of only few works that try to address this problem (Sutskever et al., 2014a; Jean et al., 2014).

Furthermore, there are some works that try to use vector models trained using recurrent neural networks (RNN) to improve decoder outputs. For instance, in (Sundermeyer et al., 2014) they build two kinds of models at word level, one based on word alignments and other one phrase-based. The authors train RNNs to obtain their models and they use them to rerank n-best lists after decoding. They report improvements in BLEU and TER scores in several language pairs, but they are not worried about context issues of a document although they do take into account both sides of the translation: source and target. In (Devlin et al., 2014) they also present joint models that augment the NNLM with a source context window to introduce a new decoding feature. They finally present improvements in BLEU score for Arabic-English language pair and show a new technique to introduce this kind of models inside MT systems in a computationally efficient way. These two last works prove the power of applying NN models as features inside MT systems.

3 Training monolingual and bilingual semantic models

As we explained before, there are several works that use monolingual WVM as language models, or the composition of monoligual models to build bilingual ones. This section shows a methodology to build directly bilingual models.

3.1 Bilingual word vector models

For our experiments we use the two algorithms implemented in the *word2vec* package, Skipgram and CBOW.

The Skipgram model trains a NN to predict the context of a given word. On the other hand, the CBOW algorithm uses a NN to predict a word given a set of its surrounding words, where the order of the words in the history does not inuence the projection.

In order to introduce semantic information in a bilingual scenario, we use a parallel corpus and automatic word alignment to extract a new training corpus of word pairs: $(w_{i,T}|w_{i,S})$. For instance, if the words *house* and *casa* are aligned in a document, we consider the new form *casa|house*.

This approach is different from (Wolf et al., 2014) who build an independent model for each language. With our method, we try to capture simultaneously the semantic information associated to the source word and the information in the target side of the translation. In this way, we hope to better capture the semantic information that is implicitly given by translating a text. To better characterize ambiguous words for MT, for instance, we expect to be able to distinguish among the different meanings that the word *desk* can have when translated in Spanish: *desk|mesa* vs. *desk|mostrador* vs. *desk|escritorio*.

3.2 Settings

The training set for our models is built from parallel corpora in the English-Spanish language pair available in Opus [1] (Tiedemann, 2012; Tiedemann, 2009). These corpora have been automatically aligned and therefore contain the aligment information necessary to build our bilingual models. We chose the one-to-one alignments to avoid noise and duplicities in the final data. Table 1 shows the size of the specific data used: EuropalV7, United Nations, Multilingual United Nations, and Subtitles-2012. Monolingual models are also build with these corpora and therefore are comparable in size. With this corpus, the final training set has 584 million words for English and 759 for Spanish.

[1] http://opus.lingfil.uu.se/

	Corpus	Documents	Sentences	English Tokens	Spanish Tokens
Training	Europarl-v7	–	1,965,734	49,093,806	51,575,748
	UN	–	61,123	5,970,000	6,580,000
	Multi UN	73,047	9,275,905	554,860,000	621,020,000
	Subtitles-2012	46,884	24,929,151	306,600,000	498,190,000
Development	NC-2009	136	2,525	65,595	68,089
Test	NC-2011	110	3,003	65,829	69,889

Table 1: Figures on the corpora used for training, development and test.

For training the models, we set to 600 the dimensionality of our vectors and we used a context window of 5 during the training (2 words before and 2 words after). Previous work (Martínez-Garcia et al., 2014b) and related experiments showed the adequacy of these parameters.

4 Cross-Lingual Lexical Subsitution Task

We evaluate the generated models described in Section 3 in a cross-lingual lexical substitution exercise. In order to do this, first, the content words of the test set which are translated in more than one different way by a baseline translation system are identified (see Section 5 for the description of the baseline system). We call these words ambiguous. The task consists in choosing the adequate translation from the set of ambiguous words. In our case, the correct choice is given by the reference translation of the test set.

To give an example, the word *desk* appears many times in a newswire document about a massive complaining for exaggerated rents. This word has here the meaning of *a service counter or table in a public building, such as a hotel*[2]. The correct translation to that meaning in Spanish would be the word *mostrador* or *ventanilla*. But, we can see that in the output of a SMT system, besides the correct translations, *desk* can appear translated as *mesa* or even as *escritorio* in the same document. If the reference translation contains *mostrador*, only this word will be considered correct in the evaluation.

Once we have identified the words that we want to translate with the vector models, we get their context target words and their aligned source word and look for vector associated to the $sw|tw$ form in our bilingual model. Then, we build a context vector as the sum of the vectors of the surrounding target words and use it to choose among the set of translation options (all the options seen within the document). We choose the best translation as the one that has associated the vector which is the closest to the context vector.

[2]Definition taken from Collins Concise English Dictionary.

Model	Top 1	Top 5
mono CBOW	47.71%	65.44%
mono Skipgram	47.71%	59.19%
bi CBOW	62.39%	85.49%
bi Skipgram	62.39%	78.36%

Table 2: Evaluation of the *word2vec* vector models. Top 1 and Top 5 accuracies of the monolingual (mono rows) in Spanish and the bilingual (bi rows) English–Spanish models trained using CBOW or Skipgram.

4.1 Results

This task is evaluated on the NewsCommentaries-2011 test set. Table 2 shows the results of the evaluation of our bilingual (*bi*) model in comparison to a monolingual (*mono*) model trained in Spanish. The accuracies show the performance of our models on the ambiguous words. For this test set, we find 8.12% of ambiguous words and, in average, 3.26 options per ambiguous word. We skip some adverbials, common verbs, the prepositions and conjunctions as ambiguous words to avoid noise in the results. In average, the monolingual model has a coverage of 90.97% and the bilingual 87.53% for this test set. Regarding to the ambiguous words, 83.97% of them are known for the bilingual model and a 87.37% for the monolingual.

The two *word2vec* algorithms have the same performance for this task when they suggest only the best option, an accuracy of 47.71% for the monolingual model and 62.39% for the bilingual one. So, bilingual models are encoding significantly more semantic information than monolingual models. It has to be said that here the most frequent translation option achieves a 59.76% of accuracy. So, it is only with bilingual models that we beat the frequentist approach.

Accuracies are significantly improved when more options are taken into account. When looking at the accuracy at Top 5, CBOW achieves 65.44% in the monolingual task and 85.49% in the bilingual one, whereas the Skipgram models have 6 less points in the monolingual case and 13 in the bilingual one. These results indicate that CBOW bilingual models are capturing better the semantics and that considering more than one option can be important in the full translation task.

5 Vector Models for Document-level Translation

We evaluate in this section the use of the word vector models described in Section 3 as language models within a document-level MT system.

5.1 Vector models as Semantic Space Language Models in Docent

The Docent decoder allows us to use a dense word vector model as a semantic language model. This language model implementation tries to reward the word choices that are closer to their context.
In a similar way to the evaluation task explained in Section 3, these models calculate a score for every word in a document translation candidate. This score is calculated as the cosine similarity between the vector representation of the word and the sum of the vectors of the previous 30 words. This parameter makes possible that the context crosses sentence boundaries. The score produced by the semantic space language model is $h(w|h) = \alpha p_{cos}(w|h)$ if w is a known word, and $h(w|h) = \epsilon$ if w is an unknown word, where α is the proportion of content words in the training corpus and ϵ is a small fixed probability, as described in (Hardmeier, 2014).

The assumption is the same here as before, the better the choice, the closer the context vector will be to the vector representation of the evaluated word. The final score for a document translation candidate is an average of the scores of its words.

5.2 Experimental Settings

Our SMT baseline system is based on Moses. The translation system has been trained with the Europarl corpus in its version 7 for the Spanish–English language pair. We used the GIZA++ software (Och and Ney, 2003) to do the word alignments. The language model is an interpolation of several 5-gram language models obtained using SRILM (Stolcke, 2002) with interpolated Kneser-Ney discounting on the target side of the Europarl corpus v7; United Nations; NewsCommentary 2007, 2008, 2009 and 2010; AFP, APW and Xinhua corpora as given by (Specia et al., 2013)[3] The optimization of the weights is done with MERT (Och, 2003) against the BLEU measure on the NewsCommentary corpus of 2009. As in the previous section, our experiments are carried out over the NewsCommentary-2011 test set. We chose the newswire documents as test set because typically they are documents with high consistency and coherence.

Regarding the document-level decoder, we use Docent. The first step in the Docent translation process is the output of our Moses baseline system. We set the initial Docent weights to be the same as the ones obtained with MERT for the Moses baseline. Finally, the word vector models used in the experiments of this section are the ones that we describe and evaluate in Section 3 using the CBOW algorithm.

5.3 Results

Table 3 shows the automatic evaluation obtained with the Asiya toolkit (González et al., 2012) for several lexical metrics (BLEU, NIST, TER, METEOR and ROUGE), a syntactic metric based on the overlap of PoS elements (SP-Op), and an average of a set of 21 lexical and syntactic metrics (ULC), including all the previous measures and many more. The first row shows the results for the Moses baseline system. The second row shows the evaluation of the Docent baseline system working with the baseline Moses output as first step. This Docent system uses only the default features that are equivalent to the ones in the Moses system but without lexical reordering. The last two rows show the evaluation of our extensions for the Docent decoder using both, monolingual vector models as semantic space language models (Docent + monoSSM) and the bilingual ones (Docent + biSSM). The results show only slight differences among the systems. However, these differences reflect the impact of our word embeddings in the translation process and are consistent across metrics. The differences are statistically signifi-

[3]Resources are available in:
http://statmt.org/wmt13/qualityestimationtask.html

system	BLEU	NIST	TER	METEOR	ROUGE	SP-Op	ULC
Moses	28.60	7.54	72.17	23.41	30.20	19.99	77.76
Docent	28.33	7.46	72.83	23.22	30.36	19.38	77.14
Docent + monoSSM	28.48	7.52	72.61	23.28	30.33	19.61	77.49
Docent + biSSM	28.58	7.66	72.56	23.31	30.38	19.78	77.89

Table 3: Automatic evaluation of the systems. See text for the system and metrics definition.

newswire	Moses	Docent	Docent+monoSSM	Docent+biSSM
news79	47.88	48.10	47.07	48.00
news88	24.18	24.60	24.18	23.26
news104	35.53	35.71	35.58	36.00
news107	19.52	19.57	19.58	19.66
news27	14.45	14.22	14.27	14.83
news68	38.91	38.39	38.58	39.73

Table 4: Evaluation of the different systems using BLEU metric on some individual newswire documents extracted from the NewsCommentary-2011 test set.

cant at the 90% confidence level, but not at higher level, between Moses and all Docent systems and, also, between the Docent baseline and both extended Docent systems. We observed that by using boostrap-resampling over BLEU and NIST metrics as described in (Koehn, 2004). We observe that Docent systems have a positive trend in their performance as long as we introduce models with more information (from only monolingual to bilingual).

Looking a little bit closer at each system, we observe that monolingual models do help Docent to find better document translation candidates. They are able to improve 0.15 point in BLEU, which is a lexical metric that is usually not sensible to document-level changes (Martínez-Garcia et al., 2014a) and also they gain 0.41 points in the syntactic metric. In a similar way, bilingual models improve a little bit more the performance over the monolingual models. In particular, they show an improvement of 0.10 in BLEU with respect to the monolingual models and 0.25 points with respect to the Docent baseline system. We observe also a similar behaviour for the rest of the metrics. For instance, regarding to the syntactic metric based on the overlap of PoS elements (SP-Op), bilingual models are able to recover 0.50 points with respect to the Docent baseline system and 0.15 points respect to the system with the monolingual models. For the average metric, ULC, the best system is Docent+biSSM, being 0.13 point over Moses and 0.75 over Docent. However, in general, there is first a slight decrease in translation quality when going from the sentence-based decoder to the document-based one probably due to the fact that Docent is not currently supporting lexicalized reordering.

In summary, we conclude from these results that the semantic information captured by our vector models help the document-level translation decoder. We also observe that bilingual models capture valuable information from the aligned data that came from the first step translation. This behaviour is coherent with the previous evaluation of the models showed in Section 3.

Table 4 shows the BLEU scores for some particular documents with some interesting cases. These results reflect the behaviour of our systems. We found some documents where the Docent systems cannot improve the Moses translation. For instance, the phrase "*House of Bones*" appears in a document about a famous building. Its correct translation is "*Casa de los Huesos*". However, Moses translates it as "*Cámara de huesos*" and Docent systems only suggest a new incorrect option "*Asamblea de huesos*". On the other hand, we find many examples where word vector models are helping. For instance, in the example of *desk* that we mentioned in Section 3, it is translated as *mostrador*, *mesa* and *escritorio* by Moses. Using the Docent baseline, it appears translated as *escritorio* and *mesa*. That shows how Docent is controling the coherence level of the translation. Using the Docent extended with the monolingual model, it appears as *escritorio*, *mesa* and *taquilla*. The word vector language model helps the system to change one translation option for a more correct one. Finally, using the bilingual vector model, we observe the word translated as *mostrador*, *mesa* and *taquilla*, obtaining here 2 good translation instead of only one. This shows how the bilingual information helps to obtain better translations. We observe how monolingual vector models improve the Docent base translation and, at the same time, how the bilingual information helps to improve the translation and even obtain better results than the ones with the Moses baseline.

6 Conclusions

We have presented an evaluation of word vector models trained with neural networks. We test them in a document-level machine translation environment. First, we build monolingual and bilingual models using the *word2vec* package implementations for the CBOW and the Skipgram algorithms. We test the models to see their capability to select a good translation option for a word that appears translated in more than one sense in a first translation of a document. The results of these evaluations show that the CBOW models perform better than the Skipgram one in our test set, achieving at most 85.49% and 78.36% respectively for the bilingual model for the accuracy at Top 5. Also, the bilingual model achieves better results than the monolingual one, with a 65.44% of accuracy for the best monolingual model trained with CBOW against the 85.49% for the bilingual model under the same conditions. These results indicate that WSM can be useful for translation tasks and it is left as future work a wider evaluation of the models considering the variation of all the parameters (context training window, vectors dimensionality, size and quality of the training data, etc.) We also want to use other techniques, like the semisupervised approach described in (Madhyastha et al., 2014), to build new bilingual models in order to compare them with the ones that are presented here.

As a second step of the process, we evaluated our word vector models inside a machine translation system. In particular, we chose the Docent decoder since it works at document-level and allows a fast integration of WVMs as semantic space language models. This option allows us to asses the vector models quality in a specific translation environment. The carried out experiments showed that WVMs models can help the decoder to improve the final translation. Although we only observe a slight improvement in the results in terms of automatic evaluation metrics, the improvement is consistent among metrics and is larger as we introduce more semantic information into the system. That is, we get the best results when using the models with bilingual information.

Summing up, the evaluation has shown the utility of word vector models for translation-related tasks. However, the results also indicate that these systems can be improved. We left as future work the effect that bilingual WVMs obtained with other methods can have in the final translation. Also, we find it interesting to apply these models to a particular document-level phenomenon such as ambiguous words. Developing a specific feature for Docent that scores the adequacy of a translation option for every ambiguous word in a document using word vector models can improve the performance of such models for translation tasks.

Acknowledgments

Supported by the TACARDI project (TIN2012-38523-C02) of the Spanish Ministerio de Economía y Competitividad (MEC). Special thanks to Christian Hardmeier and Jörg Tiedemann for their insightful comments and technical support.

References

Bahdanau, D., K. Cho, and Y. Bengio. 2014. Neural machine translation by jointly learning to align and translate. In *arXiv:1409.0473*.

Cho, K., B. van Merrienboer, D. Bahdanau, and Y. Bengio. 2014. On the properties of neural machine translation: Encoder-decoder approaches. In *Proc. of the 8th SSST*, pages 103–111.

Devlin, J., R. Zbib, Z. Huang, T. Lamar, R. Schwartz, and J. Makhoul. 2014. Fast and robust neural network joint models for statistical machine translation. In *Proc. of the 52nd ACL (Vol 1.)*, pages 1370–1380.

Gong, Z., M. Zhang, and G. Zhou. 2011. Cache-based document-level statistical machine translation. In *Proc. of the 2011 EMNLP*, pages 909–919.

González, M., J. Giménez, and L. Màrquez. 2012. A graphical interface for MT evaluation and error analysis. In *Proc. of the 50th ACL, System Demonstrations*, pages 139–144.

Hardmeier, C. and M. Federico. 2010. Modelling pronominal anaphora in statistical machine translation. In *Proc. of the 7th International Workshop on Spoken Language Translation*, pages 283–289.

Hardmeier, C., J. Nivre, and J. Tiedemann. 2012. Document-wide decoding for phrase-based statistical machine translation. In *Proc. of the EMNLP-CoNLL*, pages 1179–1190.

Hardmeier, C., S. Stymne, J. Tiedemann, and J. Nivre. 2013. Docent: A document-level decoder for phrase-based statistical machine translation. In *Proc. of the 51st ACL*, pages 193–198.

Hardmeier, C. 2014. Discourse in machine translation (PhD Thesis). Uppsala Universitet.

Jean, S., K. Cho, R. Memisevic, and Y. Bengio. 2014. On using very large target vocabulary for neural machine translation. In *arXiv (abs/1412.2007)*.

Koehn, P., H. Hoang, A. Birch, C. Callison-Burch, M. Federico, N. Bertoldi, B. Cowan, W. Shen, C. Moran, R. Zens, C. Dyer, O. Bojar, A. Constantin, and E. Herbst. 2007. Moses: open source toolkit for statistical machine translation. In *Proc. of the 45th ACL*, pages 177–180.

Koehn, Philipp. 2004. Statistical significance tests for machine translation evaluation. In *Proc. of EMNLP 2004*, pages 388–395.

Madhyastha, P. S., X. Carreras, and A. Quattoni. 2014. Learning task-specific bilexical embeddings. In *Proc. of the 25th COLING*, pages 161–171.

Martínez-Garcia, E., C. España-Bonet, and L. Màrquez. 2014a. Document-level machine translation as a re-translation process. In *Procesamiento del Lenguaje Natural, Vol. 53*, pages 103–110. SEPLN.

Martínez-Garcia, E., C. España-Bonet, J. Tiedemann, and L. Màrquez. 2014b. Word's vector representations meet machine translation. In *Proc. of the 8th SSST*, pages 132–134.

Mikolov, T., K. Chen, G. Corrado, and J. Dean. 2013a. Efficient estimation of word representations in vector space. In *Proc. of Workshop at ICLR*. http://code.google.com/p/word2vec.

Mikolov, T., Q. V. Le, and I. Sutskever. 2013b. Exploiting similarities among languages for machine translation. In *arXiv:1309.4168*.

Mikolov, T., I. Sutskever, G. Corrado, and J. Dean. 2013c. Distributed representations of words and phrases and their compositionality. In *Proc. of NIPS*, pages 3111–3119.

Mikolov, T., W. Yih, and G. Zweig. 2013d. Linguistic regularities in continuous space word representations. In *Proc. of NAACL HLT*, pages 746–751.

Nagard, R. Le and P. Koehn. 2010. Aiding pronouns translation with co-reference resolution. In *Proc. of Joint 5th Workshop on Statistical Machine Translation and MetricsMATR*, pages 252–261.

Och, F. and H. Ney. 2003. A systematic comparison of various statistical alignment models. *Computational Linguistics (Vol. 29)*.

Och, F. 2003. Minimum error rate training in statistical machine translation. In *Proc. of the ACL*.

Papineni, K., S. Roukos, T. Ward, and W.J. Zhu. 2002. Bleu: a method for automatic evaluation of machine translation. In *Proc. of the 40th ACL*, pages 311–318.

Specia, Lucia, Kashif Shah, Jose G. C. De Souza, and Trevor Cohn. 2013. Quest - a translation quality estimation framework. In *Proc. of ACL Demo Session*, pages 79–84.

Stolcke, A. 2002. SRILM – An extensible language modeling toolkit. In *Proc. Intl. Conf. on Spoken Language Processing*, pages 257–286.

Sundermeyer, M., T. Alkhouli, J. Wuebker, and H. Ney. 2014. Translation modeling with bidirectional recurrent neural networks. In *Proc. of the 2014 EMNLP*, pages 14–25. EAMNLP.

Sutskever, I., O. Vinyals, and V. Le Quoc. 2013. Recurrent continuous translation models. In *Proc. of EMNLP*, pages 1700–1709.

Sutskever, I., V. Le Quoc, O. Vinyals, and W.Zaremba. 2014a. Addressing the rareword problem in neural machine translation. In *arXiv:1410.8206*.

Sutskever, I., O. Vinyals, and V. Le Quoc. 2014b. Sequence to sequence learning with neural networks. In *Proc. NIPS 2014*, pages 1422–1430.

Tiedemann, J. 2009. News from opus - a collection of multilingual parallel corpora with tools and interfaces. In *Recent Advances in Natural Language Processing (vol V)*, pages 237–248.

Tiedemann, J. 2012. Parallel data, tools and interfaces in opus. In *Proc. of the 8th LREC*, pages 2214–2218. http://opus.lingfil.uu.se/.

Webber, B. 2014. Discourse for machine translation. In *Proc. of the 28th PACLIC*.

Wolf, L., Y. Hanani, K. Bar, and N. Derschowitz. 2014. Joint word2vec networks for bilingual semantic representations. In *Poster sessions at CICLING*.

Xiao, T., J. Zhu, S. Yao, and H. Zhang. 2011. Document-level consistency verification in machine translation. In *Proc. of MT-Summit XIII*, pages 131–138.

Xiong, D., M. Zhang, and X. Wang. 2015. Topic-based coherence modeling for statistical machine translation. In *IEEE/ACM Transactions on audio, speech and language processing (Vol. 23)*, pages 483 – 493.

The potential and limits of lay post-editing in an online community

Linda Mitchell
CNGL/School of Applied Language and Intercultural Studies
Dublin City University
Dublin, Ireland
linda.mitchell7@mail.dcu.ie

Abstract

This paper aims at exploring the potential of a lay community as post-editors. It focusses on 15 members of an online technology support forum, native speakers of the target language (TL) and some knowledge of the source language (SL) translating content that was machine translated from English into German specific to their own domain. It presents the most predominant errors remaining in the post-edited output and the impact of these on the quality of the post-edited output as measured by domain specialists evaluating adequacy and fluency. This paper further explores examples of these errors and possible solutions to reducing the occurrence of these and maximising the community's potential. The targeted post-editing quality was "'good enough", as determined in the post-editing guidelines. The PE results demonstrate that there is still room for improvement in terms of quality.

1 Introduction

User-Generated Content (UGC) is constantly growing online. With that growth, the demand for translations with fast turnaround times increases, too. Common solutions to meet this demand are MT or a combination of MT and Post-Editing (PE), the correction of automatically translated text. Previous research in the field of PE has predominantly focussed on professional translators, e.g. de Almeida (2013) who investigates correlations between translation experience and post-editing quality, Plitt and Masselot (2010) who compare results of traditional Human Translation to post-editing in an industrial setting using the example of Autodesk, or Guerberof (2009) who compares productivity between translation with Translation Memories (TM) to post-editing of MT content. Participants within these experiments have been found to experience adverse feelings towards post-editing (e.g. de Almeida 2013), which is not correlated to their often excellent performance. There have further been studies with translation students as post-editors, e.g. Koponen (2013), who investigates variation in post-editing preferences or Depraetere (2010), who seeks to establish strategies in post-editing behaviour of translation students. Recently, there have been studies investigating individual lay people or communities as post-editors, such as with subjects who have some knowledge of both the SL and the TL but who are untrained in translation (Aranberri et al. 2014) or domain specialists who are untrained in translation and have no knowledge of the SL (Schwartz 2014).

While the studies presented above have mostly been of hypothetical nature here, we are tapping into a new pool of potential post-editors by focussing on an already existent and real online community. This community is a technology support forum, the Norton[1] Community, a platform facilitating discussion on the Norton products among the users of the products in order to solve problems they may be experiencing with additional guidance from Symantec employees. It is a small community, which sets itself apart from communities discussed in previous translation research, as it is not based on social media, such as Facebook or Twit-

[1]Norton is a sub-division of Symantec Corporation.

ter. In order to determine the potential of lay post-editing, we compare the post-editing behaviour of lay post-editors[2] to that of professional translators or any other post-editor types that have been reported on. In the following, such studies are presented to facilitate a comparison with the current research.

2 Related Research

De Almeida (2013) investigates the post-editing behaviour of 18 professional translators with varying degrees of experience in translation and in PE for English → French and English → Brazilian Portuguese. She focusses on essential, preferential changes and newly introduced errors. She finds that her subjects do not only implement essential changes but that they also implement additional preferential changes, e.g. of stylistic or synonymical nature, even though they were instructed not to do so. She uncovers a tendency of professional translators to over-edit the text, which could render the post-editing process less efficient.

Groves and Schmidtke (2009) investigate common edits performed on MT output using the Microsoft Treelet MT engine focussing on EN → DE and EN → FR, employing 3 professional translators with varying degrees of translation experience and productivity. For both language pairs they identify the insertion and deletion of function words as the most common edit, 42% of which consist of determiners (for German), predominantly the insertion of the determiner *die*. They further note changes in punctuation as being among the most common edits in their data and point out the frequent deletion of the pronoun *Sie*, which is typically inserted by their MT system. They hope to resolve these issues with automatic statistical post-editing. Groves and Schmidtke do not report on any errors that remain in the post-edited output.

Depraetere (2010) focusses on post-editing training of translation students looking at the language pair English → French. Hypothetically, these students would not have established automised translation routines yet and would be more open to new translation techniques and would be closer to lay post-editors in behaviour than professional translators. She investigates the post-editing results of 10 such students, and how they intuitively approach post-editing with the view to creating appropriate post-editing guidelines that focus on the errors ignored. Depraetere finds that, in contrast to professional translators, there are few stylistic or phrasal ordering changes implemented. More importantly, she finds that the students adhered strictly to the guidelines, which were to "make sure that the source text and the target text were informationally similar and that the target text was grammatically correct" (Depraetere 2010: 3), i.e. they performed minimal edits. Their behaviour involved, for example, accepting literal translations by the MT system that are not equivalent to the source text. She concludes that there are no clear post-editing strategies present on a micro level, i.e. the types of errors corrected.

It can be concluded that professional translators tend to post-edit more systematically, frequently correcting the same errors (Groves and Schmidtke 2009) and that they tend to over-edit MT output by implementing preferential changes to render the writing style closer to their own (de Almeida 2013). Although the manner of measuring errors/changes differs between these studies and the approach taken in this paper, they give an important indication. Furthermore, translation students seem to under-edit the machine translated output and strictly adhere to the guidelines they are presented with (Depraetere 2010).

Moorkens and O'Brien (2015) also focus on differences between novice translators and professionals in the frame a post-editing user interface study. They find that professionals are more efficient but that their working habits and attitudes may prevent them from following the structure of the experiment as intended. They conclude that while novices may be the group that is more easily engaged in research, their results cannot be carried over to professionals.

Čulo et al. (2014) investigate how post-editing affects typical translation strategies for 12 professional translators and 12 translation students (English → German) by comparing translations, monolingually post-edited and bilingually post-edited (with access to the ST) texts. Čulo et al. disprove the claim that bilingual post-editing produces as high a quality as human translation (HT). Based on their examples, they hypothesise that errors and interference effects may be based on the post-editing rules for light PE and on the MT output.

[2] We define a lay post-editor as anybody who is not a professional translator or translation student.

PE rules have been addressed on a theoretical level by Rico and Ariano (2014). They seek to establish a framework for developing language dependent PE guidelines (English → Spanish) These were based on an analysis of the MT output and PE patterns that emerged incorporated into a flexible decision tool. While this approach appears to be successful, it is unsuitable for the purpose of the current study. Rico and Ariano do not deal with SMT, nor does their project support German. Their PE guidelines are targeted at professional post-editors or translators and are unsuitable for lay post-editors, as the guidelines require linguistic knowledge to be understood.

The aim of the experiment described in this paper was to uncover the post-editing approach taken by lay post-editors and how it fits into the current body of research. Furthermore, this study aims at identifying the potential of a lay community as post-editors of content that is relevant to their domain. Firstly, we aim to identify the number of errors corrected and the number of errors that remain in the post-edited output of the lay post-editors. This paper subsequently sets out to present strategies to maximise a lay community's potential for post-editing.

3 Experimental Design

The participants for this experiment were recruited online in the German Norton Community by means of private messaging and a publicly posted open call for participation. Fifteen native speakers of German with some knowledge[3] of English, who post-edited bilingually were considered only, with the aim to eliminate outliers based on their language skills. [4] The participants were members of the Norton Community and were familiar with the domain of the Norton products. Each participant post-edited 12 tasks.[5] The texts for the tasks were extracted from the English-speaking Norton community. They were machine translated from English into German using the ACCEPT baseline SMT engine, which is based on Moses, as described in ACCEPT (2012) in the ACCEPT portal.[6] The language pair English → German was chosen here, as it is particularly challenging for MT engines because of the differences in syntax between the languages.

Figure 1 displays the (German) post-editing interface the lay post-editors used to post-edit the machine translated content.

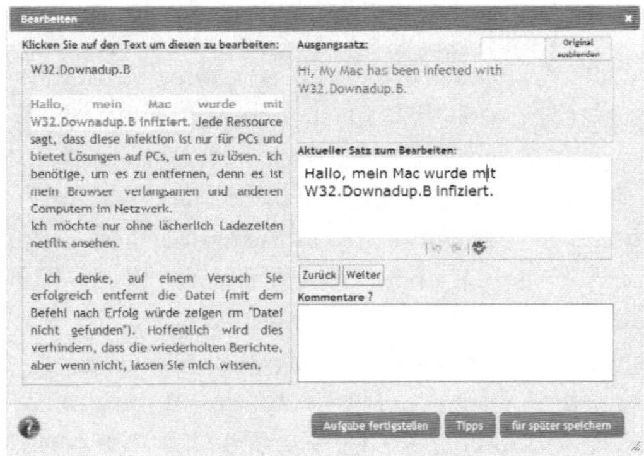

Figure 1: Post-editing Interface (German)

On the left, the machine translated text is displayed with the original version of the current segment displayed on the top right and the current segment to be edited below. Of particular importance here is the middle button on the bottom, "Tipps", which displayed the post-editing guidelines when clicked. These are presented below.

Tips for post-editing:

- Edit the text to make it more fluent and clearer based on your interpretation.
- Try to correct phrasal ordering and spelling, for example, if they make the text hard or impossible to understand.
- Use words, phrases or punctuation as they are, if they are acceptable.
- If you are working with reference to the original text, make sure that no information has been added or deleted.

These guidelines were developed for both monolingual and bilingual post-editing based on TAUS' guidelines to achieve post-editing quality that is "good enough". With these, it was hoped to keep over-editing, identified as being prevalent amongst professional translators (de Almeida 2013), to a minimum. Similar to Depraetere (2010), we sought to establish a baseline of PE behaviour in an online community of lay post-editors.

[3]'Some knowledge' here refers to the categories B1 to C2 as defined in CEDEFOP 2011.

[4]This work is based on the post-editing and post-editor data collected in a study as described in Mitchell (2015).

[5]Each 'task' contained a subject line, a question and the accepted solution to that question.

[6]www.accept-portal.eu

The post-editing results were analysed based on the error categorisation proposed by (de Almeida 2013), which was developed for investigating post-editing behaviour. The error annotation was performed by the author of this paper, a native speaker of German. While it may be argued that one annotator is not sufficient in evaluating the content, it was considered an appropriate solution here, as recent studies have shown that achieving annotator agreement is difficult, due to ambiguity of categories, disagreement on whether a construct is an error or not and disagreement on the spans of errors (e.g. Lommel 2014). Agreement on spans of errors is particularly important for phrasal ordering, an error type that was expected to be of significance in this study, due to the language pair English $\rightarrow$ German. The categories of preferential and essential changes were dropped, as the participants were assumed to be untrained in translation and would therefore not have experience of these concepts. The main categories used for this experiment were 'Language', 'Accuracy' and 'Format' (based on de Almeida 2013: 95) with the category Language including adjectives, adverbs, capitalisation, conjunctions, determiners, gender, nouns, number, phrasal ordering, prepositions, pronouns, punctuation, spelling and verb tense; the category Accuracy includes extra information, information missing, untranslated information and mistranslation; and Format consists of additional or missing spaces. For the error annotation all machine translated content (322 segments) and 44% of the post-edited content (4 post-edited versions per MT segment), approximately 72 segments per post-editor, was randomly selected and evaluated.

4 Results and Analysis

In order to demonstrate the finding that post-editing by a lay community is feasible, the errors corrected by the participants are presented here. The results can be found in Table 1, displaying the Total number of errors corrected, the number of errors in the Language, Accuracy and Format categories in both absolute numbers and percentages, compared to the errors that had been present in the raw MT output.

It is evident that the lay community was able to correct on average 73% of all errors, with the lowest number being 21% (PE13) and the highest number being 83% (PE8). The average number of errors corrected in the Language category

	Total	%	Lang.	%	Acc.	%	F.	%
PE1	199	66	95	61	100	79	-4	-44
PE2	182	69	88	65	88	74	5	63
PE3	215	81	103	80	101	81	4	80
PE4	254	81	133	81	120	90	1	10
PE5	248	78	116	70	114	88	6	75
PE6	231	87	114	84	107	91	2	40
PE7	164	57	69	44	89	75	-1	-33
PE8	223	83	116	85	94	81	6	67
PE9	215	80	107	80	102	84	-2	-40
PE10	213	77	113	74	94	85	0	0
PE11	222	78	114	75	101	86	-1	-25
PE12	234	81	122	84	105	83	-2	-33
PE13	51	21	67	48	-8	-8	-8	-800
PE14	227	71	131	76	97	75	-9	-225
PE15	193	78	98	77	86	82	1	17
Avg.	205	73	106	72	93	76	0	-57

Table 1: Errors corrected (absolute and in %) for the Total number of errors corrected, errors in the Language, Accuracy and Format category (also absolute and in %)

are 72% with 48% (PE13) as the lowest and 85% (PE8) as the highest number and 76% on average and -8% (PE13) as the lowest, i.e. 8 errors were introduced in the post-edited output, and 91% (PE6) of all errors of the Accuracy category corrected. While none of the post-editors corrected 100% of the errors and there is great variation across the lay post-editors, these results show the potential of lay post-editing, especially with the examples of PE3, PE4, PE6, PE8, PE9, PE12, who correct $\geq$ 80% of all errors. It should be noted that even in studies with professional translators acting as post-editors, it is often reported that errors remain in the post-edited output. Furthermore, the guidelines used targeted "good enough" post-editing quality, rather than aiming at the best humanly possible quality. Thus, we did not expect a correction rate of 100% of all errors.

In order to interpret this data, the need to investigate the profile of the lay post-editors arises. This was discussed in Mitchell (2015:166-176); Section 7 focusses on the post-editor profile, i.e. language competence, domain competence and psychomotor competence. While the first two were measured by self-reporting, the last was based on key logging data recorded in the ACCEPT portal. We found that there were no correlations between any of these competences and the post-editing quality, represented by both the error annotation and the domain specialist evaluation. Hence, the post-editor background was not deemed to be a helpful variable in the light of this article.

In the following, an overview of the main errors

that remain in the post-edited output and how they affect the quality of the same are presented in order to propose strategies for maximising the potential of a lay community as post-editors. Table 2 displays the average number of errors across all post-editors in the MT output they were editing, as well as in the post-edited content. These are ordered by the most frequent errors present in the MT output. It emerges that errors from the Accuracy category were the most common: mistranslation, information missing and extra information, as well as errors that emerge from the differences in syntax between English and German, i.e. phrasal ordering and verb (tense), the latter of which often manifests itself as a missing part of the verb, determining the correct tense. Additional sub-categories of Language that contained a considerable number of errors in the content annotated were determiner and pronoun.

Category	Errors (MT)	Avg.	Errors (PE)	Avg.
Mistranslation	873	58	162	11
Phrasal ordering	791	53	100	7
Information missing	526	35	161	11
Verb (tense)	271	18	40	3
Extra information	256	17	48	3
Determiner	247	16	50	3
Pronoun	150	10	28	2
Untranslated	146	10	40	3

Table 2: Errors present in MT output and after PE in total and on average across all post-editors

Figure 2 displays the absolute number of errors for the main error category Accuracy for each post-editor, in order to establish how they handled the errors present in the categories extra information, missing information, untranslated and mistranslation individually. The most frequent errors, which post-editors failed to correct/introduced, were either mistranslations or information missing. The number of remaining errors ranged between 3 and 17 for mistranslation and 2 and 13 for the category information missing. Figure 2 also reveals an outlier in the post-editing behaviour, PE13.

While PE13 accounts for nearly 30% of the errors in these two categories, the categories of untranslated and extra information contain numbers of errors that are comparable to those of the other post-editors. The category untranslated information seems to contain the lowest number of errors mostly, followed by the category of extra information, predominantly $\leq$ 10 errors per post-editor.

Compared to the number of Accuracy errors,

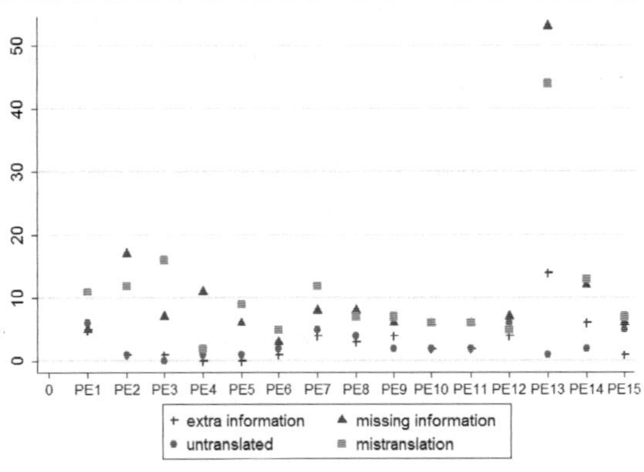

Figure 2: Errors remaining (absolute) in PE output in Accuracy category

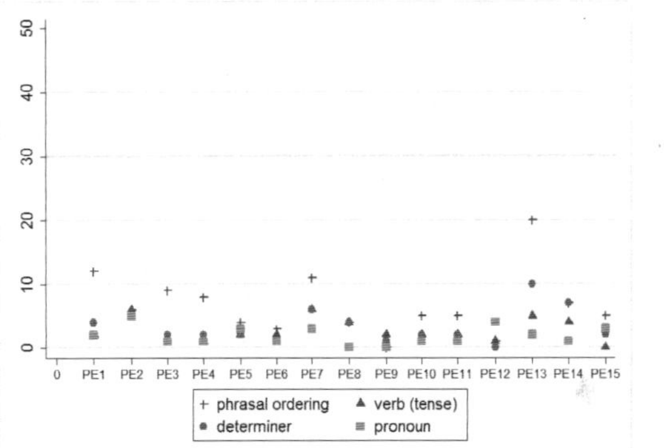

Figure 3: Predominant errors remaining (absolute) in PE output in Language category

as presented in Figure 2, considerably fewer Language errors remained in the MT output, as evident from Figure 3. Phrasal ordering errors, as expected, takes the highest rank of errors remaining in the post-edited output per evaluator. This echoes Depraetere's (2010) finding that post-editors who are not professional translators leave MT output unedited if the sentence is comprehensible and often leave literal translations untouched even though they may not convey the source text meaning accurately. The ratios of types of errors remaining (phrasal ordering, determiner and pronouns) are similar across all post-editors except for PE12 and PE13.

Examples:
The following three examples show minimal editing to no editing. For mistranslation, the error stems from the incorrect conjunction *weil* in

the MT output that was mistakenly retained; for phrasal ordering, the post-editor creates an awkward construction and did not correct the phrasal ordering; for information missing, the machine translated output was left unedited, which results in the conjunction (a function word) missing.

Mistranslation:
ST: ... I bought a new laptop *and*[7] problem was more prevalent.
MT: ... *weil* ich eine neue Laptops und Problem weiter verbreitet wurde.
HT: ... ich kaufte einen neuen Laptop *und* das Problem wurde noch schlimmer.
PE: ... *weil* das Problem durch den Kauf eines neuen Laptop schlimmer wurde.

Phrasal ordering:
ST: Purge *in progress* for 2-1/2 days... help!
MT: Bereinigung *in Fortschritt* für 2-1 / 2 Tage... zu helfen!
HT: Bereinigung seit zweieinhalb Tagen *in Arbeit*...Bitte um Hilfe!
PE: Bereinigung *in Arbeit* seit zweieinhalb Tagen.... Bitte um Hilfe!

Information missing:
ST: First, make sure Teamviewer is not running.
MT: Stellen Sie zuerst sicher TeamViewer wird nicht ausgeführt.
HT: Stellen Sie zuerst sicher, *dass* TeamViewer nicht ausgeführt wird.
PE: Stellen Sie zuerst sicher TeamViewer wird nicht ausgeführt.

The following example focusses on extra information that has been accidentally introduced by retaining the verb from the MT output and inserting it in the wrong position in the sentence. This shows that the placement of verbs not only poses problems for MT engines but also for human lay post-editors.

Extra information:
ST: In almost all cases, the events are caused by legitimate programs or Windows processes...
MT: In fast allen Fällen *verursacht* werden, die Ereignisse von legitimen Programmen oder Windows Prozesse...
HT: In fast allen Fällen werden die Ereignisse von legitimen Programmen oder Windows Prozessen verursacht...
PE: In fast allen Fällen *verursacht* werden diese Ereignisse von legitimen Programmen oder Windows Prozesse *verursacht*...

In addition to retaining errors from the MT, post-editors produce verbal errors. The next example requires a complex verb construction, which the post-editor failed to produce. While the post-editor does produce a correct sentence compared to the MT output, it does not accurately reflect the meaning of the source text. This may have also been due to insufficient knowledge of the source language.

Verb (tense):
ST: However, NU should not have been deleting this.
MT: Aber NU *sollten nicht gelöscht wurden.*
HT: Aber NU *hätte* diese *nicht löschen sollen.*
PE: NU *sollte* diese Elemente *nicht löschen.*

The following two examples involve the changing of function words, i.e. determiners and pronouns. While the first one shows that the post-editor discards the correct determiner as suggested by the MT system, the second example shows that the post-editor deemed the sentence comprehensible and left it unedited. In addition, the meaning is completely mistranslated, which was not picked up on by the post-editor.

Determiner:
ST: Check if it runs *the* scans or detects any threats.
MT: Überprüfen Sie, ob es führt *die* Scans oder erkennt Bedrohungen.
HT: Überprüfen Sie, ob *die* Scans ausgeführt oder Bedrohungen erkannt werden.
PE: Überprüfen Sie, ob *der* Scans ausgeführt wird oder Bedrohungen erkannt werden.

Pronoun:
ST: All *I* care about is the first C: drive in this list.
MT: *Ich* interessiert, ist das erste Laufwerk C: In dieser Liste enthalten.
HT: *Mich* interessiert nur das erste Laufwerk, C:, in dieser Liste.
PE: *Ich* interessiert, ist das erste Laufwerk C: in dieser Liste enthalten.

The last example shows insufficient knowledge of the source language or the domain. The post-editor left 'Antivirus License Be' unedited, possibly because they assumed it to be the correct term or were unable to translate it.

Untranslated:
ST: Can Norton Antivirus *License Be* Transferred From One Computer To Another?
MT: Kann Norton Antivirus *License Be* übertragen von One Computer So Anderer?
HT: Kann ich die Norton Antivirus *Lizenz* auf einen anderen Computer übertragen?
PE: Kann ich die Norton Antivirus *License Be* auf einen anderen Compter übertragen ?

[7] Italics were added in all examples to highlight the translation problem of interest.

In summary, errors may be caused by erroneous source texts, by insufficient knowledge of the source language (or the domain), which leads to mistranslations and retaining errors as introduced by the MT output or introduced by the post-editors. Other times errors may be caused by editing hastily and producing errors that could have been easily avoided. This is not an unexpected situation in a lay post-editing scenario as lay post-editors are assumed to be untrained in translation and proof-reading. Furthermore, post-editors often left segments unchanged that needed editing in regards to syntax, e.g. phrasal ordering and verbs. When it comes to insufficient knowledge of the SL, it would be beneficial for the post-editors to have an option to send the segments in question to another post-editor/professional translator, a solution suggested by Schwartz (2014). Errors stemming from editing too hastily and too little editing could be addressed through revised post-editing guidelines. A factor that may have influenced PE quality negatively is motivation. Revised guidelines could increase the post-editors' knowledge of how to post-edit successfully on a theoretical level. On a practical level, however, they would also need to be motivated to to implement the required changes. We believe that motivation is a complex aspect that has an impact on lay post-editing quality. While motivation was not addressed here, it would be beneficial if it were considered in the future. Hence, we developed the following amended post-editing guidelines focussing on German as a target language.[8] They focus on the most common errors that remain in the post-edited output and do not include a reference to reusing as much of the MT output as possible (cf. Depraetere 2010). The guidelines were written in a clearer and a more concise manner. Extra items have been added for the mistakes that were predominant in the post-edited output: verbs, determiners, pronouns and mistranslations.
Tips for post-editing:

- Correct spelling, grammar and word order errors.

- Pay particular attention to verbs, determiners *(e.g. der, die, das)* and pronouns *(e.g. ich, du, er, mich, dich, sich).*

- Correct any mistranslated information in the MT output.

- Ensure that no information has been added or deleted from the original text.

With these guidelines, we hope to point lay post-editors in the right direction without confusing them about the goal of their post-editing. Furthermore, they may be a first step in maximising the community's potential and aiming for post-editing quality that is better than "good enough", which is the quality that was targeted for the purpose of this experiment. These revised guidelines would only be a successful solution, however, if they were interpreted correctly by the post-editors and if they had the motivation required to implement them. It remains to be seen whether additional post-editor training in this regard would be helpful and feasible in an online community with volunteer post-editors.

5 Conclusion

It can be concluded from this sample that lay post-editors correct on average around 74% of errors in total. Furthermore, it was found that the most common errors remaining were all categories associated with Accuracy (mistranslation, information missing, extra information and untranslated information) and the following categories associated with Language; phrasal ordering, verb, determiner and pronoun. This fits with findings by Depraetere (2010), in terms of syntactical changes, and with Groves and Schmidtke (2009) in terms of the changing of function words, mainly determiners and pronouns, which occur often in our sample and are not always corrected.

Additionally, the ratios of errors remaining in both the Language and the Accuracy category are quite similar across the post-editors, i.e. they systematically leave some errors uncorrected in the MT output, which corresponds to de Almeida's findings. However, rather than over-editing the text, they adhere to the guidelines and leave literal translations or awkward sentence structures unedited, as described by Depraetere (2010).

Furthermore, the errors remaining in the post-edited output were due to unedited (portions of) segments, insufficient knowledge of English or hurried editing, which could be resolved by passing on 'complicated' segments to more competent editors and by having more 'tuned' post-editing

[8]These could be easily adapted to suit other languages by replacing the error categories here with ones specific to these languages.

guidelines, here tailored to German as a target language.

Acknowledgements This research was funded by the European Community's Seventh Framework Programme as part of the ACCEPT project under grant agreement no. 288769. It was continued in association with CNGL II.

References

ACCEPT Consortium. 2012. *Baseline machine translation systems.* Deliverable 4.1. Available from: http://www.accept.unige.ch/Products/D_4_1_Baseline_MT_systems.pdf.

Aranberri, Nora, Gorka Labaka, Arantza Diaz de Ilarraze and Kepa Sarasola 2014. Comparison of postediting productivity between professional translators and lay users. *Proceedings of the Third Workshop on Post-editing Technology and Practice*, Vancouver, Canada. 20–34.

Čulo, Oliver, Silke Gutermuth, Silvia Hansen-Schirra and Jean Nitzke 2014. The influence of post-editing on translation strategies. *IN: Post-editing of Machine Translation* Laura Winther Balling, Michael Carl, Michel Simard, Lucia Specia and Sharon O'Brien (eds.). 200–218.

de Almeida, Giselle 2013. Translating the post-editor: an investigation of post-editing changes and correlations with professional experience across two Romance languages *PhD thesis*, Dublin City University.

Depraetere, Ilse 2010. What counts as useful advice in a university post-editing training context? Report on a case study. *EAMT 2010: Proceedings of the 14th Annual conference of the European Association for Machine Translation,* 27-28 May 2010, Saint-Raphaël, France.

Groves, Declan and Dag Schmidtke 2009. Identification and Analysis of Post-Editing Patterns for MT *MT Summit XII: Proceedings of the twelfth Machine Translation Summit, August 26-30, 2009.* Ottawa, Ontario, Canada. 429–436.

Guerberof, Ana 2012. Productivity and quality in the post-editing of outputs from translation memories and machine translation. *PhD thesis*, Unversitat Rovira.

Koponen, Maarit 2013. This translation is not too bad: an analysis of post-editor choices in a machine translation post-editing task. *Proceedings of MT Summit XIV Workshop on Post-editing Technology and Practice (WPTP), 2-6 September.* S. O'Brien, M. Simard and L. Specia (eds.). Nice, France, 1–9.

Linguistic Data Consortium. 2005. Linguistic data annotation specification: assessment of fluency and adequacy in translations. Revision 1.5. Available from: http://www.ldc.upenn.edu/Catalog/docs/LDC2003T17/TransAssess02.pdf [Accessed 3 October 2012].

Lommel, Arle, Maja Popovic and Aljoscha Burchardt 2014. Assessing inter-annotator agreement for translation error annotation. *IN: Proceedings of the Ninth International Conference on Language Resources and Evaluation (LREC),* 26-31 May, Reykjavik, Iceland.

Mitchell, Linda 2015. Community Post-Editing of Machine-Translated User-Generated Content. *PhD thesis*, Dublin City University.

Moorkens, Joss and Sharon O'Brien 2015. Post-editing evaluations: trade-offs between novice and professional participants *IN: Proceedings of the 18th annual conference of the European Association for Machine Translation (EAMT 2015),* 11-13 May, Antalya, Turkey.

Plitt, Mirko and François Masselot 2010. A productivity test of statistical machine translation post-editing in a typical localisation environment *The Prague Bulletin of Mathematical Linguistics*, 93, 7–16.

Rico, Celia and Martín Ariano 2014. Defining Language dependent post-editing guidelines: the case of the language pair English-Spanish *IN: Post-editing of Machine Translation* Laura Winther Balling, Michael Carl, Michel Simard, Lucia Specia and Sharon O'Brien (eds.). 299–322.

Schwartz, Lane 2014. Monolingual post-editing by a domain expert is highly effective for translation triage. *Proceedings of the Third Workshop on Post-editing Technology and Practice*, Vancouver, Canada, 34–44.

TAUS. 2010. MT post-editing guidelines. Available from: https://www.taus.net/think-tank/best-practices/postedit-best-practices/machine-translation-post-editing-guidelines [Accessed 24 February 2015].

Post-Editing Evaluations: Trade-offs between Novice and Professional Participants

Joss Moorkens
ADAPT Centre/School of Computing
Dublin City University
Ireland
joss.moorkens@dcu.ie

Sharon O'Brien
ADAPT Centre/SALIS/CTTS
Dublin City University
Ireland
sharon.obrien@dcu.ie

Abstract

The increasing use of post-editing in localisation workflows has led to a great deal of research and development in the area, much of it requiring user evaluation. This paper compares some results from a post-editing user interface study carried out using novice and expert translator groups. By comparing rates of productivity, edit distance, engagement with the research, and qualitative findings regarding each group's attitude to post-editing, we find that there are trade-offs to be considered when selecting participants for evaluation tasks. Novices may generally be more positive and enthusiastic and will engage considerably with the research while professionals will be more efficient, but their routines and attitudes may prevent full engagement with research objectives.

1 Introduction

The use of machine translation (MT) in commercial translation and localisation workflows has grown exponentially in recent years. Relatively recent breakthroughs in the quality of statistical machine translation (SMT) output has led to the use of MT for assimilation (gisting) and MT for dissemination (post-edited MT). The growth in the amount of content to be translated and a push for cost-cutting from translation clients has meant that post-editing of MT has grown in popularity – a survey of almost 1000 language service providers (LSPs) in 2013 found that over 44% offer a post-editing (PE) service to customers (DePalma et al., 2013).

This has led to a requirement for user testing, as industry and researchers attempt to learn how translators work with MT, through the task of post-editing, and most usually within a translation memory tool (Moorkens and O'Brien, 2013). User dissatisfaction with post-editing has been widely reported (Krings, 2001; O'Brien and Moorkens, 2014) and translators tend to associate translation automation negatively with "regimentation, dependence, exploitation or impotence" (Cronin, 2013). Any new features intended to make the task more palatable to translators will naturally need to be tested for effectiveness. Automatic evaluation metrics (AEMs - such as BLEU) are typically used to measure quality improvements in MT and quality improvements, in turn, are expected to lead to higher levels of satisfaction among post-editors. However, some AEMs have been shown not to correlate well with human evaluation of quality (Tatsumi, 2009), and although automatic metrics measuring edit distance such as Human-mediated Translation Edit Rate (HTER) (Snover et al., 2006) have better correlations with human judgements (Snover et al., 2009), evaluations with real users are often necessary to gain a deeper understanding of the human/machine interaction and relationship. User evaluation also offers the possibility of eliciting valuable qualitative data, which can give insights into barriers for adoption and acceptance.

 This research is supported by the Science Foundation Ireland (Grant 12/CE/I2267) as part of the CNGL (www.cngl.ie) at Dublin City University and by the FALCON Project (falcon-project.eu), funded by the European Commission through the Seventh Framework Programme (FP7) Grant Agreement No. 610879.

Many translation user studies are carried out using translation students, often out of necessity (Morado Vázquez et al., 2013) or convenience (Bowker, 2005). On the other hand, the common orthodoxy is that, where possible, it is best to evaluate using experts – professional translators – because they are more representative of the target user group for MT. In this paper we focus on the ramifications of using one user type over another for post-editing research. We do this by comparing the results of a post-editing user evaluation study using two sets of participants, one novice group (translation students) and one expert group (professional translators and post-editors). We have chosen translation students rather than lay or untrained volunteer translators (Mitchell, 2015) as our novice group, as students are more likely to be participants in research. The purpose of the user evaluation was to test smart post-editing features that had been programmed into a beta post-editing environment in order to test their effectiveness, although we do not report results from that test here. Instead, we focus explicitly on differences between the two user groups and on their suitability as research participants. Such differences are sometimes acknowledged but sidestepped when reporting research results.

The measurements collected during the evaluations were speed (measured in source text words per second), edit distance (measured using the Translation Edit Rate (TER) metric), attitudes to post-editing (collected via a survey), and user engagement (we measure the number of clicks on experimental features in the translation interface as a proxy for user engagement).

Yamada (2012) compared novice and professional translators and found productivity increases in both groups using post-editing, although the student group tended to make fewer edits. García (2010) found that his students preferred post-editing to human translation, which might make them a more favourable group for user testing.

Jääskeläinen (2010) notes that not all professional translators can be considered expert, as they may not produce good quality translations or may fall into an automatic routine when they work. Moreover, a translator may be an expert in a specific domain, and not at all expert in another. In addition, she suggests that experts may underperform for reasons such as "inflexibility, over-confidence, or bias" (Jääskeläinen, 2010). More generally, professional users have been found to exhibit resistance when faced with change due to a bias toward the status quo (Samuelson and Zeckhauser, 1988), or if they feel they have not been involved in the decision to change (Hirschheim and Newman, 1988). This outline of previous work suggests that the use of professional translators in post-editing research needs careful consideration because not all professional translators are equal.

2 Methodology

This research follows on from an earlier study that sought to identify PE-specific features that could be incorporated into editing environments to make the task more efficient for post-editors as described in Moorkens and O'Brien (2013). Five of those features were programmed into a beta PE environment (called "PEARL") and tested in this study (change gender, change number, change case, reject MT output, and copy source punctuation to target).

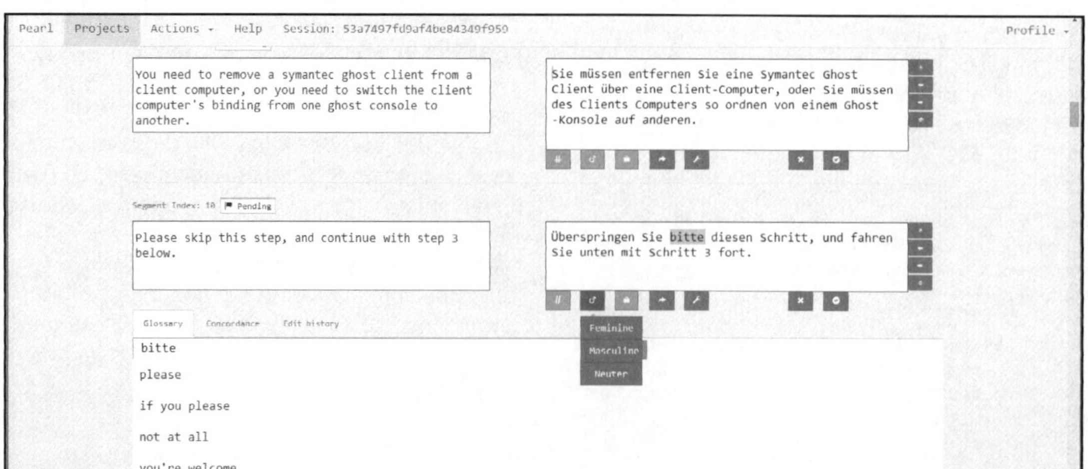

Figure 1. The PEARL test interface.

These features were selected because they represent some of the high-frequency, but tedious edits required during post-editing. They were tested in the English to German language pair using the purpose-built test interface with one group of professional and one group of student translators. English-German was selected because it is known to be one of the more demanding pairs for MT and we assumed we would see more evidence of issues regarding the features by using a demanding language pair.

2.1 Test Interface and Data

This research used the web-based interface called PEARL as a test suite for PE-specific functionality (see Figure 1). Data used were two test sets (50 US English segments each) of Norton Security helpdesk data, donated by Symantec, that had been machine translated into German using a purpose-built Moses Statistical MT engine. Features were switched on and off so that the two data sets could be tested with and without the new features.

Data Set 1 was post-edited by half of the participants with features turned off, and by half of the participants with features turned on. Then Data Set 2 was post-edited by half of the participants with features turned off, and by half of the participants with features turned on. Participants were requested not to switch applications, leave their desk, nor to ask any questions unless absolutely necessary. They were told not to worry about style, but to correct any words or grammar that was wrong or nonsensical. The researchers were present at all times during the post-editing sessions.

2.2 Participant Profiles

This research was carried out with two groups of participants. Group 1 was made up of nine expert participants, all professional English to German translators, mostly with extensive experience of localisation work who can intuitively translate and edit a text according to industry throughput expectations. In describing a five-stage process of gaining expertise, Dreyfus and Dreyfus (2005) highlight the importance of intuition as a defining characteristic of expertise. On average, the participants had 11.3 years of translation experience and four years of PE experience. Four participants had ten or more years' translation experience. The translators in Group 1 would regularly translate or post-edit texts similar to the data in this study, putting them at a further advantage when compared with the novice group, who had no experience of the specialised domain. The post-editing sessions took place in their normal place of work, on their usual computers.

Group 2 were 35 undergraduate translation students who were registered in an undergraduate translation programme in Zurich. The post-editing sessions took place in their computer lab. Very few had any professional translation experience, and the group were very reliant on procedural instruction, and as such could be considered novice according to Dreyfus and Dreyfus' taxonomy of expertise (2005).

Both groups of participants completed an online survey following the PE tasks, and the expert group also carried out a post-test interview. It was not possible to do so with the novice group due to timetable constraints.

2.3 Measurements

Participants were asked to undertake two post-editing tasks in English to German (one with the features to be tested and one without). The task comprised of 40 segments in total, although few of the novice participants completed the task within the allotted time (roughly 30 minutes per participant). From this task and from the post-task survey, we can compare our cohorts using four measurements. The first measurement is productivity or speed, which is calculated by dividing the number of words in the completed source text segments by total time in seconds, giving a words-per-second rate. The second measurement is edit distance, where raw MT and PE data are submitted to ASIYA[1], an online toolkit for MT evaluation (Giménez and Màrquez, 2010), to get a measurement using the Translation Edit Rate (TER) metric.

The third measurement is attitudes to post-editing. This was an open survey question that we have coded to a three-point Likert scale, where 1 is negative, 2 neutral, and 3 positive. More details of this coding phase are in Section 3.3. The final measurement is user engagement, looking at the number of times the participant clicked on experimental features in

[1] http://asiya.cs.upc.edu/demo/

the translation interface and using this as a proxy for user engagement. Participants were aware that feature-testing was the reason for the study, and were asked specifically to try the experimental features. Despite this, several participants chose not to try the features and post-edited as they would normally.

3 Results

3.1 Productivity

Table 1 shows the rate of source text words per second translated by Group 1, the professional post-editors, in two tasks (with/without new features). The average rate across all Group 1 users and tasks was 0.387 words per second after removing one outlier – User 2 was called away from his desk during the study, which made his second task time inaccurate and gave him a low WPS rate for that task (italicised). Table 2 shows the equivalent productivity rates for Group 2, the novice post-editors. The study with Group 2 was conducted in three university-scheduled computer lab sessions. For space reasons, we present the results for the first session of Group 2, with the average WPS rate (based on source text words translated) of 0.126. The figures for the rest of the group were very similar, with an average WPS rate across the whole group of 0.156, less than half the speed of the expert group. This is to be expected, of course, as the expert group have a great deal of experience in translation and in post-editing generally, as well as domain-specific expertise.

User	WPS Task 1	WPS Task 2
User 1	0.355	0.418
User 2	0.32	*0.109*
User 3	0.322	0.368
User 4	0.415	0.676
User 5	0.336	0.271
User 6	0.334	0.306
User 7	0.514	0.493
User 8	0.479	0.292
User 9	0.324	0.361
Average words per second for all users in both tasks		**0.387**

Table 1. Group 1 – Experts: Productivity (Words per Second)

User	WPS Task 1	WPS Task 2
User 1	0.072	0.117
User 2	0.136	0.118
User 3	0.129	0.103
User 4	0.148	0.157
User 5	0.210	0.129
User 6	0.151	0.115
User 7	0.091	0.151
User 8	0.087	0.129
User 9	0.127	0.106
User 10	0.240	0.130
User 11	0.052	0.091
User 12	0.057	0.080
User 13	0.202	0.137
Average words per second for these users in both tasks		**0.126**

Table 2. Group 2: Novices - Productivity (Words per Second)

3.2 Edit Distance

Using raw machine translated output and post-edited data, edit distance was calculated using the TER metric, defined by Snover et al. (2006, p3) as "the minimum number of edits needed to change a hypothesis so that it exactly matches one of the references".

At the document level, the average TER score for Group 1 is 30.31, calculated by dividing the number of edits by the average number of words in the reference segment (the raw MT). The most heavily edited segment received a score of 122.22. The MT output and post-edited version of this segment may be seen in Table 3.

MT output	Post-edited segment
Bitte beachten Sie die Bedingungen in Ihrem Symantec-Supportzertifikat	*Informationen zu den Bestimmungen und Bedingungen der Vereinbarung finden Sie im Symantec-Support-Zert*

Table 3. Group 1 post-edit example

The novice post-editors in Group 2 tended to edit less, with an average document-level

TER score of 27.15. The most heavily edited segment, with a score of 100.0, may be seen in Table 4.

MT output	Post-edited segment
Microsoft hat einige Sicherheitslück beheben April einen Patch veröffentlicht.	*Microsoft hat im April einen Patch veröffentlicht, mit dem mehrere Sicherheitslücken behoben wurden.*

Table 4. Group 2 post-edit example

In making fewer edits, Group 2 left more errors in the raw MT uncorrected. For example, in the segment "*Es tut mit leid, aber Ich kann bei diesem Produkt nicht weiter assistieren*", the post-editor has left the misspelled *tut mit leid* unedited, whereas all of Group 1 corrected this phrase to *tut mir leid*. Group 2 target texts contained more misspellings, such as the word *kann* spelled with a single 'n'.

3.3 Attitude to post-editing

Responses to the question 'Did you like the task of post-editing? Why/why not?' were divided into positive, neutral and negative. A response was categorised as positive if the participant answered with responses such as "Yes", "I liked it", or "it was kind of fun", neutral if they used phrases such as "so, so", "sort of", "kind of" or if they used some form of neutral description, and negative if they said "no", "not really", or "I think it is a bit useless". Comparative responses by group may be seen in Table 5.

	Group 1 (experts)	Group 2 (novices)
Positive	11%	35%
Neutral	33%	18%
Negative	56%	47%

Table 5. Attitudes to post-editing

When asked for their views on post-editing prior to the evaluation, Group 1 responses were mostly negative. Three participants said that PE can be worthwhile if the MT quality is good enough. Others disliked PE for reasons such as the lack of creativity, tediousness of the task, limited opportunity to create quality, poor quality source text rendering MT unusable, and poor term management. They considered that the main tasks during PE are tedious fixes to the word order, correcting product names, and correcting tags. They also said that they are more prone to mistakes as their "mind falls asleep", that they quickly become tired due to having to be constantly vigilant and due to the absence of any confidence indication, and that switching between mouse and keyboard was also tedious. They sometimes find it difficult to understand how to balance time and quality to find an acceptable quality level for a client.

In comparison, the novices in Group 2 were more positively disposed towards post-editing. Of those who gave positive responses, the reasons they used were that the translation was already done for them and they just needed to "improve a few things". Others liked the task because it was "new" or "challenging". Those with a neutral attitude suggested that post-editing limited the use of "imagination" or that it was "uncreative". Reasons given for negative responses can be grouped into four main categories to do with time, quality, tool functionality, and lack of context. Some participants complained about the raw MT quality saying it would be "easier to start from scratch". There was a perception among a few that the task took more time (than translation), was exhausting because it was repetitive, and made more difficult due to the lack of context for the segments.

3.4 User engagement

Participants were expressly requested to try several experimental features in the PEARL interface, but not all participants chose to engage with them. All were told that, as per DCU research ethics guidelines, they would not be penalised for non-participation, but all chose to participate. It is possible that they felt compelled by management or co-workers (in the case of Group 1) or lecturers and fellow students (in the case of Group 2). By taking part without engaging with the purpose of the research, a participant's impact is more negative and wasteful than not taking part at all. The average number of button presses on experimental features are shown in Table 6.

	Group 1 (experts)	Group 2 (novices)
Change case	2.50	7.26
Change gender	2.66	3.07
Change number	1.66	2.89

Table 6. Engagement with PE features

As can be seen, the experts in Group 1 were less likely to engage with the interface. The average number of button presses was brought down by two participants who chose not to try any of the buttons at all. All participants from Group 2 tried the feature buttons at least once, and most continued to engage with the purpose of the research despite some server problems causing an intermittent response to buttons pressed. As previously stated, one characteristic of an expert is intuition. Group 1 participants intuitively knew how to work quickly on an MT segment using familiar features (such as cut and paste), but this made them less likely to try unfamiliar features, such as those added for the purpose of this research.

4 Conclusion

User evaluation is currently continuing on post-editing with foci on areas such as adding PE-specific features (Sanchis-Trilles et al., 2014), incremental retraining (Dara et al., 2014), deciding what content should be post-edited rather than translated from scratch (Castilho et al., 2014), quality prediction (Vieira, 2014), and quality/productivity expectations in an MT/TM combination (Guerberof Arenas, 2014). Results of these evaluations may have an impact on decisions as to what remuneration is appropriate for professional post-editing. As MT deployment increases in the language industry, it makes sense to carry out user evaluations with the people who will be expected to engage with that technology. Productivity rates for experts, as seen in Section 3.1, were more than double those of the novice post-editors. In fact, the expert post-editors in Group 1 of this study worked so quickly that our server's CPU load rose worrisomely as they moved quickly and intuitively through the texts. Their segments tended to be more comprehensively edited than those of the novice group. On the other hand, their attitudes towards the technology were considerably more negative than that of the novice group and they were much more likely to adhere to an automatic routine, and less likely to engage with the research objectives. Their attitudes are possibly due to "anxiety and uncertainty regarding change" (Kim and Kankanhalli, 2009).

It is unclear whether the lower engagement with the research (in Section 3.4) by the expert group was due to their automatic routine or a negative attitude to PE/MT, but it appears that novice users are more likely to engage with new tasks and features without preconceptions. It must also be noted that, despite the comparatively positive attitude to PE among the novice group, almost half still felt negatively about the task of PE. The novice group was enthusiastic about taking part in research, and as with research in general, student groups are likely to take part in future research due to convenience and lower costs. This research suggests that, for post-editing, there are tradeoffs to be considered when using novice vs. professional groups to estimate productivity or the usefulness of a new feature in a production environment. Novices may generally be more positive and enthusiastic and will engage considerably with the research, but conclusions drawn from research with novice users cannot necessarily be carried over to experts. Professionals will be more efficient, but their routines and attitudes may prevent full engagement with research objectives. To get balanced results on user interaction with MT, it is advisable to employ adequate numbers of users with varying levels of expertise.

Acknowledgement

The authors would like to place on record their thanks to the staff and management at Alpha CRC in Cambridge, UK, and at ZHAW in Winterthur, Switzerland, for their help and participation in this research. We also thank Chris Hokamp and Ximo Planells for development work, and Dr. Lamia Tounsi and Peter Jud for assistance in Winterthur. In addition, we are grateful to Symantec for providing test data.

References

Bowker, Lynne. 2005. Productivity vs quality? A pilot study on the impact of translation memory systems. *Localisation Focus*, 4(1):13-20.

Castilho, Sheila, Sharon O'Brien, Fabio Alves, Morgan O'Brien. 2014. Does post-editing increase usability? A study with Brazilian Portuguese as Target Language. In *Proceedings of the Seventeenth Annual Conference of the European Association for Machine Translation (EAMT2014)*. Proceedings eds. Marko Tadić, Philipp Koehn, Johann Roturier, Andy Way. Dubrovnik, Croatia, June 16-18 2014, 183-190.

Cronin, Michael. 2013. *Translation in the Digital Age*. Routledge, Oxfordshire, UK.

Dara, Aswarth, Josef van Genabith, Qun Liu, John Judge, Antonio Toral. 2014. Active Learning for Post-Editing Based Incrementally Retrained MT. In *Proceedings of the 14th Conference of the European Chapter of the Association for Computational Linguistics*, Gothenburg, Sweden, April 26-30 2014, 185–189.

DePalma, Donald A., Vijayalaxmi Hegde, Hélène Pielmeier, and Robert G. Stewart. 2013. *The Language Services Market: 2013*. Common Sense Advisory, Boston, USA.

Dreyfus, Hubert, and Stuart Dreyfus. 2005. Peripheral Vision: Expertise in Real World Contexts. *Organization Studies,* 26 (5): 779–792.

Garcia, Ignacio. 2010. Is machine translation ready yet? *Target,* 22(1):7-21.

Giménez, Jesús, and Lluís Màrquez. 2010. Asiya: An Open Toolkit for Automatic Machine Translation (Meta-)Evaluation. *The Prague Bulletin of Mathematical Linguistics*, 94:77-86.

Guerberof Arenas, Ana. 2014. Correlations between productivity and quality when post-editing in a professional context. *Machine Translation*, 28(3-4): 165-186.

Hirschheim, R., and M. Newman. 1988. Information systems and user resistance: theory and practice. *The Computer Journal*, 31(5):398-408.

Jääskeläinen, Riitta. 2010. Are All Professionals Experts? Definitions of Expertise and Reinterpretation of Research Evidence in Process Studies. In *Translation and Cognition*, ed. by Gregory Shreve and Erik Angelone. John Benjamins, Amsterdam, Netherlands 213–227.

Kim, Hee-Woong, and Atreyi Kankanhalli. 2009. Investigating User Resistance To Information Systems Implementation: A Status Quo Bias Perspective. *MIS Quarterly*, 33(3):567-582.

Krings, Hans P. 2001. *Repairing Texts*. Kent State University Press, Ohio, USA.

Mitchell, Linda. 2015. The potential and limits of lay post-editing in an online community. In *Proceedings of the 18th Annual Conference of the European Association for Machine Translation (EAMT2015)*, Antalya, Turkey, May 11-13 2015.

Moorkens, Joss, and Sharon O'Brien. 2013. User Attitudes to the Post-Editing Interface, In *Proceedings of MT Summit XIV Workshop on Post-editing Technology and Practice*. Proceedings eds. Sharon O'Brien, Michel Simard, Lucia Specia. Nice, September 2, 2013, 19–25.

Morado Vázquez, Lucía, Silvia Rodríguez Vázquez, and Pierrette Bouillon. 2013. Comparing Forum Data Post-Editing Performance Using Translation Memory And Machine Translation Output: A Pilot Study. In *Proceedings of MT Summit XIV*. Nice, France, September 3-6, 2013.

O'Brien, Sharon, and Joss Moorkens. 2014. Towards Intelligent Post-Editing Interfaces. In *Proceedings of FIT XXth World Congress 2014*, 4-6 Aug 2014, Berlin, Germany.

Samuelson, William, and Richard Zeckhauser. 1988. Status Quo Bias in Decision Making. *Journal of Risk and Uncertainty*, 1:7-59.

Sanchis-Trilles, Germán, Vicent Alabau, Christian Buck, Michael Carl, Francisco Casacuberta, Mercedes García-Martínez, Jesús González-Rubio, Robin L. Hill, Philipp Koehn, Luis A. Leiva, Bartolomé Mesa-Lao, Daniel Ortiz-Martínez, Herve Saint-Amand, Chara Tsoukala. 2014. Interactive Translation Prediction vs. Conventional Post-editing in Practice: A Study with the CasMaCat Workbench. *Machine Translation*, 28(3-4):217-235.

Snover, Matthew, Bonnie Dorr, Richard Schwartz, Linnea Micciulla, and John Makhoul. 2006. A Study of Translation Edit Rate with Targeted Human Annotation. In *Proceedings of Association for Machine Translation in the Americas*, 2006, 223–231.

Snover, Matthew, Nitin Madnani, Bonnie J. Dorr, and Richard Schwartz. 2009. Fluency, Adequacy, or HTER? Exploring Different Human Judgments with a Tunable MT Metric. In *Proceedings of the Fourth Workshop on Statistical Machine Translation*, Athens, Greece, 30-31 March 2009, 259–268.

Tatsumi, Midori. 2009. Correlation between automatic evaluation scores, post-editing speed and some other factors. In *Proceedings of MT Summit XII*, Ottawa, 26–30 August 2009, 332–339.

Vieira, Lucas Nunes. 2014. Indices of cognitive effort in machine translation post-editing. *Machine Translation*, 28(3-4):187–216.

Yamada, Masaru. 2012. Revising text: An empirical investigation of revision and the effects of integrating a TM and MT system into the translation process. *PhD Thesis*, Rikkyo University, Tokyo.

Benchmarking SMT Performance for Farsi Using the TEP++ Corpus

Peyman Passban, Andy Way, Qun Liu
ADAPT Centre
School of Computing
Dublin City University
Dublin, Ireland

{ppassban,away,qliu}@computing.dcu.ie

Abstract

Statistical machine translation (SMT) suffers from various problems which are exacerbated where training data is in short supply. In this paper we address the data sparsity problem in the Farsi (Persian) language and introduce a new parallel corpus, TEP++. Compared to previous results the new dataset is more efficient for Farsi SMT engines and yields better output. In our experiments using TEP++ as bilingual training data and BLEU as a metric, we achieved improvements of +11.17 (60%) and +7.76 (63.92%) in the Farsi–English and English–Farsi directions, respectively. Furthermore we describe an engine (SF2FF) to translate between formal and informal Farsi which in terms of syntax and terminology can be seen as different languages. The SF2FF engine also works as an intelligent normalizer for Farsi texts. To demonstrate its use, SF2FF was used to clean the IWSLT–2013 dataset to produce normalized data, which gave improvements in translation quality over FBK's Farsi engine when used as training data.

1 Introduction

In SMT (Koehn et al., 2003), where the bilingual knowledge comes from parallel corpora, having large datasets is crucial. This issue is compounded when working with low-resource languages, such as Farsi. The poor performance of existing systems for the Farsi–English pair confirms the necessity of developing a large and representative dataset. Clearly all the existing problems do not originate solely from the data, but not having a reliable training set prevents us from investigating Farsi SMT to the best extent possible.

Generating datasets is a time-consuming and expensive process, especially for SMT, in which massive amount of aligned bilingual sentences are required. Accordingly instead of starting from scratch we enriched and refined the existing corpus TEP (Pilevar et al., 2011).[1] Despite having a larger alternative (the Mizan[2] corpus), TEP was selected as the basis of our work that we clarify further in Section 3 and 4.1. TEP is a collection of film subtitles in spoken/informal Farsi (SF) that have distinct structures from formal/journalistic Farsi (FF). Accordingly, training an MT engine using this type of data might provide unsatisfactory results when working with FF which is the dominant language of Farsi texts. For this reason TEP was firstly refined both manually and automatically, which Section 3 explains in detail. TEP++ is the refined version of TEP that is much closer to FF and considerably cleaner. Using both TEP and TEP++ we trained several engines for bidirectional translation of the Farsi–English pair, as well as an engine to translate between FF and SF (SF2FF). The next sections explain the challenges of dealing with SF and describe the data preparation process in detail. The structure of paper is as follows. Section 2 discusses background of MT, addressing existing systems (§2.1) and available corpora (§2.2). Section 3 explains TEP++ and our development process. Experimental results are reported in Section 4 in-

[1]TEP: Tehran English-Persian parallel corpus http://opus.lingfil.uu.se/TEP.php
[2]http://www.dadegan.ir/catalog/mizan

cluding a comparison of the various MT systems and a study of the impact of SF2FF in Farsi SMT. Finally the last section concludes the paper along with some avenues for future works.

2 Background

Building an SMT engine for Farsi is difficult due to its rich morphology and inconsistent orthography (Rasooli et al., 2013). Not only these challenges but also the complex syntax and several exceptional rules in the grammar make the process considerably complex. The lack of data is another obstacle in this field. Nevertheless there have been some previous attempts at Farsi SMT. In this section we briefly review previous works encompassing systems in the first section, as well as available resources in the second section.

2.1 Farsi MT Systems

There are a limited number of SMT systems for Farsi. Some instances translate in one direction and some others are working bidirectionally. The Pars translator[3] is a commercial rule-based engine for English–Farsi translation. It contains 1.5 million words in its database and includes specific dictionaries for 33 different fields of science. Another English–Farsi MT system was developed by the Iran Supreme Council of Information.[4] Postchi[5] is a bidirectional system listed among the EuroMatrix[6] systems for the Farsi language. These systems are not terribly robust or precise examples of Farsi SMT and are usually the by-products of research or commercial projects. The only system that has officially been reported for the purpose of Farsi SMT is FBK's system (Bertoldi et al., 2013). It was tested on a publicly available dataset and from this viewpoint is the most important system for our purposes.[7]

2.2 Parallel Corpora for Farsi SMT

The first attempts at generating Farsi–English parallel corpora are documented in the Shiraz project (Zajac et al., 2000). The authors constructed a corpus of 3000 parallel sentences, which were translated manually from monolingual online Farsi documents at New Mexico State University. More recently Qasemizadeh et al. (2007) participated in the Farsi part of MULTEXT-EAST[8] project (Erjavec, 2010) and developed about 6000 sentences. There is also a corpus available in ELRA[9] consisting of about 3,500,000 English and Farsi words aligned at sentence level (about 100,000 sentences). This is a mixed domain dataset including a variety of text types such as art, law, culture, literature, poetry, proverbs, religion etc. PEN (Parallel English–Persian News corpus) is another small corpus (Farajian, 2011) generated semi-automatically. It includes almost 30,000 sentences. Farajian developed a method to find similar sentence pairs and for quality assurance used Google Translate.[10] All these corpora are relatively small-scale datasets. However, there are two other large-scale collections, namely Mizan and TEP, that are more interesting for our purposes. Mizan is a bilingual Farsi–English corpus of more than one million aligned sentences, which was developed by the Dadegan research group.[11] Sentences are gathered from classical literature with an average length of 15 words each. Despite comprising a large amount of sentences, the results obtained from using Mizan as a training set are less satisfactory. We will discuss the structure of Mizan and analyse some translation errors that ensue in the next section. The final corpus that is the basis of our work is TEP (Pilevar et al., 2011), which consists of more than 600,000 aligned Farsi–English sentences gathered from film subtitles. Experimental results show that TEP works better than Mizan as a training corpus for SMT.

3 TEP++

TEP++ is a refined version of TEP. TEP is a quite noisy corpus and it triggers several failures in the Farsi SMT pipeline. Besides the problem of noise because it was gathered from film subtitles, it is in SF. Accordingly it would be inappropriate to use an SMT system trained on SF data for the translation of FF. Unfortunately discrepancies between formal and informal Farsi structures are quite con-

[3]http://mabnasoft.com/english/parstrans/index.htm

[4]http://www.machinetranslation.ir/

[5]http://www.postchi.com/

[6]http://matrix.statmt.org/resources/pair?l1=fa&l2=en#pair

[7]However other Farsi MT engines like the Shiraz system (Amtrup et al., 2000) or that of Mohaghegh (2012) use their own in-house datasets. As we are not able to replicate them we do not include them in our comparisons.

[8]The project started in 1998 and the last version was released in 2010 (http://nl.ijs.si/ME)

[9]http://catalog.elra.info/product_info.php?products_id=1111

[10]https://translate.google.com/

[11]A research group supported by the Iran Supreme Council of Information to provide data resources for Farsi language and speech processing (http://www.dadegan.ir)

siderable. In what follows we show some of these cases and try to illustrate the main challenges with refinements to TEP.

In terms of orthography, Farsi is one of the hardest languages. It is written with the Perso-Arabic script. Unlike Arabic, some Persian words have inter-word zero-width non-joiner spaces (or semi-spaces) (Rasooli et al., 2013). Usually semi-spaces are incorrectly written as regular space character (U+0020 and U+200c are the Unicode for space and semi-space, respectively) that can easily change the meaning of the constituent and even the syntax of the whole sentence. As an example the right form of the word greedy is آستین‌دراز ≡ /āstin-derāz/[12] with a semi-space character (between n sound and d sound). If it is written with a space as in آستین دراز ≡ /āstin e derāz/, it means long sleeve, a completely different meaning which will mislead the SMT engine. Another problem is the presence of multiple writing forms for some characters. For the character ی ≡ /y/ all forms of ی, ي and ئ are common. This inconsistent writing style exists similarly for several other characters. The diacritic problem is another issue. Words can appear both with and without diacritics, like اخیراً or اخیرا ≡ /axiran/ (recently). Clearly, these problems should be resolved in preprocessing.

In addition, SF has its own specific problems, one being lexical variation. Some words occur in SF texts that do not have any counterpart in FF e.g. ایول ≡ /eyval/ (good job). Syntax in SF is also a problem. Farsi is an SOV language but in SF, versions of sentences with SVO and VOS order are both common. For example, علی نامه رو بخون ≡ /æli nāme ro bexoun/ (Ali, read the letter) is a standard SOV sentence, but both VOS (بخون نامه رو علی) and SVO (علی بخون نامه رو) forms are very normal; even in SF these look more natural than the SOV variant. In TEP++, we tried to correct the order and syntax of the sentences as much as possible which was very challenging. Not only the order but also the internal constituents of the sentences had to be changed. For example the verb بخون ≡ /bexoun/ (read) in SF is بخوان ≡ /bexān/ in FF or آمد ≡ /āmad/ (came) is the formal version of اومد ≡ /oumad/. These types of changes do not just happen to verbs. Other cases are even worse, e.g the right form of "for them" in FF is برای آنها ≡ /barāye ānhā/ which is written as براشون ≡ /barāšoun/ in SF (two FF words are packed in a single SF word). SF suffers from word ambiguity problem as well. A word like تو ≡ /to/ (you) which in formal texts is translated only into "you" (3rd-singular person), can mean both "you" (1st and 3rd-singular person) and "inside" in SF.

Problems with SF are not limited to those discussed. However as a solution we cleaned the TEP data both automatically and manually. As a mandatory prerequisite of the refinement phase we applied knowledge of Farsi linguistics and developed a rule-based system for some of the cases. The rule-based system includes 17 general rules/templates. For the remainder a team of 20 native speaker of Farsi, manually edited the corpus. The result is TEP++ with 578,251 aligned sentences, with an average length of 7 for the English side and 9 for Farsi. It includes 4,963,693 English tokens (62,185 unique tokens) and 5,065,434 Farsi tokens (122,432 unique tokens). TEP++ covers 94% of the TEP and we neglected the remaining 6% because of the bad quality of the original TEP data.

4 Experiments

This section is divided into 3 subsections. The first part reports the BLEU scores for three main Farsi corpora, Mizan, TEP and TEP++. We also discuss the problems with Mizan in Section 4.1 and perform error analysis on the output translations, where it is used as the SMT training data. In the second part using TEP and TEP++ we carry out monolingual translation between SF and FF (SF2FF) and discuss some use-cases for this type of translation task. Finally in the last part we show how SF2FF boosts the SMT quality for Farsi and report our results on the IWSLT–2013 dataset providing a comparison with FBK's system.

4.1 Mizan, TEP and TEP++

To test the performance of our engines, they were trained using Mizan, TEP and TEP++. We used Moses (Koehn et al., 2007) with the default configuration for phrase-based translation. For the language modeling, SRILM (Stolcke and others,

[12] We used Wikipedia phonetic chart to show the spellings of Farsi words and - character to show the semi-space. http://en.wikipedia.org/wiki/Persian_phonology

2002) was used. The evaluation measure is BLEU (Papineni et al., 2002) and to tune the models, we applied MERT (Och, 2003). Table 1 summarizes our experimental results for the Mizan dataset. We evaluated with two types of language models, 3-gram (LM3) and 5-gram (LM5). Numbers for both before and after tuning are reported. For all experiments training, tuning and test sets were selected randomly from the main corpus. The size of the test set is 1,000 and the tuning set is 2000 sentences. Training set sizes are reported in tables. For all experiments BLEU scores for Google Translate are reported as a baseline.

	EN–FA		FA–EN	
	Before	After	Before	After
LM3	8.24	10.47	11.70	**13.35**
LM5	8.54	**10.53**	11.97	13.14
Google Translate	2.32		4.21	
Training set	1,016,758 parallel sentences			
Corpus	Mizan			

Table 1: Experimental Results for Mizan

From a system that is trained on almost 1M sentences, we might expect better performance. To try to gain some insight into the nature of the problem, we randomly selected 100 Farsi translations and compared them with the reference sentences. Based on the statistics of the error analysis for the subset of 100 translations, 3 main reasons of the failures present themselves:

1. In more than half of the cases (59%) the decoder does not find the correct translation of a given word. Wrong lexical choice is the most common problem for the translation.

2. Due to the rich morphology of Farsi 41% of the words are generally translated with slight errors in their forms. The problem, therefore, is wrong word formation on the target side (Farsi). To give an example translating verbs into the wrong tense or with the wrong affixes.

3. 33% of the constituents have reordering problems. Some times the translations are correct but are not in their right positions.

Such deficiencies do not only apply for Mizan; they are common in Farsi SMT (and SMT in general even), no matter what training data is. Studying the results of translation error analysis, Farzi and Faili (2015) confirm our findings.

Another issue which should be considered about the Farsi SMT evaluation is that Farsi is a free word-order language. When compiling the results of our experiments, we only had a single reference available against which the output from our various systems could be compared. Computing automatic evaluation scores when translating into a free word-order language in the single-reference scenario is somewhat arbitrary. We would expect a manual evaluation on a subset of sentences to confirm that the output translations are somewhat better than the automatic evaluation scores suggest.

Similar to Mizan we repeated the same experiments for the TEP and TEP++. Table 2 and Table 3 show the results of these related experiments. Two engines were trained using the TEP and TEP++ corpora. In order to provide a comparison between the two corpora used, tuning and test sets were selected in a way which mirror each other in both datasets, i.e. TEP sentences and their counterparts in TEP++.

	EN–FA		FA–EN	
	Before	After	Before	After
LM3	10.12	**12.14**	17.29	17.60
LM5	10.69	11.88	18.05	**18.57**
Google Translate	1.14		6.60	
Training set	609,085 parallel sentences			
Corpus	TEP			

Table 2: Experimental Results for TEP

	EN–FA		FA–EN	
	Before	After	Before	After
LM3	15.93	19.37	27.29	29.21
LM5	15.93	**19.60**	28.25	**29.74**
Google Translate	3.27		7.35	
Training set	575,251 parallel sentences			
Corpus	TEP++			

Table 3: Experimental Results for TEP++

As can be seen in the FA–EN direction we reached +11.17 (60%) improvement and in EN–FA direction the improvident is +7.76 (63.92%).[13]

[13]The best performance using TEP for FA–EN is 18.57, the best for TEP++ is 29.74 and the improvement of FA–EN direction is 60%

Another achievement is that even where using less data, the TEP++ engine performs better. TEP++ includes 94% of the TEP (§3) so even with about 33K fewer sentences pairs in the training set we obtained better results. The BLEU scores of TEP++ still are significantly better than the baseline (TEP) considering the results of paired bootstrap resampling (Koehn, 2004).[14]

This improvement is not odd and we were expecting such numbers. As it was studied in Rasooli at al. (2013) and Bertoldi et al. (2013) preprocessing and normalization have a considerable effect in Farsi SMT, as we explained in §3. Results from Google Translate is another confirmation to this issue. SF (the language of TEP) is an almost unknown language for Google Translate hence translation from/into this language will provide inappropriate results. Results are slightly better for TEP++ because the sentences are cleaner and more formal which are close to that of Google Translate. Finally it should be mentioned that Moses generally works much better than Google Translate for Farsi MT and the quality of Google Translate significantly decreases for long sentences.

4.2 SF2FF Results

Doing the refinements on TEP to produce TEP++ that as explained in §3, was very laborious. The by-product was a pair of corpora, one in SF and one in FF. We trained a phrase-based translation engine using these corpora in order to translate from SF into FF. The benefit of having such an engine is to produce the cleaned FF for free, as the TEP refinement was a costly process. Moreover, having a knowledge of Farsi linguistics was a prerequisite. This engine provides the same functionality with less cost and without applying linguistic knowledge. The trained engine works like a black box and carries out all the refinements. Similar to ours, Fancellu et al. (2014) have also worked on monolingual SMT between Brazilian and European Portuguese.

In the SF–FF direction we obtained 88.94 BLEU points and in the opposite direction systems works with BLEU score of 81.62. This process –more than an MT task– is a transformation in which words are converted into the normalized/correct forms and the order of constituents are changed in some cases. Accordingly BLEU numbers are high. SF2FF engine helps us to stablish a fully automated pipeline to make a large-scale bilingual Farsi corpus. Any type of data can be taken from the internet such as film subtitles or tweets that are usually noisy with informal writing conventions. SF2FF can normalize them. and the normalized version is good enough to be aligned with the English side (or any other language). To show the application of SF2FF and its performance, it was fed a test set from TEP (the same dataset we used in the TEP experiment). The data was normalized by SF2FF. Normalization helps to provide a more precise translation. The pipeline is illustrated in Figure 1. Selected sentences are in SF and the BLEU score for their translation by TEP is 18.57. If SF2FF translates them into FF they would be cleaner and much closer to the language of TEP++ and consequently the results of SMT would be better. Sentences in the two sets are counterpart of each other. The TEP++ engine obtains a BLEU score of 29.72 on the formal/clean version of the same sentences. If the noisy data is cleaned by SF2FF and is then translated by TEP++, the BLEU score rises to 25.36, i.e. SF2FF provides +6.79-point improvement. The BLEU score obtained the normalized data is significantly better and is 36% higher than that of the original data which demonstrates the efficiency of SF2FF.

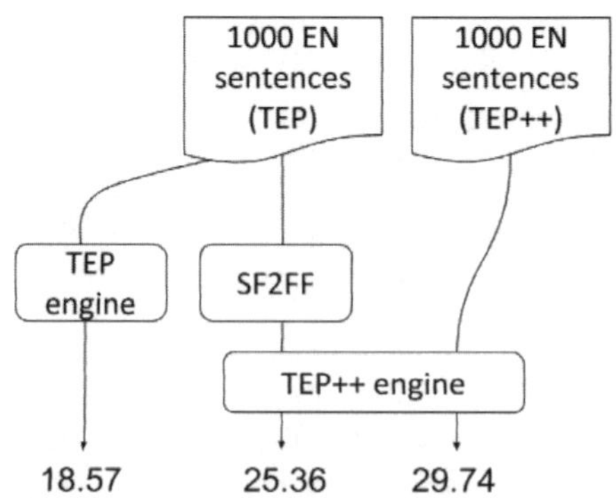

Figure 1: SF normalization by SF2FF

4.3 Comparison of SMT Performance

The only system that has been tested on a standard dataset and published is FBK's Farsi translation engine. It was reported in Bertoldi et al. (2013) and tested on the IWSLT–2013 dataset. The data has been made available by (Cettolo et al., 2012) and includes TED talk translations. In their paper,

[14]We used ARK research group codes for statistical significance testing for 1000 samples with 0.05 parameter http://www.ark.cs.cmu.edu/MT/

the FBK team explained that Farsi online data (including the IWSLT–2013 dataset) is very noisy and using requires some preprocessing, so they tried to normalize the data. Therefore, for the translation task, they used a normalized version of the IWSLT–2013 dataset along with an in-house corpus for language modeling. They also mentioned that using existing Farsi corpora such as TEP does not enhance translation quality. To compare our engines with FBK's system we firstly normalized the same dataset with SF2FF engine, and to make the language model we used the TEP++ corpus. The results for baseline,[15] FBK's system and ours (DCU) are shown in Table 4. For the FA–EN direction FBK obtained +2.0 points (16%) improvement in BLEU score, while for the same direction our improvement is +3.74 (29%). For the opposite direction we also outperform FBK, with a +1.10 difference in BLEU. The BLEU score for the EN–FA direction by DCU is 11.42, 2.29 points higher than the baseline (25%).

	Baseline	FBK	DCU
English-Farsi	9.13	10.32	**11.42**
Farsi-English	12.47	14.47	**16.21**

Table 4: Head-to-head comparison

5 Conclusion and Future Work

The contributions of this paper are threefold. First we developed a new corpus namely TEP++ and trained a translation engine. We showed that TEP++ works better than its predecessor TEP. Second we developed an engine to translate between FF and SF. SF2FF works like an intelligent preprocessor/normalizer and translates SF into FF that is a big credit for Farsi SMT. Finally we obtained better results in comparison to other reported results so far.

At the moment, in Farsi SMT data scarcity is the main challenge despite the fact that large volumes of textual data is available via the internet. Stored data on the internet for Farsi is in most cases are very noisy and also appears in SF forms. Our SF2FF engine can help to clean the internet data to generate reliable Farsi corpora. In the next step by normalizing existing Farsi corpora and aggregating them we will release a large-scale, reliable dataset for Farsi SMT. TEP++ also will be publicly available shortly. We also intended to carry out a human evaluation to investigate the correlation between the automatic score and manual findings.

[15] https://wit3.fbk.eu/score.php?release=2013-01

Acknowledgment

We would like to thank the three anonymous reviewers for their valuable comments. This research is supported by Science Foundation Ireland through the CNGL Programme (Grant 12/CE/I2267) in the ADAPT Centre (www.adaptcentre.ie) at Dublin City University.

References

Amtrup, Jan Willers, Hamid Mansouri Rad, Karine Megerdoomian, and Rémi Zajac. 2000. *Persian–English machine translation: An overview of the Shiraz project*. Computing Research Laboratory, New Mexico State University, USA.

Bertoldi, Nicola, M Amin Farajian, Prashant Mathur, Nicholas Ruiz, and Marcello Federico. 2013. Fbks machine translation systems for the IWSLT 2013 evaluation campaign. In *Proceedings of the 10th International Workshop for Spoken Language Translation*. Heidelberg, Germany.

Cettolo, Mauro, Christian Girardi, and Marcello Federico. 2012. Wit^3: Web inventory of transcribed and translated talks. In *Proceedings of the 16th Conference of the European Association for Machine Translation (EAMT)*, pages 261–268, Trento, Italy, May.

Erjavec, Toma. 2010. Multext-east version 4: Multilingual morphosyntactic specifications, lexicons and corpora. In *Proceedings of the Seventh International Conference on Language Resources and Evaluation (LREC'10)*. Malta, European Language Resources Association (ELRA).

Farajian, Mohammad Amin. 2011. PEN: parallel English–Persian news corpus. In *Proceedings of the 2011th World Congress in Computer Science, Computer Engineering and Applied Computing*. Nevada, USA.

Farzi, Saeed and Heshaam Faili. 2015. A swarm-inspired re-ranker system for statistical machine translation. *Computer Speech & Language*, 29(1):45–62.

Federico, Fancellu, O'Brien Morgan, and Way Andy. 2014. Standard language variety conversion using smt. In *Proceedings of the Seventeenth Annual Conference of the European Association for Machine Translation (EAMT)*, pages 143–149, Dubrovnik, Croatia, May.

Koehn, Philipp, Franz Josef Och, and Daniel Marcu. 2003. Statistical phrase-based translation. In *Proceedings of the 2003 Conference of the North American Chapter of the Association for Computational*

Linguistics on Human Language Technology, pages 48–54. Edmonton, Canada.

Koehn, Philipp, Hieu Hoang, Alexandra Birch, Chris Callison-Burch, Marcello Federico, Nicola Bertoldi, Brooke Cowan, Wade Shen, Christine Moran, Richard Zens, et al. 2007. Moses: Open source toolkit for statistical machine translation. In *Proceedings of the 45th annual meeting of the ACL on interactive poster and demonstration sessions*, pages 177–180. Prague, Czech Republic.

Koehn, Philipp. 2004. Statistical significance tests for machine translation evaluation. In *Proceedings of the 2004 Conference on Empirical Methods in Natural Language Processing(EMNLP)*, pages 388–395, Barcelona, Spain.

Mohaghegh, Mahsa. 2012. *English–Persian phrase-based statistical machine translation: enhanced models, search and training, Massey University, Albany (Auckland), New Zealand.* Ph.D. thesis.

Och, Franz Josef. 2003. Minimum error rate training in statistical machine translation. In *Proceedings of the 41st Annual Meeting on Association for Computational Linguistics-Volume 1*, pages 160–167. Sapporo, Japan.

Papineni, Kishore, Salim Roukos, Todd Ward, and Wei-Jing Zhu. 2002. BLEU: a method for automatic evaluation of machine translation. In *Proceedings of the 40th annual meeting on association for computational linguistics*, pages 311–318. Philadephia, Pennsylvania, USA.

Pilevar, Mohammad Taher, Heshaam Faili, and Abdol Hamid Pilevar. 2011. TEP: Tehran English–Persian parallel corpus. In *Computational Linguistics and Intelligent Text Processing*, pages 68–79. Springer.

Qasemizadeh, Behrang, Saeed Rahimi, and Behrooz Mahmoodi Bakhtiari. 2007. The first parallel multilingual corpus of persian: Toward a persian blark. In *The Second Workshop on Computational Approaches to Arabic Script-based Languages (CAASL-2)*. California, USA.

Rasooli, Mohammad Sadegh, Ahmed El Kholy, and Nizar Habash. 2013. Orthographic and morphological processing for Persian-to-English statistical machine translation. In *Proceedings of the International Joint Conference on Natural Language Processing*, pages 1047– 1051. Nagoya, Japan.

Stolcke, Andreas et al. 2002. SRILM an extensible language modeling toolkit. In *Proceedings of the International Conference on Spoken Language Processing*, pages 901–904. Denver, Colorado.

Zajac, Rémi, Steve Helmreich, and Karine Megerdoomian. 2000. Black-box/glass-box evaluation in shiraz. In *Workshop on Machine Translation Evaluation at LREC-2000*. Athens, Greece.

Dynamic Terminology Integration Methods in Statistical Machine Translation

Mārcis Pinnis
Tilde, Vienibas gatve 75a, Riga, Latvia
University of Latvia, 19 Raina Blvd., Riga, Latvia
marcis.pinnis@tilde.lv

Abstract

In this paper the author presents methods for dynamic terminology integration in statistical machine translation systems using a source text pre-processing workflow. The workflow consists of exchangeable components for term identification, inflected form generation for terms, and term translation candidate ranking. Automatic evaluation for three language pairs shows a translation quality improvement from 0.9 to 3.41 BLEU points over the baseline. Manual evaluation for seven language pairs confirms the positive results; the proportion of correctly translated terms increases from 1.6% to 52.6% over the baseline.

1 Introduction

In professional translation services, correct and consistent handling of terminology is an important indicator of translation quality. However, pure statistical machine translation (SMT) systems, such as, Moses (Koehn et al., 2007) in a general scenario cannot ensure correct and consistent handling of terminology, because statistics of large amounts of data are difficult to control if not constrained by means of, e.g., bilingual term collections or translation model or language model adaptation techniques. In cases where the context is too ambiguous (e.g., if an SMT system receives just a short translation segment or the SMT system's models are limited in the possibilities to analyse larger context) or when external knowledge is required, it can be impossible for an SMT system to guess the correct translation.

In the localisation industry customers often provide their own term collections that have to be strictly used during translation to ensure correct and consistent usage of terminology. Obviously, such collections may contain term translations that are rated as unlikely (in certain contexts) by an SMT system's models or they may even be missing in the models at all if custom adaptation of the models using the customers' provided data is not performed. If such SMT systems would be integrated in localisation service workflows, it would not be possible to ensure high terminology translation quality in the SMT suggestions. Therefore, effective methods that can benefit from custom term collections are necessary.

Researchers have tried to address the terminology integration challenge directly by using in-domain term collections and indirectly by tackling the broader challenge of domain adaptation. Significant research efforts have been focussed on using in-domain parallel and monolingual corpora (that contain in-domain terminology) to perform SMT system translation and language model adaptation to specific domains (to name but a few, Koehn & Schroeder (2007), Bertoldi & Federico (2009), Hildebrand et al. (2005), and many others). Terminology integration has been also indirectly addressed by research on multi-word unit integration in SMT. E.g., Bouamor et al. (2012) showed that for French-English it is enough to simply add multi-word unit pairs to the parallel corpus; however, they observed a limited gain of +0.3 BLEU (Papineni et al., 2002) points. In terms of direct terminology integration, Pinnis & Skadiņš (2012) have shown that the addition of terms to the parallel corpus and the introduction of a bilingual terminology identifying feature in the translation model can significantly improve translation quality of an out-of-domain system (up to +2.13 BLEU points). Their method specifically addressed morphologically rich languages by identifying terms in different inflected forms using stemming tools. Similar work that shows significant quality improvements has been recently performed by Arcan et al. (2014a) for the English-Italian language pair. They use a term collection to create a "fill-up" translation model that consists of a pre-trained SMT system's phrase table merged with a phrase table created from the bilingual terminology. However, all these methods require to re-train the whole SMT system (or at least re-tune the SMT system) if new in-domain data becomes available. For many translation tasks such a scenario is not economically justifiable. Furthermore, if we have already trained a relatively good SMT system (let it be a general domain system or a close-domain system to the domain that is needed), we should be able to tailor it to the required domain with the help of just the right bilingual terminology.

Consequently, considerable research efforts have been focussed also on dynamic integration methods for term collections in SMT that do not require re-training of SMT systems. For instance, the *Moses* SMT system supports input data (in the Moses XML format) that is enriched with externally generated translation candidates. Using this methodology, Carl & Langlais (2002) used term dictionaries to pre-process source text and achieved an increase in translation quality for the English-French language pair. Similarly, Arcan et al. (2014a) identify exactly matched terms and provide translation equivalents from the Wiki Machine[1] by performing context-based disambiguation if there are multiple translation equivalents for a single term for English-Italian. Babych & Hartley (2003) showed that inclusion of certain named entities in "*do-not-translate*" lists allowed to increase translation quality for the English-Russian language pair. Recently dynamic translation and language models (Bertoldi, 2014) have been investigated for integration of terminology into SMT (Arcan et al., 2014b) for English-Italian. It is evident that most of the related research has, however, mostly focused on languages with simple morphology or translation of phrases that are rarely translated or even left untranslated. A study in the FP7 project TTC (2013) showed that for English-Latvian such simplified methods do not yield positive results. Hálek et al. (2011) came to the same conclusion in their work on English-Czech named entity translation. This means that for morphologically rich languages more linguistically rich methods are necessary.

In this paper, the author proposes a workflow for dynamic terminology integration in SMT systems that allows to: 1) identify terms in source text (i.e., translation segments or even large documents with Moses XML tags) that is sent to the SMT system for translation, 2) generate inflected forms of terms using corpus-based and morphological synthesis-based methods, and 3) rank term translation candidates. The methods proposed have been evaluated in two different scenarios using automated SMT quality metrics for three language pairs and by performing manual comparative evaluation for seven language pairs (from English into Estonian, French, German, Italian, Latvian, Lithuanian, and Spanish). The results will show that the proposed methods are able to improve terminology translation quality and the overall sentence translation quality for morphologically rich languages. For evaluation purposes, the author uses the LetsMT SMT platform (Vasiļjevs et al., 2012), which is based on the Moses SMT system.

The paper is further structured as follows: section 2 describes the dynamic terminology integration workflow and the different modules for source text pre-processing, section 3 describes our automatic and manual evaluation efforts, and section 4 concludes the paper.

2 Dynamic Terminology Integration Workflow

The idea of the dynamic terminology integration scenario (conceptually depicted in Figure 1) is that users (e.g., translators when using SMT capabilities in a computer-assisted translation (CAT) environment, Web site owners when integrating SMT widgets in their Web sites, etc.) have to be able to assign custom bilingual term collections to pre-trained SMT systems of the LetsMT platform when there is a need to translate some content. To ensure this functionality the author utilises the capability of the Moses decoder to translate input data in the Moses XML format and introduce a new source text pre-processing workflow before

[1] The Wiki Machine is available online at: https://bitbucket.org/fbk/thewikimachine

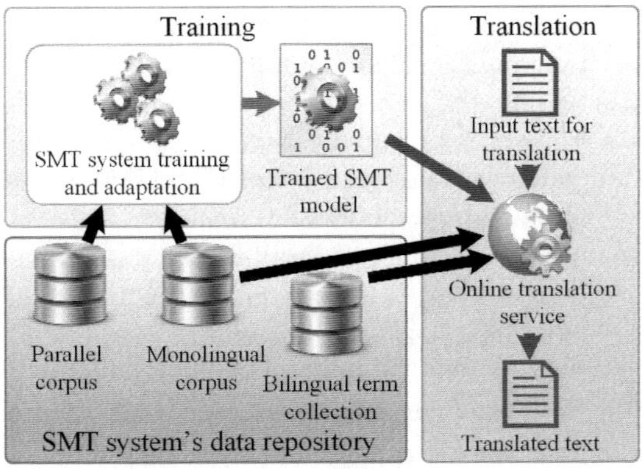

Figure 1: The conceptual design of dynamic terminology integration in SMT systems

decoding the content with the Moses decoder. The workflow (depicted in Figure 2) consists of three exchangeable modules that 1) use a bilingual term collection provided by the user to identify terms in the source text using term identification methods (see section 2.1), 2) generate inflected forms of the translations of the identified terms (see section 2.2), and 3) assign translation confidence scores to translation candidates and enrich the source text with the generated translation candidates (see section 2.3). After pre-processing the terminology enriched content is translated with the Moses decoder by explicitly using the provided translation candidates.

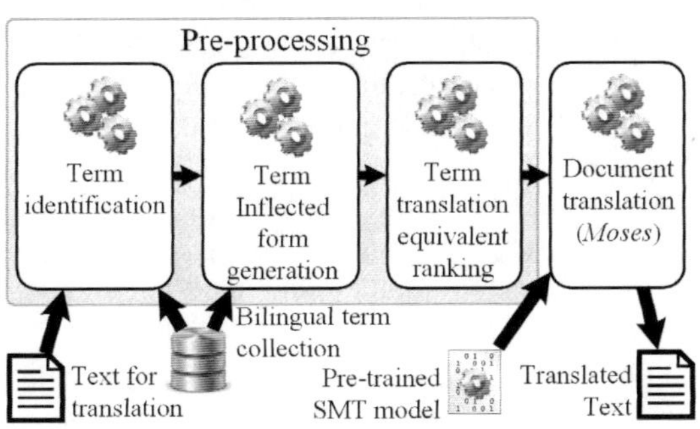

Figure 2: Source text pre-processing workflow

When using SMT capabilities in on-line scenarios, let it be translation of full Web pages, on-line pre-translation of following translation segments in CAT tools (e.g., the MateCat platform by Federico et al. (2014)), or any other scenario that requires quick SMT response, an important factor to be considered for dynamic integration methods is their impact on the overall speed of translation. For successful SMT integration in localisation scenarios, it is crucial that SMT systems can provide translations quickly as translator performance will decrease if the translators will have to wait for SMT suggestions (Skadiņš et al., 2014). To ensure that the effect on the overall translation speed is minimal, compromises between how linguistically rich term identification and ranking has to be or whether or not to perform the inflected form generation for terms in an off-line mode (i.e., when uploading a term collection to the SMT platform) have to be met. The proposed workflow allows to decide whether processing speed or linguistic richness is of greater importance.

2.1 Term Identification

The first task that has to be performed when pre-processing source text using a bilingual term collection is to identify terms. For this purpose, three methods were investigated:

- The first method (*TWSC*) performs term identification using the linguistically and statistically motivated term extraction tool *TWSC* (Pinnis et al., 2012). TWSC 1) morpho-syntactically tags and lemmatises the source text, 2) extracts term phrases that match morpho-syntactic term phrase patterns (most commonly, noun phrases), 3) performs statistic ranking using co-occurrence measures and reference corpora statistics, and 4) tags terms in a document by prioritising longer phrases. Then, the extracted term phrases are looked-up in the term collection by comparing their lemma and part of speech sequences. If the terms in the term collection do not contain morpho-syntactic information, terms are morphologically analysed and lemmatised, after which all matching term phrase patterns from TWSC are identified and used for look-up purposes.

- As the source text may be too short to perform statistical analysis and because we only search for term phrases that are included in the user provided term collections, the second method (*Valid Phrase-Based Term Identification* or *Phrase*) starts by performing the two steps from TWSC, however then it directly looks-up, whether the morpho-syntactically valid term phrases actually correspond to a term from the term collection.

- The first two methods rely heavily on linguistic tools that can significantly affect the translation speed. Therefore, the third method (*Fast Term Identification* or *Fast*) performs a left-to-right search in the source text using minimal linguistic support from language-specific stemming tools to identify terms in different inflected forms.

2.2 Inflected Form Generation

The next pre-processing step after term identification is the generation of translation candidates for the identified terms. Previous research (Nikoulina et al., 2012; Carl & Langlais, 2002; Babych & Hartley, 2003) on source text pre-processing has not given special attention to this question, because the bilingual term collections already *"provide"* translation equivalents. However, the issue is that the terms that are provided in the bilingual term collections are usually in their canonical forms. For morphologically rich languages the canonical forms in many contexts are not the required inflected forms. Because of the focus on language pairs that do not require (or require very limited) morphological generation (e.g., English-French, English-German, etc.), previous research has not seen the need to address these issues. Therefore, the author investigated three different methods for acquisition of inflected forms of terms:

- The first method (*Synthesis*) uses a morphological analyser and synthesiser and inflected form generation rules to generate inflected forms of a term from its canonical form. E.g., the Latvian term 'datu tips' (in English: 'data type') corresponds to the term phrase pattern '`^N...g.* ^N.*`' consisting of two nouns (the first word is in a genitive case). The term phrase pattern corresponds to the inflection rule '`***** ***00`'. The rule specifies that the first word has to be kept as is (the '*'), however the second word is allowed to be in any inflected form of a noun ('0' indicates that any value for a morphological category is acceptable; in the positional tagset used for Latvian the fourth and fifth positions correspond to case and number). The rules allow defining also morpho-syntactic agreements between different morphological categories (e.g., in Latvian adjectives in a noun phrase have to have the same gender, number, and case as the head noun). For Latvian there are in total 18 inflection rules specified for 99 term phrase patterns from TWSC.

- The second method (*Corpus*) is language independent and relies on the SMT system's monolingual corpus (e.g., the corpus that is used for language modelling) to identify inflected forms of terms using a similar method to the *Fast Term Identification*.

- Both previous methods may not be able to generate inflected forms for all terms. For instance, the first method may lack a term phrase pattern necessary for a specific term, whereas, when applying the second method, some inflected forms may be missing in the corpus or the stemming tool may not be able to identify all forms. Therefore, the third method (*Combined*) is a combination (using union) of both previous methods.

2.3 Term Translation Equivalent Ranking

As the last pre-processing step, the generated translation candidates have to be ranked by assigning translation confidence scores. For this purpose two methods were investigated:

- The first method (*Equal*) assigns equal translation likelihood scores to all translation candidates of a term. This method is used as a baseline method for translation candidate ranking. When assigning equal weights to all translation candidates, we rely on the language model to select the most likely translation.

- The second method (*Simple*) uses a large monolingual corpus and calculates for each translation candidate of a term its relative frequency among all translation candidates of the term. This method allows assigning higher scores for more common translations.

It is evident that both methods rely only on the language model and important statistics that may come from the translation model (e.g., source to target language transfer information) are lost. We also lose important information from the source language's context as that could help identifying, which translation candidate is more likely in a given context. However, the potentially more sophisticated methods are left for future work.

3 Evaluation

To evaluate the dynamic terminology integration methods, two evaluation tasks were carried out: 1) automatic evaluation that identifies the combination of the different methods that allows achieving the highest results, and 2) manual evaluation that focusses on term translation qualitative analysis using production SMT systems and an authoritative term collection. The following subsections describe both evaluation efforts.

3.1 Automatic Evaluation

The automatic evaluation was performed for three language pairs (English-German, Latvian, and Lithuanian) using general domain SMT systems that were trained in the LetsMT platform using the DGT-TM parallel corpus (Steinberger et al., 2012) (the releases of 2007, 2011, and 2012). For evaluation, the author uses a proprietary parallel corpus of 872 sentence pairs in the automotive domain (technical documentation from car service manuals). The original data set was available for English-Latvian, therefore, the remaining two data sets for German and Lithuanian were prepared by professional translators. For English-Latvian an in-domain tuning set of 1,745 sentence pairs was available; for the remaining systems held-out sets of 2,000 sentence pairs from the training data were used for SMT system tuning. The results of the baseline systems are given in Table 1. It is evident that the results for English-Latvian are significantly higher (although still relatively low) than for the other language pairs. This is mainly due to the fact that an automotive domain tuning set was available for the English-Latvian experiments. As the results for the other language pairs are very low, Table 1 includes also automatic evaluation results using 1000 held-out sentence pairs from the DGT-TM corpus to show that the systems on in-domain data perform relatively well. This shows just how different the writing styles and the language complexity between different domains can be.

Lang. pair	EN-DE	EN-LT	EN-LV
BLEU (a)	8.27	6.94	12.68
BLEU (g)	54.03	48.12	-

Table 1: Baseline system performance (“*(a)*” - automotive domain evaluation sets; “*(g)*” - SMT system in-domain evaluation sets from the DGT-TM corpus)

Next, the author analysed, which pre-processing configuration allows achieving better results (see Figure 3). This analysis was performed for English-Latvian using a term collection that was created by a professional translator from the tuning-data. The term collection consists of 644 term pairs (terms were included only in their canonical forms). The results show that all combinations performed better than the baseline system. It is evident that the *Fast Term Identification* allows achieving better results than the other term identification methods. The method also allows to identify more terms in the source text (1,404; compared to 1,261 for *Phrase* and 620 for *TWSC*). We see also that the *Synthesis* method for inflected form generation achieves lower results than the *Corpus* method for which there are two possible reasons: 1) data ambiguity for the SMT system by providing significantly more inflected forms is increased, and 2) the implemented ranking methods do not allow effectively estimating, which inflected form is more or less likely due to not taking the language transfer characteristics into account.

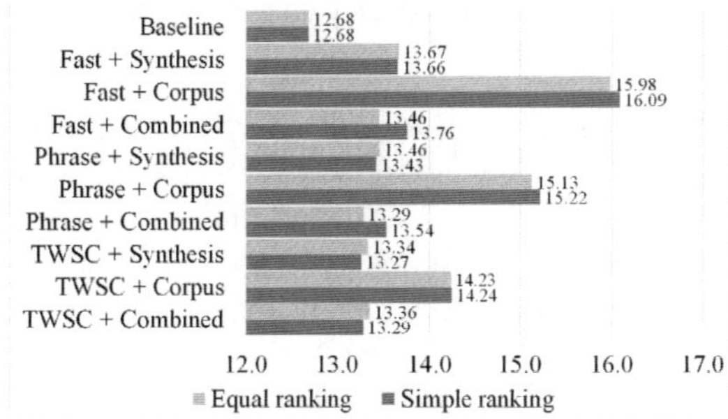

Figure 3: Automatic evaluation results using three different term collections for English-Latvian (BLEU scores)

Next, professional translators were asked to prepare professional term collections for English-German (692 term pairs) and English-Lithuanian (662 term pairs) and performed automatic evaluation experiments. The results in Figure 4 are limited to the configurations with ‘*Corpus+Simple*’ that showed to achieve the best results for English-Latvian.

3.2 Manual Evaluation

The automatic evaluation showed positive results. However, the SMT systems in the baseline scenario achieved relatively low scores and the term collections were relatively small (although fo-

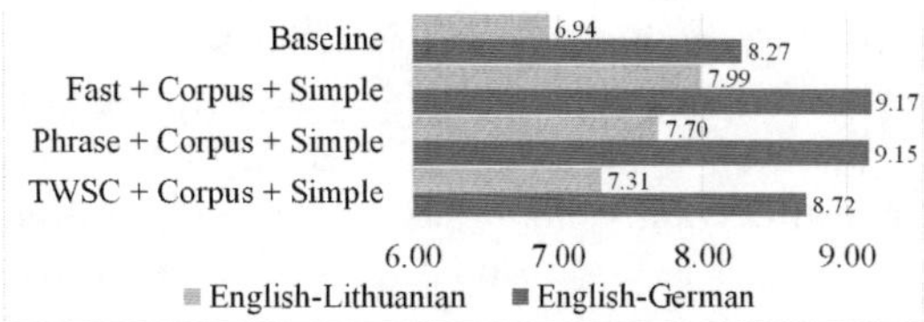

Figure 4: Automatic evaluation results using different term identification methods and corpus-based inflected form generation and ranking

cussed to a narrow domain). Therefore, the manual evaluation was performed for seven language pairs using production level in-domain SMT systems (contrary to out-of-domain systems before) in the information technology domain. For terminology integration, the freely available Microsoft Terminology Collection[2] was used.

As the term collection contains many ambiguous terms that can be confused with general language words and phrases (e.g., '*AND*', '*about*', '*name*', '*form*', '*order*', etc.), it is important to filter such candidates out as the dynamic integration workflow (contrary to methods that perform SMT system model adaptation) is sensitive to the level of ambiguity of the included terms. The collections for the different language pairs were filtered using a term pair specificity estimation method that is based on inverse document frequency (IDF) scores (Spärck Jones, 1972) from a broad domain corpus. The formula is given in (1); it was first introduced by Pinnis & Skadiņš (2012).

$$R\left(p_s, p_t\right) = min\left(\sum_{i=1}^{|p_s|} IDF_s\left(p_s\left(i\right)\right), \sum_{j=1}^{|p_t|} IDF_t\left(p_t\left(j\right)\right)\right) \quad (1)$$

The baseline system performance and the term collection statistics are given in Table 2.

Lang. pair	BLEU	Terms (filtered)	Terms (initial)
EN-ES	74.61	18,871	23,094
EN-FR	68.76	19,665	24,160
EN-ET	55.23	10,175	12,648
EN-LT	60.42	10,352	12,726
EN-LV	66.98	10,497	12,926
EN-RU	60.79	18,416	22,669
EN-DE	61.35	20,308	24,997

Table 2: Baseline system performance (on 1,000 held-out sentence pairs) and statistics of the term collections before and after filtering

[2]The Microsoft Terminology Collection can be downloaded from: http://www.microsoft.com/Language/en-US/Terminology.aspx

The manual evaluation is performed by comparing the SMT system performance without (the baseline scenario) and with (the improved scenario) integrated terminology. The '*Fast+Corpus+Simple*' configuration was used in this experiment. The evaluation data for each language pair consists of 100 in-domain sentences for which the outputs of the SMT systems in the two scenarios differed (different translations were produced in average for 56% of sentences). For each language pair two professional translators were involved in the evaluation.

For the evaluation, translators were asked to perform three ratings:

- For each sentence, translators had to decide which scenario produced a better translation. If both scenarios produced translations of equal quality, the translators had to decide whether both scenarios produced acceptable or not acceptable translations.
- Similarly to the sentence level, for each term that was identified in the source text using the '*Fast*' method, translators had to decide which scenario produced a better translation.
- The first two are quantitative analysis measures, therefore as a third rating translators were asked to rate the term translation quality in both scenarios separately. The translators had to decide whether the term is translated correctly, whether a wrong inflectional form is used, whether it is not translated, whether it is split up or its words are in a wrong order, whether a wrong lexical choice is made, whether the marked phrase is actually not a term and has been wrongly identified as a term, or whether there is another issue.

The sentence level evaluation summary in Table 3 shows that the translations of the improved scenario were preferred more for six language pairs. Because of spatial restrictions, the paper features only results from the analysis where evaluators were in full agreement. It is evident that the task of comparing sentence level quality is a very challenging task for evaluators, because the Free Kappa (Randolph, 2005) agreement scores are mainly in the levels of fair to moderate.

The term level evaluation summary is given in Table 4. It is evident that translation quality has improved over the baseline scenario for all language pairs evaluated. Even more, the agreement

Lang. pair	Bas.	Imp.	Both	None	Total	Free Kappa
EN-ES	11	8	15	19	53	0.38
EN-FR	8	21	35	18	82	0.16
EN-ET	8	16	3	36	63	0.50
EN-LT	6	8	23	16	53	0.37
EN-LV	1	9	9	57	76	0.68
EN-RU	9	17	7	27	60	0.47
EN-DE	5	15	29	9	58	0.45

Table 3: Evaluation summary for sentence level ratings where evaluators were in agreement

Lang. pair	Bas.	Imp.	Both	None	Total	Free Kappa
EN-ES	4	34	77	0	115	0.64
EN-FR	4	71	141	4	220	0.44
EN-ET	21	51	53	0	125	0.70
EN-LT	1	40	54	3	98	0.49
EN-LV	6	46	67	4	123	0.75
EN-RU	1	49	93	0	143	0.82
EN-DE	2	30	87	0	119	0.70

Table 4: Evaluation summary for term level ratings where evaluators were in agreement

scores for evaluators show that the task of comparing in which system terms were translated better was fairly easy and in general well understood.

The summary of the term translation quality evaluation for the individual scenarios is given in Table 5. The results show that the proportion of correct term translations has improved for all language pairs from +1.6% for English-Estonian to +52.6% for English-Lithuanian. The minimal improvement for English-Estonian is mainly due to selection of wrong inflected forms (which is a lesser quality issue, but an issue nonetheless) rather than wrong term lexical choices (which is a greater quality issue). The author believes that the relatively low performance for English-Estonian is caused by the under-performance of the word stemming component for Estonian that is used for inflectional form acquisition for terms (however, deeper investigation is necessary). It is evident that in terms of using the correct lexical choice, the quality has improved from +26.4% for English-German to +65.2% for English-Lithuanian. This means that the method allows ensuring terminology translation consistency better than in the baseline scenario.

4 Conclusions

The paper presented a source text pre-processing workflow for dynamic terminology integration in SMT systems. To evaluate the methods, the author performed automatic evaluation in the automotive domain. The results show that the best combination of pre-processing methods achieved a translation quality improvement from 0.9 to 3.41 BLEU points (depending on the language pair) over the baseline scenario. Manual evaluation for seven language pairs indicates that the proportion of correctly translated terms increased from 1.6% to 52.6% over the baseline scenario.

Although the results are positive, the best results were achieved using lightly linguistic methods (i.e., stemming tools). The linguistically more advanced methods could either identify less terms or produced too many inflected forms of terms, thus making it more difficult for the SMT decoder to select the correct form. The author believes that a language transfer based term ranking method and a method that combines the different term identification methods could improve the results even further. However, this is an area for future work.

5 Acknowledgements

This work has been supported by the European Social Fund within the project "*Support for Doctoral Studies at University of Latvia*". The research has been supported by the ICT Competence Centre (www.itkc.lv) within the project "*2.6. Multilingual Machine Translation*" of EU Structural funds, contract nr. L-KC-11-0003. The author would like thank Valters Šics for training SMT systems that were used in the manual evaluation task.

References

Arcan, M., Giuliano, C., Turchi, M., and Buitelaar, P. 2014a. Identification of Bilingual Terms from Monolingual Documents for Statistical Machine Translation. In *Proceedings of CompuTerm 2014*.

Arcan, M., Turchi, M., Tonelli, S., and Buitelaar, P. 2014b. Enhancing Statistical Machine Translation with Bilingual Terminology in a CAT Environment. In *Proceedings of AMTA 2014* (pp. 54–68).

Babych, B., and Hartley, A. 2003. Improving Machine Translation Quality With Automatic Named Entity Recognition. In *Proceedings of the 7th International EAMT workshop on MT and other Language Technology Tools, Improving MT through other Language Technology Tools: Resources and Tools for Building MT*.

Bertoldi, N. 2014. Dynamic models in Moses for Online Adaptation. In *The Prague Bulletin of Mathematical Linguistics* (Vol. 101(1), pp. 7–28).

% of terms	EN-ES		EN-FR		EN-ET		EN-LT		EN-LV		EN-RU		EN-DE	
	B	I	B	I	B	I	B	I	B	I	B	I	B	I
Term correct	71.3	85.4	55.9	75.0	39.8	40.4	42.1	64.2	51.3	67.9	60.2	89.2	70.3	85.6
Wrong inflection	1.9	11.5	1.6	5.8	19.4	50.3	7.9	18.4	11.3	27.5	6.0	8.7	1.6	5.2
Not translated	8.6	0.6	19.2	14.3	9.9	1.2	0.6	0.0	4.6	0.0	16.3	0.9	7.8	0.3
Term split up or re-ordered	2.2	0.3	6.7	0.9	2.2	0.3	1.9	2.2	2.6	0.0	6.6	0.6	0.7	1.0
Wrong lexical choice	7.3	1.3	13.3	1.6	18.8	4.6	30.4	2.8	20.9	0.0	10.8	0.6	5.9	5.6
Not a term	6.4	0.6	1.7	1.7	0.6	0.6	10.8	10.8	1.7	1.7	0.0	0.0	0.7	1.0
Other	2.2	0.3	1.6	0.7	9.3	2.5	6.3	1.6	7.6	3.0	0.0	0.0	13.1	1.3
Rel. impr. of correct term translations (%)	19.6		34.1		1.6		52.6		32.3		48.0		21.9	
Rel. impr. of correct lexical choice (%)	32.2		40.5		53.1		65.2		52.4		47.7		26.4	
Rel. red. of errors (%)	48.9		43.3		1.0		38.3		34.0		72.7		51.6	

Table 5: Evaluation summary for term translation quality

Bertoldi, N., and Federico, M. 2009. Domain Adaptation for Statistical Machine Translation with Monolingual Resources. In *Proceedings of the 4th Workshop on Statistical Machine Translation* (pp. 182189).

Bouamor, D., Semmar, N., and Zweigenbaum, P. 2012. Identifying bilingual Multi-Word Expressions for Statistical Machine Translation. In *Proceedings of LREC 2012* (pp. 674–679).

Carl, M., and Langlais, P. 2002. An Intelligent Terminology Database as a Pre-processor for Statistical Machine Translation. In *COLING-02 on COMPUTERM 2002: 2nd international workshop on computational terminology*. (Vol. 14, pp. 1–7).

Cattelan, A., Farina, A., Lupinetti, D., Martines, A., Massidda, A., Schwenk, H., Barrault, L., Blain, F., Koehn, P., Buck, C., and Germann, U. 2014. The MateCat Tool. In *Proceedings of COLING 2014* (pp. 129–132).

Hálek, O., Rosa, R., Tamchyna, A., and Bojar, O. 2011. Named Entities from Wikipedia for Machine Translation. In *Proceedings of ITAT 2011* (pp. 23–30).

Hildebrand, A. S., Eck, M., Vogel, S., and Waibel, A. 2005. Adaptation of the Translation Model for Statistical Machine Translation Based on Information Retrieval. In *Proceedings of EAMT* (pp. 133–142).

Koehn, P., Hoang, H., Birch, A., Callison-Burch, C., Federico, M., Bertoldi, N., Cowan, B., Shen, W., Moran, C., Zens, R., Dyer, C., Bojar, O., Constantin, A., and Herbst, E. 2007. Moses: Open Source Toolkit for Statistical Machine Translation. In *Proceedings of the ACL 2007 Interactive Poster and Demonstration Sessions* (pp. 177–180).

Koehn, P., and Schroeder, J. 2007. Experiments in Domain Adaptation for Statistical Machine Translation. In *Proceedings of the 2nd Workshop on Statistical Machine Translation* (pp. 224–227).

Nikoulina, V., Sandor, A., and Dymetman, M. 2012. Hybrid Adaptation of Named Entity Recognition for Statistical Machine Translation. In *Proceedings of ML4HMT-12* (pp. 116).

Papineni, K., Roukos, S., Ward, T., and Zhu, W.-J. 2002. BLEU: a Method for Automatic Evaluation of Machine Translation. In *Proceedings of ACL 2002* (pp. 311–318).

Pinnis, M., Ljubešić, N., Ştefănescu, D., Skadiņa, I., Tadić, M., and Gornostay, T. 2012. Term Extraction, Tagging, and Mapping Tools for Under-Resourced Languages. In *Proceedings of TKE 2012* (pp. 193–208).

Pinnis, M., and Skadiņš, R. 2012. MT Adaptation for Under-Resourced Domains What Works and What Not. In *Proceedings of Baltic HLT 2012* (pp. 177–180).

Randolph, J. J.. 2005. Free-Marginal Multirater Kappa (multirater K[free]): An Alternative to Fleiss' Fixed-Marginal Multirater Kappa. In *Joensuu Learning and Instruction Symposium*.

Skadiņš, R., Skadiņa, I., Pinnis, M., Vasiļjevs, A., and Hudík, T. 2014. Application of Machine Translation in Localization into Low-resourced Languages. In *Proceedings of EAMT 2014* (pp. 209–216).

Spärck Jones, K. 1972. A Statistical Interpretation of Term Specificity and Its Application in Retrieval. In *Journal of Documentation* 28, 11–21.

Steinberger, R., Eisele, A., Klocek, S., Pilos, S., and Schlter, P. 2012. DGT-TM: A Freely Available Translation Memory in 22 Languages. In *Proceedings of LREC 2012* (pp. 454–459).

TTC. 2013. Public Deliverable D7.3: Evaluation of the Impact of TTC on Statistical MT (p. 38). *TTC Project: Terminology Extraction, Translation Tools and Comparable Corpora*.

Vasiļjevs, A., Skadiņš, R., and Tiedemann, J. 2012. LetsMT!: a Cloud-Based Platform for Do-It-Yourself Machine Translation. In *Proceedings of the ACL 2012 System Demonstrations* (pp. 43–48).

Identifying main obstacles for statistical machine translation of morphologically rich South Slavic languages

Maja Popović
DFKI – Language Technology Lab
Berlin, Germany
maja.popovic@dfki.de

Mihael Arčan
Insight Centre for Data Analytics
National University of Galway, Ireland
mihael.arcan@insight-centre.org

Abstract

The best way to improve a statistical machine translation system is to identify concrete problems causing translation errors and address them. Many of these problems are related to the characteristics of the involved languages and differences between them. This work explores the main obstacles for statistical machine translation systems involving two morphologically rich and under-resourced languages, namely Serbian and Slovenian. Systems are trained for translations from and into English and German using parallel texts from different domains, including both written and spoken language. It is shown that for all translation directions structural properties concerning multi-noun collocations and exact phrase boundaries are the most difficult for the systems, followed by negation, preposition and local word order differences. For translation into English and German, articles and pronouns are the most problematic, as well as disambiguation of certain frequent functional words. For translation into Serbian and Slovenian, cases and verb inflections are most difficult. In addition, local word order involving verbs is often incorrect and verb parts are often missing, especially when translating from German.

1 Introduction

The statistical approach to machine translation (SMT), in particular phrase-based SMT, has become widely used in the last years: open source tools such as Moses (Koehn et al., 2007) have made it possible to build translation systems for any language pair, domain or text type within days. Despite the fact that for certain language pairs, e.g. English-French, high quality SMT systems have been developed, a large number of languages and language pairs have not been (systematically) investigated. The largest study about European languages in the Digital Age, the META-NET Language White Paper Series[1] in year 2012 showed that only English has good machine translation support, followed by moderately supported French and Spanish. More languages are only fragmentary supported (such as German), whereby the majority of languages are weakly supported. Many of those languages are also morphologically rich, which makes the SMT task more complex, especially if they are the target language. A large part of weakly supported languages consists of Slavic languages, where both Serbian and Slovenian belong. Both languages are part of to the South Slavic language branch, Slovenian[2] being the third official South Slavic language in the EU and Serbian[3] is the official language of a candidate member state. For all these reasons, a systematic investigation of SMT systems involving these two languages and defining the most important errors and problems can be very very beneficial for further studies.

In the last decade, several SMT systems have been built for various South Slavic languages and English, and for some systems certain morpho-syntactic transformations have been applied more

[1] http://www.meta-net.eu/whitepapers/key-results-and-cross-language-comparison
[2] together with Croatian and Bulgarian
[3] together with Bosnian and Montenegrin

or less successfully. However, all the experiments are rather scattered and no systematic or focused research has been carried out in order to define actual translation errors as well as their causes.

This paper reports results of an extensive error analysis for four language pairs: Serbian and Slovenian with English as well as with German, which is also a challenging language – complex (both as a source and as a target language) and still not widely supported. SMT systems have been built for all translation directions using publicly available parallel texts originating from several different domains including both written and spoken language.

2 Related work

One of the first publications dealing with SMT systems for Serbian-English (Popović et al., 2005) and Slovenian-English (Sepesy Maučec et al., 2006) are reporting first results using small bilingual corpora. Improvements for translation into English are also reported by reducing morpho-syntactic information in the morphologically rich source language. Using morpho-syntactic knowledge for the Slovenian-English language pair was shown to be useful for both translation directions in (Žganec Gros and Gruden, 2007). However, no analysis of results has been carried out in terms of what were actual problems caused by the rich morphology and which of those were solved by the morphological preprocessing.

Through the transLectures project,[4] the Slovenian-English language pair became available in the 2013 evaluation campaign of IWSLT.[5] They report the BLEU scores of TED talks translated by several systems, however a deeper error analysis is missing (Cettolo et al., 2013).

Recent work in SMT also deals with the Croatian language, which is very closely related to Serbian. First results for Croatian-English are reported in (Ljubešić et al., 2010) on a small weather forecast corpus, and an SMT system for the tourist domain is presented in (Toral et al., 2014). Furthermore, SMT systems for both Serbian and Croatian are described in (Popović and Ljubešić, 2014), however only translation errors caused by language mixing are analysed, not the problems related to the languages themselves.

[4]https://www.translectures.eu/

[5]International Workshop on Spoken Language Translation, http://workshop2013.iwslt.org/

Different SMT systems for subtitles were developed in the framework of the SUMAT project,[6] including Serbian and Slovenian (Etchegoyhen et al., 2014). However, only the translations between them have been carried out as an example of closely related and highly inflected languages.

3 Language characteristics

Serbian (referred to as “sr”) and Slovenian (“sl”), as Slavic languages, have quite free word order and are highly inflected. The inflectional morphology is very rich for all word classes. There are six distinct cases affecting not only common nouns, but also proper nouns as well as pronouns, adjectives and some numbers. Some nouns and adjectives have two distinct plural forms depending on the number (less than five or not). There are also three genders for the nouns, pronouns, adjectives and some numbers leading to differences between the cases and also between the verb participles for past tense and passive voice.

As for verbs, person and many tenses are expressed by the suffix, and, similarly to Spanish and Italian, the subject pronoun (e.g. I, we, it) is often omitted. In addition, negation of three quite important verbs, “*biti* (sr/sl)” (to be), “*imati* (sr) / *imeti* (sl)” (to have) and “*hteti* (sr) / *hoteti* (sl)” (to want), is formed by adding the negative particle to the verb as a prefix. In addition, there are two verb aspects, namely many verbs have perfective and imperfective form(s) depending on the duration of the described action. These forms are either different although very similar or are distinguished only by prefix.

As for syntax, both languages have a quite free word order, and there are no articles, neither indefinite nor definite.

Although the two languages share a large degree of morpho-syntactic properties and mutual intelligibility, a speaker of one language might have difficulties with the other. The language differences are both lexical (including a number of false friends) as well as grammatical (such as local word order, verb mood and/or tense formation, question structure, dual in Slovenian, usage of some cases).

4 SMT systems

In order to systematically explore SMT issues related to the targeted languages, five different domains were used in total. However, not all do-

[6]http://www.sumat-project.eu

(a) number of sentences

# of Sentences	sl-en	sl-de	sr-en	sr-de
DGT	3.2M	3M	/	/
Europarl	600k	500k	/	/
EMEA	1M	1M	/	/
OpenSubtitles	1.8M	1.8M	1.8M	1.8M
SEtimes	/	/	200k	/

(b) average sentence length

Avg. Sent. Length	sl	sr	en	de
DGT	16.0	/	17.3	16.6
Europarl	23.4	/	27.0	25.4
EMEA	12.7	/	12.3	11.8
OpenSubtitles	7.7	7.6	9.2	8.9
SEtimes	/	22.4	23.8	/

Table 1: Corpora characteristics.

mains were used for all language pairs due to unavailability. It should be noted that according to the META-NET White Papers, both languages have minimal support, with only fragmentary text and speech resources. For the Slovenian-English and Slovenian-German language pairs, four domains were investigated: DGT translation memories provided by the JRC (Steinberger et al., 2012), Europarl (Koehn, 2005), European Medicines Agency corpus (EMEA) in the pharmaceutical domain, as well as the OpenSubtitles[7] corpus. All the corpora are downloaded from the OPUS web site[8] (Tiedemann, 2012). For the Serbian language, only two domains were available: the enhanced version of the SEtimes corpus[9] (Tyers and Alperen, 2010) containing "news and views from South-East Europe" for Serbian-English, and OpenSubtitles for the Serbian-English and Serbian-German language pairs. It should be noted that all the corpora contain written texts except OpenSubtitles, which contains transcriptions and translations of spoken language thus being slightly peculiar for machine translation. On the other hand, this is the only corpus containing all language pairs of interest.

Table 1 shows the amount of parallel sentences for each language pair and domain (a) as well as the average sentence length for each language and domain (b). For each domain, a separate system has been trained and tuned on an unseen portion of in-domain data. Since the sentences in OpenSubtitles are significantly shorter than in other texts, the tuning and test sets for this domain contain 3000 sentences whereas all other sets contain 1000 sentences. Another remark regarding the OpenSubtitles corpus is that we trained our systems only on those sentence pairs, which were available in English as well as in German in order to have a completely same condition for all systems.

All systems have been trained using phrase-based Moses (Koehn et al., 2007), where the word alignments were build with GIZA++ (Och and Ney, 2003). The 5-gram language model was build with the SRILM toolkit (Stolcke, 2002).

5 Evaluation and error analysis

The evaluation has been carried out in three steps: first, the BLEU scores were calculated for each of the systems. Then, the automatic error classification has been applied in order to estimate actual translation errors. After that, manual inspection of language related phenomena leading to particular errors is carried out in order to define the most important issues which should be addressed for building better systems and/or develop better models.

5.1 BLEU scores

As a first evaluation step, the BLEU scores (Papineni et al., 2002) have been calculated for each of the translation outputs in order to get a rough idea about the performance for different domains and translation directions.

The scores are presented in Table 2:

- the highest scores are obtained for translations into English;
- the scores for translations into German are similar to those for translations into Slovenian and Serbian;
- the scores for Serbian and Slovenian are better when translated from English than when translated from German;
- the best scores are obtained for DGT (which contains a large number of repetitions), followed by EMEA (which is very specific domain); the worst scores are obtained for spoken language OpenSubtitles texts.

[7]http://www.opensubtitles.org/
[8]http://opus.lingfil.uu.se/
[9]http://nlp.ffzg.hr/resources/corpora/setimes/

Domain/Lang. pair	sl-en	sr-en	sl-de	sr-de	en-sl	de-sl	en-sr	de-sr
DGT	77.3	/	59.3	/	72.1	58.6	/	/
Europarl	58.9	/	33.8	/	56.0	36.5	/	/
EMEA	69.7	/	53.8	/	66.0	56.2	/	/
OpenSubtitles	38.4	33.2	21.5	22.4	26.2	19.6	22.8	18.4
SEtimes	/	43.8	/	/	/	/	35.8	/

Table 2: BLEU scores for all translation outputs.

In addition, all the BLEU scores are compared with those of Google Translate[10] outputs of all tests. All systems built in this work outperform the Google translation system by absolute difference ranges from 1 to 10%, confirming that the languages are weakly supported for machine translation.

5.2 Automatic error classification

Automatic error classification has been performed using Hjerson (Popović, 2011) and the error distributions are presented in Figure 1. For the sake of brevity and clarity, as well as for avoiding redundancies, the error distributions are not presented for all translation outputs, but have been averaged in the following way: since no important differences were observed neither between domains (except that OpenSubtitles translations exhibit more inflectional errors than others) nor between Serbian and Slovenian (neither as source nor as the target language), the errors are averaged over domains and two languages called "x". Thus, four error distributions are shown: translation from and into English, and translation from and into German.

The following can be observed:

- translations into English are "the easiest", mostly due to the small number of morphological errors; however, the English translation outputs contain more word order errors than Serbian and Slovenian ones;
- all error rates are higher in German translations than in English ones, but the mistranslation rate is especially high;
- German translation outputs have less morphological errors than Serbian and Slovenian translations from German; on the other hand, more reordering errors can be observed in German outputs;
- all error rates are higher in translations from German than from English, except inflections.

[10]`http://translate.google.com`, performed on 27th February 2015

The results of the automatic error analysis are valuable and already indicate some promising directions for improving the systems, such as word order treatment and handling morphologic generation. Nevertheless, more improvement could be obtained if more precise guidance about problems and obstacles related to the language properties and differences were available (apart from the general ones already partly investigated in related work).

5.3 Identifying linguistic related issues

Automatic error analysis has already shown that that different language combinations show different error distributions. This often relates to linguistic characteristics of involved languages as well as to divergences between them. In order to explore those relations, manual inspection of about 200 sentences from each domain and language pair annotated by Hjerson together with their corresponding source sentences has been carried out.

As the result of this analysis, the following has been discovered:

- there is a number of frequent error patterns, i.e. obstacles (issues) for SMT systems
- nature and frequency of many issues depend on language combination and translation direction
- some of translation errors depend on the domain and text type, mostly differing for written and spoken language
- issues concerning Slovenian and Serbian both as source and as target languages are almost

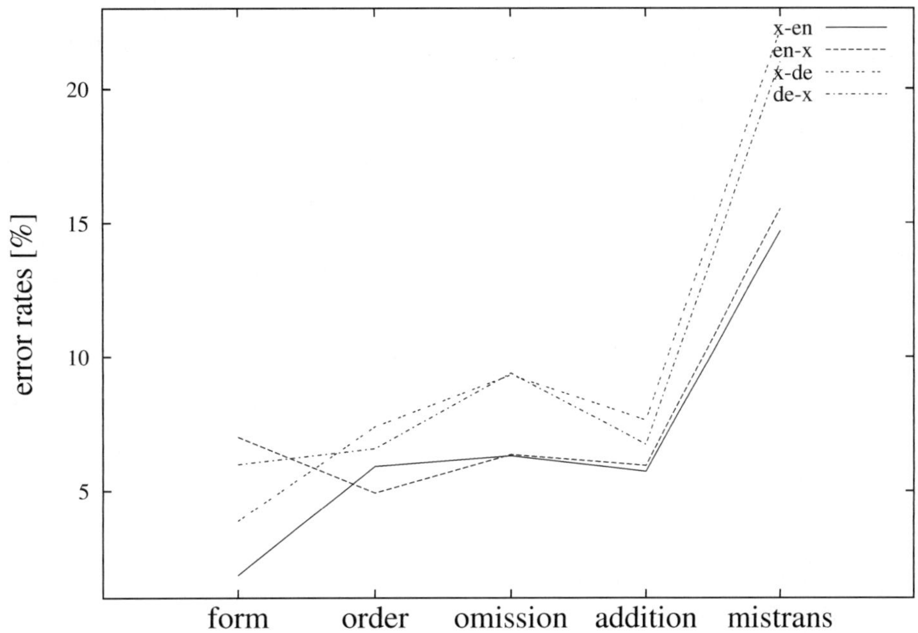

Figure 1: Error rates for five error classes: word form, word order, omission, addition and mistranslation; each error rate represents the percentage of particular (word-level) error type normalised over the total number of words.

the same – there are only few language specific phenomena.

The most frequent general issues[11], i.e. relevant for all translation directions, are:

- **noun collocations** (written language)

  Multi-word expressions consisting of a head noun and additional nouns and adjectives in English poses large problems for all translation directions, especially from and into English. Their formation is different in other languages and often the boundaries are not well detected so that they are translated to unintelligible phrases.

source	12th "Tirana Fall" art and music festival
output*	12th "Tirana collection fall of art and a music festival
reference	the ratings agency's first Emerging Europe Sensitivity Index (EESI)
output	the first Index sensitivity Europe in the development of (EESI) this agency

[11]Non-English parts of examples are literally translated into English and marked with *.

- **negation**

  Due to the distinct negation forming, mainly concerning multiple negations in Serbian and Slovenian, negation structures are translated incorrectly.

reference	the prosecution has done nothing so far
source*	the prosecution has not done nothing so far
output	the prosecution is not so far had done nothing
source	Being a rector does not give someone the freedom
reference*	Being a rector does not give nobody the freedom
output*	Being a rector does not give some freedom

- **phrase boundaries and order**

  Phrase boundaries are not detected properly so that the group(s) of words are misplaced, often accompanied with morphological errors and mistranslations.

reference	of which about a fifth is used for wheat production
output	of which used to produce about one fifth of wheat
reference	But why have I brought this thing here?
output	This thing, but why am I here?
reference	The US ambassador to Sofia said on Wednesday .
output	Said on Wednesday , US ambassador to Sofia .

- **prepositions**

  Prepositions are mostly mistranslated, sometimes also omitted or added.

- **word order**

  Local word permutations mostly affecting verbs and surrounding auxiliary verbs, pronouns, nouns and adverbs.

Some of the frequent issues are strongly dependent on translation direction. For translation into English and German the issues of interest are:

- **articles**

  Due to the absence of articles in Slavic languages, a number of articles in English and German translation outputs are missing, and a certain number is mistranslated or added.

- **pronouns**

  The source languages are pro-drop, therefore a number of pronouns is missing in the English and German translation outputs.

- **possessive pronoun *"svoj"***

  This possessive pronoun can be used for all persons ("my", "your", "her", "his", "our", "their") and it is difficult to disambiguate.

- **verb tense**

  Due to different usage of verb tenses in some cases, the wrong verb tense from the source language is preserved, or sometimes mistranslated. The problem is more prominent for translation into English.

- **agreement** (German target)

  A number of cases and gender agreements in German output is incorrect.

- **missing verbs** (German target)

  Verbs or verb parts are missing in German output, especially when they are supposed to appear at the end of the clause.

- **conjunction *"i"* (and)** (Serbian source)

  The main meaning of this conjunction is "and", but another meaning "also, too, as well" is often used too; however, it is usually translated as "and".

- **adverb *"lahko"*** (Slovenian source)

  This word is used for Slovenian conditional phrases which correspond to English constructions with modal verbs "can", "might", "shall", or adverbs "possibly"; the entire clause is often not translated correctly due to incorrect disambiguation.

For translation into Serbian and Slovenian, the most important obstacles are:

- **case**

  Incorrect case is used, often in combination with incorrect singular/plural and/or gender agreement.

- **verb inflection**

  Verb inflection does not correspond to the person and/or the tense; a number of past participles also has incorrect singular/plurar and/or gender agreement.

- **missing verbs**

  Verb or verb parts are missing, especially for constructions using auxiliary and/or modal verbs. The problem is more frequent when translating from German.

- **question structure** (spoken language)

  Question structure is incorrect; the problem is more frequent in Serbian where additional particles ("li" and "da li") should be used but are often omitted.

- **conjunction *"a"*** (Serbian target)

  This conjunction does not exist in other languages, it can be translated as "and" or "but", and its exact meaning is something in between. Therefore it is difficult to disambiguate the corresponding source conjunction.

- **"-*ing*" forms** (English source)

  English present continuous tense does not exist in other languages, and in addition, it is often difficult to determine if the word with the suffix "-ing" is a verb or a noun. Therefore words with the "-ing" suffix are difficult for machine translation.

- **noun-verb disambiguation** (English source)

  Apart from the words ending with the suffix "-ing", there is a number of other English words which can be used both as a noun as well as a verb, such as "offer", "search", etc.

- **modal verb "*sollen*"** (German source)

  This German modal verb can have different meanings, such as "should", "might" and "will" which is often difficult to disambiguate.

It has to be noted that some of the linguistic phenomena known to be difficult are not listed – the reason is that their overall number of occurrences in the analysed texts is low and therefore the number of related errors too. For example, German compounds are well known for posing problems to natural language processing tasks among which is machine translation – however, in the given texts only a few errors related to compounds were observed, as well as a low total number of compounds. Another similar case is the verb aspect in Serbian and Slovenian – some related errors were detected, but their count as well as the overall count of such verbs in the data is very small.

Therefore the structure and nature of the texts for a concrete task should always be taken into account. For example, for improvements of spoken language translation more effort should be put in question treatment than in noun collocation, and in technical texts the compound problem would probably be significant.

6 Conclusions and future work

In this work, we have examined several SMT systems involving two morphologically rich and under-resourced languages in order to identify the most important language related issues which should be dealt with in order to build better systems and models. The BLEU scores are reported as a first evaluation step, followed by automatic error classification which has captured interesting language related patterns in distributions of error types. The main part of the evaluation consisted of (manual) analysis of errors taking into account linguistic properties of both target and source language. This analytic analysis has defined a set of general issues which are causing errors for all translation directions, as well as sets of language dependent issues. Although many of these issues are already known to be difficult, they can be addressed only with the precise identification of concrete examples.

The main general issues are shown to be structural properties concerning multi-noun collocations and exact phrase boundaries, followed by negation formation, wrong, missing or added preposition as well as local word order differences. For translation into English and German, article and pronoun omissions are the most problematic, as well as disambiguation of certain frequent functional words. For translation into Serbian and Slovenian, cases and verb inflections are most difficult to handle. In addition, other problems concerning verbs are frequent as well, such as local word order involving verbs and missing verb parts (which is especially difficult when translating from German).

In future work we plan to address some of the presented issues practically and analyse the effects. An important thing concerning system improvement is that although most of the described issues are common for various domains, the exact nature of the texts desired for the task at hand should always be kept in mind. Analysis of issues for domains and text types not covered by this paper should be part of future work too.

Acknowledgments

This publication has emanated from research supported by the QT21 project – European Union's Horizon 2020 research and innovation programme under grant number 645452 as well as a research grant from Science Foundation Ireland (SFI) under grant number SFI/12/RC/2289. We are grateful to the anonymous reviewers for their valuable feedback.

References

Cettolo, Mauro, Jan Niehues, Sebastian Stüker, Luisa Bentivogli, and Marcello Federico. 2013. Report on the 10th IWSLT evaluation campaign. In *Proceedings of the International Workshop on Spoken Language Translation (IWSLT)*, Heidelberg, Germany, December.

Etchegoyhen, Thierry, Lindsay Bywood, Mark Fishel, Panayota Georgakopoulou, Jie Jiang, Gerard Van Loenhout, Arantza Del Pozo, Mirjam Sepesy Maučec, Anja Turner, and Martin Volk. 2014. Machine Translation for Subtitling: A Large-Scale Evaluation. In *Proceedings of the Ninth International Conference on Language Resources and Evaluation (LREC14)*, Reykjavik, Iceland, May.

Koehn, Philipp, Hieu Hoang, Alexandra Birch, Chris Callison-Burch, Marcello Federico, Nicola Bertoldi, Brooke Cowan, Wade Shen, Christine Moran, Richard Zens, Chris Dyer, Ondřej Bojar, Alexandra Constantin, and Evan Herbst. 2007. Moses: Open source toolkit for statistical machine translation. In *Proceedings of the 45th Annual Meeting of the ACL on Interactive Poster and Demonstration Sessions*, Stroudsburg, PA, USA.

Koehn, Philipp. 2005. Europarl: A Parallel Corpus for Statistical Machine Translation. In *Proceedings of the 10th Machine Translation Summit*, pages 79–86, Phuket, Thailand, September.

Ljubešić, Nikola, Petra Bago, and Damir Boras. 2010. Statistical machine translation of Croatian weather forecast: How much data do we need? In Lužar-Stiffler, Vesna, Iva Jarec, and Zoran Bekić, editors, *Proceedings of the ITI 2010 32nd International Conference on Information Technology Interfaces*, pages 91–96, Zagreb. SRCE University Computing Centre.

Och, Franz Josef and Hermann Ney. 2003. A Systematic Comparison of Various Statistical Alignment Models. *Computational Linguistics*, 29(1):19–51, March.

Papineni, Kishore, Salim Roukos, Todd Ward, and Wie-Jing Zhu. 2002. BLEU: a method for automatic evaluation of machine translation. pages 311–318, Philadelphia, PA, July.

Popović, Maja and Nikola Ljubešić. 2014. Exploring cross-language statistical machine translation for closely related South Slavic languages. In *Proceedings of the EMNLP14 Workshop on Language Technology for Closely Related Languages and Language Variants*, pages 76–84, Doha, Qatar, October.

Popović, Maja, David Vilar, Hermann Ney, Slobodan Jovičić, and Zoran Šarić. 2005. Augmenting a Small Parallel Text with Morpho-syntactic Language Resources for Serbian–English Statistical Machine Translation. pages 41–48, Ann Arbor, MI, June.

Popović, Maja. 2011. Hjerson: An Open Source Tool for Automatic Error Classification of Machine Translation Output. *The Prague Bulletin of Mathematical Linguistics*, (96):59–68, October.

Sepesy Maučec, Mirjam, Janez Brest, and Zdravko Kačič. 2006. Slovenian to English Machine Translation using Corpora of Different Sizes and Morpho-syntactic Information. In *Proceedings of the 5th Language Technologies Conference*, pages 222–225, Ljubljana, Slovenia, October.

Steinberger, Ralf, Andreas Eisele, Szymon Klocek, Spyridon Pilos, and Patrick Schlüter. 2012. DGT-TM: A freely available Translation Memory in 22 languages. In *Proceedings of the 8th International Conference on Language Resources and Evaluation (LREC12)*, pages 454–459, Istanbul, Turkey, May.

Stolcke, Andreas. 2002. SRILM – an extensible language modeling toolkit. volume 2, pages 901–904, Denver, CO, September.

Tiedemann, Jörg. 2012. Parallel data, tools and interfaces in OPUS. In *Proceedings of the 8th International Conference on Language Resources and Evaluation (LREC12)*, pages 2214–2218, May.

Toral, Antonio, Raphael Rubino, Miquel Esplà-Gomis, Tommi Pirinen, Andy Way, and Gema Ramirez-Sanchez. 2014. Extrinsic Evaluation of Web-Crawlers in Machine Translation: a Case Study on CroatianEnglish for the Tourism Domain. In *Proceedings of the 17th Conference of the European Association for Machine Translation (EAMT)*, pages 221–224, Dubrovnik, Croatia, June.

Tyers, Francis M. and Murat Alperen. 2010. South-East European Times: A parallel corpus of the Balkan languages. In *Proceedings of the LREC Workshop on Exploitation of Multilingual Resources and Tools for Central and (South-) Eastern European Languages*, pages 49–53, Valetta, Malta, May.

Žganec Gros, Jerneja and Stanislav Gruden. 2007. The voiceTRAN machine translation system. In *Proceedings of the 8th Annual Conference of the International Speech Communication Association (INTERSPEECH 07)*, pages 1521–1524, Antwerp, Belgium, August. ISCA.

Poor man's lemmatisation for automatic error classification

Maja Popović[1] **Mihael Arčan**[2] **Eleftherios Avramidis**[1]
Aljoscha Burchardt[1] **Arle Lommel**[1]

[1] DFKI – Language Technology Lab, Berlin, Germany
firstname.lastname@dfki.de
[2] Insight Centre for Data Analytics, National University of Galway, Ireland
mihael.arcan@insight-centre.org

Abstract

This paper demonstrates the possibility to make an existing automatic error classifier for machine translations independent from the requirement of lemmatisation. This makes it usable also for smaller and under-resourced languages and in situations where there is no lemmatiser at hand. It is shown that cutting all words into the first four letters is the best method even for highly inflective languages, preserving both the detected distribution of error types within a translation output as well as over various translation outputs.

The main cost of not using a lemmatiser is the lower accuracy of detecting the inflectional error class due to its confusion with mistranslations. For shorter words, actual inflectional errors will be tagged as mistranslations, for longer words the other way round. Keeping all that in mind, it is possible to use the error classifier without target language lemmatisation and to extrapolate inflectional and lexical error rates according to the average word length in the analysed text.

1 Introduction

Future improvement of machine translation (MT) systems requires reliable automatic evaluation and error classification tools in order to minimise efforts of time and money consuming human classification. Therefore automatic error classification tools have been developed in recent years (Zeman et al., 2011; Popović, 2011) and are being used to facilitate the error analysis. Although these tools are completely language independent, for obtaining a precise error distribution over classes a lemmatiser for the target language is required. For the languages strongly supported in language resources and tools this does not pose a problem. However, for a number of languages a lemmatiser might not be at hand, or it does not exist at all. This paper investigates possibilities for obtaining reasonable error classification results without lemmatisation. To the best of our knowledge, this issue has not been investigated so far.

2 Motivation and explored methods

We investigate the edit-distance i.e. word error rate (WER) approach implemented in the Hjerson tool (Popović, 2011), which enables detection of five error categories: *inflectional errors*, *word order errors*, *missing words* (omissions), *extra words* (additions) and *lexical errors* (mistranslations). For a given MT output and reference translation, the classication results are provided in the form of the five error rates, whereby the number of errors for each category is normalised over the total number of words.

The detailed description of the approach can be found in (Popović and Ney, 2011). The starting point is to identify actual words contributing to the Word Error Rate (WER), recall (reference) error rate (RPER) and precision (hypothesis) error rate (HPER). The WER errors are marked as substitutions, deletions and insertions. Then, the lemmas are used: first, to identify the inflectional errors – if the lemma of an erroneous word is correct and the full form is not. Second, the lemmas are also used for detecting omissions, additions and mistranslations. It is also possible to calculate WER

Method	
full	The visit will reach its peak in the afternoon .
$lemma$	The visit will reach its peak in the afternoon .
$4let$	The visi will reac its peak in the afte .
$2thirds$	Th vis wi rea it pe in th aftern .
$stem$	The visi wil rea its pea in the afternoo .
full	President is receiving the Minister of Finance .
$lemma$	President be receive the Minister of Finance .
$4let$	Pres be rece the Mini of Fina .
$2thirds$	Presid is receiv th Minis of Fina .
$stem$	Presiden is receiv the Minist of Financ .

Table 1: Examples for each of the word reduction methods.

based on lemmas instead of full words in order to increase the precision with regard to human error annotation, which makes the algorithm even more susceptible to possible lack of lemmas.

If the full word forms were used as a replacement for lemmas, it would not be possible to detect any inflectional error thus setting the inflectional error rate to zero, and noise would be introduced in omission, addition and mistranslation error rates. Therefore, a simple use of the full forms instead of lemmas is not advisable, especially for the highly inflective languages. The goal of this work is to examine possible methods for processing of the full words in a more or less simple way in order to yield a reasonable error classification results by using them as a replacement for lemmas. Following methods for word reduction are explored:

- first four letters of the word ($4let$)

  The simplest way for word reduction is to use only its first n letters. The choice of first four letters has been shown to be successful for improvement of word alignments (Fraser and Marcu, 2005), therefore we decided to set n to four.

- first two thirds of the word length ($2thirds$)

  In order to take the word length into account, the words are reduced to 2/3 of their original length (rounded down).

- word stem ($stem$)

  A more refined method which splits words into stems and suffixes based on harmonic mean of their frequencies is used, similar to the compound splitting method described in (Koehn and Knight, 2003). The suffix of each word is removed and only the stem is preserved. For calculation of stem and suffix frequencies, both the translation output and its corresponding reference translation are used.

Examples of two English sentences processed by each of the methods is shown in Table 1.

The methods are tested on various distinct target languages and domains, some of the languages being very morphologically rich. Detailed description of the texts can be found in the next section.

3 Experiments and results

The two main objectives of automatic error classifier are:

- to estimate the error distribution within a translation output
- to compare different translation outputs in terms of error categories

Therefore we tested the described methods for both these aspects by comparing the results with those obtained when using lemmatised words, i.e. we used the error rates obtained with lemmas as the "reference" error rates. The best way for the assessment would be, of course, a comparison with human error classification. Nevertheless, this has not been done for two reasons: first, the original method using lemmas is already thoroughly tested in previous work (Popović and Ney, 2011) and is shown to correlate well with human judgements. Second, human evaluation is resource and time-consuming.

The explored target languages in this work are English, Spanish, German, Slovenian and Czech originating from news, technical texts, client data of Language Service Providers, pharmaceutical domain, Europarl (Koehn, 2005), as well as the OpenSubtitles[1] spoken language corpus. In addition, one Basque translation output from technical domain has been available as well. The publicly available texts are described in (Callison-Burch et al., 2011), (Specia, 2011) and (Tiedemann, 2012). The majority of translation outputs has been created by statistical systems but a number of translations has been produced by rule-based systems. It should be noted that not all target languages were available for all domains, however the total amount of texts and the diversity of languages and domains are sufficient to obtain reliable results – about 36000 sentences with average number of words ranging from 8 (subtitles) through 15 (domain-specific corpora) up to 25 (Europarl and news) have been analysed.

Lemmas for English, Spanish and German texts are generated using TreeTagger,[2] Slovenian lemmas are produced by the Obeliks tagger (Grčar et al., 2012), and Czech texts are lemmatised using the COMPOST tagger (Spoustová et al., 2009).

It should be noted that all the reported results are calculated using WER of lemmas (or corresponding substitutions) since no changes related to lemma substitution techniques were observed in comparison with the use of the standard full word WER.

3.1 Error distributions within a translation output

Our first experiment consisted of calculating distributions of five error rates within one translation output using all word reduction methods described in Section 2 and comparing the obtained results with the reference distributions of error rates obtained using lemmas. The results for three distinct target languages are presented in Table 2: English as the least inflective, Spanish having very rich verb morphology, and Czech as generally highly inflective.

Reference distributions are presented in the first row, followed by the investigated word reduction methods; in the last row the results obtained using full words are shown as well, and the intuitively suspected effects can be clearly seen: no inflectional errors are detected, and the vast majority of them are tagged as lexical error (mistranslation). Furthermore, it is confirmed that the variations in word order errors, omissions and additions are small, whereas the most affected error classes are inflections and mistranslations.

As for different target languages, in the English output the differences between the error rates are small for all error classes, but for the more inflected Spanish text and the highly inflected Czech text the situation is fairly different: $4let$ distribution is closest to the reference lemma error distribution, whereas $2thirds$ and $stem$ distributions are lying between the lemma and the full word distributions. In addition, it can be observed that the $stem$ method performs better than the $2thirds$ method.

In Table 3, the parts of the reference translations from Table 1 containing inflectional errors are shown together with the corresponding parts of the translation output in order to better understand the different performance of the methods. Each of the sentences contains one (verb) inflectional error. The first error, "receives" instead of "receiving", is correctly detected by all methods. The second one, "reached" instead of "reach" is correctly tagged by all methods except by $2thirds$ because the reduced word forms are not the same in the translation and in the reference. The $stem$ method often exhibits the same problem, however less frequently.

3.2 Comparing translation outputs

For the comparison of different translation outputs, only the $4let$ method has been investigated because it produces the best error distributions (closest to those obtained by lemmas) and it is also the simplest to perform.

Figure 1 illustrates the results for the two highly inflectional languages, namely Slovenian (above) and Czech (below). Slovenian translations originating from six statistical MT systems (dealing with three different domains and two source languages) and Czech outputs produced by four different MT systems have been analysed. Only the two most critical error classes are presented, namely inflectional (left) and lexical (right) error rates – for other error categories no significant performance differences between the reduction methods were observed.

For the Slovenian translations, the correlation between $4let$ and reference lemma system rankings is 1, both for the inflectional and for the lexical error rates. The same applies to Czech lex-

[1] `http://www.opensubtitles.org/`

[2] `http://www.ims.uni-stuttgart.de/projekte/corplex/TreeTagger/`

Target Language	Method	infl	order	miss	add	lex
		Error Rates [%]				
English	*lemma* (ref)	1.5	7.6	5.2	3.0	8.7
	4let	1.9	7.6	5.2	3.0	8.2
	2thirds	0.9	7.5	5.3	3.0	9.3
	stem	1.2	7.6	5.3	3.0	9.0
	full	0	7.6	5.4	3.1	10.1
Spanish	*lemma* (ref)	4.6	6.4	5.9	3.6	13.5
	4let	4.0	6.6	6.0	3.6	13.9
	2thirds	2.6	6.4	6.0	3.5	15.5
	stem	3.1	6.6	6.1	3.6	14.8
	full	0	6.7	6.1	3.6	17.9
Czech	*lemma* (ref)	10.4	10.6	7.1	7.6	36.4
	4let	10.0	10.8	7.0	7.7	36.9
	2thirds	5.6	11.0	6.8	7.6	41.4
	stem	7.2	10.9	7.0	7.7	39.7
	full	0	11.3	6.8	7.6	47.1

Table 2: Comparison of error rates obtained by each of the described word reduction methods with the reference lemma error rates for three translation outputs: English (above), Spanish (middle) and Czech (below). Error rates using full words as lemma replacement are shown as well, illustrating why this method is not recommended.

Method	Reference translation	MT output
full	The visit will <u>reach</u>	Visit <u>reached</u>
lemma	The visit will *reach*	Visit *reach*
4let	The visi will *reac*	Visit *reac*
2thirds	Th vis wi *rea*	Vis *rea*
stem	The visi will *rea*	Vis *rea*
full	President is <u>receiving</u>	President <u>receives</u>
lemma	President be *receive*	President *receive*
4let	Pres be *rece*	Pres *rece*
2thirds	Presid is **receiv**	President **recei**
stem	Presiden is *receiv*	President *receiv*

Table 3: Illustration of the main problem for inflectional error detection: if the reduced word form is not exactly the same in the reference and in the translation output (bold), the error will not be tagged as inflectional. This phenomenon occurs most frequently for the *2thirds* method, therefore this method exibits the poorest performance.

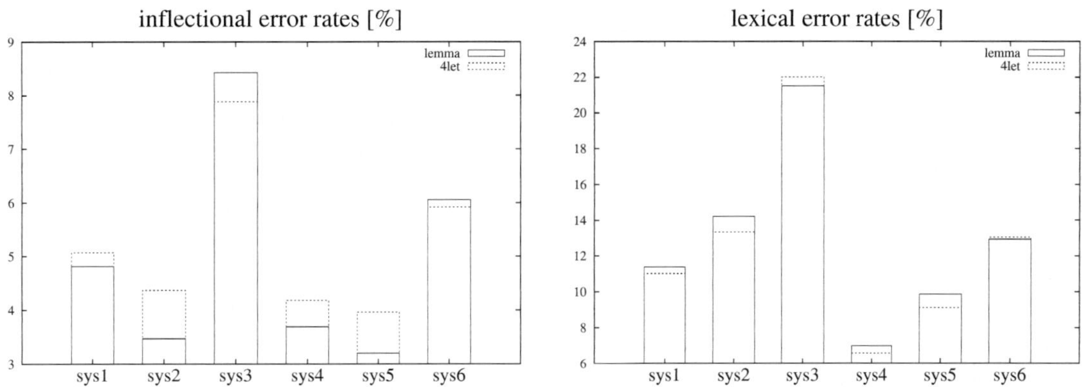

(a) Comparing six Slovenian MT outputs

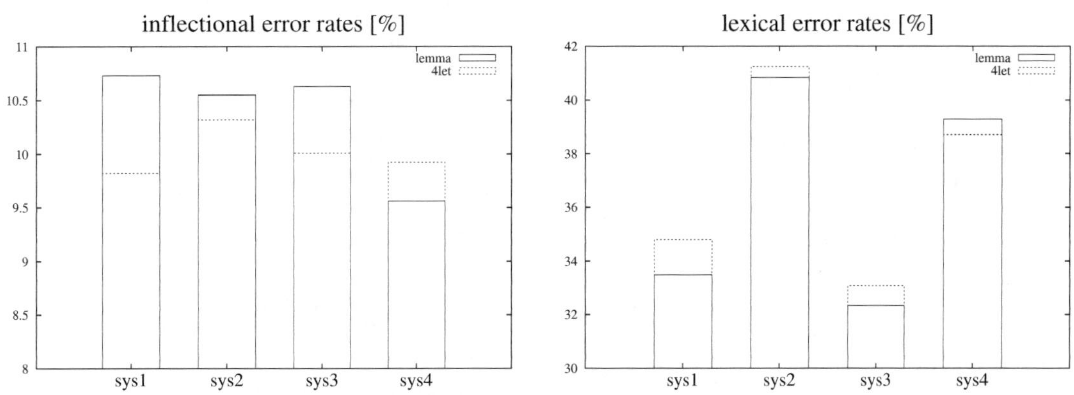

(b) Comparing four Czech MT outputs

Figure 1: Comparison of translation outputs for highly inflective languages based on the two most critical error classes, i.e. inflectional (left) and lexical errors (right) – six Slovenian (above) and four Czech (below) translation outputs. Reference lemma error rates are presented by full lines, $4let$ error rates by dashed lines.

ical error rates, but not for the Czech inflections though: lemma method ranks the error rates (from highest to lowest) *1, 3, 2, 4* whereas the $4let$ ranking is *2, 3, 4, 1*. However, the important fact is that the relative differences between the systems are very small for inflectional errors; all the systems contain a high number of inflectional errors (between 9.6 and 10.8%), whereas the absolute differences between the systems range only between 0.2 and 1%. This means that the $4let$ method is generally well capable of system comparison, but it is not able to capture very small relative differences correctly.

3.3 Analysis of confusions

In previous sections it is shown that the $4let$ method, despite certain disadvantages, is well capable to substitute the lemmas both for estimating error distributions within an output as well as for comparing error rates across the translation outputs. However, an important remaining question is: what is exactly happening? Results presented in previous sections indicate that a number of inflectional errors is substituted by lexical errors. However, they also show that the $4let$ inflectional error rates sometimes are lower and sometimes higher than the lemma-based ones, thus indicating that not only a simple substitution of inflectional errors by mistranslations is taking place.

In order to explore these underlying phenomena, accuracies and confusions between error classes are calculated and confusion matrix is presented in Table 4. Since there are practically no variations in reordering error rates, the confusions are presented only for inflections, additions[3] and lexical errors.

As a first step, the confusions are calculated for all merged texts and the results are presented in the first row. It is confirmed that the low accuracy of the inflections and their confusions with mistranslations are indeed the main problems, however there is a number of reverse confusions, i.e. certain mistranslations are tagged as inflectional errors. Apart from that, there is also certain amount of confusions between inflections and additions.

Since some of the used reference translations were independent ("free") human translations and some were post-edited translation outputs, we separated the texts into two sets and calculated confusions for each one. Nevertheless, no important differences could be observed, as it can be seen in the corresponding rows in Table 4.

The next step was to analyse each of the target languages separately, and the results are presented further below in the table. Although the numbers are more diverse, all the important phenomena are practically same for all languages, namely low accuracy of inflections due to confusion with mistranslations. Only for the Basque translation the percentage is similar for confusions in both directions.

Last step was division of texts into written text and spoken language transcriptions, and, contrary to the other set-ups, several notable differences were observed. First of all, the accuracy of inflections is significantly lower for spoken language, and the percentage of confusions with mistranslations is much higher. On the other hand, in written text much more mistranslations are substituted by inflections.

3.3.1 Word length effects

The differences between written and spoken language, together with the observations about Basque where the words can be very long, showed that the word length is an important factor which is neglected by the simple cutting of words into first four letters. The inflections of very short words such as articles and auxiliary verbs cannot be captured, and some long words which are not related at all can be easily tagged as inflectional errors only because they share the first four characters – see Table 5. Furthermore, *reception*, *receipt*, *recent* and *receiver* all share first four letters and could possibly be tagged as inflectional error. On the other hand, such coincidences are not very frequent and therefore there are less substitutions of lexical errors. We calculated the average lengths of words for which each of the two substitution types occur, and obtained an average word length of 3.44 for inflection→mistranslation substitution and 8.64 for the reverse one.

Neglecting the word length by the $4let$ method was the reason to explore the other two methods ($2thirds$ and $stem$) in the first place. However, they produced significantly worse error distributions due to the often inconsistent word cutting. Since the $stem$ method could be potentially improved (contrary to the $2thirds$ method), we analysed its confusions and compared with those of the $4let$ method in order to better understand the differences. The confusions for all merged translation

[3]The situation regarding omissions is analogous to the one regarding additions.

4let	infl	infl→lex	infl→add	lex	lex→infl	add	add→infl
Overall	**57.1**	**36.0**	5.6	89.5	8.0	88.9	8.0
Reference	56.2	37.4	5.5	90.5	7.2	90.4	3.7
Post-edit	57.9	34.3	5.8	87.5	9.8	86.8	6.1
English	47.1	46.8	5.5	93.2	5.4	94.7	2.8
Spanish*	55.6	35.2	5.3	89.4	8.6	91.8	2.6
German	43.2	47.0	7.3	87.9	8.5	84.9	8.1
Slovenian	51.6	41.8	6.2	91.9	6.2	86.7	2.1
Czech*	66.3	28.4	5.2	90.0	7.3	81.3	6.3
Basque*	79.2	**16.4**	3.8	84.0	**13.4**	86.3	5.6
Written	65.7	27.4	5.0	**87.0**	**10.1**	87.6	**6.4**
Spoken	**44.4**	**49.2**	6.0	94.1	4.6	89.7	1.6

Table 4: Accuracies and confusions between reference lemma error categories and those obtained by the *4let* method; for all texts (Overall), separately for post-editions and for references, separately for each target language, and separately for written and spoken language.

Method	Reference translation	MT output
full	There were ergonomic problems .	There was ergonomische problems .
lemma	There be ergonomic problem .	There be_{infl} $ergonomische_{lex}$ problem .
4let	Ther were ergo prob .	Ther was_{lex} $ergo_{infl}$ prob .

Table 5: Illustration of the word length problem for the *4let* method: inflectional errors for short words (*were/was*) are impossible to detect and are considered as lexical errors; on the other hand, a lexical error (untranslated German word *ergonomische*) is tagged as inflectional error because it shares first four letters with the reference translation *ergonomic*.

	Method	infl	infl→lex	infl→add	lex	lex→infl	add	add→infl
Overall	*4let*	**57.1**	**36.0**	**5.6**	89.5	8.0	88.9	8.0
	stem	48.4	44.2	6.0	**94.2**	**4.8**	**89.7**	**4.3**

Table 6: Comparison of overall *4let* and *stem* accuracies and confusions.

outputs (Overall) presented in Table 6 show that the *stem* method is better in avoiding substitutions of mistranslations and additions with inflections, but the problem with low inflection error accuracy is worse. One possible reason is that the stem and the suffix frequencies are estimated from the very small amount of data (only the reference and the translation output) and therefore is often not able to perform consistent cuttings for all words. This method should be investigated in future work, trained on the large target language corpus as well as in combination with the *4let* method.

4 Conclusions and Future Work

The experiments presented in this paper show that it is possible to use an existing automatic error classifier without target language lemmas. It is shown that cutting all words into first four letters is the best method even for highly inflective languages, preserving both the distribution of error types within a system as well as distribution of each error type over various systems. However, it might not be able to capture very small variations correctly.

The main issue is the low accuracy of inflectional error class due to confusions with mistranslations. For shorter words, actual inflectional errors tend to be tagged as mistranslations, for longer words the other way round. Keeping all that in mind, it is possible to use the error classifier without target language lemmatisation and to extrapolate inflectional and lexical error rates according to the dominant word length in the analysed text.

Our further work will concentrate on combining the *4let* method with more refined methods which take into account the word length, and also investigating other fixed reduction lengths, e.g. 5 and 6. Comparison with human error classification results as well as manual inspection of problematic words and error confusion types should be carried out as well.

Acknowledgments

This publication has emanated from research supported by QTLEAP project – ECs FP7 (FP7/2007-2013) under grant agreement number 610516: "QTLEAP: Quality Translation by Deep Language Engineering Approaches" and by a research grant from Science Foundation Ireland (SFI) under Grant Number SFI/12/RC/2289. We are grateful to the reviewers for their valuable feedback.

References

Callison-Burch, Chris, Philipp Koehn, Christof Monz, and Omar Zaidan. 2011. Findings of the 2011 Workshop on Statistical Machine Translation. In *Proceedings of the Sixth Workshop on Statistical Machine Translation (WMT 2011)*, pages 22–64, Edinburgh, Scotland, July.

Fraser, Alexander and Daniel Marcu. 2005. ISI's Participation in the Romanian-English Alignment Task. In *Proceedings of the ACL Workshop on Building and Using Parallel Texts*, pages 91–94, Ann Arbor, Michigan, June.

Grčar, Miha, Simon Krek, and Kaja Dobrovoljc. 2012. Obeliks: statistični oblikoskladenjski označevalnik in lematizator za slovenski jezik. In *Proceedings of the 8th Language Technologies Conference*, pages 89–94, Ljubljana, Slovenia, October.

Koehn, Philipp and Kevin Knight. 2003. Empirical methods for compound splitting. In *Proceedings of the 10th Conference of the European Chapter of the Association for Computational Linguistics (EACL 03)*, pages 347–354, Budapest, Hungary, April.

Koehn, Philipp. 2005. Europarl: A Parallel Corpus for Statistical Machine Translation. In *Proceedings of the 10th Machine Translation Summit*, pages 79–86, Phuket, Thailand, September.

Popović, Maja and Hermann Ney. 2011. Towards Automatic Error Analysis of Machine Translation Output. *Computational Linguistics*, 37(4):657–688, December.

Popović, Maja. 2011. Hjerson: An Open Source Tool for Automatic Error Classification of Machine Translation Output. *The Prague Bulletin of Mathematical Linguistics*, (96):59–68, October.

Specia, Lucia. 2011. Exploiting Objective Annotations for Measuring Translation Post-editing Effort. In *Proceedings of the 15th Annual Conference of the European Association for Machine Translation (EAMT 11)*, pages 73–80, Leuven, Belgium, May.

Spoustová, Drahomíra "Johanka", Jan Hajič, Jan Raab, and Miroslav Spousta. 2009. Semi-Supervised Training for the Averaged Perceptron POS Tagger. In *Proceedings of the 12th Conference of the European Chapter of the ACL (EACL 2009)*, pages 763–771, Athens, Greece, March.

Tiedemann, Jörg. 2012. Parallel data, tools and interfaces in OPUS. In *Proceedings of the 8th International Conference on Language Resources and Evaluation (LREC12)*, pages 2214–2218, May.

Zeman, Daniel, Mark Fishel, Jan Berka, and Ondřej Bojar. 2011. Addicter: What Is Wrong with My Translations? *The Prague Bulletin of Mathematical Linguistics*, 96:79–88, October.

Truly Exploring Multiple References for Machine Translation Evaluation

Ying Qin
Dept. of Computer Science
Beijing Foreign Studies University
qinying@bfsu.edu.cn

Lucia Specia
Dept. of Computer Science
University of Sheffield
l.specia@sheffield.ac.uk

Abstract

Multiple references in machine translation evaluation are usually under-explored: they are ignored by alignment-based metrics and treated as bags of n-grams in string matching evaluation metrics, none of which take full advantage of the recurring information in these references. By exploring information on the n-gram distribution and on divergences in multiple references, we propose a method of n-gram weighting and implement it to generate new versions of the popular BLEU and NIST metrics. Our metrics are tested in two into-English machine translation datasets. They lead to a significant increase in Pearson's correlation with human fluency judgements at system-level evaluation. The new NIST metric also outperforms the standard NIST for document-level evaluation.

1 Introduction

Quality evaluation plays a critical role in Machine Translation (MT). Since its conception, the BLEU metric (Papineni et al., 2002) has had a significant impact on MT development. Although human evaluation has been used in recent evaluation campaigns such as WMT (Workshop on Statistical MT) (Bojar et al., 2014) and other forms of reference-less metrics have been proposed (Gamon et al., 2005; Specia et al., 2010), the merit of language and resource-independent n-gram based metrics such as BLEU is undeniable. Despite its criticisms, BLEU is thus still considered the *de facto* or at least a baseline metric for MT quality evaluation.

Due to the cost of human translation, often only one reference translation is available at evaluation time. However, generally there are numerous valid translations for a given sentence or document. Different references provide valid variations in linguistic aspects such as style, word choice and word order. Therefore, having multiple reference translations is key to improve the reliability of n-gram based evaluation metrics: the more references, the more chances for n-grams correctly translated to be captured. HyTER, an n-gram matching metric based on an exponential number of reference translations for a given target sentence, demonstrates the potential for better machine translation evaluation results from having as many references as possible (Dreyer and Marcu, 2012). Nevertheless, in the more realistic case where only a few references are available, if these are simply taken as bags of n-grams, increasing the number of references will not lead to the best possible results, as pointed out by Doddington (2002).

In this paper we explore how to use multiple references by means other than simply viewing them as bags of n-gram like BLEU, NIST (Doddington, 2002) and other n-gram co-occurrence based metrics do. Our assumption is that each reference reflects the complete meaning of the source segment. The semantic entirety of the translation will be adversely affected if all the n-grams from various references are simply put together. We propose a method of modifying the weight assignment strategy in BLEU and NIST by taking into account the n-gram distributions and divergences over different references.

Experiments were performed on two into-

English translation datasets released by LDC, leading to promising results. In the remainder of this paper we will first review BLEU and related n-gram based evaluation metrics (Section 2). We then describe the method we propose to explore multiple references by reassigning the weights of n-grams that are common in system translations and references (Section 3), and the experiments performed and their results (Section 4). These illustrate how the modified BLEU and NIST scores compare against standard BLEU and NIST scores at the system, document and sentence levels.

2 N-gram based evaluation

2.1 BLEU

The BLEU metric applies a straightforward method of counting the n-grams that overlap in the system translation and given human translations under the assumption that human translations precisely reproduce the meaning of the source text. The closer to the reference, the higher the translation quality of the system translation will be. The core formula is given in Eq. 1 (Papineni et al., 2002), so that we can subsequently compare it to our approach.

$$S\_B = BP \times exp\sum_{n=1}^{N} w_n log P_n, \tag{1}$$

where

$$P_n = \frac{\sum_{C \in Candi} \sum_{ngram \in C} Count_{clip}(ngram)}{\sum_{C \in Candi} \sum_{ngram' \in C'} Count(ngram')}$$

$$BP = \begin{cases} 1, if|c| \geq |r| \\ e^{(1-|r|/|c|)}, if|c| < |r| \end{cases}$$

w_n is a weighting factor usually set as $1/N$, where N is the longest possible n-gram considered by the matching method. N is usually set to 4 to avoid data sparseness issues resulting from longer n-grams. P_n is the n-gram precision at a given n and in essence represents the proportion of n-grams in the candidate translation that also appear in the reference translation. BP is a penalty factor for shorter segments. c and r are the length of the candidate segment and reference segment, respectively.

When multiple references are available, $Count_{clip}(ngram)$ is clipped at the maximum count of n-grams which occurs in a single reference, and r is set as the length of the reference closest in size to the candidate translation.

Due to the sparsity of n-grams with large n and the geometric average of n-gram precisions, BLEU is not suitable for sentence-level evaluation. Several smoothing approaches have been proposed to alleviate this issue, such as the standard plus-one smoothing (Lin and Och, 2004) and combinations of smoothing techniques (Chen and Cherry, 2014).

A great deal of methods have been proposed to improve the performance of BLEU. These include metrics such as m-bleu (Agarwal and Lavie, 2008) and Amber (Chen and Kuhn, 2011). However, these metrics still treat n-grams in different references equally, regardless of whether the n-gram appears only once or is found in all references.

2.2 NIST

The NIST metric weights n-grams that occur less frequently in references more heavily (Doddington, 2002), as shown in Eq. 2.

$$S\_N = \sum_{n=1}^{N} \left\{ \sum_{\substack{w_1 \dots w_n \\ co-occur}} Info(w_1 \dots w_n) / \sum_{\substack{w_1 \dots w_n \\ \text{in system}}} (1) \right\} \times exp\left\{ \beta log_2 \left[min(\frac{L_{sys}}{\overline{L_{ref}}}, 1) \right] \right\}, \tag{2}$$

where

$$Info(w_1 \dots w_n) = log(\frac{\text{\# of occur of } w_1 \dots w_{n-1}}{\text{\# of occur of } w_1 \dots w_n})$$

and $\overline{L_{ref}}$ is the average number of words in all references, L_{sys} is the number of words in the system translation, β is used as a weight for the penalty factor, and N is often 5.

The NIST metric focuses on non-popular n-grams in references and assumes that highly frequent n-grams, such as function words, tend to carry little meaning. However, this method consequently weakens the validity of n-grams that recur in multiple references. Since all references are valid translations for the same source text, one would expect multiple references to share common words and phrases that convey core meaning. Therefore, reducing the importance of these common n-grams is not beneficial to quality evaluation.

2.3 Improvements on n-gram based metrics

Current improvements on the n-gram co-occurrence evaluation metrics can be divided into three categories. The first category extends the scope of similarity detection by using a more flexible matching strategy, for example using WordNet to capture synonyms as in METEOR (Banerjee and Lavie, 2005). The second category uses different functions to calculate the degree of similarity, for example edit distance, error rate, semantic distance (Nießen et al., 2000; Leusch et al., 2003; Snover et al., 2006; Snover et al., 2009). And the last category weights or combines the outcome of similarity functions as features (Liu et al., 2010; Giménez and Màrquez, 2010).

These methods focus on different forms of comparison between candidates and references. However, to our knowledge there are no other attempts to mine recurring information from multiple references if these are provided. Assuming all the possible translations form a "semantic" space, each reference only covers a subspace. The recurring n-grams among them should constitute the core part of this semantic space, which is more likely to represent the meaning of the source text. It is this kind of information that we want to explore and apply with our n-gram weighting technique.

3 Exploring information from multiple references

Although references can vary with translators and styles, many essential words and expressions are usually expected to be identical or similar for the same source text. For example, consider the segments below from our datasets: four references and one system (Sys) translation.

Ref1: *The gunman was shot to death by the police.*

Ref2: *Police killed the gunman.*

Ref3: *The gunman was shot dead by the police.*

Ref4: *The gunman was shot to death by the police.*

Sys: *Gunman is shot dead by police.*

Four unigrams appear in all four references: ., *the, gunman, police*. The words *shot* and *by* appear three times whilst *dead* only appears once. The most recurring content unigrams in the references convey most of the meaning of the sentence. For the system output, there are six unigrams matching those in references, among them *gunman, police*, which occur in all references. However these are equally counted by BLEU and set as to have the lowest information value by NIST, compared to other unigrams such as *dead*, which only occurs once in one reference. This results in very low scores. The smoothed BLEU score for this segment is 0.3217 since there are no 3/4-grams matchings. The NIST score is 2.8867. However this is a rather good translation, with human judgements on fluency and accuracy of 4 and 4.7, respectively (human judgement ranges over 1-5). Taking into account the recurring n-grams in multiple references and assigning them heavier weights could thus be helpful to capture the quality of this system translation.

If function words are disregarded, an n-gram that recurs in most of the references could represent the core meaning of the source. The more often an n-gram is found in multiple references, the higher the probability that a matching n-gram appears in a high quality translation. Therefore, focusing on common n-grams found in multiple references, we propose a modified n-gram weighting approach for BLEU and NIST on the basis of the following factors.

3.1 Frequency of recurring n-grams in references

The degree of n-gram recurrence among references is represented by the number of times an n-gram appears in the references M divided by the total number of references $refno$. Nevertheless, it is unlikely that the number of times an n-gram occurs in references increases the significance of the respective n-gram by that number compared to an n-gram that occurs only once. Therefore we use the logarithm ratio instead. As an n-gram may be contained in all references, the add-one approach is then applied to avoid the expression in the logarithm returning a value of zero, as in Eq. 3.

$$log(1 + M/refno) \qquad (3)$$

This attempt to reweight n-grams in BLEU and information content in NIST however did not lead to satisfactory results. Upon further analysis of the weighting strategy, we discovered that it is biased towards n-grams with a small n whose co-occurrence probability may be much higher than n-grams with a large n. In other words, the weighting is biased towards high-frequent function words, thus deviating from our original intention of assigning heavier weight to content (recurring) n-grams. As a result, using frequency as the only factor for n-gram reweighting is insufficient to capture useful information in multiple references.

3.2 Divergence of n-grams

In order to reduce the weight of most frequent function words, the distribution of n-grams is taken into account to improve Eq. 3. Less overlap among references may indicate that the translation is difficult, or that several different valid translations exist. In this scenario, recurring n-grams tend to be function words rather than content words. For instance, only function words repeat in the three references below, which may indicate that the source can be translated in many ways:

a. *At this time, the police have blocked the bombing scene.*

b. *They have now sealed off the spot.*

c. *The police has already blockaded the scene of the explosion.*

To address the problem, a unit called n-gram divergence is defined as in Eq. 4 to describe the degree of concentration of n-grams among references. The more divergent the distribution of n-grams in the references, the lower weight that is assigned to the most frequent common n-grams in the references.

$$Ngram_{diver} = \frac{\text{\# type of n-gram}}{\text{\# total of n-gram}}, \qquad (4)$$

i.e. the count of different n-grams divided by total number of n-grams. The higher the number of n-gram types found in multiple references, the more flexible or variable the translation will be, resulting in a higher value for n-gram divergence. This unit is used to measure the degree to which multiple references are similar.

3.3 Length of n-grams

The quality of the translation improves with the length of the matching n-grams, both in terms of fluency and accuracy evaluation. An additional modification of Eq. 3 is performed by replacing the constant 1 with the length of n-gram n, as depicted in Eq. 5,

$$log(n + M/refno). \qquad (5)$$

Eq. 6, denoted as R, is the final expression applied to reweight n-grams in BLEU and NIST and incorporates all of the factors described above.

$$R = Ngram_{diver} \times log(n + M/refno) \qquad (6)$$

3.4 Using Zipf's law

An alternative approach of neutralising function words in references is to use the Zipf's law. Ha et al. (2002) verify Zipf's law on n-grams by ranking all n-grams ($n \geq 1$). So the n-grams recurring in references in Eq. 3 can be represented by the product between frequency f and the ranking order r of n-grams divided by $refno$, as in Eq. 7.

$$R' = log(1 + r \times f/refno) \qquad (7)$$

The new BLEU score, denoted as S_{BM}, i.e., Score of BM, is rewritten in Eq. 8,

$$S\_{BM} = BP \times exp(\sum_{n=1}^{N} w_n log(R \times P_n)), \qquad (8)$$

where BP, w_n and P_n are as stated as in Eq. 1. Add-one smoothing is applied to the segment level evaluation. In the equation, R can be replaced by R'. We compare the performance of the two weighting approaches in our experiments.

The modified NIST score formula, denoted as S_{NM} (Score of metric NM), is shown as Eq. 9.

$$S\_{NM} = \sum_{n=1}^{N} \left\{ \sum_{\substack{w_1 \ldots w_n \\ co-occur}} Info(w_1 \ldots w_n) / \sum_{\substack{w_1 \ldots w_n \\ \text{in system}}} (1) \right\} \times R \times exp\left\{ \beta log_2 \left[min(\frac{L_{sys}}{\overline{L}_{ref}}, 1) \right] \right\} \qquad (9)$$

3.5 Arithmetic mean BLEU

Another modification in NIST with respect to BLEU is the fact that it uses arithmetic instead of geometric mean (Doddington, 2002). Although our method focuses on scenarios with multiple references in evaluation, further comparison to NIST is made by changing the averaging strategy in BM to that of NIST, denoted as BMA (BLEU Multi-reference Arithmetic mean).

4 Experiments and results

4.1 Data

Despite of the shortage of multiple references for MT evaluation, two datasets are found suitable to conduct experiments to test our reweighting strategy. The first dataset is Multiple-Translation Chinese Part 2 (MTC-P2) (LDC2003T17), including 4 sets of human translations for a single set of Mandarin Chinese source materials, 100 stories with 212-707 Chinese characters, totally 878 segments. There are three system translations P2-05,

P2-09 and P2-14 with human judgements on fluency and accuracy respectively. The other dataset is Multiple-Translation Chinese Part 4 (MTC-P4) (LDC2006T04), also with 4 references, 100 news stories each with 280-605 characters, totally 919 segments. Six system translations P4-09, P4-11, P4-12, P4-14, P4-15 and P4-22 are judged by 2-3 human annotators.

Human judgements for the nine system translations were carried out at segment level within limited time. Hence we firstly check the agreement among human annotators. We considered an agreement when two out of two judgements or two out of three judgements are same. The agreement proportion at system level is the number of segments agreed upon divided by the total number of segments in the system. This agreement proportion is normalised by the degree of agreement by chance, i.e., using Cohen's kappa coefficient which is commonly applied in WMT. Since the scale of human annotation is 1 to 5, the agreement by chance value is set as 0.2. Table 1 shows the kappa agreement of human annotators on all system translations. Note that the average agreement on fluency is only fair, while the agreement on accuracy is even worse. Given the subjectivity of the task, however, this range of figures is not uncommon.

	Flu	Acc
p2-05	0.311	0.254
p2-09	0.320	0.257
p2-14	0.294	0.280
p4-09	0.132	0.123
p4-11	0.143	0.094
p4-12	0.218	0.053
p4-14	0.247	0.106
p4-15	0.150	0.120
p4-22	0.229	0.264
Mean	0.227	0.172

Table 1: Kappa agreement of human judgement on system translations

Our evaluation is performed at the system, document and segment levels. Different human judgements are averaged for the final score of a segment, and all segment scores in a text are averaged for the final document score. While scores for smoothed BLEU and standard BLEU are similar at system and document levels, the standard BLEU score is generally below the smoothed BLEU score for segment level. BM is derived from smoothed BLEU.

4.2 System level

We compare the Pearson correlation for various automatic evaluation scores with human scores at system level in terms of fluency (Flu) and accuracy (Acc), as shown in Table 2.

	BLEU	BM	BMA	NIST	NM
Flu	0.7021	0.7090	**0.7136**	0.5657	0.5938
Acc	0.6957	0.6947	0.7114	**0.7941**	0.7756

Table 2: Pearson correlation at system level

For fluency judgements, BMA displays the highest correlation with human scores, 26.14% higher than NIST score and 1.64% better than BLEU. These results are promising. Compared to BLEU, BM is slightly better. NM scores also outperform NIST. The results are not as positive when measuring correlation to accuracy judgements. NIST still performs the best, however, the gap between BMA and NIST is much lower for accuracy than for fluency.

When we apply Eq. 7 to reweight BLEU, the correlation with human scores at system level achieves 0.6926 on fluency and 0.7391 on accuracy. This represents a distinct increase in correlation for accuracy judgements, making the gap to the best performing metric (NIST) even smaller. However, it leads to a slight decrease in correlation for fluency evaluation. Overall, our results demonstrate that the proposed methods is effective for fluency evaluation at system level.

4.3 Document level

Tables 3 and 4 shows the metrics comparison for document level evaluation. For fluency (Table 3), BM outperforms BLEU in 6 out of 9 systems, and its average correlation exceeds that of standard BLEU. BMA leads to even more promising results compared to BLEU. However at document level the BMA metric does not perform as well as NIST even using the same averaging method. Note that the performance of NM is better than standard NIST, indicating that the use of recurring n-grams in multiple references works. In fact, NM leads to the best fluency evaluation for all systems.

For accuracy evaluation (Table 4), the performance of BM, BMA and NM varies with different system outputs. NM still performs the best overall.

The reweighting approach in Eq. 7 is clearly inferior to BM at document level, with only 2 out of 9 outputs sightly better than BM both on fluency and accuracy evaluation. We speculate that this may be because Zipf's law is less applicable to small scale datasets such as ours. Nevertheless, the n-gram weighting approach proposed in Eq. 6 proved effective.

	BLEU	BM	BMA	NIST	NM
p2-05	0.1510	0.1637	0.1627	**0.2495**	0.2401
p2-09	0.0990	0.0867	**0.0992**	0.0467	0.0653
p2-14	0.1666	0.1707	0.2102	0.2644	**0.2474**
p4-09	0.3423	0.3392	0.3716	**0.4343**	0.4291
p4-11	0.1310	0.1423	0.1492	0.1486	**0.1681**
p4-12	0.1479	0.1424	0.1711	0.1955	**0.2032**
p4-14	0.1168	0.1191	0.1373	**0.1610**	0.1577
p4-15	0.2384	0.2397	0.2703	**0.3189**	0.3163
p4-22	0.1568	0.1589	0.1660	0.2202	**0.2211**
Mean	0.1722	0.1736	0.1931	0.2266	**0.2276**

Table 3: Doc-level Pearson correlation on fluency

	BLEU	BM	BMA	NIST	NM
p2-05	0.2571	0.2621	0.2778	0.3334	**0.3549**
p2-09	0.0942	0.0874	**0.1015**	0.0936	0.0850
p2-14	0.2613	0.2633	0.2943	**0.3161**	0.3015
p4-09	0.3867	0.3808	0.4186	**0.4928**	0.4844
p4-11	0.1656	0.1825	0.1890	0.1604	**0.2016**
p4-12	0.3218	0.3197	0.3537	0.3751	**0.3847**
p4-14	0.1532	0.1495	0.1719	**0.1934**	0.1828
p4-15	0.2367	0.2292	0.2730	**0.4010**	0.3887
p4-22	0.0887	0.0922	0.0829	**0.2428**	0.2363
Mean	0.2184	0.2185	0.2403	0.2898	**0.2911**

Table 4: Doc-level Pearson correlation on accuracy

4.4 Segment level

In all datasets, BM performs worse at segment level than smoothed BLEU. The average gap in correlation between BM and BLEU is 4.5% on fluency and 2.9% on accuracy. NM outperforms NIST at segment level on 4 out of 9 systems on fluency, but overall, NM is slightly worse than NIST, for both fluency and accuracy.

We believe the main reason is that data sparsity of recurring n-grams at segment level is more severe than at document and system levels. The second possible cause is that the smoothed BLEU score is not based on actual n-gram matching between the candidates and references, but a predictable score computed even if there is no n-gram matching. It is hard to apply common information in multiple references to this score. Closer investigation is presented in the following section. Also important, the low agreement among humans on quality judgements might pose more challenges to evaluation than the methods themselves.

4.5 Discussion

Fluency and accuracy evaluation At system and document level, the reweighting strategy by considering multiple references yields better results than both BLEU and NIST. The improvements on fluency are much promising than on accuracy.

We examine the recurring n-grams in the four references in MTC-P2 in detail. Taking unigrams as example, among the unigrams in all references, 48.7% occur in a single reference, 17.8% are covered by any two references. As expected, the percentage of common n-grams decreases as we increase the number of references. There is a sharp drop when the number of references changes from one to two, indicating that most n-grams appear only in one reference. This becomes a more severe limitation of the dataset for n-grams with larger n, as depicted in Figure 1. 91.86% of 4-grams appear in a single reference, while only 0.24% are covered by the four references.

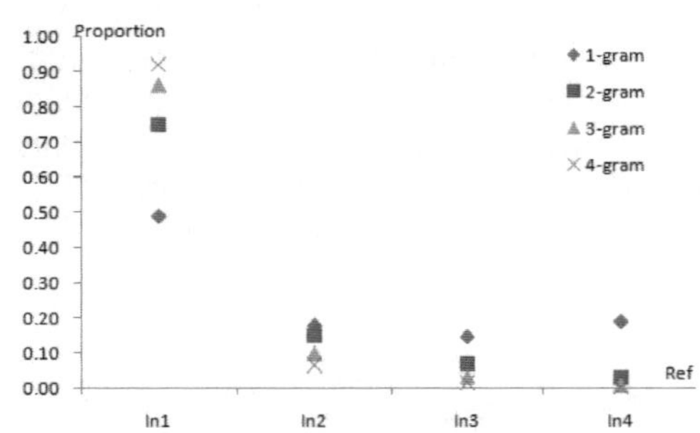

Figure 1: Common 1-4grams in references of MTC P2 (InX denotes covered by X references)

For the matching n-grams between a candidate and references, all n-gram counts but unigram counts go down as we increase the number of references. Figure 2 illustrates the distribution of matching n-grams for the P2-05 system as an instance. Among the matching unigrams, 20% appear in one of the references, 17% appear in two of them, 22% in three, and 41% are covered by all references. Notice that the matching unigrams that occur in all four references exceed the unigrams that appear in less than four references. However, most of these unigrams are function words and punctuation. Weighting them more heavily has a negative effect on accuracy evaluation, especially at segment level. This also explains the increase in correlation for accuracy when Zipf's law is applied to deduce the effect of function words. On the other hand, many higher-order n-grams were found in more than one reference, which explains the improvements on fluency evaluation.

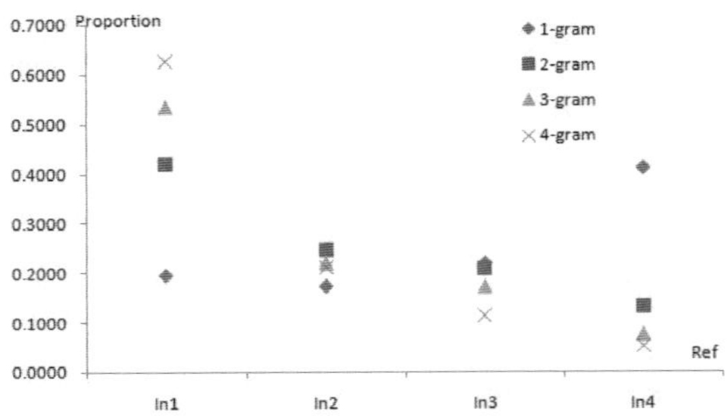

Figure 2: Matching n-grams distribution of P2-05

Content vs functional n-grams Using Eq. 7 to assign heavier weight to content n-grams improves the correlation for accuracy evaluation at system level, but leads to a drop in correlation for document and segment level evaluations. Thus there is no clear advantage for using such an approach to weighting function words and content n-grams differently, at least for the datasets used in the experiments.

Influence of number of references Our experiments use four references, only a small portion of the valid translations for the source texts. This somewhat limited the exploration of the proposed reweighting method.

Eq. 5 indicates that the larger the number of references, the lower the weighting ratio for recurring n-grams. For instance, for bigrams appearing twice in 10 references, the outcome of Eq. 5 is 0.3424, while for bigrams appearing once, the outcome of Eq. 5 is 0.3222. However since there are only four references, the weighting ratio is larger, 0.3979/0.3522. In other words, the larger the number of references, the lower the impact of the reweighting method on the results.

Increasing the number of references could help discriminate function words and content words as well. To check the recurrence of n-grams in larger numbers of references, we investigate the devset1-3 of BTEC (Takezawa et al., 2002), which contains 1512 source sentences, each with 16 English references. We show the average 1-4grams distribution over 2 to 16 translations in Figure 3. As expected, the proportion of n-grams covered by multiple references decreases as the number of references increases, showing that more translation variety is obtained with more references. The total number of 1-4grams found in three references (In3) is still as high as 28.4%, demonstrating the potential benefits of exploring multiple references.

5 Conclusions and future work

Recurring n-grams in references can help capture important words and sequences of words that are chosen by various translators. By combining recurrence distributions, divergence information and the length of n-grams, a modified weighting strategy for BLEU and NIST was proposed to make better use of multiple references in translation evaluation. This strategy was tested with different reweighting schemes. The results on two datasets proved promising.

Overall, the strategy favours fluency evaluation over accuracy evaluation. To address that, in future work we will further improve the metric by tackling common n-grams carrying lower information content. We also observed how the weaknesses of exact n-gram matching affects the performance of the proposed metrics. In future work, in addition to the n-gram distributions, divergence information and length of n-grams, synonym recurrence information will also be explored. Adapting this approach to other metrics such as METEOR is another direction for future work.

Acknowledgements

Ying Qin's work is supported by a Beijing Social Science Funding Project (15WYA006) and the National Research Centre for Foreign Language Education, BFSU.

References

Agarwal, A and A Lavie. 2008. Meteor, m-bleu and m-ter: Evaluation metrics for high-correlation with human rankings of machine translation output. In *Proceedings of the Third Workshop on Statistical Machine Translation. ACL*, pages 115–118.

Banerjee, S and A Lavie. 2005. Meteor: An automatic metric for mt evaluation with improved correlation with human judgments. In *Proceedings of the ACL Workshop on Intrinsic and Extrinsic Evaluation Measures for Machine Translation and/or Summarization*, pages 65–72.

Bojar, Ondrej, Christian Buck, Christian Federmann, et al. 2014. Findings of the 2014 workshop on statistical machine translation. In *Proceedings of the Ninth Workshop on Statistical Machine Translation*, pages 12–58.

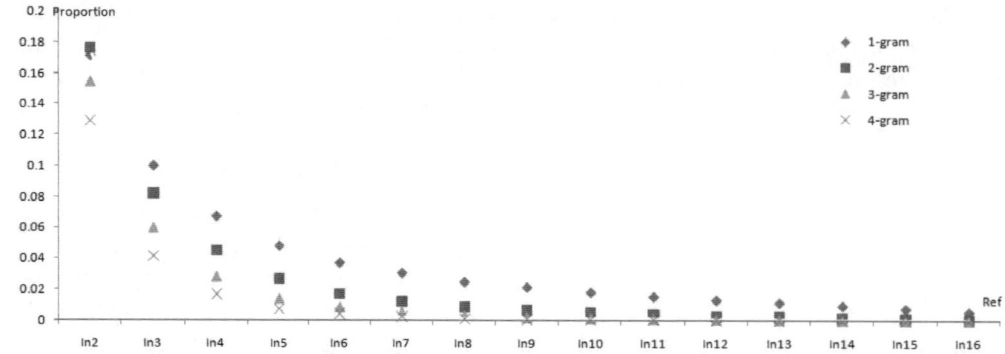

Figure 3: 1-4grams distribution in the BTEC corpus

Chen, Boxing and Colin Cherry. 2014. A systematic comparison of smoothing techniques for sentence-level bleu. In *ACL 2014*, page 362.

Chen, Boxing and Roland Kuhn. 2011. Amber: A modified bleu, enhanced ranking metric. In *Proceedings of the 6th Workshop on Statistical Machine Translation*, pages 71–77.

Doddington, G. 2002. Automatic evaluation of machine translation quality using n-gram co-occurrence statistics. In *Proceedings of the second international conference on Human Language Technology Research*, pages 138–145.

Dreyer, Markus and Daniel Marcu. 2012. Hyter: Meaning-equivalent semantics for translation evaluation. In *2012 Conference of the North American Chapter of the ACL: Human Language Technologies*, pages 162–171.

Gamon, Michael, Anthony Aue, and Martine Smets. 2005. Sentence-level mt evaluation without reference translations: Beyond language modeling. In *Proceedings of EAMT*, pages 103–111.

Giménez, Jesús and Lluís Màrquez. 2010. Asiya: An Open Toolkit for Automatic Machine Translation (Meta-)Evaluation. *The Prague Bulletin of Mathematical Linguistics*, (94):77–86.

Ha, Le Quan, Elvira I Sicilia-Garcia, Ji Ming, and F Jack Smith. 2002. Extension of zipf's law to words and phrases. In *Proceedings of the 19th international conference on Computational linguistics*, pages 1–6. ACL.

Leusch, G, N Ueffing, and H Ney. 2003. A novel string-to-string distance measure with applications to machine translation evaluation. In *Proceedings of MT Summit IX*, pages 33–40.

Lin, Chin Yew and Franz Josef Och. 2004. Orange: a method for evaluating automatic evaluation metrics for machine translation. In *Proceedings of the 20th international conference on Computational Linguistics.ACL*, pages 501–507.

Liu, C, D Dahlmeier, and H. T. Ng. 2010. Tesla: Translation evaluation of sentences with linear-programming-based analysis. In *Proceedings of the Joint Fifth Workshop on Statistical Machine Translation and MetricsMATR. ACL*, pages 354–359.

Nießen, Sonja, Franz Josef Och, Gregor Leusch, Hermann Ney, et al. 2000. An evaluation tool for machine translation: Fast evaluation for mt research. In *LREC*.

Papineni, K, S Roukos, T Ward, et al. 2002. Bleu: a method for automatic evaluation of machine translation. In *Proceedings of the 40th annual meeting on ACL*, pages 311–318.

Snover, Matthew, Bonnie Dorr, Richard Schwartz, Linnea Micciulla, and John Makhoul. 2006. A study of translation edit rate with targeted human annotation. In *Proceedings of association for machine translation in the Americas*, pages 223–231.

Snover, Matthew, Nitin Madnani, Bonnie J Dorr, and Richard Schwartz. 2009. Fluency, adequacy, or hter?: exploring different human judgments with a tunable mt metric. In *Proceedings of the Fourth Workshop on Statistical Machine Translation*, pages 259–268. ACL.

Specia, L, D Raj, and M. Turchi. 2010. Machine translation evaluation versus quality estimation. *Machine translation*, 24(1):39–50.

Takezawa, Toshiyuki, Eiichiro Sumita, Fumiaki Sugaya, Hirofumi Yamamoto, and Seiichi Yamamoto. 2002. Toward a broad-coverage bilingual corpus for speech translation of travel conversations in the real world. In *LREC*, pages 147–152.

Searching for Context: a Study on Document-Level Labels for Translation Quality Estimation

Carolina Scarton[1], Marcos Zampieri[2,3], Mihaela Vela[2], Josef van Genabith[2,3] and Lucia Specia[1]
[1]University of Sheffield / Regent Court, 211 Portobello, Sheffield, UK
[2]Saarland University / Campus A2.2, Saarbrücken, Germany
[3]German Research Centre for Artificial Intelligence / Saarbrücken, Germany
{c.scarton,l.specia}@sheffield.ac.uk
{marcos.zampieri,m.vela}@uni-saarland.de
josef.van_genabith@dfki.de

Abstract

In this paper we analyse the use of popular automatic machine translation evaluation metrics to provide labels for quality estimation at document and paragraph levels. We highlight crucial limitations of such metrics for this task, mainly the fact that they disregard the discourse structure of the texts. To better understand these limitations, we designed experiments with human annotators and proposed a way of quantifying differences in translation quality that can only be observed when sentences are judged in the context of entire documents or paragraphs. Our results indicate that the use of context can lead to more informative labels for quality annotation beyond sentence level.

1 Introduction

Quality estimation (QE) of machine translation (MT) (Blatz et al., 2004; Specia et al., 2009) is an area that focuses on predicting the quality of new, unseen machine translation data without relying on human references. This is done by training models using features extracted from source and target texts and, when available, from the MT system, along with a quality label for each instance.

Most current work on QE is done at the sentence level. A popular application of sentence-level QE is to support post-editing of MT (He et al., 2010). As quality labels, Likert scores have been used for post-editing effort, as well as post-editing time and edit distance between the MT output and the final version – HTER (Snover et al., 2006).

There are, however, scenarios where quality prediction beyond sentence level is needed, most notably in cases when automatic translations without post-editing are required. This is the case, for example, of quality prediction for an entire product review translation in order to decide whether or not it can be published as is, so that customers speaking other languages can understand it.

The quality of a document is often seen as some form of aggregation of the quality of its sentences. We claim, however, that document-level quality assessment should consider more information than sentence-level quality. This includes, for example, the topic and structure of the document and the relationship between its sentences. While certain sentences are considered perfect in isolation, their combination in context may lead to incoherent text. Conversely, while a sentence can be considered poor in isolation, when put in context, it may benefit from information in surrounding sentences, leading to a document that is fit for purpose.

Document-level quality prediction is a rather understudied problem. Recent work has looked into document-level prediction (Scarton and Specia, 2014; Soricut and Echihabi, 2010) using automatic metrics such as BLEU (Papineni et al., 2002) and TER (Snover et al., 2006) as quality labels. However, their results highlighted issues with these metrics for the task at hand: the evaluation of the scores predicted in terms of mean error was inconclusive. In most cases, the prediction model only slightly improves over a simple baseline where the average BLEU or TER score of the training documents is assigned to all test documents.

Other studies have considered document-level information in order to improve, analyse or automatically evaluate MT output (not for QE purposes). Carpuat and Simard (2012) report that MT output is overall consistent in its lexical choices, nearly as consistent as manually translated texts. Meyer and Webber (2013) and Li et al. (2014) show that the translation of connectives differs from humans to MT, and that the presence of explicit connectives correlates with higher HTER values. Guzmán et al. (2014) explore rhetorical structure (RST) trees (Mann and Thompson, 1987) for automatic evaluation of MT into English, outperforming traditional metrics at system-level evaluation.

Thus far, no previous work has investigated ways to provide a global quality score for an entire document that takes into account document structure, without access to reference translations. Previous work on document-level QE use automatic evaluation metrics as quality labels that do not consider document-level structures and are developed for inter-system rather than intra-system evaluation. Also, previous work on evalution of MT does not focus on complete evaluation at document-level.

In this paper, we show that the use of BLEU and other automatic metrics as quality labels do not help to successfully distinguish different quality levels. We discuss the role of document-wide information for document-level quality estimation and present two experiments with human annotators.

In the first experiment, translators are asked to subjectively assess paragraphs in terms of cohesion and coherence (herein, SUBJ). In the second experiment, a two-pass post-editing experiment is performed in order to measure the difference between corrections made with and without wider contexts (the tow passes are called PE1 and PE2, repectively).

The task of assessing paragraphs according to cohesion and coherence is highly subjective and thus the results of the first study did not show high agreement among annotators. The results of the two-stage post-editing experiment showed significant differences from the post-editing of sentences without context to the second stage where sentences were further corrected in context. This is an indication that certain translation issues can only be solved by relying on wider contexts, which is a crucial information for document-level QE. A manual analysis was conducted to evaluate differences between PE1 and PE2. Although several of the changes were found to be related to style or other non-discourse related phenomena, many discourse related changes were performed that were only possible given the wider context available.

In the remainder of this paper we first present related work in Section 2. In Section 3 we discuss the use of BLEU-style metrics for QE at document level. Section 4 describes the experimental set up used in the paper. Section 5 presents the first study were the annotators assess quality in terms of cohesion and coherence, while Section 6 shows the two-pass post-editing experiment and its results. The conclusions and future work are presented in Section 7.

2 Related work

The research reported here is about quality estimation at document-level. Therefore, work on document-level features and document-level quality prediction are both relevant, as well as studies on how discourse phenomena manifest in the output of MT systems.

Soricut and Echihabi (2010) propose document-level features to predict document-level quality for ranking purposes, having BLEU as quality label. While promising results were reported for ranking of translations for different source documents, the results for predicting absolute scores proved inconclusive. For two out of four domains, the prediction model only slightly improves over a baseline where the average BLEU score of the training documents is assigned to all test documents. In other words, most documents have similar BLEU scores, and therefore the training mean is a hard baseline to beat.

Scarton and Specia (2014) propose a number of discourse-informed features in order to predict BLEU and TER at document level. They also found the use of these metrics as quality labels problematic: the error scores of several QE models were very close to that obtained by the training mean baseline. Even when mixing translations from different MT systems, BLEU and TER were not found to be discriminative enough.

Carpuat and Simard (2012) provide a detailed evaluation of lexical consistency in translations of documents produced by a statistical MT (SMT) system, i.e., on the consistency of words and phrases in the translation of a given source text. SMT was found to be overall consistent in its lexical choices, nearly as consistent as manually translated texts.

Meyer and Webber (2013) present a study on implicit discourse connectives in translation. The phenomenon is evaluated using human references and machine translations for English-French and English-German. They found that humans translated explicit connectives in the source (English) into implicit connectives in the target (German and French) in 18% of the cases. MT systems translated explicit connectives into implicit ones less often.

Li et al. (2014) study connectives in order to improve MT for Chinese-English and Arabic-English. They show that the presence of explicit connectives correlates with high HTER for Chinese-English only. Chinese-English also showed correlation between ambiguous connectives and higher HTER. When comparing the presence of discourse connectives in translations and post-editions, they found that cases of connectives only appearing in the translation or post-edition also show correlation with high HTER scores.

Guzmán et al. (2014) explore RST trees (Mann and Thompson, 1987) for automatic evaluation of MT into English, with a discourse parser to annotate RST trees at sentence level in English. They compare the discourse units of machine translations with those in the references by using tree kernels to compute the number of common subtrees between the two trees. This metric outperformed others at system-level evaluation.

In summary, no previous work has investigated ways to provide a global quality score for an entire document that takes into account document structure, neither for evaluation nor for estimation purposes.

3 Automatic evaluation metrics as quality labels for document-level QE

As discussed in Section 2, although the use of BLEU-style metrics as quality scores for document-level QE clearly seems inadequate, previous work resorted to these automatic metrics because of the lack of better labels. In order to better understand this problem, we conducted an experiment with French-English translations from the LIG corpus (Potet et al., 2012). We took the first part of the corpus containing 119 source documents on the news domain (from various WMT news test sets), their MT by a phrase-based SMT system, a post-edited version of these translations by a human translator, and a reference translation. We used a range of automatic metrics such as BLEU, TER, METEOR-ex (exact match) and METEOR-st (stem match), which are based on a comparison between machine translations and human references, and the "human-targeted" version of BLEU and TER, where machine translations are compared against their post-editions: HBLEU and HTER. Table 1 shows the results of the average score (AVG) for each metric considering all documents, as well as the standard deviation (STDEV).

	AVG	STDEV
BLEU (↑)	0.27	0.05
TER (↓)	0.53	0.07
METEOR-ex (↑)	0.29	0.03
METEOR-st (↑)	0.30	0.03
HTER (↓)	0.21	0.03
HBLEU (↑)	0.64	0.05

Table 1: Average metric scores in the LIG corpus.

We conducted a similar analysis on the English-German (EN-DE) news test set from WMT13 (Bojar et al., 2013), which contains 52 documents, both at document and paragraph levels. Three MT systems were considered in this analysis: **UEDIN** (an SMT system), **PROMT** (a hybrid system) and **RBMT-1** (a rule-based system). Average metric scores are shown in Table 2.

For all the metrics and corpora, the STDEV values for documents are very small (below 0.1), indicating that all documents are considered similar in terms of quality according to these metrics (the scores are all very close to the mean).

At paragraph level (Table 2), the scores variation increases, with BLEU showing the highest variation. However, the very high STDEV values for BLEU (very close to the actual average score for all documents) is most likely due to the fact that BLEU does not perform well for short segments such as a paragraph due to the n-gram sparsity at this level, as shown in Stanojević and Sima'an (2014).

Overall, it is important to emphasise that BLEU-style metrics were created to evaluate different MT systems based on the same input, as opposed to evaluating different outputs of a single MT system, as we do here. The experiments in Section 6 attempt to shed some light on alternative ways to accurately measure document-level quality, with an emphasis on designing a label for document-level quality prediction.

	UEDIN				PROMT				RBMT-1			
	Document		Paragraph		Document		Paragraph		Document		Paragraph	
	AVG	STDEV	AVG	STDEV	AVG	STDEV	AVG	STDEV	AVG	STDEV	AVG	STDEV
BLEU (↑)	0.2	0.048	0.2	0.16	0.19	0.05	0.2	0.16	0.15	0.04	0.16	0.14
TER (↓)	0.62	0.063	0.63	0.24	0.61	0.07	0.62	0.25	0.66	0.06	0.67	0.23
METEOR-ex (↑)	0.37	0.056	0.37	0.16	0.36	0.06	0.37	0.16	0.32	0.05	0.33	0.15
METEOR-st (↑)	0.39	0.058	0.39	0.16	0.38	0.06	0.39	0.16	0.34	0.05	0.35	0.15

Table 2: Average metric scores for automatic metrics in the WMT13 EN-DE corpus.

4 Experimental settings

In the following experiments, we consider a paragraph as a "document". This decision was made to make the annotation feasible, given the time and resources available. Although the datasets are different for the two subtasks, they were taken from the same larger corpus and annotated by the the same group of translators.

4.1 Methods

The SUBJ experiment (Section 5) consists in assessing the quality of paragraphs in terms of cohesion and coherence. We define cohesion as the linguistic marks (cohesive devices) that connect clauses, sentences or paragraphs together; coherence captures whether clauses, sentences or paragraphs are connected in a logical way, i.e. whether they make sense together (Stede, 2011). In order to assess these two phenomena, we propose a 4-point scale. For coherence: 1=Completely coherent; 2=Mostly coherent; 3=Little coherent, and 4=Incoherent; for cohesion: 1=Flawless; 2=Good; 3=Disfluent and 4=Incomprehensible.

PE1 and PE2 (Section 6) consist in objective assessments through the post-editing of MT sentences in two rounds: in isolation and in context. In the first round (PE1), annotators were asked to post-edit sentences which were shown to them out of context. In the second round (PE2), they were asked to further post-edit the same sentences now given in context and fix any other issues that could only be solved by relying on information beyond individual sentences. For this, each annotator was given as input the output of their PE1, i.e. the sentences they had previously post-edited themselves.

4.2 Data

The datasets were extracted from the test set of the EN-DE WMT13 MT shared task. EN-DE was chosen given the availability of in-house annotators for this language pair. Outputs of the **UEDIN** SMT system were chosen as this was the best participating system for this language pair (Bojar et al., 2013). For the SUBJ experiment, paragraphs were randomly selected from the full corpus.

For PE1 and PE2, only source (English) paragraphs with 3-8 sentences were selected (filter S-NUMBER) to ensure that there is enough information beyond sentence-level to be evaluated and make the task feasible for the annotators. These paragraphs were further filtered to select those with cohesive devices. Cohesive devices are linguistic units that play a role in establishing cohesion between clauses, sentences or paragraphs (Halliday and Hasan, 1976). Pronouns and discourse connectives are examples of such devices. A list of pronouns and the connectives from Pitler and Nenkova (2009) was considered for that. Finally, paragraphs were ranked according to the number of cohesive devices they contain and the top 200 paragraphs were selected (filter C-DEV). Table 3 shows the statistics of the initial corpus and the resulting selection after each filter.

	Number of Paragraphs	Number of Cohesive devices
FULL CORPUS	1,215	6,488
S-NUMBER	394	3,329
C-DEV	200	2,338

Table 3: WMT13 English source corpus.

For the PE1 experiment, the paragraphs in C-DEV were randomised. Then, sets containing seven paragraphs each were created. For each set, the sentences of its paragraphs were also randomised in order to prevent annotators from having access to wider context when post-editing. The guidelines made it clear to annotators that the sentences they were given were not related, not necessarily part of the same document, and that therefore they should not try to find any relationships among them. For PE2, sentences were put together in their original paragraphs and presented to the annotators as a complete paragraph.

4.3 Annotators

The annotators for both experiments are students of "Translation Studies" courses (TS) in Saarland University, Saarbrücken, Germany. All students were familiar with concepts of MT and with post-editing tools. They were divided in two sets: (i) *Undergraduate students (B.A.)*, who are native speakers of German; and (ii) *Master students (M.A.)*, the majority of whom are native speakers of German. Non-native speakers have at least seven years of German language studies. B.A. and M.A. students have on average 10 years of English language studies. Only the B.A. group did the SUBJ experiment. PE1 and PE2 were done by all groups.

PE1 and PE2 were done using three CAT tools: PET (Aziz et al., 2012), Matecat (Federico et al., 2014) and memoQ.[1] These tools operate in very similar ways in terms of their post-editing functionalities, and therefore the use of multiple tools was only meant to make the experiment more interesting for students and did not affect the results. SUBJ was done without the help of tools.

5 Coherence/cohesion judgements

Our first attempt to access quality beyond sentence level was to explicitly guide annotators to consider discourse, where the notion of "discourse" covers various linguistic phenomena observed across discourse units. Discourse units can be clauses (intra-sentence), sentences or paragraphs.

Six sets with 17 paragraphs each were randomly selected from FULL CORPUS and given to 25 annotators from the B.A. group (each annotator evaluated one set). The task was to assess the paragraphs in terms of cohesion and coherence, using the scale given. The annotators could also rely on the source paragraphs. The agreement for the task in terms of Spearman's rank correlation and the number of students per set are presented in Table 4. The number of annotators per set is different because some of them did not complete the task.

	Set 1	Set 2	Set 3	Set 4	Set 5	Set 6
Annotators	3	3	4	7	6	2
Coherence	0.07	0.05	0.16	0.16	0.28	0.58
Cohesion	0.38	0.43	0.28	0.09	0.38	0.12

Table 4: Spearman's correlation for the SUBJ task.

A low agreement in terms of Spearman's ρ rank correlation was found for both cohesion (ranging from 0.09 to 0.43) and coherence (ranging from 0.05 to 0.28, having 0.58 as an outlier) evaluations. Naturally, these concepts are very abstract, even for humans, offering substantial room for subjective interpretations. In addition, the existence of (often many) errors in the MT output can hinder the understanding of the text altogether, rendering judgements on any specific quality dimension difficult to make.

6 Quality assessment as a two-stage post-editing task

Using HTER, we measured the edit distance between the post-edited versions with and without context. The hypothesis is that differences between the two versions are likely to be corrections that could only be performed with information beyond sentence level.

For PE1, paragraphs from C-DEV set were divided in sets of seven and the sentences were randomised in order to prevent annotators from having access to context when post-editing. For PE2, sentences were put together in their original paragraphs and presented to annotators in context. A total of 112 paragraphs were evaluated in 16 different sets, but only sets where more than two annotators completed the task are presented here (SET1, SET2, SET7, SET9, SET14 and SET15).[2]

6.1 Task agreement

Table 5 shows the agreement for the PE1 and PE2 tasks using Spearman's ρ rank correlation. It was calculated by comparing the HTER values of PE1 against MT and PE2 against PE1. "Annotators" shows the number of annotators per set.

The HTER values of PE1 against PE2 are low, as expected, since the changes from PE1 to PE2 are only expected to reflect discourse related issues. In other words, no major changes were expected during the PE2 task. The correlation in HTER between PE1 and MT varies from 0.22 to 0.56, whereas the correlation in HTER between PE1 and PE2 varies between -0.14 and 0.39. The negative figures mean that the annotators strongly disagreed regarding the changes made from PE1 to PE2. This can be related to stylistic choices made by annotators, although further analysis is needed to study that (see Section 6.3).

[1] https://www.memoq.com/

[2] Sets with only two annotators are difficult to interpret.

	SET1	SET2	SET5	SET6	SET9	SET10	SET14	SET15	SET16
Annotators	3	3	3	4	4	3	3	3	3
PE1 x MT - HTER	0.63	0.57	0.22	0.32	0.28	0.18	0.30	0.24	0.18
PE1 x PE2 - HTER	0.05	0.07	0.05	0.03	0.10	0.06	0.09	0.07	0.05
PE1 x MT - Spearman	0.52	0.50	0.52	0.56	0.37	0.41	0.71	0.22	0.46
PE2 x PE1 - Spearman	0.38	0.39	−0.03	−0.14	0.25	0.15	0.14	0.18	−0.02

Table 5: HTER values for PE1 against MT and PE1 against PE2 and Spearman's rank correlation values for PE2 against PE1.

6.2 Issues beyond sentence level

The values for HTER among annotators in PE2 against PE1 were averaged in order to provide a better visualisation of changes made in the paragraphs from PE1 to PE2. Figure 1 shows the results for individual paragraphs in all sets. The majority of the paragraphs were edited in the second round of post-editions. This clearly indicates that information beyond sentence-level can be helpful to further improve the output of MT systems. Between 0 and 19% of the words have changed from PE1 to PE2 (on average 7% of the words changed).

An example of changes from PE1 to PE2 related to discourse phenomena is shown in Table 6. In this example, two changes are related to the use of information beyond sentence level. The first is related to the substitution of the sentence *"Das ist falsch"* - literal translation of *"This is wrong"* - by *"Das ist nicht gut"*, which fits better into the context. The other change is related to explicitation of information. The annotator decided to change from *"Hier ist diese Schicht ist dünn"* - literal translation of *"Here, this layer is thin"* - to *"Hier ist die Anzahl solcher Menschen gering"*, a translation that better fits the context of the paragraph *"Here, the number of such people is low"*.

6.3 Manual analysis

In order to better understand the changes made by the annotators from PE1 to PE2 and also better explain the negative values in Table 5, we manually inspected the post-edited data. This analysis was done by senior translators who were not involved in the actual post-editing experiments. They counted modifications performed and categorised them into three classes:

Discourse/context changes: changes related to discourse phenomena, which could only be made by having the entire paragraph text.

Stylistic changes: changes related to translator's stylistic or preferential choices. These changes can be associated with the paragraph context, although they are not strictly necessary under our post-editing guidelines.

Other changes: changes that could have been made without the paragraph context (PE1), but were only performed during PE2.

The results are shown in Table 7. Low agreement in the number of changes and the type of changes among annotators is found in most sets. Although annotators were asked not to make unnecessary changes (stylistic), some of them made changes of this type (especially annotators 2 and 3 from sets 5 and 6, respectively). These sets are also the ones that show negative values in Table 5. Since stylistic changes do not follow a pattern and are related to the background and preferences of the translator, the high number of this type of change for these sets can be the reason for the negative correlation figures. In the case of SET6, annotator 2 also performed several changes classified as "other changes". This may have also led to negative correlation values. However, the reasons behind the negative values in SET16 could include other phenomena, since overall the variation in the changes performed is low. Further analysis considering the quality of the post-edition needs to be done in order to better explain these results.

7 Conclusions

This paper focused on judgements of translation quality at document level with the aim to produce labels for QE datasets. We highlighted issues with the use of automatic evaluation metrics for the task, and proposed and experimented with two methods for collecting labels using human annotators.

Our pilot study for quality assessment of paragraphs in terms of coherence and cohesion proved a very subjective and difficult task. Definitions of cohesion and coherence are vague and the annotators' previous knowledge can play an important role during the annotation task.

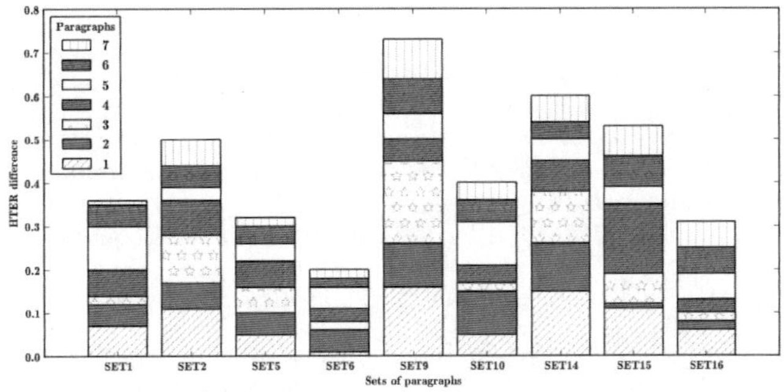

Figure 1: HTER between PE1 and PE2 for each of the seven paragraphs in each set.

PE1: - St. Petersburg bietet nicht viel kulturelles Angebot, Moskau hat viel mehr Kultur, es hat eine Grundlage.
Es ist schwer fr die Kunst, sich in unserem Umfeld durchzusetzen.
Wir brauchen das kulturelle Fundament, aber wir haben jetzt mehr Schriftsteller als Leser.
Das ist falsch.
In Europa gibt es viele neugierige Menschen, die auf Kunstausstellungen, Konzerte gehen.
Hier ist diese Schicht ist dünn.

PE2: - St. Petersburg bietet nicht viel kulturelles Angebot, Moskau hat viel mehr Kultur, es hat eine Grundlage.
Es ist schwer fr die Kunst, sich in unserem Umfeld durchzusetzen.
Wir brauchen das kulturelle Fundament, aber wir haben jetzt mehr Schriftsteller als Leser.
Das ist nicht gut.
In Europa gibt es viele neugierige Menschen, die auf Kunstausstellungen, Konzerte gehen.
Hier ist die Anzahl solcher Menschen gering.

SRC: - St. Petersburg is not a cultural capital, Moscow has much more culture, there is bedrock there.
It's hard for art to grow on our rocks.
We need cultural bedrock, but we now have more writers than readers.
This is wrong.
In Europe, there are many curious people, who go to art exhibits, concerts.
Here, this layer is thin.

Table 6: Example of changes from PE1 to PE2.

	SET1			SET2			SET5			SET6				SET9				SET10			SET14			SET15			SET16		
Annotators	1	2	3	1	2	3	1	2	3	1	2	3	4	1	2	3	4	1	2	3	1	2	3	1	2	3	1	2	3
Discourse/context	2	3	1	0	6	2	2	1	0	2	2	0	0	1	7	1	0	4	0	0	1	0	1	2	1	2	0	1	1
Stylistic	2	0	1	1	0	1	3	11	0	0	3	9	3	5	10	1	3	1	2	2	6	0	0	3	3	2	2	1	3
Other	1	2	4	0	2	2	2	2	6	0	6	0	1	2	0	4	2	1	0	2	2	0	1	1	2	1	1	1	0
Total errors	5	5	6	1	8	5	7	14	6	2	11	9	4	8	17	6	5	6	2	4	9	0	2	6	6	5	3	3	4

Table 7: Manual analysis of PE1 and PE2.

Our second method for collecting labels using human annotators is based on post-editing and showed promising results on uncovering issues that rely on wider context to be identified (and fixed). Although some annotators did not follow the task specification and made unnecessary modifications or did not correct relevant errors at sentence level, overall the results showed that several issues could only be solved with paragraph-wide context. Moreover, even though stylistic changes can be considered unnecessary, some of them could only be made based on wider context.

We will now turn to studying how to use the information reflecting differences between the two rounds of post-editing as labels for QE at document level. One possibility is to use the HTER between the second and first rounds directly, but this can lead to many "0" labels, i.e. no edits made. Another idea is to devise a function that combines the HTER without context (PE1 x MT) and the difference between PE1 and PE2.

Our findings reveal important discourse dependencies in translation that go beyond QE, with relevance for MT evaluation and MT in general.

Acknowledgments

This work was supported by the EXPERT (EU Marie Curie ITN No. 317471) project.

References

Aziz, Wilker, Sheila Castilho Monteiro de Sousa, and Lucia Specia. 2012. Cross-lingual Sentence Compression for Subtitles. In *The 16th Annual Conference of the European Association for Machine Translation*, pages 103–110, Trento, Italy.

Blatz, John, Erin Fitzgerald, George Foster, Simona Gandrabur, Cyril Goutte, Alex Kulesza, Alberto Sanchis, and Nicola Ueffing. 2004. Confidence Estimation for Machine Translation. In *The 20th International Conference on Computational Linguistics*, pages 315–321, Geneva, Switzerland.

Bojar, Ondřej, Christian Buck, Chris Callison-Burch, Christian Federmann, Barry Haddow, Philipp Koehn, Christof Monz, Matt Post, Radu Soricut, and Lucia Specia. 2013. Findings of the 2013 Workshop on Statistical Machine Translation. In *The Eighth Workshop on Statistical Machine Translation*, pages 1–44, Sofia, Bulgaria.

Carpuat, Marine and Michel Simard. 2012. The Trouble with SMT Consistency. In *The Seventh Workshop on Statistical Machine Translation*, pages 442–449, Montreal, Quebec, Canada.

Federico, Marcello, Nicola Bertoldi, Mauro Cettolo, Matteo Negri, Marco Turchi, Marco Trombetti, Alessandro Cattelan, Antonio Farina, Domenico Lupinetti, Andrea Martines, Alberto Massidda, Holger Schwenk, Loïc Barrault, Frederic Blain, Philipp Koehn, Christian Buck, and Ulrich Germann. 2014. THE MATECAT TOOL. In *The 25th International Conference on Computational Linguistics: System Demonstrations*, pages 129–132, Dublin, Ireland.

Guzmán, Francisco, Shafiq Joty, Lluís Màrquez, and Preslav Nakov. 2014. Using Discourse Structure Improves Machine Translation Evaluation. In *The 52nd Annual Meeting of the Association for Computational Linguistics*, pages 687–698, Baltimore, MD.

Halliday, Michael A. K. and Ruqaiya Hasan. 1976. *Cohesion in English*. English Language Series. Longman, London, UK.

He, Yifan, Yanjun Ma, Josef van Genabith, and Andy Way. 2010. Bridging SMT and TM with Translation Recommendation. In *The 48th Annual Meeting of the Association for Computational Linguistics*, pages 622–630, Uppsala, Sweden.

Li, Junyi Jessy, Marine Carpuat, and Ani Nenkova. 2014. Assessing the Discourse Factors that Influence the Quality of Machine Translation. In *The 52nd Annual Meeting of the Association for Computational Linguistics*, pages 283–288, Baltimore, MD.

Mann, Willian C. and Sandra A. Thompson. 1987. *Rhetorical Structure Theory: A Theory of Text Organization*. Cambridge University Press, Cambridge, UK.

Meyer, Thomas and Bonnie Webber. 2013. Implicitation of Discourse Connectives in (Machine) Translation. In *The Workshop on Discourse in Machine Translation*, pages 19–26, Sofia, Bulgaria.

Papineni, Kishore, Salim Roukos, Todd Ward, and Wei jing Zhu. 2002. BLEU: a Method for Automatic Evaluation of Machine Translation. In *The 40th Annual Meeting of the Association for Computational Linguistics*, pages 311–318, Philadelphia, PA.

Pitler, Emily and Ani Nenkova. 2009. Using Syntax to Disambiguate Explicit Discourse Connectives in Text. In *The Joint conference of the 47th Annual Meeting of the Association for Computational Linguistics and the Fourth International Joint Conference on Natural Language Processing of the Asian Federation of Natural Language Processing*, pages 13–16, Suntec, Singapore.

Potet, Marion, Emmanuelle Esperança-Rodier, Laurent Besacier, and Hervé Blanchon. 2012. Collection of a Large Database of French-English SMT Output Corrections. In *The 8th International Conference on Language Resources and Evaluation*, pages 23–25, Istanbul, Turkey.

Scarton, Carolina and Lucia Specia. 2014. Document-level translation quality estimation: exploring discourse and pseudo-references. In *The 17th Annual Conference of the European Association for Machine Translation*, pages 101–108, Dubrovnik, Croatia.

Snover, Matthew, Bonnie Dorr, Richard Schwartz, Linnea Micciulla, and John Makhoul. 2006. A Study of Translation Edit Rate with Targeted Human Annotation. In *Proceedings of the Seventh biennial conference of the Association for Machine Translation in the Americas*, AMTA 2006, pages 223–231, Cambridge, MA.

Soricut, Radu and Abdessamad Echihabi. 2010. TrustRank: Inducing Trust in Automatic Translations via Ranking. In *The 48th Annual Meeting of the Association for Computational Linguistics*, pages 612–621, Uppsala, Sweden.

Specia, Lucia, Marco Turchi, Nicola Cancedda, Marc Dymetman, and Nello Cristianini. 2009. Estimating the Sentence-Level Quality of Machine Translation Systems. In *The 13th Annual Conference of the European Association for Machine Translation*, pages 28–37, Barcelona, Spain.

Stanojević, Miloš and Khalil Sima'an. 2014. Fitting Sentence Level Translation Evaluation with Many Dense Features. In *2014 Conference on Empirical Methods in Natural Language Processing*, pages 202–206, Doha, Qatar.

Stede, Manfred. 2011. *Discourse Processing*, volume 4 of *Synthesis Lectures on Human Language Technologies*. Morgan & Claypool Publishers.

Stripping Adjectives: Integration Techniques for Selective Stemming in SMT Systems

Isabel Slawik **Jan Niehues** **Alex Waibel**
Institute for Anthropomatics and Robotics
KIT - Karlsruhe Institute of Technology, Germany
firstname.lastname@kit.edu

Abstract

In this paper we present an approach to reduce data sparsity problems when translating from morphologically rich languages into less inflected languages by selectively stemming certain word types. We develop and compare three different integration strategies: replacing words with their stemmed form, combined input using alternative lattice paths for the stemmed and surface forms and a novel hidden combination strategy, where we replace the stems in the stemmed phrase table by the observed surface forms in the test data. This allows us to apply advanced models trained on the surface forms of the words.

We evaluate our approach by stemming German adjectives in two German→English translation scenarios: a low-resource condition as well as a large-scale state-of-the-art translation system. We are able to improve between 0.2 and 0.4 BLEU points over our baseline and reduce the number of out-of-vocabulary words by up to 16.5%.

1 Introduction

Statistical machine translation (SMT) is currently the most promising approach to automatically translate text from one natural language into another. While it has been successfully used for a lot of languages and applications, many challenges still remain. Translating from a morphologically rich language is one such challenge where the translation quality of modern systems is often still not sufficient for many applications.

Traditional SMT approaches work on a lexical level, that is every surface form of a word is treated as its own distinct token. This can create data sparsity problems for morphologically rich languages, since the occurrences of a word are distributed over all its different surface forms. This problem becomes even more apparent when translating from an under-resourced language, where parallel training data is scarce.

When we translate from a highly inflected language into a less morphologically rich language, not all syntactic information encoded in the surface forms may be needed to produce an accurate translation. For example, verbs in French must agree with the noun in case and gender. When we translate these verbs into English, case and gender information may be safely discarded.

We therefore propose an approach to overcome these sparsity problems by stemming different morphological variants of a word prior to translation. This allows us to not only estimate translation probabilities more reliably, but also to translate previously unseen morphological variants of a word, thus leading to a better generalization of our models. To fully maximize the potential of our SMT system, we looked at three different integration strategies. We evaluated hard decision stemming, where all adjectives are replaced by their stem, as well as soft integration strategies, where we consider the words and their stemmed form as translation alternatives.

2 Related Work

The specific challenges arising from the translation of morphologically rich languages have been widely studied in the field of SMT. The factored translation model (Koehn and Hoang, 2007) enriches phrase-based MT with linguistic information. By translating the stem of a word and its morphological components separately and then applying generation rules to form the correct surface form of the target word, it is possible to generate translations for surface forms that have not been seen in training.

Talbot and Osborne (2006) address lexical redundancy by automatically clustering source words with similar translation distributions, whereas Yang and Kirchhoff (2006) propose a backoff model that uses increasing levels of morphological abstractions to translate previously unseen word forms.

Niehues and Waibel (2011) present quasi-morphological operations as a means to translate out-of-vocabulary (OOV) words. The automatically learned operations are able to split off potentially inflected suffixes, look up the translation for the base form using a lexicon of Wikipedia[1] titles in multiple languages, and then generate the appropriate surface form on the target side. Similar operations were learned for compound parts by Macherey et al. (2011).

Hardmeier et al. (2010) use morphological reduction in a German→English SMT system by adding the lemmas of every word output as a byproduct of compound splitting as an alternative edge to input lattices. A similar approach is used by Dyer et al. (2008) and Wuebker and Ney (2012). They used word lattices to represent different source language alternatives for Arabic→English and German→English respectively.

Weller et al. (2013a) employ morphological simplification for their French→English WMT system, including replacing inflected adjective forms with their lemma using hand-written rules, and their Russian→English (Weller et al., 2013b) system, removing superfluous attributes from the highly inflected Russian surface forms. Their systems are unable to outperform the baseline system trained on the surface forms. Weller et al. argue that human translators may prefer the morphologically reduced system due to better generalization ability. Their analysis showed the Russian system often produces an incorrect verb tense, which indicates that some morphological information may be helpful to choose the right translation even if the information seems redundant.

[1]http://www.wikipedia.org

3 Stemming

In order to address the sparsity problem, we try to cluster words that have the same translation probability distribution, leading to higher occurrence counts and therefore more reliable translation statistics. Because of the respective morphological properties of our source and target language, word stems pose a promising type of cluster. Moreover, stemming alleviates the OOV problem for unseen morphological variants. Because of these benefits, we chose stem clustering in this paper, however, our approach can work on different types of clusters, e.g. synonyms.

Morphological stemming prior to translation has to be done carefully, as we are actively discarding information. Indiscriminately stemming the whole source corpus hurts translation performance, since stemming algorithms make mistakes and often too much information is lost.

Adding the stem of every word as an alternative to our source sentence greatly increases our search space. Arguably the majority of the time we need the surface form of a word to make an informed translation decision. We therefore propose to keep the search space small by only stemming selected word classes which have a high diversity in inflections and whose additional morphological information content can be safely disregarded.

For our use case of translating from German to English, we chose to focus only on stemming adjectives. Adjectives in German can have five different suffixes, depending on the gender, number and case of the corresponding noun, whereas in English adjectives are only rarely inflected. We can therefore discard the information encoded in the suffix of a German adjective without losing any vital information for translation.

3.1 Degrees of Comparison

While we want to remove gender, number and case information from the German adjective, we want to preserve its comparative or superlative nature. In addition to its base form (e.g. *schön* [*pretty*]), a German adjective can have one of five suffixes (*-e, -em, -en, -er, -es*). However, we cannot simply remove all suffixes using fixed rules, because the comparative base form of an adjective is identical to the inflected masculine, nominative, singular form of an attributive adjective.

For example, the inflected form *schöner* of the adjective *schön* is used as an attributive adjective in the phrase *schöner Mann* [*handsome man*] and as a comparative in the phrase *schöner wird es nicht* [*won't get prettier*]. We can stem the adjective in the attributive case to its base form without any confusion (*schön Mann*), as we generate a form that does not exist in proper German. However, were we to apply the same stemming to the comparative case, we would lose the degree of comparison and still generate a valid German sentence (*schön wird es nicht* [*won't be pretty*]) with a different meaning than our original sentence. In order to differentiate between cases in which stemming is desirable and where we would lose information, a detailed morphological analysis of the source text prior to stemming is vital.

3.2 Implementation

We used readily available part-of-speech (POS) taggers, namely the TreeTagger (Schmid, 1994) and RFTagger (Schmid and Laws, 2008), for morphological analysis and stemming. In order to achieve accurate results, we performed standard machine translation preprocessing on our corpora before tagging. We discarded exceedingly long sentences and sentence pairs with a large length difference from the training data. Special dates, numbers and symbols were normalized and we smart-cased the first letter of every sentence. Typically preprocessing for German also includes splitting up compounds into their separate parts. However, this would confuse the POS taggers, which have been trained on German text with proper compounds. Furthermore, our compound splitting algorithm might benefit from a stemmed corpus, providing higher occurrence counts for individual word components. We therefore refrain from compound splitting before tagging and stemming.

We only stemmed words tagged as attributive adjectives, since only they are inflected in German. Predicative adjectives are not inflected and therefore were left untouched. Since we want to retain the degree of comparison, we used the fine-grained tags of the RFTagger to decide when and how to stem. Adjectives tagged as comparative or superlative were stemmed through the use of fixed rules. For all others, we used the lemma output by the TreeTagger, since it is the same as the stem and was already available in our system.

Finally, our usual compound splitting (Koehn and Knight, 2003) was trained and performed on the stemmed corpus.

4 Integration

After clustering the words into groups that can be translated in the same or at least in a similar way, there are different possibilities to use them in the translation system. A naive strategy is to replace each word by its cluster representative, called *hard decision stemming*. However, this carries the risk of discarding vital information. Therefore we investigated techniques to integrate both, the surface forms as well as the word stems, into the translation system. In the *combined input*, we add the stemmed adjectives as translation alternatives to the preordering lattices. Since this poses problems for the application of more advanced translation models during decoding, we propose the novel *hidden combination* technique.

4.1 Hard Decision Stemming

Assuming that the translation probabilities of the word stems can be estimated more reliably than those of the surface forms, the most intuitive strategy is to consequently replace each surface form by its stem. In our case, we replaced all adjectives with their stems. This has the advantage that afterwards the whole training pipeline can be performed in exactly the same manner as it is done in the baseline system. For tuning and testing, the adjectives in the development and test data are stemmed and replaced in the same manner as in the training data.

4.2 Combined Input

Mistakes made during hard decision stemming cannot be recovered. Soft integration techniques avoid this pitfall by deferring the decision whether to use the stem or surface form of a word until decoding. We enable our system to choose by combining both the surface form based (default) phrase table and the word stem based (stemmed) phrase table log-linearly. The weights of the phrase scores are then learned during optimization.

In order to be able to apply both phrase tables at the same time, we need to modify the input of the decoder. Our baseline system already uses preordering lattices, which encode different reordering possibilities of the source sentence. We replaced every edge in the lattice containing an adjective by two edges: one containing the surface form and the other the word stem. This allows the decoder to choose which word form to use depending on the word and its context.

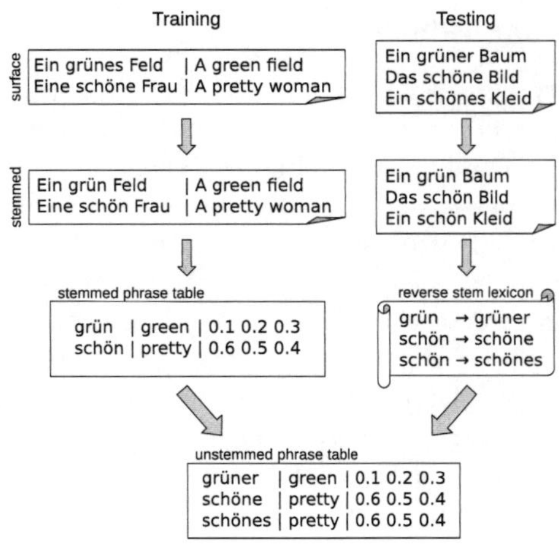

Figure 1: Workflow for unstemming the PT.

4.3 Hidden Combination

While we are able to modify our phrase table to use both surface forms and stems in the last strategy, other models in our log-linear system suffer from the different types of source input. For example, the bilingual language model (Niehues et al., 2011) is based on tokens of target words and their aligned source words. In training, we can use either the stemmed corpus or the original one, but during decoding a mixture of stems and surface forms occurs. For the unknown word forms the scores will not be accurate and the performance of our model will suffer. Similar problems occur when using other translation models such as neural network based translation models.

We therefore developed a novel strategy to integrate the word stems into the translation system. Instead of stemming the input to fit the stemmed phrase table, we modified the stemmed phrase table so that it can be applied to the surface forms. The workflow is illustrated in Figure 1. We extracted all the stem mappings from the development and test data and compiled a stem lexicon. This maps the surface forms observed in the dev and test data to their corresponding stems. We then applied this lexicon in reverse to our stemmed phrase table, in effect duplicating every entry containing a stemmed adjective with the inflected form replacing the stem. Afterwards this "unstemmed" phrase table is log-linearly combined with the default phrase table and used for translation.

This allows us to retain our generalization won by using word clusters to estimate phrase probabilities, and still use all models trained on the surface forms. Using the hidden combination strategy, stemming can easily be implemented into current state-of-the-art SMT systems without the need to change any of the advanced models beyond the phrase table. This makes our approach highly versatile and easy to implement for any number of system architectures and languages.

5 Experiments

Since we expect stemming to have a larger impact in cases where training data is scarce, we evaluated the three presented strategies on two different scenarios: a low-resource condition and a state-of-the-art large-scale system. In both scenarios we stemmed German adjectives and translated from German to English.

In our low-resource condition, we trained an SMT system using only training data from the TED corpus (Cettolo et al., 2012). TED translations are currently available for 107 languages[2] and are being continuously expanded. Therefore, there is a high chance that a small parallel corpus of translated TED talks will be available in the chosen language.

In the second scenario, we used a large-scale state-of-the-art German→English translation system. This system was trained on significantly more data than available in the low-resource condition and incorporates several additional models.

5.1 System Description

The low-resource system was trained only on the TED corpus provided by the IWSLT 2014 machine translation campaign, consisting of 172k lines. As monolingual training data we used the target side of the TED corpus.

The large-scale system was trained on the European Parliament Proceedings, News Commentary, TED and Common Crawl corpora provided for the IWSLT 2014 machine translation campaign (Cettolo et al., 2014), encompassing 4.69M lines. For the monolingual training data we used the target side of all bilingual corpora as well as the News Shuffle and the Gigaword corpus.

Before training and translation, the data is preprocessed as described in Section 3.2. The noisy Common Crawl corpus was filtered with an SVM classifier as described by Mediani et al. (2011). After preprocessing, the parallel corpora are word-aligned with the GIZA++ toolkit (Gao and Vo-

[2]http://www.ted.com/participate/translate

gel, 2008) in both directions. The resulting alignments are combined using the *grow-diag-final-and* heuristic. The Moses toolkit (Koehn et al., 2007) is used for phrase extraction. For the large-scale system, phrase table adaptation combining an in-domain and out-of-domain phrase table is performed (Niehues and Waibel, 2012). All translations are generated by our in-house phrase-based decoder (Vogel, 2003).

We used 4-gram language models (LMs) with modified Kneser-Ney smoothing, trained with the SRILM toolkit (Stolcke, 2002) and scored in the decoding process with KenLM (Heafield, 2011).

All our systems include a reordering model which automatically learns reordering rules based on part-of-speech sequences and, in case of the large-scale system, syntactic parse tree constituents to better match the target language word order (Rottmann and Vogel, 2007; Niehues and Kolss, 2009; Herrmann et al., 2013). The resulting reordering possibilities for each source sentence are encoded in a lattice.

For the low-resource scenario, we built two systems. One small baseline with only one phrase table and language model, as well as aforementioned POS-based preordering model, and an advanced system using an extended feature set of models that are also used in the large-scale system. The extended low-resource and the large-scale system include the following additional models.

A bilingual LM (Niehues et al., 2011) is used to increase the bilingual context during translation beyond phrase boundaries. It is built on tokens consisting of a target word and all its aligned source words. We also used a 9-gram cluster LM built on 100 automatically clustered word classes using the MKCLS algorithm (Och, 1999).

The large-scale system also uses an in-domain LM trained on the TED corpus and a word-based model trained on 10M sentences chosen through data selection (Moore and Lewis, 2010).

In addition to the lattice preordering, a lexicalized reordering model (Koehn et al., 2005) which stores reordering probabilities for each phrase pair is included in both extended systems.

We tune all our systems using MERT (Venugopal et al., 2005) against the BLEU score. Since the systems have a varying amount of features, we reoptimized the weights for every experiment.

For the low-resource system, we used IWSLT test 2012 as a development set and IWSLT test 2011 as test data. For the large-scale system, we used IWSLT test 2011 as development data and IWSLT test 2012 as test data.

System	Dev	Test
Baseline	28.91	30.25
Hard Decision	29.01	30.30
Combined Input	29.13	30.47
Hidden Combination	**29.25**	**30.62**

Table 1: TED low-resource small systems results.

All results are reported as case-sensitive BLEU scores calculated with one reference translation.

5.2 Low-resource Condition

The results for the systems built only on the TED corpus are summarized in Table 1 for the small system and Table 2 for the extended system. The baseline systems reach a BLEU score on the test set of 30.25 and 31.33 respectively.

In the small system we could slightly improve to 30.30 using only stemmed adjectives. However, in the extended system the hard decision strategy could not outperform the baseline. This indicates that for words with sufficient data it might be better to translate the surface forms.

Adding the stemmed forms as alternatives to the preordering lattice leads to an improvement of 0.2 BLEU points over the small baseline system. In the larger system with the extended features set, the combined input performed better than the hard decision stemming, but is still 0.1 BLEU points below the baseline. With this strategy we do not tap the full potential of our extended system, as there is still a mismatch between the combined input and the training data of the advanced models.

The hidden combination strategy rectifies this problem, which is reflected in the results. Using the hidden combination we could achieve our best BLEU score for both systems. We could improve by almost 0.4 BLEU points over the small baseline system and 0.3 BLEU points on the system using extended features.

System	Dev	Test
Baseline	29.73	31.33
Hard Decision	29.74	30.84
Combined Input	**29.97**	31.22
Hidden Combination	29.87	**31.61**

Table 2: TED extended features systems results.

System	Dev	Test
Baseline	38.30	30.89
Hard Decision	38.25	30.82
Combined Input	**38.65**	**31.10**
Hidden Combination	38.40	31.08

Table 3: IWSLT large-scale systems results.

5.3 Large-scale System

In order to assess the impact of our stemming on a state-of-the-art system, we tested our techniques on a large-scale system using training data from several domains. The results of these experiments are summarized in Table 3. The baseline system achieved a BLEU score of 30.89 on the test set.

As in the low-resource condition, the hard decision to use only the stems causes a slight drop in performance. Given the large amount of training data, the problem of having seen a word few times is much less severe than before.

When we combine the inputs, we can improve the translation quality to our best score of 31.10 BLEU points. The hidden combination performs similarly. By using combined input or hidden combination, we achieved a gain of 0.2 BLEU points over the baseline.

5.4 Further Analysis

In this work we have focused on selectively stemming only a small subset of our input text, namely adjectives. We therefore do not expect to see a large difference in BLEU score in our systems and indeed the improvements, while existent, are moderate. It is a well known shortcoming of automatic metrics that they cannot differentiate between acceptable translation alternatives and errors. Since time and monetary constraints did not allow us to perform a full-scale human evaluation, we use the OOV rate and manual inspection to demonstrate the benefits of our approach.

For a monolingual user of machine translation systems, even an imperfect translation will be better than no translation at all. We therefore looked at the out-of-vocabulary (OOV) rate of our systems.

477 OOV words occurred in the test set of the low-resource baseline. This means of the 1433 lines in our test set, on average every third contained an untranslated word. With stemming we were able to translate 79 of those words and reduce the number of OOV words by 16.5%. Even in the large-scale system, which is trained on a large amount of data and therefore has an already low OOV rate, we achieved a decrease of 4%. Figure 2 shows an example sentence where we managed to translate two previously OOV words using the hidden combination strategy. Furthermore, stemming can also improve our word choices as shown in the example in Figure 3.

SRC	Aber es war sehr traurig .
REF	But it was very sad .
BASE	But it was really upset .
H.C.	But it was very sad .

Figure 3: Example of improved word choice.

Stemming certain words in a corpus not only affects the translation of that word, but the whole system. For example, stemming changes the occurrence statistics of the stemmed words, and therefore the output of empirical algorithms such as compound splitting and word alignment is subject to change. By combining the stemmed and default phrase tables, we gave our decoder the chance to use a phrase from the stemmed phrase table even if the phrase contains no stemmed words. A manual evaluation of the output of the hidden combination system compared to the hard decision stemmed system showed that the difference was largely in word order as exemplified in Figure 4.

6 Conclusion

In this paper we addressed the problem of translating from morphologically rich languages into less inflected languages. The problem of low occur-

SRC	Während Schimpansen von großen , **furchteinflößenden** Kerlen geführt werden , wird die Bonobo - Gesellschaft von **ermächtigten** Weibchen geführt .
REF	While chimpanzees are dominated by big , **scary** guys , bonobo society is run by **empowered** females .
BASE	As chimpanzees by large , **fear einflößenden** guys are , the Bonobo-society led by **ermächtigten** females .
H.C.	During the chimpanzees of big , **scary** guys are , the Bonobo is society of **empowered** females .

Figure 2: Example translations of the baseline and hidden combination low-resource systems. OOV phrases have been marked in bold.

SRC	Nun ja , eine Erleuchtung ist für gewöhnlich etwas , dass man findet weil man es irgendwo fallen gelassen hat .
REF	And you know , an epiphany is usually something you find that you dropped someplace .
H.D.	Well , there is an epiphany usually , something that you can find because it has somewhere dropped .
H.C.	Well , an epiphany is usually something that you can find because it has dropped somewhere .

Figure 4: Example of improved word order of the hidden combination over the hard decision system.

rence counts for surface forms and high out-of-vocabulary rates for unobserved surface forms can be alleviated by stemming words.

We showed that stemming has to be done carefully, since SMT systems are highly sensitive to lost information. Given our use case of German to English translation, we chose to only stem adjectives, which can have five suffixes depending on gender, number and case of the corresponding noun. We took special care to ensure comparative and superlative adjectives retained their degree of comparison after stemming.

As an alternative to the hard decision strategy, where every word is replaced by its stem, we proposed two soft integration techniques incorporating the stems and surface forms as alternative translation paths in the preordering lattices. State-of-the-art SMT systems consist of a log-linear combination of many advanced models. Combining the surface forms and word stems posed problems for models relying on source side tokens. We therefore developed a novel hidden combination technique, where the word stems in the phrase table are replaced by the observed surface forms in the test data. This allowed us to use the more reliably estimated translation probabilities calculated on the word stems in the decoder while simultaneously applying all our other models to the surface forms of the words.

We evaluated our approach on German→English translation in two scenarios, one low-resource condition and a large-scale state-of-the-art SMT system. Given the low-resource condition, we evaluated a small, basic system as well as a more sophisticated system using an extended feature set. Using the hidden combination strategy, we were able to outperform the baseline systems in all three experiments by 0.2 up to 0.4 BLEU points. While these improvements may seem moderate, they were achieved solely through the modification of adjectives. We were also able to show that our systems generalized better than the baseline as evidenced by the OOV rate, which could be decreased by 16.5% in the low-resource condition.

Acknowledgments

The project leading to this application has received funding from the European Union's Horizon 2020 research and innovation programme under grant agreement n° 645452.

References

Cettolo, M., C. Girardi, and M. Federico. 2012. WIT3: Web Inventory of Transcribed and Translated Talks. In *Proceedings of the 16th Annual Meeting of the European Association for Machine Translation*, Trento, Italy.

Cettolo, M., J. Niehues, S. Stüker, L. Bentivogli, and M. Federico. 2014. Report on the 11th IWSLT Evaluation Campaign, IWSLT 2014. In *Proceedings of the 11th International Workshop on Spoken Language Translation*, Lake Tahoe, California, USA.

Dyer, C., S. Muresan, and P. Resnik. 2008. Generalizing Word Lattice Translation. In *Proceedings of the 46th Annual Meeting of the ACL: Human Language Technologies*, Columbus, Ohio, USA.

Gao, Q. and S. Vogel. 2008. Parallel Implementations of Word Alignment Tool. In *Proceedings of the Software Engineering, Testing, and Quality Assurance for Natural Language Processing*, Columbus, Ohio, USA.

Hardmeier, C., A. Bisazza, M. Federico, and F.B. Kessler. 2010. FBK at WMT 2010: Word Lattices for Morphological Reduction and Chunk-based Reordering. In *Proceedings of the Fifth Workshop on Statistical Machine Translation and Metrics MATR*, Uppsala, Sweden.

Heafield, K. 2011. KenLM: Faster and Smaller Language Model Queries. In *Proceedings of the Sixth Workshop on Statistical Machine Translation*, Edinburgh, UK.

Herrmann, T., J. Niehues, and A. Waibel. 2013. Combining Word Reordering Methods on Different Linguistic Abstraction Levels for Statistical Machine Translation. In *Seventh Workshop on Syntax, Semantics and Structure in Statistical Translation*, Atlanta, Georgia, USA.

Koehn, P. and H. Hoang. 2007. Factored Translation Models. In *Proceedings of the Joint Conference on Empirical Methods in Natural Language Processing and Computational Natural Language Learning*, Prague, Czech Republic.

Koehn, P. and K. Knight. 2003. Empirical Methods for Compound Splitting. In *Proceedings of the 10th Conference of the European Chapter of the ACL*, Budapest, Hungary.

Koehn, P., A. Axelrod, A.B. Mayne, C. Callison-Burch, M. Osborne, and D. Talbot. 2005. Edinburgh System Description for the 2005 IWSLT Speech Translation Evaluation. In *Proceedings of the 2nd International Workshop on Spoken Language Translation*, Pittsburgh, Pennsylvania, USA.

Koehn, P., H. Hoang, A. Birch, C. Callison-Burch, M. Federico, N. Bertoldi, B. Cowan, W. Shen, C. Moran, R. Zens, C. Dyer, O. Bojar, A. Constantin, and E. Herbst. 2007. Moses: Open Source Toolkit for Statistical Machine Translation. In *Proceedings of the 45th Annual Meeting of the ACL*, Prague, Czech Republic.

Macherey, K., A. Dai, D. Talbot, A. Popat, and F. Och. 2011. Language-independent Compound Splitting with Morphological Operations. In *Proceedings of the 49th Annual Meeting of the ACL: Human Language Technologies*, Portland, Oregon, USA.

Mediani, M., E. Cho, J. Niehues, T. Herrmann, and A. Waibel. 2011. The KIT English-French Translation Systems for IWSLT 2011. In *Proceedings of the Eights International Workshop on Spoken Language Translation*, San Francisco, California, USA.

Moore, R.C. and W. Lewis. 2010. Intelligent Selection of Language Model Training Data. In *Proceedings of the 48th Annual Meeting of the ACL*, Uppsala, Sweden.

Niehues, J. and M. Kolss. 2009. A POS-based Model for Long-Range Reorderings in SMT. In *Proceedings of the Fourth Workshop on Statistical Machine Translation*, Athens, Greece.

Niehues, J. and A. Waibel. 2011. Using Wikipedia to Translate Domain-Specific Terms in SMT. In *Proceedings of the Eights International Workshop on Spoken Language Translation*, San Francisco, California, USA.

Niehues, J. and A. Waibel. 2012. Detailed Analysis of Different Strategies for Phrase Table Adaptation in SMT. In *Proceedings of the Tenth Conference of the Association for Machine Translation in the Americas*, San Diego, California, USA.

Niehues, J., T. Herrmann, S. Vogel, and A. Waibel. 2011. Wider Context by Using Bilingual Language Models in Machine Translation. In *Proceedings of the Sixth Workshop on Statistical Machine Translation*, Edinburgh, UK.

Och, F.J. 1999. An Efficient Method for Determining Bilingual Word Classes. In *Proceedings of the Ninth Conference of the European Chapter of the ACL*, Bergen, Norway.

Rottmann, K. and S. Vogel. 2007. Word Reordering in Statistical Machine Translation with a POS-Based Distortion Model. In *Proceedings of the 11th International Conference on Theoretical and Methodological Issues in Machine Translation*, Skövde, Sweden.

Schmid, H. and F. Laws. 2008. Estimation of Conditional Probabilities with Decision Trees and an Application to Fine-Grained POS Tagging. In *Proceedings of the 22nd International Conference on Computational Linguistics*, Manchester, UK.

Schmid, H. 1994. Probabilistic Part-of-Speech Tagging Using Decision Trees. In *Proceedings of the International Conference on New Methods in Language Processing*, Manchester, UK.

Stolcke, A. 2002. SRILM – An Extensible Language Modeling Toolkit. In *Proceedings of the International Conference of Spoken Language Processing*, Denver, Colorado, USA.

Talbot, D. and M. Osborne. 2006. Modelling Lexical Redundancy for Machine Translation. In *Proceedings of the 21st International Conference on Computational Linguistics and the 44th Annual Meeting of the ACL*, Sydney, Australia.

Venugopal, A., A. Zollman, and A. Waibel. 2005. Training and Evaluation Error Minimization Rules for Statistical Machine Translation. In *Proceedings of the Workshop on Data-driven Machine Translation and Beyond*, Ann Arbor, Michigan, USA.

Vogel, S. 2003. SMT Decoder Dissected: Word Reordering. In *Proceedings of the IEEE International Conference on Natural Language Processing and Knowledge Engineering*, Beijing, China.

Weller, M., A. Fraser, and S. Schulte im Walde. 2013a. Using Subcategorization Knowledge to Improve Case Prediction for Translation to German. In *Proceedings of the 51st Annual Meeting of the ACL*, Sofia, Bulgaria.

Weller, M., M. Kisselew, S. Smekalova, A. Fraser, H. Schmid, N. Durrani, H. Sajjad, and R. Farkas. 2013b. Munich-Edinburgh-Stuttgart Submissions of OSM Systems at WMT13. In *Proceedings of the Eighth Workshop on Statistical Machine Translation*, Sofia, Bulgaria.

Wuebker, J. and H. Ney. 2012. Phrase Model Training for Statistical Machine Translation with Word Lattices of Preprocessing Alternatives. In *Proceedings of the Seventh Workshop on Statistical Machine Translation*, Montreal, Canada.

Yang, M. and K. Kirchhoff. 2006. Phrase-Based Backoff Models for Machine Translation of Highly Inflected Languages. In *Proceedings of the 11th Conference of the European Chapter of the ACL*, Trento, Italy.

Evaluating machine translation for assimilation via a gap-filling task

Ekaterina Ageeva
School of Linguistics
Higher School of Economics
Moscow, Russia
evageeva_2@edu.hse.ru

Mikel L. Forcada
Dept. Llenguatges i Sistemes Informàtics
Universitat d'Alacant
E-03071 Alacant, Spain
mlf@dlsi.ua.es

Francis M. Tyers
HSL-fakultetet
UiT Norgga árktalaš universitehta
9017 Romsa, Norway
francis.tyers@uit.no

Juan Antonio Pérez-Ortiz
Dept. Llenguatges i Sistemes Informàtics
Universitat d'Alacant
E-03071 Alacant, Spain
japerez@dlsi.ua.es

Abstract

This paper provides additional observations on the viability of a strategy independently proposed in 2012 and 2013 for evaluation of machine translation (MT) for assimilation purposes. The strategy involves human evaluators, who are asked to restore keywords (to fill gaps) in reference translations. The evaluation method is applied to two language pairs, Basque–Spanish and Tatar–Russian. To reduce the amount of time required to prepare tasks and analyse results, an open-source task management system is introduced. The evaluation results show that the gap-filling task may be suitable for measuring MT quality for assimilation purposes.

1 Introduction

As suggested by Church and Hovy (1993), modern machine translation (MT) systems may be divided into two broad categories according to their purpose: post-editing and assimilation systems. The output of the former is intended to be transformed into text comparable to human translation; the latter systems' goal is to enhance user's comprehension of text. Both kinds may be evaluated, either to control for quality in the development process or to compare the systems. Importantly, according to Church and Hovy (1993), the evaluation methods must closely consider the system's primary purpose.

Despite the fact that, as a result of widespread usage of online MT, assimilation (or gisting) is currently the most frequent application of MT (in 2012, daily output of Google Translate matched the yearly output of human translations[1]), few methodologies are established for assimilation evaluation of MT. The methods include post-editing and comparison by bilingual experts (Ginestí-Rosell et al., 2009), and multiple choice tests (Jones et al., 2007; Trosterud and Unhammer, 2012). These approaches are often costly and prone to subjectivity: see the discussion by O'Regan and Forcada (2013). As an alternative, the modification of *cloze* testing (Taylor, 1953) was introduced for assimilation evaluation, first by Trosterud and Unhammer (2012) as a supplementary technique, and then by O'Regan and Forcada (2013) as a stand-alone method. Prior to this, cloze tests have been used to evaluate raw MT quality (Van Slype, 1979; Somers and Wild, 2000). While these authors ask informants to fill gaps in MT output, Trosterud and Unhammer (2012) and O'Regan and Forcada (2013) ask informants to fill gaps in the reference (human) translation. A designated number of keywords is removed from the human-translated sentences. The evaluators are then asked to fill the gaps with suitable words with and without the help of MT output. The gap-filling task models how well users comprehend the key points of the text, as it is roughly equivalent with answering questions. Thus, the method does not directly evaluate the quality of machine-produced text, but rather its usefulness in understanding the meaning of the original text.

The gap-filling method has been successfully used to evaluate the Basque–English Apertium language pair. In this work we extend the evalua-

[1] http://googleblog.blogspot.co.uk/2012/04/breaking-down-language-barriersix-years.html

tion to two more language pairs: Basque–Spanish and Tatar–Russian. The former pair, while not producing output suitable for post-editing, is a good example of an assimilation MT system. In addition, Basque and Spanish are not mutually understandable, and therefore constitute a good pair for evaluation. For the latter pair, the evaluation served as a quality check in the period of active development during the Google Summer of Code 2014 programme. In addition to evaluating, we explore the previously unconsidered aspects of the experiment: the correlation between evaluators' scores, and the effects of the linguistic domain of texts and the percentage of gaps in a sentence. To facilitate the evaluation, we introduce an automated system which creates task sets from parallel corpora given a range of parameters (number of gaps in a sentence, hint type, gap filler, etc.), checks evaluators' answers, and calculates and reports generalized results. This system is integrated into the Appraise MT evaluation platform (Federmann, 2012); the code is open-source and is available on GitHub.[2]

We anticipate that the assessed MT systems will contribute to the users' understanding of text, that is, the users will show better results in gap-filling tasks when assisted with MT. We also expect to see different results depending on text domain and the relative number of gaps in a sentence.

The paper is organised as follows: in section 2 we describe the gap-filling method for assimilation evaluation: the task layout, the choice of words, and how the tasks are generated. Section 3 introduces the experimental material, the evaluators, the distribution of tasks and the evaluation procedure. In section 4 we describe and discuss the experiment results. Finally, section 5 draws some conclusions. This paper is concerned primarily with assimilation evaluation; for a deeper discussion on evaluation see e.g. (Koehn, 2010, ch. 8).

2 Methodology

This section discusses the reasoning behind the gap-filling method and task structure. The gap-filling method of evaluating machine translation for assimilation purposes is based on the following hypothesis: a reader's understanding of a given text correlates with the number of words they are able to correctly restore in the text. Therefore, the base of an assimilation task is a (reference) sentence, where some of the words are blacked out, or removed. The sentence is produced by a human (as opposed to machine-translated), and it is in the language known to evaluators, which is also the *target language* of the machine translation system. The additional elements of the task are what we call hints, or extra sentences that help the participant to understand the main sentence. There are two types of hints: first, the *source*, which is semantically equivalent to the *reference*, also human-produced, but in the source language of the pair. The second type is the *machine-translated* hint, which comes from the machine translation of the *source* sentence. Table 1 shows a sample task, and Figure 1 shows the task in the online evaluation environment.

In the course of the experiment, following O'Regan and Forcada (2013), we offer these hint combinations:

Reference sentence only: The participants are asked to fill the gaps without being given any context. This task serves as a baseline score and as an indicator of gaps that can be completed using common knowledge or language intuition (e.g. idioms and strong collocations). For example, in an English phrase 'Jack ordered <...> and chips', one of the natural answers would be 'fish'. Such an answer, however, may be unrelated to the meaning of the source text, and may be given on the basis of collocation only.

Reference sentence and source sentence: By setup, the participants have no command of the source language, however, it may help them to fill in proper nouns or loan words.

Reference sentence and MT hint: In addition to the reference sentence, the participants see the source sentence translated via the MT system, in this case Apertium (Forcada et al., 2011). This type of task is used for measuring the contribution of machine translation to understanding the gist of the text.

Reference sentence and both hints: This task is added to check whether MT and source provide complementary hints.

In order to prepare the evaluation questions, we determine and remove keywords from the reference sentences. We consider two parameters: the list of allowed parts of speech (PoS), and the number of gaps relative to sentence length ("gap den-

[2] `https://github.com/Sereni/Appraise`

Ref	Ayudas económicas para el tratamiento de toxicomanías en comunidades terapéuticas no concertadas.
Task	Ayudas económicas para el { } de toxicomanías en comunidades terapéuticas no concertadas.
Src	Komunitate terapeutiko itundu gabeetan toxikomaniak tratatzeko diru-laguntzak ematea.
MT	Comunidad terapéutico pactar gabeetan toxikomaniak las-ayudas de dinero para tratar dar.

Table 1: An example group of sentences showing the gapped sentence and hint types. Reference, MT and task sentences are in Spanish, the source sentence is in Basque.

Ref	Примерно полчаса; вам нужно выйти через 7 остановок, потом пройти ещё около 100 метров.
10%	Примерно полчаса; вам нужно выйти через 7 { }, потом пройти ещё около 100 метров.
20%	{ } полчаса; вам нужно { } через 7 остановок, { } пройти ещё около 100 метров.
30%	Примерно полчаса; вам нужно { } через 7 { }, потом пройти { } около 100 { }.

Table 2: Example of different gap percentage settings for a Russian reference sentence.

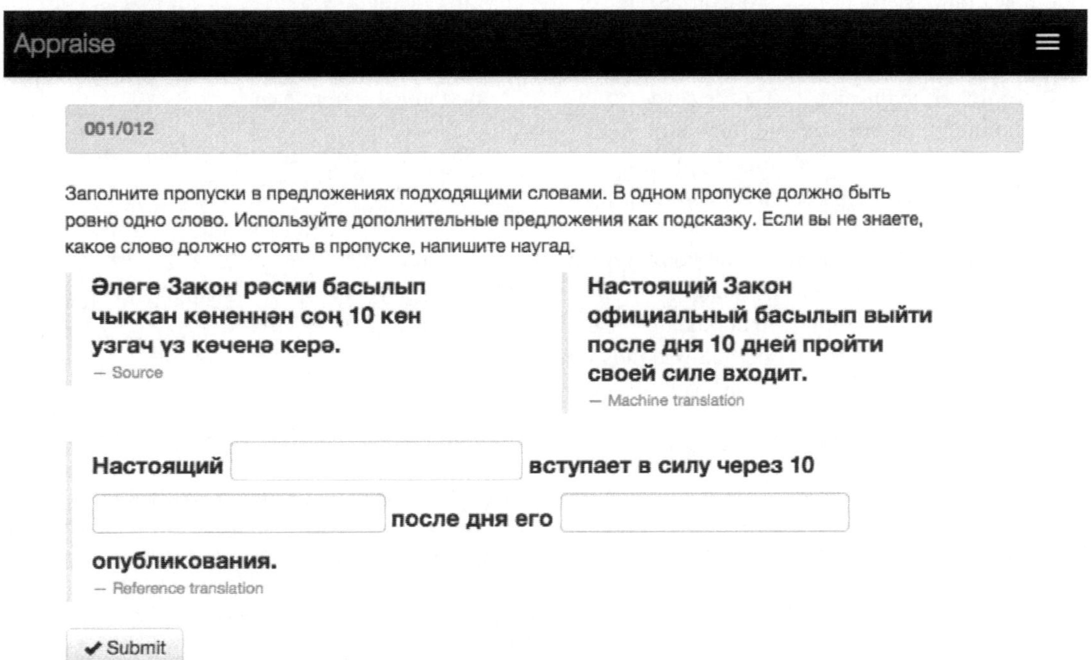

Figure 1: An example set of sentences in the online environment. The task is Russian legal text with 30% gaps.

sity"). For the evaluations described in this paper we use gap densities of 10, 20 and 30 percent (Table 2), and the following parts of speech: noun (including proper nouns), adjective, adverb and lexical verb (as opposed to auxiliary verb).

For each sentence, the list of candidate keywords is prepared. It is composed of all the words that fall into the allowed PoS list. The number of gaps in the sentence is calculated based on sentence length and specified gap density. All reference sentences are longer than 10 words. Finally, the required number of keywords is selected from the candidate list in such a manner that the gaps are distributed evenly throughout the sentence. We start at a random word in a sentence and check whether it is a keyword candidate. If yes, we remove it, and move *n* words forward, going back to the beginning of sentence if necessary. The step length *n* is the sentence length divided by the desired number of gaps. If the word is not a keyword, or has already been removed, we look at the next word instead. The process is repeated until the designated number of words has been removed, or until there are no more words in the keyword list.

Keyword removal could be one of the most time-consuming steps in task preparation. It normally requires human effort, because we would like to determine the words that contribute the most to understanding the text as opposed to removing random words. In our automatic setup, the above procedure is performed by a script integrated into the task generation pipeline. Parts of speech are determined with Apertium's morphological analysers. To control for homonymy, we only allow the word into the candidate list if all of its possible part of speech attributions are on the PoS list. For example, if we only allow nouns on the word list, and the word "fly" receives two possible part of speech attributions from the tagger, noun and verb, it is not considered for the candidate list.

Having prepared the sentence sets, we assemble them into XML formatted for the Appraise platform.

3 Experimental set-up

In this section we will discuss the evaluators, the evaluation procedure, and the tasks in more detail.

For each experiment we called for native speakers of target language of the language pair (i.e. Spanish and Russian) who had no command of source language of the pair (Basque and Tatar, respectively). The knowledge was self-reported, and the participants were not asked about any other languages they may know. Eleven evaluators participated in the Basque–Spanish experiment, and 28 in Tatar-Russian (although not everyone completed the task in full, see discussion). The majority of Russian participants were aged 20–25, with university degrees or in the process of obtaining them. Although we have not asked the participants about their knowledge of languages other than Tatar and Russian, it is reasonable to assume that most Russian participants knew English to some extent. The Spanish participants were university staff with background in computer science.

By design, our gap-filling tasks require a human translation (reference) of source sentences. Calling for a human translator, however, would significantly increase the resources needed for evaluation. We therefore use parallel text sources, which provide the same sentence in two languages simultaneously:

1. For Basque–Spanish, from the corpus of legal texts "Memorias de traducción del Servicio Oficial de Traductores del IVAP";[3]

2. For Tatar-Russian, from the following sources on three different topics:

   (a) Casual conversations, from a textbook[4] of spoken Tatar;

   (b) Legal texts, from the Constitution and laws[5] of Tatarstan;

   (c) News, from the President of Tatarstan website[6].

Each set features 36 pairs of sentences. For the Basque–Spanish experiment the pairs were drawn randomly from the corpora; for Tatar–Russian, compiled by hand by the developer of the language pair in Apertium. The Basque–Spanish experiment featured 94, 181 and 272 gaps in the 10, 20 and 30 % tasks, respectively. For Tatar–Russian these numbers are 272, 396 and 724, due to longer sentences used in task creation.

[3] http://tinyurl.com/ivaptm2

[4] Литвинов И.Л. Я начинаю говорить по-татарски. Казань: Татарское кн. изд-во, 1994. — 320 с. ISBN 5–298–00463–6 (стр. 219, 220, 232, 233, 234)

[5] http://tatarstan.ru

[6] http://president.tatarstan.ru/

3.1 Procedure

The evaluations took place online, in a system called Appraise (Federmann, 2012), which is designed specifically for various MT evaluation tasks. We adapted the code of Appraise to accommodate for the gap-filling tasks. The tasks were uploaded into the system and manually distributed between the participants by the following rules:

1. Each participant evaluates every sentence (understood as a succession of words), a total of 36;
2. these sentences are divided into 4 groups of 9, one for each evaluation mode (see section 2);
3. in total, all sentences of the set are evaluated with 10, 20 and 30% of words removed;
4. each participant may encounter a given sentence in only one of the percentage variations;
5. each sentence-mode-percentage combination is evaluated by more than one participant.

The participants are given the instructions in their native language; these instructions are repeated above each task in the evaluation system. For the participants' convenience, the body of questions is split into smaller groups which allow multiple evaluation sessions. The instructions are the following: read all the available hints and fill each gap with one suitable word, guessing if unsure. Participants' answers are recorded and marked correct or incorrect automatically. In addition, the time taken to fill the gaps in one sentence is recorded.

This variety of the gap-filling task requires open answers, and it is therefore possible that the participants may provide words that fit the gaps well, but do not match the original answer. To account for these cases, we process all the answers to detect possible synonyms (a method suggested by O'Regan and Forcada (2013)). An answer is considered a candidate synonym if it is given by two or more evaluators, and it does not match the answer word. We record each candidate synonym along with the answer key and the context sentence. For example, the word *asumir* is the original answer in the Spanish sentence *Aprender a jugar y divertirse en el agua sin asumir riesgos* ('Learning to play and have fun in the water without taking risks'). However, two or more evaluators gave a different answer, *correr* (*correr riesgos*, 'running risks'). Based on this data, an expert, who is native speaker of the target language and who has not participated in the evaluations, decides whether the candidate synonym is an acceptable replacement to the answer key in the given context. We then check participants' results against the compiled synonym list and increase scores where appropriate. On average, the scores improve by three percentage points in all evaluation modes. Candidate synonyms are extracted automatically from the evaluators' responses, and each individual score is automatically updated according to the synonym list.

The synonym lists for Basque–Spanish and Tatar–Russian contain 52 and 25 words, respectively. The time taken to compile each list depends on the number of candidate synonyms, and in our case was approximately 30 minutes.

4 Results and discussion

The results are presented in this section. Table 3 shows the proportion and standard deviation of correct answers depending on evaluation mode and gap density. The evaluators' correct answer percentage is averaged over the number of evaluators. In addition to the percentage of correct answers we kept a record of the time taken to fill the gaps in one sentence. To reduce the noise from participants who were distracted during evaluation, when calculating times we remove all the results over 6 minutes (the statistical mode is approximately two minutes). The typical time taken to complete one question varies from under one minute for tasks without hints and few gaps, to approximately two minutes for tasks with more hints and gaps.

We expect the scores obtained in different task modes inside one gap density to decrease when going from tasks with MT and source hint to tasks with MT hint only, to tasks with source hint only, and finally, to tasks with no hint. We also expect that with the increase in gap density, the time taken to fill the gaps should also increase, and the percentage of correct answers should decrease.

The latter trend holds: the average time taken to fill the gaps increases and the average percentage of correct answers decreases as the relative number of gaps goes up. The larger number of gaps in the sentence makes it more difficult to predict the answer based on the context, and also leaves more room for mistakes. Exploring different percentage-mode combinations, we may note that the 10% no-hint tasks take the least time to complete. We would have expected longer completion time, since the participant must come up

Density	Basque–Spanish				Tatar–Russian			
	MT & Src	MT	Src	No hint	MT & Src	MT	Src	No hint
10%	62 ± 32	58 ± 28	40 ± 39	49 ± 40	57 ± 42	64 ± 41	54 ± 43	46 ± 41
20%	65 ± 30	70 ± 27	31 ± 28	31 ± 30	65 ± 31	60 ± 33	46 ± 31	39 ± 32
30%	48 ± 26	40 ± 24	26 ± 20	18 ± 18	59 ± 28	56 ± 26	40 ± 28	35 ± 30

Table 3: Average number of gaps successfully filled (%), using a synonym list, for each language pair in all four task modes.

with their own answer unassisted. However, in the no-hint task the participant is required to read only one (reference) sentence, as opposed to two or three (reference and hints) in other tasks. Also, the number of gaps in 10%-gap tasks is low, as it never exceeds three. We found that, as opposed to trying to devise the best word for no-hint gaps, the participants often resorted to filing these gaps with random words, which takes little time.

We will now discuss the percentage of correct answers based on task type. In general, tasks with MT hints score higher than tasks without MT hints. This aligns well with our expectations and suggests than machine translation helps to understand the provided text. In addition, tasks with source hints are completed better than tasks without hints, and the same relation holds between MT+source and MT-only types of tasks. In view of the relatively large standard deviations, the significance of the hints' contribution was tested using a linear regression model. The data points (y) were represented as an individual evaluator's average score (the number of correct answers divided by the total number of answers) in each of the percentage-hint combinations. Two separate models were created: one for no-hint ($x = 0$) vs MT-hint ($x = 1$) tasks, and another for no-hint ($x = 0$) vs source-hint ($x = 1$) tasks. Given the null hypothesis that the slope b of the regression line $y = a + bx$ equals zero, the contribution of MT hint is found to be significant on the $p < 0.001$ level, while the contribution of the source hint is significant only with $p < 0.162$.

Two records in the data do not align with our expectations: the no-hint 10% sentences in Basque–Spanish, which scored significantly higher than the source-hint in the same category, and MT+source 10% sentences in Tatar–Russian, which we would have expected to score higher than the corresponding MT-only task. In the first case, this is largely due to the use of synonyms list. Before taking synonyms into account, the scores were 32 and 35 percent for source and no-hint tasks, respectively. This still shows a small difference in favor of no-hint tasks. However, the latter percentage increases significantly after we extend the answer list with synonyms. Such an increase suggests that, in this case, the content words were restored by semantic context rather than through strong collocation. The second pattern, low scores in Tatar–Russian 10% MT+source, does not stem from the task content. Instead, it is the result of the fixed order of tasks: the participants have always been given MT+source 10% sentences first, followed by other task types. The participants have not received any training tasks before the main evaluations. Therefore, it is possible that the accommodation period is responsible for lower-than-expected scores in this mode of evaluation.

It remains questionable whether we can compare results for different gap densities. The 10%, 20%, and 30% sets contained the same sentences. However, in each case different words were removed. It appears that some content words are easier to fill than the others. This may explain why in Basque–Spanish the 20% MT tasks are completed with better accuracy than 10% tasks.

It is worth noting that many participants reported feeling frustrated in the course of evaluations, especially while working on the no-hint tasks. The latter required suggesting the words with very little context, which led some of the participants to giving random words for answers, or leaving the space blank. 6 out of 49 participants quit the experiment before completing it. Considering the importance of receiving the full set of evaluations, we must address the issue of participant motivation in the upcoming experiments. It may be beneficial to offer monetary compensation for the evaluators' efforts (in our case, they were volunteers).

4.1 Annotator agreement

After obtaining the results we calculated Krippendorff's alpha (Krippendorff, 1970) measure to represent annotator agreement, shown in Table 4.

We selected this measure because of its compatibility with more than two annotators per task

Density	Basque–Spanish				Tatar–Russian			
	MT & Src	**MT**	**Src**	**No hint**	**MT & Src**	**MT**	**Src**	**No hint**
10%	0.496	0.517	0.400	0.124	0.598	0.459	0.711	0.517
20%	0.714	0.700	0.358	0.275	0.740	0.667	0.473	0.261
30%	0.559	0.430	0.406	0.300	0.534	0.581	0.411	0.412

Table 4: Krippendorff Alpha measure of annotator agreement, for each language pair in all four task modes.

and missing data (not all the gaps were evaluated). To calculate Krippendorff's alpha we used an algorithm implementation by Thomas Grill,[7] dividing the answers in each gap into two categories: correct and incorrect. The previously obtained synonym lists were taken into account, i.e. if the two answers are different but both correct, they fall into one category. The measure was calculated separately for each hint and percentage combination.

The interpretation of Krippendorff's alpha varies depending on the application. One of the general guidelines suggested by Landis and Koch (1977) for kappa-like measures (which includes Krippendorff's Alpha) is as follows: $k < 0$ indicates "poor" agreement, 0 to 0.2 "slight", 0.21 to 0.4 "fair", 0.41 to 0.6 "moderate", 0.61 to 0.8 "substantial", and 0.81 to 1 "near perfect".

In general, the level of annotator agreement is relatively high. As the MT and MT+source hints are introduced, the agreement increases (measures closer to 1): the annotators are more consistently correct or incorrect in each given sentence. The agreement measure for the same sentences without hints is closer to zero, which attests to the reliability of our methodology. We note the outlier score in Tatar–Russian 10% source tasks, which has the most contribution from the news texts. This set of sentences contains many loan words, which have similar form in Tatar and Russian (e.g. president, minister, championship), and are understood by Russian speakers. The gaps with loan words have mostly been filled correctly, while there was some disagreement in other gaps.

4.2 Results for different domains

For the Tatar–Russian language pair the participants were offered texts from three different domains (in equal proportions): casual conversations, legal texts and news. The results by domains are displayed in table 5. The MT system used in the evaluation has been targeted to translate texts from all three of the domains. Taking into consideration the above discussion of 10% MT+Source tasks, we observe similar results across the three categories. Note that the source sentences paired with MT improve participants' performance in casual texts, compared to MT-only task mode. This may be due to the fact that many words are borrowed from Russian into Tatar, and are in fact understood by Russian speakers.

5 Conclusions

We have conducted assimilation evaluation of two Apertium translation directions: Basque–Spanish and Tatar–Russian. The results suggest that this evaluation method reflects the contribution of MT to users' understanding of text. The version of the toolkit used in this experiment may be downloaded from our repository.[8]

The experiments may easily be repeated for any language pair (provided a parallel corpus) and any machine translation system. Based on our experience, we would like to suggest the following amendments to the procedure:

1. As reported by O'Regan and Forcada (2013), unless the evaluation is targeted at a specific text domain, it may be beneficial to include a stylistic variety of texts in the initial corpus. Neighboring sentences on the same topic may assist the users in gap-filling tasks;
2. If possible, increase the number of evaluators, or reduce the number of questions per participant. In the above experiments each participant filled from 110 to 187 gaps, divided into small groups. Reducing the amount of work may increase task completion rate;
3. To account for the adaptation period, provide training tasks before the main evaluations take place.

As a consideration for future work, it may be beneficial to compare the results of evaluation by

[7] http://grrrr.org/data/dev/krippendorff_alpha/

[8] https://github.com/Sereni/Appraise/tree/1e9d735faee64d1b97fb343ab111ace6a64509d7

		Evaluation mode			
Domain	Gap percentage	MT & Src	MT	Src	No hint
Casual	10%	64 ± 45	64 ± 43	62 ± 46	53 ± 44
	20%	73 ± 32	63 ± 36	41 ± 28	38 ± 31
	30%	70 ± 31	60 ± 24	39 ± 27	38 ± 33
Legal	10%	53 ± 40	68 ± 35	39 ± 38	33 ± 35
	20%	61 ± 25	66 ± 24	50 ± 34	48 ± 34
	30%	50 ± 26	48 ± 29	40 ± 27	34 ± 29
News	10%	53 ± 38	60 ± 44	57 ± 42	49 ± 39
	20%	59 ± 34	49 ± 35	47 ± 32	29 ± 29
	30%	58 ± 22	61 ± 22	41 ± 30	35 ± 27

Table 5: Tatar–Russian Average number of gaps successfully filled (%), using a synonym list, for three different domains, in all four task modes.

gap-filling method with the traditional evaluation metrics, as well as with human evaluation.

Acknowledgments: This work has been partly funded by the Spanish Ministerio de Economía y Competitividad through project TIN2012-32615. Ekaterina Ageeva's work has been supported by Google Summer of Code 2014 through the Apertium project. We thank the volunteers who participated in the evaluations.

References

Church, K. W. and Hovy, E. H. (1993). Good applications for crummy machine translation. *Machine Translation*, 8(4):239–258.

Federmann, C. (2012). Appraise: an open-source toolkit for manual evaluation of MT output. *The Prague Bulletin of Mathematical Linguistics*, 98:25–35.

Forcada, M. L., Ginestí-Rosell, M., Nordfalk, J., O'Regan, J., Ortiz-Rojas, S., Pérez-Ortiz, J. A., Sánchez-Martínez, F., Ramírez-Sánchez, G., and Tyers, F. M. (2011). Apertium: a free/open-source platform for rule-based machine translation. *Machine translation*, 25(2):127–144.

Ginestí-Rosell, M., Ramırez-Sánchez, G., Ortiz-Rojas, S., Tyers, F. M., and Forcada, M. L. (2009). Development of a free Basque to Spanish machine translation system. *Procesamiento del Lenguaje Natural*, 43:187–195.

Jones, D., Herzog, M., Ibrahim, H., Jairam, A., Shen, W., Gibson, E., and Emonts, M. (2007). ILR-based MT comprehension test with multi-level questions. In *HLT 2007: The Conference of the North American Chapter of the Association for Computational Linguistics; Companion Volume, Short Papers*, pages 77–80. Association for Computational Linguistics.

Koehn, P. (2010). *Statistical machine translation*. Cambridge University Press.

Krippendorff, K. (1970). Estimating the reliability, systematic error and random error of interval data. *Educational and Psychological Measurement*, 30(1):61–70.

Landis, J. R. and Koch, G. G. (1977). The measurement of observer agreement for categorical data. *biometrics*, pages 159–174.

O'Regan, J. and Forcada, M. L. (2013). Peeking through the language barrier: the development of a free/open-source gisting system for Basque to English based on `apertium.org`. *Procesamiento del Lenguaje Natural*, 51:15–22.

Somers, H. and Wild, E. (2000). Evaluating machine translation: the Cloze procedure revisited. In *Translating and the Computer 22: Proceedings of the Twenty-second International Conference on Translating and the Computer*.

Taylor, W. L. (1953). "Cloze procedure": a new tool for measuring readability. *Journalism quarterly*.

Trosterud, T. and Unhammer, K. B. (2012). Evaluating North Sámi to Norwegian assimilation RBMT. In *Proceedings of the Third International Workshop on Free/Open-Source Rule-Based Machine Translation (FreeRBMT 2012)*.

Van Slype, G. (1979). Critical study of methods for evaluating the quality of machine translation. *Prepared for the Commission of European Communities Directorate General Scientific and Technical Information and Information Management. Report BR*, 19142.

Unsupervised training of maximum-entropy models for lexical selection in rule-based machine translation

Francis M. Tyers
HSL-fakultehta,
UiT Norgga árktalaš universitehta,
N-9018 Romsa

Felipe Sánchez-Martínez
Dept. Lleng. i Sist. Inform.,
Universitat d'Alacant,
E-03071 Alacant

Mikel L. Forcada
Dept. Lleng. i Sist. Inform.,
Universitat d'Alacant,
E-03071 Alacant

Abstract

This article presents a method of training maximum-entropy models to perform lexical selection in a rule-based machine translation system. The training method described is unsupervised; that is, it does not require any annotated corpus. The method uses source-language monolingual corpora, the machine translation (MT) system in which the models are integrated, and a statistical target-language model. Using the MT system, the sentences in the source-language corpus are translated in all possible ways according to the different translation equivalents in the bilingual dictionary of the system. These translations are then scored on the target-language model and the scores are normalised to provide fractional counts for training source-language maximum-entropy lexical-selection models. We show that these models can perform equally well, or better, than using the target-language model directly for lexical selection, at a substantially reduced computational cost.

1 Introduction

Corpus-based machine translation (MT) has been the primary research direction in the field of MT in recent years. However, rule-based MT (RBMT) systems are still being developed, and there are many successful commercial and non-commercial systems. One reason for the continued development of RBMT systems is that in order to be successful, corpus-based MT requires parallel corpora in the order of tens of millions of words. Although for some language pairs these exist, they only exist for a fraction of the world's languages.

An RBMT system typically consists of an analysis component,[1] a transfer component and a generation component. As part of the transfer component it is necessary to make choices regarding words in the source language (SL) which may have more than one translation in the target language (TL).

Lexical selection is the task of choosing, for a given SL word, the most adequate translation in the TL among a known set of alternatives. The task is related to the task of word-sense disambiguation (Ide and Véronis, 1998). However, it is different to word-sense disambiguation in that lexical selection is a bilingual problem, not a monolingual problem: its aim is to find the most adequate translation, not the most adequate sense. Thus, it is not necessary to choose among a series of fine-grained senses if all these senses result in the same final translation; however, it may sometimes be necessary to choose a different translation for the same sense, for example in a collocation.

1.1 Prior work

Dagan and Itai (1994) used the term *word sense disambiguation* to refer to what is actually lexical selection in MT; they used a parser to identify syntactic relations such as subject–object or subject–verb. After generating all the possible translations for a given input sentence using an ambiguous bilingual dictionary, they extract the syntactic tuples from the TL and count the frequency in a previously-trained TL model of tuples. They use maximum-likelihood estimation to calculate the probability that a given

[1] Such as a morphological or syntactic analyser.

TL tuple is the translation of a given SL tuple, with an automatically determined confidence threshold.

Later, Berger et al. (1996) illustrated the use of maximum-entropy classifiers on the specific problem of lexical selection in IBM-style word-based statistical MT. Other authors (Melero et al., 2007) have used TL models to rank the translations resulting from all possible combinations of lexical selections. Nowadays, in state-of-the-art phrase-based statistical MT (Koehn, 2010), lexical selection is taken care of by a combination of the translation model and the language model. The translation model provides probabilities of translation between words or word sequences (often referred to as *phrases*) in the source and target language. The TL model provides probabilities of word sequences in the TL. Mareček et al. (2010) trained a maximum-entropy lexical selector for their dependency-grammar-based transfer system TectoMT using a bilingual corpus. More recently, Tyers et al. (2012) presented a method of lexical selection for RBMT based on rules which select or remove translations in fixed-length contexts, along with a training method for learning the rules from a word-aligned parallel corpus.[2]

2 Method

Lexical selection in this paper considers for each word a simple SL context made up of neighbouring lemma+part-of-speech combinations. Contexts considered include up to two words to the left and up to two words to the right of the word to be translated.

Let the probability of a word t being the translation of a word s in a SL context c be $p_s(t|c)$. In principle, this value could be estimated directly from the available corpora for every combination of (s, t, c). This would however present two questions: (1) how should the relevant contexts be chosen? and (2) what should be done when (s, t, c) is not found in the corpus? A maximum-entropy model answers both of these questions. It allows the contexts that we consider to be linguistically interesting to be defined *a priori* and then integrate these seamlessly into a probabilistic model (Manning and Schütze, 1999). In answer to the second question, a maximum-entropy model maximises the entropy subject to match the expected counts of the designed features with those found in the training data. That is, if there is no information in the training data, then it assumes that all outcomes —that is, all possible translations— are equally likely. As previously mentioned, the principle of maximum entropy has been applied to the problem of lexical selection before; in particular, Berger et al. (1996) cast the problem of lexical selection in statistical MT as a classification problem. They learn a separate maximum-entropy classifier for each SL word form, using SL context to distinguish between possible translations. These classifiers are then incorporated into the translation model of their word-based statistical MT system. In their approach, a classifier consists of a set of binary feature functions and corresponding weights for each feature. In both Berger et al. (1996) and our method, features are defined in the form $h_k^s(t, c)$,[3] where t is a translation, and c is a SL context. One difference is that Berger et al. (1996) take s, t and c to be based on word forms, whereas in our method they are based on lemma forms. An example would be the following feature where the Spanish word *pez* ('fish' as a living animal) is seen as the translation of *arrain* ('fish') in the context *arrain handi* 'big fish' and would therefore be defined as:

$$h^{\text{arrain}}_{\text{+handi}}(t, c) = \begin{cases} 1 & \text{if } \begin{cases} t = \textit{pez} \\ \text{and} \\ \textit{handi} \text{ follows } \textit{arrain} \end{cases} \\ 0 & \text{otherwise} \end{cases} \tag{1}$$

This feature considers a context of zero words to the left of the problem word and one word (+ *handi*) to the right of it.

As a result of training, each of the n_F features $h_k^s(t, c)$ in the classifier is assigned a weight λ_k^s. Combining these weights of active features as in equation (2) yields the probability of a translation t for word s in context c.

$$p_s(t|c) = \frac{1}{Z^s(c)} \exp \sum_{k=1}^{n_F} \lambda_k^s h_k^s(t, c) \tag{2}$$

In this equation, $Z^s(c)$ is a normalising constant. Thus, the most probable translation $t^\star$ can be found using

$$t^\star = \arg\max_{t \in T_s(s)} p_s(t|c) = \arg\max_{t \in T_s(s)} \sum_{k=1}^{n_F} \lambda_k^s h_k^s(t, c), \tag{3}$$

[2]The work by Ravi and Knight (2011) and Nuhn and Ney (2014), who decipher word-ciphered text using monolingual corpora only may be seen as a generalised version of the problem of lexical selection without parallel corpora.

[3]We follow the notation of Berger et al. (1996)

$$S \rightarrow \boxed{\textit{pre-lexsel}} \rightarrow (\{g_i\}_{i=1}^{i=|G|}, S) \rightarrow \boxed{\textbf{\textit{lexsel}}} \rightarrow (g^\star, S) \rightarrow \boxed{\textit{post-lexsel}} \rightarrow \tau(g^\star, S)$$

Figure 1: A schema of the lexical selection process: source sentence S has $|G|$ lexical selection paths g_i: *lexsel* selects one of them $g^\star$, which is used to generate translation $\tau(g^\star, S)$.

where $T_s(s)$ is the set of possible translations for SL word s.

The approaches by Berger et al. (1996) and by Mareček et al. (2010) cited above both take advantage of a parallel corpus to collect counts of contexts and translations in order to train maximum-entropy models. However, parallel corpora are not available for the majority of the world's written languages. In this section we describe an unsupervised method to learn the models using only monolingual corpora and the components from the RBMT system in which they are used.

The input to our method consists of a collection of samples, $\mathcal{G} = (S, G)$, where $S = (s_1, s_2, \ldots s_{|S|})$ is a sequence of SL words, and $G = \{g_1, g_2, \ldots g_{|G|}\}$ is a set of possible *lexical-selection paths*. A lexical-selection path $g = (t_1, t_2, \ldots, t_{|S|})$ is a sequence of lexical-selection choices of those SL words, where t_i is an element of $T_s(s_i)$, the set of possible translations of s_i.[4] This is produced in the first stages of RBMT, just after morphological analysis, part-of-speech tagging, and bilingual dictionary lookup, and before any structural transfer takes place (we will call this *pre-lexsel*). In our model, it is after these first stages that lexical selection (*lexsel*) occurs. After lexical selection, structural transfer and generation take place; a function $\tau(g_i, S)$ represents the result of these last stages, which we will call *post-lexsel*, and returns a finished translation of a specific lexical-selection path g_i of sentence S. Figure 1 shows this process schematically.

As our method is unsupervised, and therefore the occurrences of specific lexical selection events (s, t, c) cannot be counted, a TL model $P_{\mathrm{TL}}(\cdot)$ is used to compute a value for the fractional count for disambiguation path g_i, $p(g_i|S)$ after suitable normalisation:

$$p(g_i|S) = \frac{P_{\mathrm{TL}}(\tau(g_i, S))}{\sum_{g_i \in G} P_{\mathrm{TL}}(\tau(g_i, S))} \quad (4)$$

The maximum-entropy model is trained instead using the fractional count $p(g_i|S)$ for the events (s, t, c) found in g_i, that is, when in g_i the translation for s in context c is t. That is, as if event (s, t, c) had been seen a fractional number $p(g_i|S)$ of times. We prune (s, t, c) occurring less than a certain number of times in the corpus, using a development corpus to guide pruning (see section 4). The method used here for lexical selection is analogous to the method used by Sánchez-Martínez et al. (2008) to train a hidden-Markov-model-based part-of-speech tagger in a RBMT system.

3 Experimental setting

This section describes the training and evaluation settings used in the remainder of this paper. The primary motivation behind the evaluation is that it should be automatic, meaningful, and be performed over a test set which is large enough to be representative. It should evaluate both performance on the specific subtask of lexical selection, and on the whole translation task. Evaluating lexical-selection performance is an *intrinsic* module-based evaluation. It measures how well the lexical selection module disambiguates the lexical-transfer output as compared to a gold-standard corpus. The lexical transfer output is the result of looking up the translations of the SL *lexical forms* — lemmas and tags — in the bilingual dictionary.

The whole translation task evaluation is an *extrinsic* evaluation, which tests how the system improves as regards final translation quality in a real system.

The lexical-selection module should be as language-independent as possible. To that end, the language pairs tested show a wide variety of linguistic phenomena. It is also important that the methodology be as applicable to lesser-resourced and marginalised languages as to major languages.

This section begins with a short description of the Apertium platform (Forcada et al., 2011). This is followed by an overview of each of the language pairs chosen for the evaluation. The corpora to be used for training and evaluation will subsequently be described, along with the method used for annotating them. This is followed by a description of the performance measures to be used in the evaluation, and the reference results using these metrics for

[4]We deal only with single-word translations in this paper.

each of the language pairs.

3.1 Apertium

Apertium is a free/open-source RBMT platform, it comprises an engine, a toolbox and data to build RBMT systems. Translation is implemented as a pipeline consisting of the following modules: morphological analysis, morphological disambiguation, lexical transfer, lexical selection, structural transfer and morphological generation.

3.2 Language pairs

Evaluation will be performed using four Apertium (Forcada et al., 2011) language pairs. These pairs have been selected as they include languages with different morphological complexity, and different amounts of resources available — although for all pairs there is a parallel corpus available for evaluation (see Section 3.3).[5]

Breton–French (Tyers, 2010): Bilingual dictionaries were not built with polysemy in mind from the outset, but some entries were added later to start work on lexical selection.[6]

Macedonian–English: The Macedonian–English pair in Apertium was created specifically for the purposes of running lexical-selection experiments. The lexical resources for the pair were tuned to the SETimes parallel corpus (Tyers and Alperen, 2010). The most probable entry from automatic word alignment of this corpus using GIZA++ (Och and Ney, 2003) was checked to ensure that it was an adequate translation, and if so marked as the default.[7] As a result of attempting to include all possible translations, the average number of translations per word is much higher than in other pairs.[8]

Basque–Spanish (Ginestí-Rosell et al., 2009): alternative translations were included in the bilingual dictionary.[9]

English–Spanish: The English–Spanish pair was developed from a combination of the English–Catalan and Spanish–Catalan pairs, and contains a number of entries in the bilingual dictionary with more than one translation.[10]

3.3 Performance measures

This section describes the measures that will be used to evaluate the performance of the lexical selection method proposed here: a (intrinsic) *lexical selection performance* measure and an (extrinsic) *machine translation performance* measure.

3.3.1 Lexical-selection performance

This is an intrinsic module-based evaluation of the performance of the lexical-selection module. It measures how well the lexical-selection module disambiguates the output of the lexical-transfer module as compared to a gold-standard corpus. For this task, we define a metric, the lexical-selection error rate (LER), that focuses on the problem of lexical selection by restricting the evaluation to this feature; other features of the MT system, such as the transfer rules and morphological generation, are not taken into account.

The lexical-selection error rate is the fraction of times the given system chooses a translation for a word which is not the one found in an annotated reference. The process uses a SL sentence, $S = (s_1, s_2, \ldots, s_{|S|})$ and three functions. The first function, $T_s(s_i)$, returns all possible translations of s_i according to the bilingual dictionary. The second function, $T_t(s_i)$, returns the translations of s_i selected by the lexical-selection module: $T_t(s_i) \subseteq T_s(s_i)$; and usually $|T_t(s_i)| = 1$. If the lexical-selection module returns more than one translation, the first translation is selected. The function $T_r(s_i)$ returns the set of reference translations which are acceptable for s_i in sentence S.[11] For a single sentence, we define the lexical selection error rate (LER) of that sentence as

$$\mathrm{LER} = \frac{\sum_{i=1}^{|S|} \mathrm{amb}(s_i)\ \mathrm{diff}(T_r(s_i), T_t(s_i))}{\sum_{i=1}^{|S|} \mathrm{amb}(s_i)}, \quad (5)$$

where

$$\mathrm{amb}(s_i) = \begin{cases} 1 & \text{if } |T_s(s_i)| > 1 \\ 0 & \text{otherwise} \end{cases} \quad (6)$$

[5] The Apertium revision (version) used is given in footnotes.

[6] Revision 41375; `https://svn.code.sf.net/p/apertium/svn/trunk/apertium-br-fr`

[7] Bilingual dictionaries in Apertium (Forcada et al., 2011) may contain several translations for a given word. Dictionary writers may mark as *linguistic default* the most general or most frequent translation among the set of possible translations.

[8] Revision 41476; `https://svn.code.sf.net/p/apertium/svn/trunk/apertium-mk-en`

[9] Revision 44846; `https://svn.code.sf.net/p/apertium/svn/trunk/apertium-eu-es`

[10] Revision 41387; `https://svn.code.sf.net/p/apertium/svn/trunk/apertium-en-es`

[11] Depending on how the reference is built, the set returned by $T_r(s_i)$ may not include all possible acceptable translations.

L'estiu és una estació llarga						
S	*el*	*estiu*	*ser*	*un*	*estació*	*llarg*
$T_s(s_i)$	{the}	{summer}	{be}	{a}	{station, season}	{long, lengthy}
$T_r(s_i)$	{the}	{summer}	{be}	{a}	{season}	{long}
$T_t(s_i)$	{the}	{summer}	{be}	{a}	{station}	{long}
$\text{amb}(s_i)$	0	0	0	0	1	1
$\text{diff}(T_r(s_i), T_t(s_i))$	0	0	0	0	1	0

Figure 2: An example input sentence in Catalan and the three sets of English translations used for calculating the lexical-selection error rate. The source sentence $S = (s_1, s_2, \ldots, s_{|S|})$ has two ambiguous words, *estació* and *llarg* ($\text{amb}(s_i) = 1$, eq. (6)). There is one difference ($\text{diff}(T_r(s_i), T_t(s_i)) = 1$, eq. (7)) between the reference set $T_r(s_i)$ and the test set $T_t(s_i)$ of translations; thus, the error rate for this sentence is 50%.

tests if a word is ambiguous, and the function

$$\text{diff}(T_r(s_i), T_t(s_i)) = \begin{cases} 1 & \text{if } T_r(s_i) \cap T_t(s_i) = \emptyset \\ 0 & \text{otherwise} \end{cases} \quad (7)$$

states that there is a difference if the intersection between the set of reference translations $T_r(s_i)$ and the set of translations from the lexical selection module $T_t(s_i)$ is empty. Recall that, although $T_t(s_i)$ returns a set, this set will be a singleton, as when the lexical-selection module returns more than one translation, Apertium will select the default one if marked or the first one of not.[12]

The table in Figure 2 gives an overview of the inputs.In the description it is assumed that the reference translation has been annotated by hand. However, hand annotation is a time-consuming process, and was not possible. A description of how the reference was built is given in Section 3.4.

3.3.2 Machine translation performance

This is an extrinsic evaluation, which ideally would test how much the system improves as regards an approximate measurement of final translation quality in a real system. For this task, we use the widely-used BLEU metric (Papineni et al., 2002). This is not ideal for evaluating the task of a lexical selection module as the performance of the module will depend greatly on (a) the coverage of the bilingual dictionaries of the RBMT system in question, and (b) the number of reference translations. It is also worth noting that successful lexical selections may not lead to successful translations due to inadequate transfer of morphological features. The BLEU metric is included only as it is commonly used to evaluate MT systems.

[12]In practice this does not happen as each ambiguous word has a *default* translation.

3.3.3 Confidence intervals

Confidence intervals for both metrics will be calculated through *bootstrap resampling* (Efron and Tibshirani, 1994) as described by Koehn (2004). In all cases, bootstrap resampling will be carried out for 1,000 iterations. Where the $p = 0.05$ confidence intervals overlap, we will also perform paired bootstrap resampling (Koehn, 2004).

3.4 Corpora

For creating the test corpora, providing a SL corpus for training, and a TL corpus for scoring, we used four parallel corpora:

- **Ofis ar Brezhoneg** (`OAB`): This parallel corpus of Breton and French has been collected specifically for lexical-selection experiments from translations produced by *Ofis ar Brezhoneg* 'The Office of the Breton language'. The corpus has recently been made available online through OPUS.[13]
- **South-East European Times** (`SETimes`): Described in Tyers and Alperen (2010), this corpus is a multilingual corpus of the Balkan languages (and English) in the news domain. The Macedonian and English part will be used.
- **Open Data Euskadi** (`OpenData`): This is a Basque–Spanish parallel corpus made from the translation memories of the *Herri Arduralaritzaren Euskal Erakundea* 'Basque Institute of Public Administration'.[14]
- **European Parliament Proceedings** (`EuroParl`): Described by Koehn (2005), this is a multilingual corpus of the European Union official languages. We are using the English–Spanish data from version 7.[15]

[13]`http://opus.lingfil.uu.se`
[14]`http://tinyurl.com/eu-es-tm`
[15]`http://www.statmt.org/europarl/`

There are a number of approaches to creating evaluation corpora for lexical selection in the literature. Vickrey et al. (2005) use a parallel corpus to make annotated test and training sets for experiments in lexical selection applied to a simplified translation problem in statistical MT. They use word alignments from GIZA++ (Och and Ney, 2003) to annotate SL words with their translations from the reference translation in the parallel corpus. One disadvantage of this method is that only one translation is annotated per SL word, meaning that accuracies may be lower because of missing translations — this happens when the system chooses a translation which is adequate, but is not found in the reference translation. A second disadvantage is that the word alignments may not be 100% reliable, which decreases the accuracy of the annotated corpus. An alternative method is described by Zinovjeva (2000), who manually tags ambiguous words in English sentences with their translation in Swedish.

Ideally we would have had a hand-annotated evaluation corpus, as described by Zinovjeva (2000), but as this did not exist, we decided to automatically annotate a test set using a process similar to that described by Vickrey et al. (2005).

The annotation process proceeds as follows: First we word-align the corpus to extract a set of word alignments, which are correspondences between words in sentences in the source side of the parallel corpus and those in the target side. Any aligner may be used, but in this paper we use GIZA++ (Och and Ney, 2003).[16] We then use these alignments along with the bilingual dictionary of the MT system in question to extract only those sentences where: (a) there is at least one ambiguous word; (b) that ambiguous word is aligned to a single word in the TL; and (c) the word it is aligned to in the TL is found in the bilingual dictionary of the MT system. Sentences where there are no ambiguous words (approximately 90%, see Table 1) are discarded. The source side of the extracted sentence is then passed through the lexical transfer module, which returns all the possible translations, and for each ambiguous word, the translation is selected which is found aligned in the reference.

After this process, we selected 1,000 sentence pairs at random for testing (`test`), 1,000 for development (`dev`)[17] and left the remainder for training. Table 1 gives statistics about the size of the input corpora, and how many sentences were left after processing for testing, training and development. Table 2 gives information about the test corpora.

Pair	SL	TL	Amb.	% amb.
`br-fr`	13,854	13,878	1,163	8.39
`mk-en`	13,441	14,228	3,872	28.80
`eu-es`	7,967	11,476	1,360	17.07
`en-es`	19,882	20,944	1,469	7.38

Table 2: Statistics about the test corpora. The columns **SL** and **TL** give the number of tokens in the source and target languages respectively. The columns **amb. words** and **% ambig** gives the number of word with more than one translation and the percentage of SL words which have more than one translation respectively.

3.5 Reference systems

We compare our method to the following reference (or baseline) systems:

- **Linguist-chosen defaults**. A bilingual dictionary in an Apertium language pair contains correspondences between lexical forms. The dictionaries allow many lexical forms to translate to one lexical form. But a single lexical form may not have more than one translation without further processing. If there are many possible translations of a lexical form, then one must be marked as the *default* translation.
- **Oracle**. The results for the oracle system are those achieved by passing the automatically annotated reference translation through the rest of the modules of the MT system. This is included to show the upper bound for the performance of the lexical-selection module.
- **Target language model** (TLM). One method of lexical selection is to use the existing MT system to generate all the possible translations for an input sentence, and then score these translations *on-line* on a model of the TL. The highest scoring sentence is then output. This is the method used by Melero et al. (2007).

4 Results

As we are working with binary features, we use the implementation of generalised iterative scaling

[16]The exact configuration of GIZA++ used is equivalent to running the MOSES toolkit (Koehn et al., 2007) in default configuration up to step three of training.

[17]The development corpus was used for checking the value for frequency pruning of features.

Pair	Lines	Extract.	train	dev	test	No. amb	Av. amb
br-fr	57,305	4,668	2,668	1,000	1,000	603	3.06
mk-en	190,493	19,747	17,747	1,000	1,000	13,134	3.06
eu-es	765,115	87,907	85,907	1,000	1,000	1,806	3.11
en-es	1,467,708	312,162	310,162	1,000	1,000	2,082	2.28

Table 1: Statistics about the source corpora. The column **no. amb** gives the number of unique tokens with more than one possible translation. The column **av. amb** gives the average number of translations per ambiguous word. This is calculated by looking up each word in the corpus in the bilingual dictionary of the MT system and dividing the total number of translation by the number of words. Both **av. amb** and **no. amb** are calculated over the whole corpus.

Pair	Pruned	# features
br-fr	< 5	5,277
mk-en	< 7	205,494
eu-es	< 7	196,024
en-es	< 7	195,605

Table 3: Features in each rule set and pruning frequency.

available in the YASMET[18] to calculate the feature weights. After learning the feature sets and weights, we compute the evaluation measures described in Section 3.3. There is an option to remove events (s, t, c) which occur less than a certain number of times in the training corpus. This is referred to as the feature pruning frequency threshold — features occurring less than the threshold are discarded. The value was set experimentally. Values of between two and seven were tested, and the ones which provided the best improvement on the development corpus were selected; they happen to come close to the rule-of-thumb value of five that Manning and Schütze (1999, p. 596) found to be effective. Table 3 shows the number of features that have eventually been used for each language pair.

Evaluation results are presented in table 4, which compares the results of the new approach with respect to the *default behaviour* (the linguist-chosen defaults), with respect to the *oracle* (which represents the upper bound to performance), and with respect to the results obtained by using the TL model online, for each of the language pairs in Apertium with respect to our two evaluation metrics. Note that the high error rate for the Breton–French pair may be as a result of having the linguistic defaults tuned to a different domain than that of the corpus.

Significant improvements with respect to the results obtained using the TL model online are apparent with the Breton–French —the pair with the least data— and the English–Spanish language pairs. In the remaining cases, the maximum-entropy method comes close to the TL model performance in terms of similar or better BLEU and LER scores, at a much smaller computational cost.

Improvements with respect to the TL model performance are likely due to the effective use that the maximum-entropy model makes of information about the relevant SL contexts and their translations, through the weighting of features representing those SL contexts across the whole corpus.

5 Conclusions

This paper has presented a method to perform lexical selection in RBMT, and one that can be trained in an unsupervised way, that is, without the need for an annotated corpus, (in this case a word-aligned bilingual corpus): one just needs a SL corpus, a statistical TL model, and the RBMT system itself. The input to the method is simply the part-of-speech tagged source text in which each word is annotated with all the translations provided by the bilingual dictionary in the system: this makes it applicable to almost any RBMT system. The system uses a maximum-entropy formalism for lexical selection, as Berger et al. (1996) and Mareček et al. (2010), but instead of counting actual lexical selection events in an annotated corpus, it counts fractional occurrences of these events as estimated by a TL model. The method is evaluated both intrinsically (just looking at the actual lexical selection events) and extrinsically (measuring the quality of MT). Results on four language pairs using the Apertium (Forcada et al., 2011) MT system show that the method obtains similar or better results than those expensively obtained by scoring an exponential number of lexical selections for each sentence using the TL model online.

[18] http://www-i6.informatik.rwth-aachen.de/web/Software/YASMET.html; the compilable version we used is available as part of the Apertium lex-tools package, http://downloads.sourceforge.net/project/apertium/apertium-lex-tools/apertium-lex-tools-0.1.0.tar.gz.

Pair	Metric	System			
		Ling	TLM	MaxEnt	Oracle
br-fr	LER (%)	[54.8, 60.7]	[44.2, 50.5]	**[40.8, 46.9]**	[0.0, 0.0]
	BLEU (%)	[14.5, 16.4]	[15.4, 17.3]	[14.8, 16.6]	[16.7, 18.6]
mk-en	LER (%)	[28.8, 32.6]	[26.8, 30.5]	[25.2, 28.8]	[0.0, 0.0]
	BLEU (%)	[28.6, 31.0]	[30.7, 32.3]	[29.1, 31.5]	[30.9, 33.3]
eu-es	LER (%)	[43.6, 48.8]	[38.8, 44.2]	[40.9, 46.2]	[0.0, 0.0]
	BLEU (%)	[10.1, 12.0]	[10.6, 12.6]	[10.3, 12.2]	[11.5, 13.5]
en-es	LER (%)	[20.5, 24.9]	[15.1, 18.9]	**[10.4, 13.8]**	[0.0, 0.0]
	BLEU (%)	[21.5, 23.4]	[21.9, 23.8]	**[22.2, 24.1]**	[22.8, 24.7]

Table 4: LER and BLEU scores with 95% confidence intervals for the reference systems on the test corpora. The `max-ent` system has been trained using fractional counts. The results in bold face show statistically significant improvements for the maximum-entropy model compared to the TL model according to pair-bootstrap resampling.

Acknowledgements: We acknowledge support from the Spanish Ministry of Industry and Competitiveness through project Ayutra (TIC2012-32615) and from the European Commission through project Abu-Matran (FP7-PEOPLE-2012-IAPP, ref. 324414) and thank all three anonymous referees for useful comments on the paper.

References

Berger, A., Pietra, S. D., and Pietra, V. D. (1996). A maximum entropy approach to natural language processing. *Computational Linguistics*, 22(1):39–71.

Dagan, I. and Itai, A. (1994). Word sense disambiguation using a second language monolingual corpus. *Computational Linguistics*, 20(4):563–596.

Efron, B. and Tibshirani, R. J. (1994). *An Introduction to the Bootstrap*. CRC Press.

Forcada, M. L., Ginestí-Rosell, M., Nordfalk, J., ORegan, J., Ortiz-Rojas, S., Pérez-Ortiz, J. A., Sánchez-Martínez, F., Ramírez-Sánchez, G., and Tyers, F. M. (2011). Apertium: a free/open-source platform for rule-based machine translation. *Machine Translation*, 25(2):127–144.

Ginestí-Rosell, M., Ramírez-Sánchez, G., Ortiz-Rojas, S., Tyers, F. M., and Forcada, M. L. (2009). Development of a free Basque to Spanish machine translation system. *Procesamiento de Lenguaje Natural*, (43):185–197.

Ide, N. and Véronis, J. (1998). Word sense disambiguation: The state of the art. *Computational Linguistics*, 24(1):1–41.

Koehn, P. (2004). Statistical significance tests for machine translation evaluation. In *Proc. of the Conference on EMNLP*, pages 388–395.

Koehn, P. (2005). Europarl: A parallel corpus for statistical machine translation. In *Proc. of the 10th MT Summit*, pages 79–86.

Koehn, P. (2010). *Statistical machine translation*. Cambridge University Press.

Koehn, P., Hoang, H., Birch, A., Callison-Burch, C., Federico, M., Bertoldi, N., Cowan, B., Shen, W., Moran, C., Zens, R., Dyer, C., Bojar, O., Constantin, A., and Herbst, E. (2007). Moses: Open source toolkit for statistical machine translation. In *Proc. of the Annual Meeting of the ACL, demonstration session*.

Manning, C. D. and Schütze, H. (1999). *Foundations of Statistical Natural Language Processing*. MIT Press.

Mareček, D., Popel, M., and Žabokrtský, Z. (2010). Maximum entropy translation model in dependency-based MT framework. In *WMT '10 Proc. of the Joint 5th Workshop on SMT and MetricsMATR*, pages 201–206.

Melero, M., Oliver, A., Badia, T., and Suñol, T. (2007). Dealing with bilingual divergences in MT using target language n-gram models. In *Proc. of the METIS-II Workshop*, pages 19–26.

Nuhn, M. and Ney, H. (2014). Em decipherment for large vocabularies. In *Proceedings of the 52nd Annual Meeting of the Association for Computational Linguistics (Short Papers)*, pages 759–764.

Och, F. J. and Ney, H. (2003). A systematic comparison of various statistical alignment models. *Computational Linguistics*, 29(1):19–51.

Papineni, K., Roukos, S., Ward, T., and Zhu, W. J. (2002). "BLEU: a method for automatic evaluation of machine translation. In *ACL-2002: 40th Annual meeting of the ACL*, pages 311–318.

Ravi, S. and Knight, K. (2011). Deciphering foreign language. In *Proceedings of the 49th Annual Meeting of the Association for Computational Linguistics: Human Language Technologies-Volume 1*, pages 12–21. Association for Computational Linguistics.

Sánchez-Martínez, F., Pérez-Ortiz, J. A., and Forcada, M. L. (2008). Using target-language information to train part-of-speech taggers for machine translation. *Machine Translation*, 22(1-2):29–66.

Tyers, F. M. (2010). Rule-based Breton to French machine translation. In *Proc. of the 14th Annual Conference of the EAMT*, pages 174–181.

Tyers, F. M. and Alperen, M. S. (2010). SETimes: A parallel corpus of Balkan languages. In *Workshop on Exploitation of multilingual resources and tools for Central and (South) Eastern European Languages at the Language Resources and Evaluation Conference*, pages 1–5.

Tyers, F. M., Sánchez-Martínez, F., and Forcada, M. L. (2012). Flexible finite-state lexical selection for rule-based machine translation. In *Proc. of the 16th Annual Conference of the EAMT*, pages 213–220, Trento, Italy.

Vickrey, D., Biewald, L., Teyssier, M., and Koller, D. (2005). Word-sense disambiguation for machine translation. In *Proc. of HLT Conference and Conference on EMNLP*, pages 771–778.

Zinovjeva, N. (2000). Learning sense disambiguation rules for machine translation. Master's thesis, Uppsala University.

Assessing linguistically aware fuzzy matching in translation memories

Tom Vanallemeersch, Vincent Vandeghinste
Centre for Computational Linguistics, University of Leuven
Blijde Inkomststraat 13
B-3000 Leuven, Belgium
{tom,vincent}@ccl.kuleuven.be

Abstract

The concept of fuzzy matching in translation memories can take place using linguistically aware or unaware methods, or a combination of both.

We designed a flexible and time-efficient framework which applies and combines linguistically unaware or aware metrics in the source and target language.

We measure the correlation of fuzzy matching metric scores with the evaluation score of the suggested translation to find out how well the usefulness of a suggestion can be predicted, and we measure the difference in recall between fuzzy matching metrics by looking at the improvements in mean TER as the match score decreases. We found that combinations of fuzzy matching metrics outperform single metrics and that the best-scoring combination is a non-linear combination of the different metrics we have tested.

1 Introduction

Computer-aided translation (CAT) has become an essential aspect of translators' working environments. CAT tools speed up translation work, create more consistent translations, and reduce repetitiveness of the translation work. One of the core components of a CAT tool is the translation memory system (TMS). It contains a database of already translated fragments, called the translation memory (TM), which consists of translation units: segments of a text together with their translation.

Given a sentence to be translated, the traditional TMS looks for source language sentences in a TM which are identical (exact matches) or highly similar (fuzzy matches), and, upon success, suggests the translation of the matching sentence to the translator (Sikes, 2007).

Formally, a TM consists of a set of source sentences $S_1, ..., S_n$ and target sentences $T_1, ..., T_n$, where (S_i, T_i) form a translation unit. Let us call the sentence that we want to translate Q (the query sentence).

The TMS checks whether Q already occurs in the TM, i.e. whether $\exists S_i \in S_1, ..., S_n : Q = S_i$. If this is the case, Q needs no new translation and the translation T_i can be retrieved and used as the translation of Q. This is an exact match. If the TMS cannot find a perfect match, fuzzy matching is applied using some function Sim, which calculates the best match S_b of Q in the TM, i.e. the most similar match, as in (1):

$$S_b = \max_{S_i} Sim(Q, S_i) \qquad (1)$$

If $Sim(Q, S_b) >= \theta$ (a predefined minimal threshold, which is typically 0.7 in CAT tools)[1]), T_b, the translation of S_b, is retrieved from the TM and provided as a suggestion for translating Q. If the threshold is not reached, the TMS assumes that T_b is of no value for the translator and does not provide it as a translation suggestion.

Similarity calculation can be done in many ways. In current TMS systems, fuzzy matching techniques mainly consider sentences as simple sequences of words and contain very limited linguistic knowledge. The latter is for instance present in

[1] In CAT tool interfaces, this is usually expressed as a percentage, 70%, which may be modified by the user. Developers may determine the threshold empirically, but their use of a 70% threshold may also be a matter of convention.

the form of stop word lists. Few tools use more elaborate linguistic knowledge.[2]

2 Related work

There is a large variety of methods that can be used for comparing sentences to each other. They are designed for comparing any pair of sequences or trees (not necessarily sentences and their parse trees), for fuzzy matching in a TM, or for comparing machine translation (MT) output to a reference translation. As pointed out by Simard and Fujita (2012), the third type, MT automatic evaluation metrics, can also be used in the context of TMs, both as fuzzy matching metric and as metric for comparing the translation of a fuzzy match with the desired translation. Some matching methods specifically support the integration of fuzzy matches within an MT system (example-based or statistical MT); see for instance Aramaki et al. (2005), Smith and Clark (2009), Zhechev and van Genabith (2010), Ma et al. (2011).

Some matching methods are linguistically unaware. Levenshtein distance (Levenshtein, 1966), which calculates the effort needed to convert one sequence into another using the operations insertion, deletion and substitution, is the most commonly used fuzzy matching method (Bloodgood and Strauss, 2014). Tree edit distance (Klein, 1998) applies this principle to trees; another tree comparison method is tree alignment (Jiang et al., 1995).[3]

To allow using string-based matching methods on trees, there are several ways of converting trees into strings without information loss, as described in Li et al. (2008), who applies a method designed by Prüfer (1918) and based on post-order tree traversal.

Examples of matching methods specifically designed for fuzzy matching are percent match and ngram precision (Bloodgood and Strauss, 2014), which act on unigrams and longer ngrams. Baldwin (2010) compares bag-of-words fuzzy matching metrics with order-sensitive metrics, and word-based with character-based metrics. Examples of well-known MT evaluation metrics are BLEU (Papineni et al., 2002) and TER, i.e. Translation Error Rate[4] (Snover et al., 2006).

Linguistically aware matching methods make use of several layers of information. The "subtree metric" of Liu and Gildea (2005) compares subtrees of phrase structure trees. We devised a similar method, *shared partial subtree matching*, described in Section 3.1.2. Matching can also involve dependency structures, as in the approach of Smith and Clark (2009), head word chains (Liu and Gildea, 2005), semantic roles, as in the HMEANT metric (Lo and Wu, 2011), and semantically similar words or paraphrases, as in the MT evaluation metric Meteor (Denkowski and Lavie, 2014). The latter aligns MT output to one or more reference translations, not only by comparing word forms, but also through shallow linguistic knowledge, i.e. by calculating the stem of words (in some cases using language-specific rules), and by using lists with function words, synonyms and paraphrases.

Some MT evaluation metrics, such as VERTa (Comelles et al., 2014) and LAYERED (Gautam and Bhattacharyya, 2014), and some fuzzy matching methods, like the one of Gupta et al. (2014), are based on multiple linguistic layers. The layers are assigned weights or combined using a support vector machine.

Different types of metrics can be combined in order to join their strengths. For instance, the Asiya toolkit (Giménez and Márquez, 2010) contains a large number of matching metrics of different origins and applies them for MT evaluation. An optimal metric set is determined by progressively adding metrics to the set if that increases the quality of the translation.

3 Experimental setup

3.1 Independent variables

In Sections 3.1.1, 3.1.2, and 3.1.3, we describe the independent variables of our experiment.

3.1.1 Linguistically unaware metrics

Levenshtein (baseline) Given the Levenshtein distance $\Delta_{LEV}(S, T_i)$, we define Levenshtein score (i.e. similarity) as in (2):

$$Sim_{LEV}(Q, S_i) = 1 - \frac{\Delta_{LEV}(Q, S_i)}{\max(|Q|, |S_i|)} \quad (2)$$

[2]One example of such a tool is *Similis* (http://www.similis.org), which determines constituents in sentences and allows to retrieve (S_i, T_i) when S_i shares constituents with Q.

[3]We implemented the Tree Edit Distance algorithm of Klein from its description in Bille (2005), as well as the Tree Alignment Distance algorithm. However, both were too slow to be useful for parse trees unless severe optimization takes place.

[4]While the developers of TER call it *Translation Edit Rate*, the name *Translation Error Rate* is often used, through the influence of the metric name *Word Error Rate*, which is used in automatic speech recognition.

Levenshtein distance, which is based on three operation types (insertion, deletion and substitution), and its variants, assign a specific cost to each type of operation. Typically, each type has a cost of 1. Certain costs may be changed in order to obtain a specific behaviour. For instance, the cost of a substitution may depend on the similarity of words.

Translation Error Rate Given a sentence Q output by an MT system and a reference translation R, TER keeps on applying shifts to Q as long as $\Delta_{LEV}(Q, R)$ keeps decreasing.[5] The TER distance $\Delta_{TER}(Q, R)$, which equals $\Delta_{LEV}(Q, R)$ plus the cost of the shifts, is normalized as in (3):

$$Score_{TER}(Q, R) = \frac{\Delta_{TER}(Q, R)}{|R|} \quad (3)$$

We convert $Score_{TER}$ into a similarity score between 0 and 1 as in (4). This formula assumes a very high upper bound for $Score_{TER}$.[6]

$$Sim_{TER}(Q, R) = 1 - \frac{log(1 + Score_{TER}(Q, R))}{3} \quad (4)$$

Percent match calculates the percent of unigrams in Q that are found in S_i, as in (5):[7]

$$Sim_{PM}(Q, S_i) = \frac{|Q_{1grams} \cap S_{i,1grams}|}{|Q_{1grams}|} \quad (5)$$

Ngram precision compares $n$grams, i.e. subsequences of one or more elements, of length 1 up till N, as in (6), where the precision for $n$grams of length n is calculated as in (7).

$$Sim_{NGP}(Q, S_i) = \sum_{n=1}^{N} \frac{1}{N} p_n \quad (6)$$

$$p_n = \frac{|Q_{ngrams} \cap S_{i,ngrams}|}{Z * |Q_{ngrams}| + (1 - Z) * |S_{i,ngrams}|} \quad (7)$$

Q_{ngrams} is the set of $n$grams in Q. $S_{i,ngrams}$ is the set of $n$grams in S_i, and Z is a parameter to control normalization. Setting Z to a high value prefers longer translations.[8]

Bloodgood and Strauss propose weighted variants for the Sim_{PM} and Sim_{NGP} metrics, using IDF weights, which reflect the relevance of the matching words. We will refer to one of these variants later on, calling it Sim_{PMIDF}.

3.1.2 Linguistically aware metrics

Adaptations of linguistically unaware metrics We investigated Levenshtein, percent match, and TER not only on sequences of word forms, but also on sequences of lemmas. We will refer to these lemma-based metrics as Sim_{LEVLEM}, Sim_{PMLEM} and Sim_{TERLEM}.

Shared partial subtree matching We devised a method which aims specifically at comparing two parse trees. In order to perform this comparison in an efficient way, we apply the following steps: (1) check whether pairs of subtrees in the two parses share a partial subtree; (2) determine the scores of the shared partial subtrees, based on lexical and non-lexical similarity of the nodes, on the relevance of the words, and on the number of nodes in the shared partial subtree; (3) perform a greedy search for the best combination of shared partial subtrees.

Based on the scores of the partial subtrees in the final combination, we determine the shared partial subtree similarity, as in (8). In this equation, $Score_{SPS}(Q, S_i)$ stands for the sum of the scores of the partial subtrees in the combination and $MaxScore_{SPS}(Q, S_i)$ stands for the score we obtain if Q and S_i are equal.

$$Sim_{SPS}(Q, S_i) = \frac{Score_{SPS}(Q, S_i)}{MaxScore_{SPS}(Q, S_i)} \quad (8)$$

Levenshtein for Prüfer sequences Extracting information from a tree and gathering it into a sequence allows us to apply string-based methods, which are less time-costly than tree-based methods, and which come in a great variety.

When comparing the structures in two Prüfer sequences, we may use either a cost of 0 (identity of structures) or 1. However, some structures which

[5] An implementation of TER can be found here: http://www.cs.umd.edu/~snover/tercom. We used version 0.7.25 for our experiment.

[6] Setting the denominator to 3 ensures that Sim_{TER} is a non-negative number unless $Score_{TER}$ exceeds the upper bound of 19. We chose this arbitrary bound in order to have an integer as denominator in the formula.

[7] This metric is similar to the metric PER, *position-independent word error rate* (Tillmann et al., 1997). The difference between both metrics lies in the fact that PER takes account of multiple occurrences of a token in a sentence, does not calculate a normalized value between 0 and 1, and does not ignore words which are present in S_i but not in Q.

[8] For our experiment, we set N to 4 and Z to 0.5. Setting its value experimentally, however, would be more appropriate.

are not identical may have some degree of similarity (for instance, a terminal node with equal part-of-speech but different lemmas). Therefore, we assign costs between 0 and 1 when calculating the Levenshtein distance. We refer to Levenshtein calculation on Prüfer sequences as $Sim_{LEVPRFC}$.

Ngram precision for head word chains Head word chains can be considered as ngrams. Therefore, we apply a variant of ngram precision to them which we call Sim_{NGPHWC}.

Meteor For brevity's sake we do not provide the formulas on which Sim_{METEOR} is based. We use the standard settings including shallow linguistic knowledge and paraphrases.[9]

3.1.3 Combinations of metrics

Could a combination of matching metrics perform better than the metrics on their own? We checked this by creating regression trees.[10] The training examples provided for building the tree are the matches of sentences to translate, the features (independent variables) are matching metrics, and their values are the matching score. The regression trees model decisions for predicting the evaluation score of the translation of the match (the dependent variable) in a non-linear way. We consider the predicted evaluation score as a new fuzzy match score.

3.2 Dependent variable

The dependent variable of our experiment is the evaluation score of the translation suggestion. We use Sim_{TER} as evaluation metric. It reflects the effort required to change a translation suggestion into the desired translation. It should be noted that the usefulness of a translation suggestion should ultimately be determined by a translator working with a CAT tool. However, human evaluation is time-consuming. We therefore use an automatic evaluation metric as a proxy for human evaluation, similarly to the modus operandi in the development of MT systems.

In order to assess the usefulness of an indvidual or combined fuzzy matching metric, we apply a leave-one-out test to a set of parallel sentences and investigate how well each metric correlates with the evaluation score. For each $Q_i \in Q_1, \ldots, Q_n$, we select the best match produced by the metric, which we call $S_{b,i}$. We call its match score $M_{b,i}$ and its translation in the TM $T_{b,i}$. We call Q_i's translation R_i. The evaluation score of the translation is $E_{b,i} = Sim_{TER}(T_{b,i}, R_i)$. We compute the Pearson correlation coefficient between M and E. A higher coefficient indicates a more useful fuzzy matching metric.

A second way for assessing the usefulness of metrics is considering their mean evaluation score and investigating the significance of the difference between metrics through bootstrap resampling. This approach consists of taking a large number of subsets of test sentences and comparing the mean evaluation score of their best matches across metrics. For instance, if one metric has a higher mean in at least 95% of the subsets than another one, the first metric is significantly better than the second one at confidence level 0.05.

A third way we study the usefulness of metrics is by investigating the degree to which the mean evaluation score decreases as we keep adding sentences with diminishing match score. If the decrease in mean evaluation score is slower in one metric than in another, the first metric has a higher recall than the second metric, as we need to put less effort in editing the translation suggestions to reach the desired translation.

3.3 Speed of retrieval

We developed a filter called *approximate query coverage* (AQC). Its purpose is to select candidate sentences in the TM which are likely to reach a minimal matching threshold when submitting them to a fuzzy matching metric, in order to increase the speed of matching. A candidate sentence is a sentence which shares one or more $n$grams of a minimal length N with Q, and which shares enough $n$grams with Q so as to cover the latter sufficiently.

The implementation of the filter uses a suffix array (Manber and Myers, 1993), which allows for a very efficient search for sentences sharing $n$grams with Q.[11] This approach is similar to the one used in the context of fuzzy matching by Koehn and Senellart (2010).

In order to measure the usefulness of the AQC filter, we measured the tradeoff between the gain

[9] We use version 1.5 of Meteor. See http://www.cs.cmu.edu/~alavie/METEOR.

[10] We used complexity parameter 0.001, retained 500 competitor splits in the output and applied 100 cross-validations.

[11] We used the SALM toolkit (Zhang and Vogel, 2006) for building and consulting suffix arrays in our experiment.

in speed and the loss of potentially useful matches. We used a sample of about 30,000 English-Dutch sentence pairs selected from Europarl (Koehn, 2005), and a threshold of 0.2. After applying a leave-one-out test, which consists of considering each S_i in the sample as a Q and comparing it to all the other S_i in the sample, it appeared that the AQC filter selected about 9 candidate sentences per Q. The gain in speed is very significant: after filtering, a fuzzy matching metric like Sim_{LEV} only needs to be applied to 0.03% of the sentences in the sample. As for the loss of potentially useful matches, we considered each S_i for which $Sim_{LEV}(Q, S_i) >= 0.3$ to be such a match. It appears that most of these S_i are still available after filtering: 93% of all pairs (Q, S_i) with a Sim_{LEV} value between 0.3 and 0.4 have an AQC score $>= 0.2$. For pairs between 0.4 and 0.6, this is 98%, and for pairs above 0.6 100%. Hence, there is a very good tradeoff between gain in speed and loss of potentially useful matches.

3.4 Preprocessing data

We use the Stanford parser (Klein and Manning, 2003) to parse English sentences. We divide a sample of sentences into two equally sized sets: a training set, from which regression trees are built, and a test set, to which individual metrics and combined metrics derived from regression trees are applied. We derive IDF weights from the full sample.

4 Results

We tested the setup described in the previous section on a sample of 30,000 English-Dutch sentence pairs from Europarl. We built regression trees for different combinations of metrics. The combined metrics either involve the baseline and an individual metric or a larger set of metrics. The results are shown in Table 1. The leftmost column shows the metric used:

- Individual metrics: LEV (Levenshtein), TER, METEOR, PM (percent match), PMIDF (percent match with weights), NGP (ngram precision), NGPHWC (head word chains), LEVLEM (lemma-based Levenshtein), PMLEM, TERLEM, SPS (shared partial subtree matching)
- Combination of baseline and individual metric: TER+LEV, SPS+LEV, ...
- Combination of all linguistically aware metrics: LING

Table 1: Comparison of metrics with baseline

Sim	$Corr(M_{b,i}, E_{b,i})$	$Score_{TER}$
	Baseline	
LEV	0.278	1.007
	Linguistically aware metrics	
LEVLEM	0.279	1.009
LEVPRFC	0.283	0.983
METEOR	0.058	1.066
NGPHWC	0.291	1.028
PMLEM	0.420	0.927*
SPS	0.275	0.987
TERLEM	**0.500**	**0.926***
	Linguistically unaware metrics	
NGP	0.222	1.035
PM	0.424	**0.926***
PMIDF	0.335	0.963*
TER	**0.502**	**0.926***
	Metrics combined using regression tree	
LEVLEM+LEV	0.362	**0.869***
LEVPRFC+LEV	0.386	0.905*
METEOR+LEV	0.391	0.910*
NGPHWC+LEV	0.347	**0.869***
PMLEM+LEV	0.478	0.916*
SPS+LEV	0.363	0.908*
TERLEM+LEV	0.562	0.894*
NGP+LEV	0.376	0.903*
PM+LEV	0.455	0.906*
PMIDF+LEV	0.405	0.906*
TER+LEV	0.561	0.894*
LING	0.564	0.899*
NONLING	**0.571**	0.889*
ALL	0.563	0.899*
		$^*p < 0.05$

- Combination of all linguistically unaware metrics (except for the baseline): NONLING
- Combination of all metrics (including the baseline): ALL

The middle column of Table 1 shows the Pearson correlation coefficient between the match score and the evaluation score (Sim_{TER}). The rightmost column shows the means of $Score_{TER}$ values (which reflect the estimated editing effort) instead of the means of the Sim_{TER} values. We used the latter primarily to facilitate the calculation of certain statistics regarding TER, such as correlations.

Let us first have a look at the individual metrics in Table 1. The Sim_{PM} and Sim_{TER} metrics, and their lemma-based variants, have the highest correlation with the evaluation score; their correlation is markedly higher than that of the baseline. Interestingly, IDF weights do not seem to help percent match, on the contrary. The correlation of most other individual metrics is close to that of the baseline. Looking at the worst-performing two metrics, Sim_{NGP} and Sim_{METEOR}, it is striking that the latter has an extremely low correlation compared to the baseline. This needs further investigation. The high score of Sim_{TER} and Sim_{TERLEM} raises the question whether an evaluation metric favors a fuzzy matching metric which is identical or similar to it.

The means of the $Score_{TER}$ values for individual metrics more or less confirm the differences observed for correlation. Sim_{PM}, Sim_{TER} and their lemma-based variants have the lowest mean. As shown by the asterisks in the table, the difference in mean with the baseline is significant at the 0.05 level for about half of the individual metrics.

Looking at the combined metrics in Table 1, we see that all of them have a higher correlation with the evaluation score than the baseline, and a lower $Score_{TER}$ mean; the difference in mean with the baseline is always significant. Of all two-metric combinations, the ones involving Sim_{TER} and its lemma-based variant perform the best. The combinations Sim_{LING} and $Sim_{NONLING}$ perform slightly better than the best two-metric combinations. Sim_{ALL}, which includes the baseline itself, comes close to Sim_{LING} and $Sim_{NONLING}$ but does not exceed their performance. From the regression tree involving the combination of all metrics, it appears that it uses 9 of the 12 individual metrics, including the baseline, to predict the evaluation score. There is no clearcut association between the correlation values of the combined metrics and their $Score_{TER}$ mean. For instance, Sim_{NGPHWC} has the lowest correlation but also the lowest $Score_{TER}$ mean.

Figure 1 shows the mean $Score_{TER}$ increase (i.e. increase in editing effort) that we obtain when adding baseline matches with decreasing match score. When we order all test sentences according to the baseline score of their best match, the mean $Score_{TER}$ of the first 1000 sentences (the 1000 top sentences) is 0.74. When we order the test sentences according to Sim_{ALL}, the mean $Score_{TER}$ of the 1000 top sentences is 0.67. As we add more sentences to the top list, the $Score_{TER}$ mean for the baseline increases more strongly than that of Sim_{ALL}. The recall of Sim_{ALL} increases, as we need to put less effort in editing the translation suggestions of the top list. For instance, the recall for 1000 sentences is 10% lower for the baseline (0.74/0.67=1.10). For 2000 sentences, the difference increases to 11%, and for 3000 to 13%. The *oracle* line in Figure 1 indicates the mean $Score_{TER}$ increase in case we know the evaluation score of the best match beforehand; this is the upper bound for a matching metric.

From the results in Table 1, we can conclude that, though linguistically unaware metrics help a long way in improving on the baseline, linguistic metrics clearly have added value. A question that arises here, and to which we already pointed previously, is whether the use of an identical metric for fuzzy matching and for evaluation favors that fuzzy matching metric with respect to others. If that is the case, it may be better to optimize fuzzy matching methods towards a combination of evaluation metrics rather than a single metric. Ideally, human judgment of translation should also be involved in evaluation.

5 Conclusion and future

Our comparison of the baseline matching metric, Levenshtein distance, with linguistically aware and unaware matching metrics, has shown that the use of linguistic knowledge in the matching process provides clear added value. This is especially the case when several metrics are combined into a new metric using a regression tree. The correlation of combined metrics with the evaluation score is much stronger than the correlation of the baseline. Moreover, significant improvement is observed in terms of mean evaluation score, and the difference in recall with the baseline increases as match scores decrease.

Considering the fact that there is added value in linguistic information, we may further improve the performance of matching metrics by testing more metric configurations, by using additional metrics or metric combinations built for MT evaluation, and by building regression trees using larger training set sizes. Testing on an additional language, for instance a highly inflected one, may also shed light on the value of fuzzy metrics.

Our experiments were performed using a single evaluation metric, TER. We may also use other metrics for evaluation, such as percent match, Meteor or shared partial subtree matching, in order to assess to which degree the use of an identical metric for fuzzy matching and for evaluation affects results. In this respect, we will also investigate the low correlation between Meteor as a fuzzy matching metric and TER as an evaluation score, and select a new metric which we use for evaluation only and which applies matching techniques absent from the other metrics. An example of such a

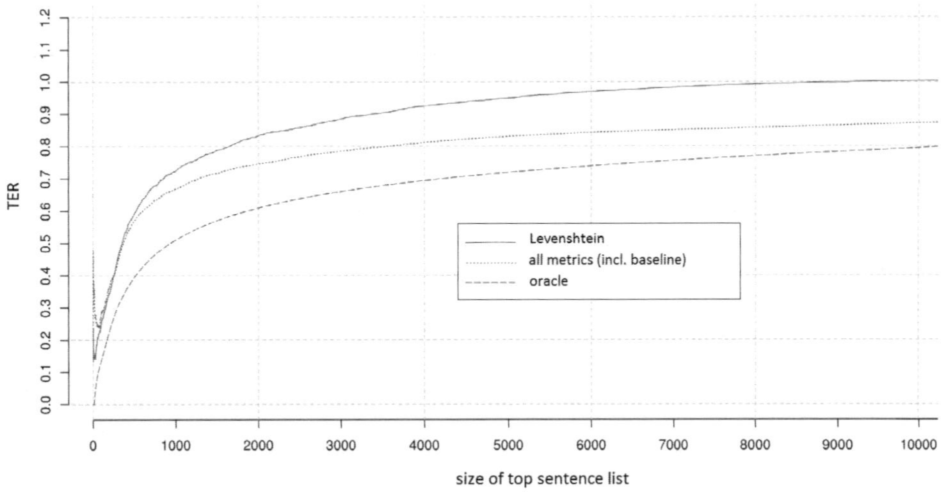

Figure 1: Mean $Score_{TER}$ increase

metric is the recently developed BEER (Stanojević and Sima'an, 2014), which is based on permutation of tree nodes. Human judgment of translation suggestions will also be taken into account.

Last but not least, we would like to point out that we have created an innovative fuzzy matching framework with powerful features: integration of matching metrics with different origins and levels of linguistic information, support for different types of structures (sequences, trees, trees converted into sequences), combination of metrics using regression trees, use of any metric in the source or target language (fuzzy matching metric or evaluation metric), and fast filtering through a suffix array.

6 Acknowledgements

This research is funded by the Flemish government agency IWT (project 130041, SCATE). See http://www.ccl.kuleuven.be/scate.

References

Aramaki, Eiji, Sadao Kurohashi, Hideki Kashioka and Naoto Kato. 2005. Probabilistic Model for Example-based Machine Translation. *Proceedings of the 10th Machine Translation Summit*, Phuket, Thailand. pp. 219–226.

Baldwin, Timothy. 2010. The Hare and the Tortoise: Speed and Accuracy in Translation Retrieval. *Machine Translation*, 23(4):195–240.

Bille, Philip. 2005. A Survey on Tree Edit Distance and Related Problems. *Theoretical Computer Science*, 337(1-3):217–239.

Bloodgood, Michael and Benjamin Strauss. 2014. Translation Memory Retrieval Methods. *Proceedings of the 14th Conference of the European Association for Computational Linguistics*, Gothenburg, Sweden. pp. 202–210.

Comelles, Elisabet, Jordi Atserias, Victoria Arranz, Irene Castellón, and Jordi Sesé. 2014. VERTa: Facing a Multilingual Experience of a Linguistically-based MT Evaluation. *Proceedings of the 9th International Conference on Language Resources and Evaluation*, Reykjavik, Iceland. pp. 2701–2707.

Denkowski, Michael and Alon Lavie. 2014. Meteor Universal: Language Specific Translation Evaluation for Any Target Language. *Proceedings of the 9th Workshop on Statistical Machine Translation*, Baltimore, Maryland, USA. pp. 376–380.

Gautam, Shubham and Pushpak Bhattacharyya. 2014. LAYERED: Metric for Machine Translation Evaluation. *Proceedings of the 9th Workshop on Statistical Machine Translation*, Baltimore, Maryland, USA. pp. 387-393.

Giménez, Jesús and Lluís Márquez. 2010. Asiya: An Open Toolkit for Automatic Machine Translation (Meta-)Evaluation. *The Prague Bulletin of Mathematical Linguistics*, 94:77–86.

Gupta, Rohit, Hanna Bechara and Constantin Orasan. 2014. Intelligent Translation Memory Matching and Retrieval Metric Exploiting Linguistic Technology. *Proceedings of Translating and the Computer 36*, London, UK. pp. 86–89.

Jiang, Tao, Lushen Wang, and Kaizhong Zhang. 1995. Alignment of Trees – An Alternative to Tree Edit. *Theoretical Computer Science*, 143(1):137-148.

Klein, Dan and Christopher Manning. 2003. Fast Exact Inference with a Factored Model for Natural Language Parsing. *Advances in Neural Information Processing Systems 15 (NIPS)*, MIT Press. pp. 3–10.

Klein, Philip. 1998. Computing the Edit Distance between Unrooted Ordered Trees. *Proceedings of the 6th Annual European Symposium on Algorithms*, Venice, Italy. pp. 91–102.

Koehn, Philipp. 2005. Europarl: A Parallel Corpus for Statistical Machine Translation. *Proceedings of the 10th Machine Translation Summit*, Phuket, Thailand. pp. 79–86.

Koehn, Philipp and Jean Senellart. 2010. Fast Approximate String Matching with Suffix Arrays and A*Parsing. *Proceedings of the 9th Conference of the Association for Machine Translation in the Americas*, Denver, Colorado. 9 pp. [http://www.mt-archive.info/AMTA-2010-Koehn.pdf]

Levenshtein, Vladimir I. 1966. Binary Codes Capable of Correcting Deletions, Insertions, and Reversals. *Soviet Physics Doklady*, 10(8):707–710.

Li, Guoliang, Xuhui Liu, Jianhua Feng, and Lizhu Zhou. 2008. Efficient Similarity Search for Tree-Structured Data. *Proceedings of the 20th International Conference on Scientific and Statistical Database Management*, Hong Kong, China. pp. 131–149.

Liu, Ding and Daniel Gildea. 2005. Syntactic Features for Evaluation of Machine Translation. *Proceedings of ACL 2005 Workshop on Intrinsic and Extrinsic Evaluation Measures for Machine Translation and/or Summarization*, Ann Arbor, Michigan, USA. pp. 25–32.

Lo, Chi-kiu and Dekai Wu. 2011. MEANT: An Inexpensive, High-accuracy, Semi-automatic Metric for Evaluating Translation Utility via Semantic Frames. *Proceedings of the 49th Annual Meeting of the Association for Computational Linguistics: Human Language Technologies – Volume 1*, Portland, Oregon, USA. pp. 220–229.

Ma, Yanjun, Yifan He, Andy Way, and Josef van Genabith. 2011. Consistent Translation using Discriminative Learning: a Translation Memory-inspired Approach. *Proceedings of the 49th Annual Meeting of the Association for Computational Linguistics: Human Language Technologies – Volume 1*, Portland, Oregon. pp. 1239–1248.

Manber, Udi and Gene Myers. 1993. Suffix Arrays: A New Method for On-line String Searches. *SIAM Journal on Computing*, 22:935–948.

Papineni, Kishore, Salim Roukos, Todd Ward, and Wei-Jing Zhu. 2002. BLEU: a Method for Automatic Evaluation of Machine Translation. *Proceedings of the 40th Annual Meeting of the Association for Computational Linguistics*, Philadelphia, Pennsylvania, USA. pp. 311–318.

Prüfer, Heinz. 1918. Neuer Beweis eines Satzes über Permutationen. *Archiv der Mathematik und Physik*, 27:742–744.

Sikes, Richard. 2007. Fuzzy Matching in Theory and Practice. *Multilingual*, 18(6):39–43.

Simard, Michel and Atsushi Fujita. 2012. A Poor Man's Translation Memory Using Machine Translation Evaluation Metrics. *Proceedings of the 10th Conference of the Association for Machine Translation in the Americas*, San Diego, California, USA. 10 pp. [http://www.mt-archive.info/AMTA-2012-Simard.pdf]

Smith, James and Stephen Clark. 2009. EBMT for SMT: a new EBMT-SMT hybrid. *Proceedings of the 3rd International Workshop on Example-Based Machine Translation*, Dublin, Ireland. pp. 3–10.

Snover, Matthew, Bonnie Dorr, Richard Schwartz, Linnea Micciula, and John Makhoul. 2006. A Study of Translation Edit Rate with Targeted Human Annotation. *Proceedings of the 7th Conference of the Association for Machine Translation in the Americas*, Cambridge, Massachusetts, USA. pp. 223–231.

Stanojević, Miloš and Khalil Sima'an. 2014. BEER: BEtter Evaluation as Ranking. *Proceedings of the 9th Workshop on Statistical Machine Translation*, Baltimore, Maryland, USA. pp. 414–419.

Tillmann, Christoph, Stephan Vogel, Hermann Ney, Alex Zubiaga, and Hassan Sawaf. 1997. Accelerated Dp Based Search For Statistical Translation. *Proceedings of the 5th European Conference on Speech Communication and Technology*, Rhodes, Greece. pp. 2667–2670.

Zhang, Ying and Stephan Vogel. 2006. Suffix Array and its Applications in Empirical Natural Language Processing. *Technical Report CMU-LTI-06-010*, Language Technologies Institute, School of Computer Science, Carnegie Mellon University.

Zhechev, Ventsislav and Josef van Genabith. 2010. Maximising TM Performance through Sub-Tree Alignment and SMT. *Proceedings of the 9th conference of the Association for Machine Translation in the Americas*, Denver, Colorado, USA. 10 pp. [http://www.mt-archive.info/AMTA-2010-Zhechev.pdf]

Re-assessing the WMT2013 Human Evaluation with Professional Translators Trainees

Mihaela Vela
Saarland University
m.vela@mx.uni-saarland.de

Josef van Genabith
German Research Center for Artificial Intelligence
Josef.Van_Genabith@dfki.de

Abstract

This paper presents experiments on the human ranking task performed during WMT2013. The goal of these experiments is to re-run the human evaluation task with translation studies students and to compare the results with the human rankings performed by the WMT development teams during WMT2013. More specifically, we test whether we can reproduce, and if yes to what extent, the WMT2013 ranking task and whether specialised knowledge from translation studies influences the results in terms of intra- and inter-annotator agreement as well as in terms of system ranking. We present two experiments on the English-German WMT2013 machine translation output. Analysis of the data follows the methods described in the official WMT2013 report. The results indicate a higher inter- and intra-annotator agreement, less ties and slight differences in ranking for the translation studies students as compared to the WMT development teams.

1 Introduction

Machine translation evaluation is an important element in the process of building MT systems. The Workshop for Statistical Machine Translation (WMT) compares new techniques for MT through human and automatic MT evaluation and provides also tracks for evaluation metrics, quality estimation of MT as well as post-editing of MT.

To date, the most popular MT evaluation metrics essentially measure lexical overlap between reference and hypothesis translation such as IBM BLEU (Papineni et al., 2002), NIST (Doddington, 2002), Meteor (Denkowski and Lavie, 2014), WER (Levenshtein, 1966), position-independent error rate metric PER (Tillmann et al., 1997) and the translation edit rate metric TER (Snover et al., 2006) and TERp (Snover et al., 2009). Gonzàlez et al. (2014) as well as Comelles and Atserias (2014) introduce their fully automatic approaches to machine translation evaluation using lexical, syntactic and semantic information when comparing the machine translation output with reference translations.

Human machine translation evaluation can be performed with different methods. Lo and Wu (2011) propose HMEANT, a metric based on MEANT (Lo et al., 2012) that measures meaning preservation between hypothesis and reference translation on the basis of verb frames and their role fillers. Another method is HTER (Snover et al., 2006) which produces targeted reference translations by post-editing MT output. Another method is HTER (Snover et al., 2006) which produces targeted reference translations by post-editing MT output. Human evaluation can also be performed by measuring post-editing time, or by asking evaluators to assess the fluency and adequacy of a hypothesis translation on a Likert scale. Another popular human evaluation method is ranking: ordering a set of translation hypotheses according to their quality. This is also the method applied during the recent WMTs, where humans are asked to rank machine translation output by using APPRAISE (Federmann, 2012), a software tool that integrates facilities for such a ranking task. In WMT, human MT evaluation is carried out by the MT development teams, usually computer scientists or computational linguists, sometimes involving crowd-sourcing based on Amazon's Mechanical Turk.

Being aware of the two communities, machine translation and translation studies, we took the available online data from the WMT2013[1] and tried to reproduce the ranking task with translation studies students for the English to German translations. The three questions we want to answer are:

- Can we reproduce at all the WMT2013 results for the language pair English-German?
- Are translation studies students (future translators) evaluating different from the WMT development teams, or in other words does specialised knowledge from translation studies influence the outcome of the ranking task?
- Are translation studies students more consistent as a group and with themselves in terms of intra- and inter-agreement?

We concentrate on English-German data since the majority of our evaluators were native speakers of German and since, from a translation studies point of view, professional translation should be performed only into the mother tongue.

2 The WMT2013 English-German Data

Before presenting the experimental setting and outcomes, we present the WMT data. We are aware of the fact that the main objective of the WMT is to evaluate the state-of-the-art in machine translation. In this context evaluation plays an important role, since a robust and reliable evaluation method makes it easier to perform a more in-depth differentiation between different machine translation outputs.

In 2013 during the WMT human evaluation campaign, the evaluation was performed both by the WMT development teams (further named researchers) and by turkers. The researcher group comprised all the participants in the WMT machine translation task. The turkers group was composed of non-experts on Amazon's Mechanical Turk (MTurk). Both groups were asked to rank randomly selected machine translation outputs, organised as quintuples of 5 outputs produced by different MT systems. The researchers were asked to rank quintuples for 300 source sentences whereas the turkers were paid per MTurk unit. Such a unit is called a human intelligence Task (HIT) and consisted of three source sentences and the corresponding quintuples. For each HIT turkers were paid $0.25.

[1]http://www.statmt.org/wmt13/

In our experiments we focus on the language pair English-German, we compare our results with those obtained in the English-German human evaluation task. We concentrate on the evaluation performed by researchers, assuming that translation studies students will be at least as consistent as researchers and having in mind that intra- and inter-annotator agreement for the turkers' group was lower than for the researchers' group. Researchers are a well defined group, or at least a better defined group, than the turkers about whom we had no information.

From the WMT2013 English-German data, which we took as reference for our experiments, we observed that there were in total 38 researchers taking part in the English-German manual evaluation task. The range of the evaluated source sentences and their quintuples is from 3 to 1059. From the 38 evaluators 12 evaluated the same sentences more than once, the range in this case being from 3 to 240 repeated sentences. From here we can conclude that for the English-German task just 12 researchers can be considered for the intra-annotator agreement. The sentence overlap between researchers (relevant for the inter-annotator agreement) has also a wide range: from sentences evaluated in common with 2 researchers to sentences evaluated in common with 36 researchers. In total the researchers in WMT2013 produced 39582 ranking pairs, without counting ties, based on which the final agreement scores and the system ranking was computed.

Another observation from the WMT2013 data is related to the systems researchers had to rank. The data shows that researchers ranked only 14 out of the 21 participating systems. The anonymised commercial and online systems were excluded from the human evaluation task.

The main criticism towards this kind of evaluation of MT output is that the evaluation does not provide evidence of the absolute quality of the MT output, but evidence of the quality of a machine translation system compared to other MT systems. If the evaluators had to decide on the ranking of 5 bad MT outputs, it might happen that even the MT system ranked first, scores bad in terms of adequacy and fluency. On the other hand, in such ranking tasks the specific skills, required for example in translation studies, are not necessary activated, since the ranking task is in fact a comparison task. Therefore, we assume that researchers and translations studies students will achieve at least comparable scores since no task-specific knowledge is required and the two groups, different from the turkers' group, can be considered homogeneous groups.

3 Experimental Design

We conducted the experiments as similar as possible to the manual ranking task in WMT2013. Like in WMT2013, evaluators were presented with a source sentence, a reference translation and five outputs produced by five anonymised and randomised machine translations systems. The instructions for the evaluators remained the same as in WMT2013:

You are shown a source sentence followed by several candidate translations. Your task is to rank the translations from best to worst (ties are allowed)

For performing the ranking task we implemented the Java-based ranking tool depicted in Figure 1.[2] Similar to APPRAISE (Federmann, 2012) the ranking can be performed on a scale from 1 to 5, with 1 being the best translation and 5 being the worst translation.

For a given source sentence, each ranking of the five MT outputs has the potential to produce 10 ranking pairs. Before applying the corresponding formulas on the data, the ranking pairs from all evaluators and for all systems are collected in a matrix like the one in Table 1. The matrix records the number of times system S_i was ranked better than S_j and vice-versa.

For example, if we look at the two systems S_1 and S_3 in the matrix, we can see that S_3 was ranked 2 times higher (from the left triangle) and 4 times lower (from the right triangle) than system S_1.

From the matrix, the final score for each system - as defined by Koehn (2012) and applied in WMT2013 - can be computed. From the matrix in Table 1 the score for system S_1 is computed by counting for each pair of systems (S_1, S_2), (S_1, S_3), (S_1, S_4), (S_1, S_5) the number of times S_1 was ranked higher than the other system divided by the total number of rankings for each pair. The results for each pair of systems including S_1 are then summed and divided by the number of systems, this being the final score for S_1.

	S_1	S_2	S_3	S_4	S_5
S_1	0	3	4	2	2
S_2	0	0	1	0	1
S_3	2	2	0	2	2
S_4	4	3	4	0	5
S_5	1	2	1	1	0

Table 1: Representation of the ranking pairs as a matrix

Considering having a system S_i from a set of systems S of size k and a set of rankings for each system pair (S_i, S_j), where $j = 1 \ldots k$, $S_j \in S$ and $i \neq j$ the score for S_i is defined as follows:

$$score(S_i) = \frac{1}{k} \sum_{i,j \neq i}^{k} \frac{|\, S_i > S_j \,|}{|\, S_i > S_j \,| + |\, S_i < S_j \,|}$$

Based on Koehn's (2012) formula each system gets a score and a ranking among the set of systems. After performing the ranking the systems are clustered by using bootstrap resampling, thus returning the final score and the cluster for each system.

Different from WMT2013 we run two evaluation rounds for the ranking task. The first round was a pilot study on which all evaluators had to evaluate the same set of randomised and anonymised sentences selected from the published WMT2013 ranking task data set. The set contained 200 source sentences and five anonymised and randomised MT outputs for each source sentence. In the pilot study we selected, as in WMT2013, only the above mentioned 14 machine translation systems for evaluation, disregarding the remaining anonymised commercial and online systems.

Regarding the sampling of the data, the second evaluation round followed the ranking task performed in WMT2013: each evaluator ranked a different randomised and anonymised sample consisting of 200 source sentences and five anonymised and randomised MT outputs for each source sentence. The individual samples were built out of all 21 machine translations outputs of the 3000 source sentences provided for the translation task.

[2]The implementation of a new tool was motivated by the accessibility of a server for the evaluators. This way each evaluator had his own evaluation set containing both the tool and the data set.

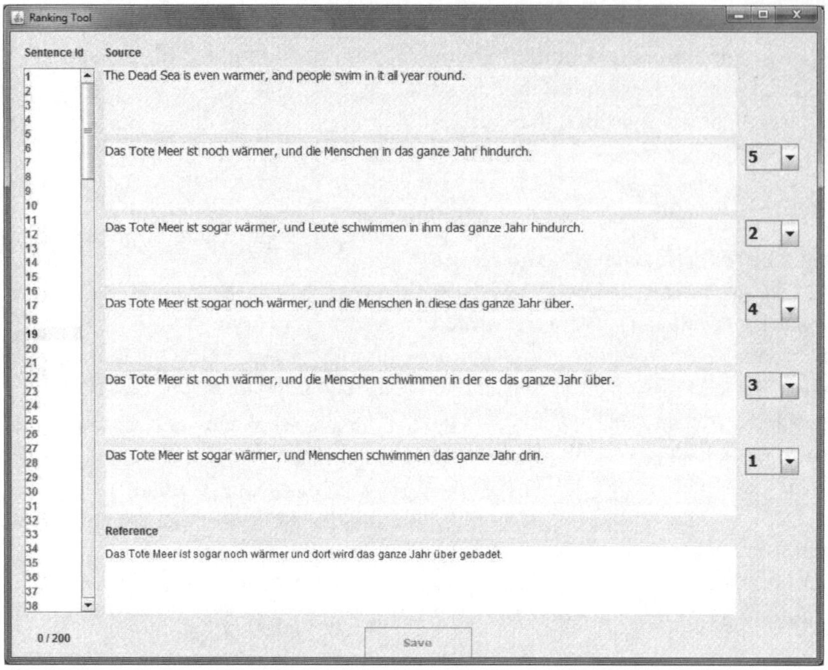

Figure 1: The Java-based ranking tool.

3.1 The Pilot Study

During the pilot study, the translation studies students had to manually rank 200 source sentences and their corresponding randomised and anonymised 5 translations. The specifics of the pilot was that each evaluator received the same data set for evaluation. In fact we randomly retrieved 180 sentences and their 5 corresponding machine translation outputs from the WMT2013 manual evaluation data set, from the rankings performed by the researchers. Out of the 180 sentences we randomly selected 20 sentences which were repeated in the data set. Based on the 200 source sentences, out of which 10% were repeated, we could compute both the inter-annotator agreement and the intra-annotator agreement. For the inter-annotator agreement we took all 200 sentences into consideration, whereas for the intra-annotator agreement we considered the preselected 20 sentences which were repeated in the data set.

During the pilot study 25 translation students and a translation lecturer took part in the experiment. Except for three students, the remaining 23 evaluators were native speakers of German with at least a B2 level[3] for English. The three non-native speakers of English had at least a C1 knowledge level of German and B2 for English. Out of the 26 evaluators 14 completed the task by ranking the quintuples for all 200 source sentences, the remaining group evaluated between 2 and 26 source sentences. In total we collected 25780 ranking pairs in the pilot study.

Based on the collected rankings the intra-annotator agreement could be computed just for 17 evaluators, the ones who evaluated sentences more than once. On the other hand, the inter-agreement was computed pairwise between all evaluators, the fact that all evaluators received the same set of sentences made this possible.

Both types of agreement (intra and inter) were measured by computing Cohen's kappa coefficient (Cohen, 1960), as it was defined by Bojar et al. (2013)

$$\kappa = \frac{P_{\text{agree}}(S_{\text{i}}, S_{\text{j}}) - P_{\text{chance}}(S_{\text{i}}, S_{\text{j}})}{1 - P_{\text{chance}}(S_{\text{i}}, S_{\text{j}})} \quad (1)$$

where $P_{agree}(S_i,S_j)$ is the proportion of times that evaluators agree on the ranking of the systems S_i and S_j ($S_i < S_j$ or $S_i = S_j$ or $S_i > S_j$) and

[3] http://en.wikipedia.org/wiki/Common_European_Framework_of_Reference_for_Languages#Common_reference_levels

$P_{chance}(S_i,S_j)$ is the number of times they agree by chance. $P_{chance}(S_i,S_j)$ itself is defined as

$$P_{\text{chance}}(S_\text{i}, S_\text{j}) = P(S_\text{i} > S_\text{j})^2 + P(S_\text{i} = S_\text{j})^2 + P(S_\text{i} < S_\text{j})^2 \quad (2)$$

Table 2 list the values for P_{agree}, P_{chance} and κ. The final κ is then the arithmetic mean of the fourth column, resulting in an overall intra-annotator agreement of 0.745 as compared to 0.649 during WMT2013.

User	P_{agree}	P_{chance}	κ
uds1	1.000	0.431	1.000
uds2	0.915	0.387	0.861
uds3	0.674	0.157	0.613
uds4	0.661	0.148	0.602
uds5	1.000	0.360	1.000
uds6	0.746	0.271	0.651
uds7	0.710	0.199	0.637
uds8	0.638	0.142	0.578
uds9	1.000	0.467	1.000
uds10	0.520	0.095	0.469
uds11	0.974	0.392	0.957
uds12	0.884	0.373	0.815
uds13	0.792	0.302	0.702
uds14	0.710	0.172	0.649
uds15	0.792	0.302	0.702
uds19	0.900	0.352	0.845
uds25	0.666	0.190	0.579

Table 2: Intra-annotator agreement for the pilot study.

For the inter-annotator agreement κ is computed by comparing each evaluator with other evaluators with whom she/he shared sentences in the ranking task. Each evaluator has been compared with the other 25 evaluators, the pairwise comparison of the 26 evaluators resulting in 325 evaluators pairs. For each of these pairs we calculated Cohen's κ, the overall inter-annotator agreement being the arithmetic mean from the inter-annotator agreement of the evaluator pairs. In the pilot study the inter-annotator agreement achieved a value of 0.494 as compared to 0.454 during WMT2013.

The system scores were calculated according to Koehn (2012). The results are listed in Table 3. In this stage we performed no clustering, since the experiments with bootstrap resampling have shown, that the cluster varied a lot depending on the sample size. Since we had no information about the sample size during bootstrap resampling performed during WMT2013 and because we collected less rankings (25780 vs. 39582 during WMT2013), we stopped here with the computation of system rankings.

Rank	Score	System
1	0.647	PROMT
2	0.572	UEDIN-SYNTAX
3	0.546	ONLINE-B
4	0.516	LIMSI-SOUL
5	0.505	STANFORD
6	0.504	UEDIN
7	0.490	KIT
8	0.462	CU-ZEMAN
9	0.456	TUBITAK
10	0.453	MES-REORDER
11	0.404	JHU
12	0.331	SHEF-WPROA
13	0.314	RWTH-JANE
14	0.294	UU

Table 3: System ranking in the pilot study without bootstrap resampling

The pilot study proved that performing the re-ranking of the English to German MT output from WMT2013 is a feasible task. Moreover, the κ scores indicate that translation studies students are more consistent when ranking MT output.

3.2 Main Study

In the main phase of our re-ranking experiment each evaluator received a different sample consisting of 200 source sentences, the reference translation for each source sentence and five anonymised and randomised machine translation outputs. Because we sampled the data from the 3000 source sentences and the 21 available system outputs, during the main study we collected information about all systems and ignored the fact, that in WMT2013 evaluators were shown only preselected systems. The software as well as the requirements for performing the ranking task remained the same as in the pilot study.

Similar to the pilot study, in each sample consisting of the 200 source sentences and the corresponding 5 machine translation outputs 10% of the data was repeated, in order to compute the intra-annotator agreement. For inter-annotator agreement we selected 20 source sentences and their corresponding reference translation as well as the corresponding 5 machine translation outputs which were common to each sample. In this phase we had 37 evaluators, all of them being 2nd or 3rd BA translation studies students. With the exception of 3 students, all of the students were native speakers of German with at least a B2 level of English. The three non-native speaker of German had a C1 level of English. From the 37 students, 19 ranked all 200 sentences completing the task. The other 18 students ranked between between 20 and 60 sentences. From all the rankings performed by the evaluators in the main study we collected 37318 ranking pairs[4], a comparable number to the 39582 ranking pairs collected during WMT2013.

From the collected data we computed Cohen's κ for the intra-annotator agreement based on the rankings collected from 22 evaluators. We obtain a κ of 0.772 for the intra-annotator agreement. From all possible pairs of evaluators, here 666, only 536 pairs had ranked sentences in common and had therefore an inter-annotator κ greater than 0. The arithmetic mean of these pairs gave us the overall inter-annotator agreement resulting in κ of 0.510.

Since in the second run of the experiment we collected almost the same number of ranking pairs as during WMT2013, we performed the ranking of the systems with and without bootstrap resampling. Table 4 lists the ranking scores without bootstrap resampling.

For bootstrap resampling we sampled from the set of pairwise rankings (S_i, S_j) collected from all evaluators and computed the score for each system with the formula in equation 3. By iterating this procedure a 1000 times, we determined the range of ranks into which a system falls in 95% of the cases[5], corresponding to a p-level of $p \leq 0.05$. The systems with overlapping ranges we clustered by taking into account that Bojar et al. (2013) recommend to build the largest set of clusters. Actually we performed the bootstrap resampling twice, once by picking 100 rankings pairs from each evaluator[6], and once by selecting 200 ranking pairs for each evaluator. The results show that the difference between 100 and 200 ranking pairs had no impact on the final ranking of the systems, and a minimal one on the way how systems were grouped to clusters. On the right side of Table 5 we present the ranking and clustering results based on samples build of 100 randomly picked rankings pairs per evaluator.

Rank	Score	System
1	0.593	ONLINE-B
3	0.573	UEDIN-SYNTAX
4	0.552	PROMT
5	0.541	UEDIN
6	0.511	KIT
7	0.480	MES-REORDER
8	0.478	LIMSI-SOUL
9	0.465	CU-ZEMAN
10	0.463	STANFORD
11	0.426	TUBITAK
12	0.422	JHU
13	0.352	UU
14	0.345	SHEF-WPROA
15	0.311	RWTH-JANE

Table 4: System ranking in the main study without bootstrap resampling

4 Discussion on Results

The motivation for running the experiments presented in the previous sections was guided by the main question whether future translators, in our case translations studies students, would rank MT output differently than the WMT2013 development teams. Being aware that translation studies students are language and translation experts, we expected them to be more consistent and more discriminative in their decisions as the WMT development teams.

With this in mind, we conducted two experiments, a pilot study and a main study, for the language pair English-German investigating whether translation studies students would evaluate MT output very differently from the WMT development teams and if yes, to what extent and how could we quantify these differences. During the pilot study we observed that the results are similar to those from WMT2013, achieving an intra-annotator agreement of 0.745 and an inter-annotator agreement of 0.494 as compared to 0.649 and 0.457 during WMT2013, we run the main study described in Section 3.2. The results from the main experiment show that translation

[4]For the 14 systems evaluated by researchers during WMT2013 we collected 24202 ranking pairs

[5]This means that the best and worst 2.25% scores for a system are not taken into consideration

[6]Repetitions were allowed.

WMT2013			Main Study		
Rank	Score	System	Rank	Score	System
1	0.637	ONLINE-B	1	0.594	ONLINE-B
	0.636	PROMT	2	0.572	UEDIN-SYNTAX
3	0.614	UEDIN-SYNTAX		0.556	PROMT
	0.571	UEDIN		0.540	UEDIN
	0.571	KIT	6	0.510	KIT
7	0.523	STANFORD	7	0.482	MES-REORDER
8	0.507	LIMSI-SOUL		0.480	LIMSI-SOUL
9	0.477	MES-REORDER		0.460	STANFORD
	0.476	JHU		0.459	CU-ZEMAN
	0.460	CU-ZEMAN	11	0.427	TUBITAK
	0.453	TUBITAK		0.426	JHU
13	0.361	UU	13	0.351	UU
14	0.329	SHEF-WPROA		0.344	SHEF-WPROA
	0.323	RWTH-JANE	15	0.308	RWTH

Table 5: System ranking with bootstrap resampling in WMT2013 and in the main study

studies students achieve an intra-annotator agreement of 0.772 and an inter-annotator agreement of 0.510. The values are slightly higher than the ones of the researchers during WMT2013, but the differences are not really that pronounced. One interpretation of these results is that this task did not require specialised knowledge neither from the researchers nor from the translation studies students. Although researchers are probably not so familiar with translation studies theories and translation students are not specialists in machine translation, from the results, we notice an overlap in decision taking/making between the two groups. This overlap can be, as mentioned before, due to the nature of the evaluation task, since evaluators from both groups had to rank the machine translation output given the source text and the reference translation and the knowledge about the source and target language was enough.

The higher agreement values for the students' group can be an indicator that students ranked the machine translation output more thoroughly, a fact that was confirmed also by the non-formal feedback we got from the evaluators. Most of them them complained that it was very difficult to rank machine translation output of roughly similar overall quality. They reported that they had first to rank for themselves the errors they saw in the machine translation output before ranking the sentences.

Another aspect which probably influenced the results is the number of evaluators (for intra-annotator agreement) and evaluator pairs (for the inter-annotator agreement) considered in the computation of κ. The lower the number of evaluators and evaluator pairs the higher the influence of each evaluator and pair on the final κ.

Concerning the system rankings presented by Bojar et al. (2013) and computed based on the expected wins described by Koehn (2012), we can remark a shifting of ranks between the systems listed in the WMT2013 report and the rankings obtained by the translation studies students. Still, this rank shifting is more preeminent in the middle part of the table, than at the bottom, proving that systems with similar quality of MT output are harder to rank than MT output which is very different. Table 5 gives an overview of the WMT2013 system rankings as well as of the system rankings in our main experiment. ONLINE-B was ranked by both groups as the best system, UEDIN-SYNTAX and UEDIN kept their ranks as well as KIT, UU, SHEF-WPROA and RWTH. Although the other systems changed their rankings by moving up or down, there is no real striking position change in the ranking list. From Table 5 we can also notice that the scores for the systems have suffered a slight decrease in our main experiment as compared to the WMT2013 results. This is due to the fact that students made a clearer distinction between good and bad translations by trying to avoid ties, this being reflected into the final systems scores.

	WMT2013	Pilot	Main Study
Total number of evaluators	38	26	37
Total number of rankings pairs	39582	25780	37318
Evaluators considered for intra-annotator agreement	12	16	22
κ (Intra-annotator agreement)	0.649	0.745	0.772
Evaluators pairs considered for inter-annotator agreement	372	325	536
κ (Inter-annotator agreement)	0.457	0.494	0.510

Table 6: Overview over collected data and Cohen's κ for the language pair English-German

5 Conclusion

From our pilot study as well as from our main experiment on evaluating machine translation by ranking sentence level machine translation output we found that the MT development teams in WMT2013 are not so different from the translation studies students we had as evaluators in our experiments. Turning back to the questions we asked in Section 1, we can say that our experiments overall reproduced the WMT2013 ranking task with some differences in the results. Indeed, we observed that the group of students achieved higher agreement score κ meaning that they were more consistent individually and as a group. On the other hand, from the computation of the system rankings the students confirmed at least the first and last places in the WMT2013 system ranking, although the scores achieved by all systems were slightly lower. The slight decrease of ranking scores is due to the fact that translation studies students were more discriminative and produced less ties. Based on the results presented in the previous sections we consider that the human ranking task does not required any specialised knowledge. Moreover, we argue that a homogeneous group and a good command of the source and target language are enough to replicate the results of the ranking task in the WMT2013.

References

Bojar, Ondřej, Christian Buck, Chris Callison-Burch, Barry Haddow, Philipp Koehn, Christof Monz, Matt Post, Hervé Saint-Amand, Radu Soricut, and Lucia Specia, editors. 2013. *Proceedings of the 8th Workshop on SMT*. ACL.

Cohen, Jacob. 1960. A Coefficient of Agreement for Nominal Scales. *Educational and Psychological Measurement*, 20(1):37–46, April.

Comelles, Elisabet and Jordi Atserias. 2014. Verta participation in the wmt14 metrics task. In *Proceedings of the Ninth Workshop on Statistical Machine Translation*, pages 368–375, Baltimore, Maryland, USA, June. Association for Computational Linguistics.

Denkowski, Michael and Alon Lavie. 2014. Meteor universal: Language specific translation evaluation for any target language. In *Proceedings of the EACL 2014 Workshop on Statistical Machine Translation*.

Doddington, George. 2002. Automatic evaluation of machine translation quality using n-gram co-occurrence statistics. In *Proceedings of the 2nd International Conference on HLT*, pages 138–145.

Federmann, Christian. 2012. Appraise: An open-source toolkit for manual evaluation of machine translation output. *PBML*, 98:25–35, 9.

Gonzàlez, Meritxell, Alberto Barrón-Cedeño, and Lluís Màrquez. 2014. Ipa and stout: Leveraging linguistic and source-based features for machine translation evaluation. In *Proceedings of the Ninth Workshop on Statistical Machine Translation*, pages 394–401, Baltimore, Maryland, USA, June. Association for Computational Linguistics.

Koehn, Philipp. 2012. Simulating human judgment in machine translation evaluation campaigns. In *IWSLT*, pages 179–184.

Levenshtein, Vladimir Iosifovich. 1966. Binary codes capable of correcting deletions, insertions and reversals. *Soviet Physics Doklady*, 10(8):707–710.

Lo, Chi-Kiu and Dekai Wu. 2011. MEANT: An inexpensive, high-accuracy, semi-automatic metric for evaluating translation utility based on semantic roles. In *Proceedings of the 49th Annual Meeting of the ACL*, pages 220–229.

Lo, Chi-kiu, Anand Karthik Tumuluru, and Dekai Wu. 2012. Fully automatic semantic MT evaluation. In *Proceedings of the Seventh Workshop on Statistical Machine Translation*, pages 243–252, Montréal, Canada, June. Association for Computational Linguistics.

Papineni, Kishore, Salim Roukos, Todd Ward, and Wei-Jing Zhu. 2002. Bleu: a method for automatic evaluation of machine translation. In *Proceedings of the 40th Annual Meeting of the ACL*, pages 311–318.

Snover, Matthew, Bonnie Dorr, Richard Schwartz, Linnea Micciulla, and John Makhoul. 2006. A study of translation edit rate with targeted human annotation. In *Proceedings of AMTA*, pages 223–231.

Snover, Matthew, Nitin Madnani, Bonnie Dorr, and Richard Schwartz. 2009. Fluency, adequacy, or HTER? Exploring different human judgments with a tunable MT metric. In *Proceedings of the 4th Workshop on SMT*, pages 259–268.

Tillmann, Christoph, Stephan Vogel, Hermann Ney, Alexander Zubiaga, and Hassan Sawaf. 1997. Accelerated DP based search for statistical translation. In *Proceedings of the EUROSPEECH*, pages 2667–2670.

Integrating a Large, Monolingual Corpus as Translation Memory into Statistical Machine Translation

Katharina Wäschle and **Stefan Riezler**
Department of Computational Linguistics
Heidelberg University
69120 Heidelberg, Germany
{waeschle, riezler}@cl.uni-heidelberg.de

Abstract

Translation memories (TM) are widely used in the localization industry to improve consistency and speed of human translation. Several approaches have been presented to integrate the bilingual translation units of TMs into statistical machine translation (SMT). We present an extension of these approaches to the integration of partial matches found in a large, monolingual corpus in the target language, using cross-language information retrieval (CLIR) techniques. We use locality-sensitive hashing (LSH) for efficient coarse-grained retrieval of match candidates, which are then filtered by fine-grained fuzzy matching, and finally used to re-rank the n-best SMT output. We show consistent and significant improvements over a state-of-the-art SMT system, across different domains and language pairs on tens of millions of sentences.

1 Introduction

A translation memory (TM) is a computational tool used by professional translators to speed up translation of repetitive texts. At its core is a database, in which source and target of previously translated segments of text are stored. TMs are capable of retrieving not only exact, but also partial matches, where only a certain percentage of source words overlap with the query, called fuzzy matches. A computer-assisted translation (CAT) tool presents possible matches found in the database to a user, if the match is considered similar enough to the current source sentence. Even if the presented target sentence is not a perfect translation, a fuzzy match can be a good starting point for the translation of the current sentence and reduce translation time and effort. Furthermore, the approach can help with translation consistency and terminology control. In contrast to statistical machine translation (SMT), TM tools are widely used in the translation industry, since the results presented to the translator are fluent translations. They are especially successful for translation of texts from repetitive domains, e.g. technical documents such as IT manuals, that are the predominant use case in the localization industry.

The idea of combining the strengths of TM and SMT tools has been successfully explored in recent years. In this paper, we extend these approaches to the integration of a large, monolingual corpus in the target language as a TM into an SMT system using cross-language information retrieval (CLIR). Our approach utilizes locality-sensitive hashing (LSH) as an efficient coarse retrieval technique to select candidate translations. In a next step, search is performed at a finer-grained level using distance metrics customary in CAT. Given a match, our model re-ranks the n-best list output by an SMT decoder using features modeling the closeness of the hypothesis and the target of the TM match. Since our approach does not rely on an alignment between source and target side of the TM match, we are able to search for potential matches in large, monolingual corpora that might only be available in the target language. We show consistent and significant improvements on different domains (IT, legal, patents) for different language pairs (including Chinese, Japanese, English, French, and German), achieving results comparable to or better than using a target-language reference of source-side matches.

2 Related Work

Work on integrating MT and SMT can be divided into approaches at the sentence level that decide whether to pass SMT or TM output to the user (He et al., 2010a,b), and approaches that merge both techniques at a sub-sentential level (Smith and Clark, 2009; Koehn and Senellart, 2010; Zhechev and van Genabith, 2010; Wang et al., 2013). While the goal of the former is to improve human translation effort in a CAT environment, the second line of research aims to improve SMT performance.

Biçici and Dymetman (2008) were among the first to propose a combined system. They start by identifying matching subsequences between the current sentence and a fuzzy match retrieved from a translation memory. Source and target of the match together with the corresponding alignment are used to construct a non-contiguous bi-phrase, which is added to the SMT grammar with a strong weight. The decoder is then run as usual using the augmented grammar. The approaches of Koehn and Senellart (2010), Zhechev and van Genabith (2010), and Ma et al. (2011), force the SMT system to translate only the unmatching segments of the source, either by restricting translation or by adding a very high feature weight to rules or bi-phrases extracted from the TM match. While all presented approaches make use of the alignment between source and target of the fuzzy match, our approach uses only the target side to restrict the translation, making it possible to use matches that can be found in a target-only corpus.

The use of TM matches to generate additional features for SMT has been explored by Simard and Isabelle (2009), Wang et al. (2013), Wang et al. (2014) and Li et al. (2014). Our re-ranking approach is very similar, with the novelty of using not only matches found by querying the source side of the corpus, but also the target.

The idea of directly searching for translations in a monolingual target language corpus has been explored by Dong et al. (2014). They retrieve target side translation candidates using a lattice representation of possible translations of a source sentence. The system is successfully applied to the task of identifying parallel sentences, but no SMT experiments are reported.

3 Integrating monolingual TM into SMT

Our integrated model uses a coarse-to-fine approach for integrating TM information into an SMT system: First, efficient retrieval is done using locality-sensitive hashing on large corpora. Second, a more fine-grained search for the best match is performed for a given sentence. Lastly, a re-ranking step uses this information to re-score the n-best list output of an SMT decoder.

3.1 Coarse-grained retrieval using LSH

In order to be able to use large corpora as translation memory, a fast method is needed to retrieve matches. In CAT practice, the goodness of a TM match is calculated using the so-called fuzzy match score (Sikes, 2007),

$$\mathrm{FMS}(s_1, s_2) = 1 - \frac{\mathrm{LD}(s_1, s_2)}{\max(|s_1|, |s_2|}))$$

which is based on the Levenshtein distance LD, i.e. the minimum number of operations[1] needed to transform the sequence s_1 into the sequence s_2. Levenshtein distance can be computed with dynamic programming in $O(mn)$ time. However, computing edit distance against a corpus of tens of millions of sentences is too slow for real-time use, especially for long sentences that appear e.g. in patent data. This leads us to a two-step approach with a coarse pre-retrieval that delivers candidates for good fuzzy matches for a given sentence in milliseconds. For a smaller candidate set we can then compute the exact fuzzy match score.

MinHash (Broder, 1997) is a way to estimate the similarity of two documents by reducing the dimensionality of the document signature using sampling. It is an instance of locality-sensitive hashing, where similar items hash to the same bucket, which makes comparison extremely fast, since only hashes have to be compared. It is usually employed for tasks such as near-duplicate detection of websites, but can be applied to our task as well. MinHash approximates the Jaccard similarity of two sets X and Y,

$$\mathrm{JC}(X, Y) = \frac{|X \cap Y|}{|X \cup Y|}$$

by generating signatures of each set, from which the Jaccard similarity can be estimated. The signature is gained by repeatedly hashing each member

[1] Allowed operations are removal, insertion, substitution or transposition.

of the set and storing only the minimal resulting hash. By representing each sentence as a set of n-grams we can use this technique to efficiently approximate the n-gram overlap of two sentences. n-gram overlap has been found to be a good predictor of TM match quality (Bloodgood and Strauss, 2014). In our experiments we used 3-grams to represent sentences in corpora with high average sentence length (legal, patent) and 1-grams for data sets featuring short sentences (IT).

To efficiently estimate the Jaccard Similarity from the MinHash signatures, we apply the banding technique described in Rajaraman and Ullman (2012, Chapter 3), where similar items are likely to get hashed to the same bucket. When setting the similarity threshold t, which regulates how similar two items have to be in order to become candidates, we are faced with a effectiveness-efficiency trade-off (Ture et al., 2011), where we find false positives, which slow down the second retrieval step, and also false negatives, which will cost overall performance. We set the t for each dataset on a held-out development set by choosing a setting in which a candidate match is returned for at least 90% of the sentences. We then compute the actual Jaccard Similarity for the set of match candidates returned by the hashing step and rank them accordingly. We take the 100 best matches for each query q_i and choose the best match from them in the fine-grained step described in the following.

3.2 Fine-grained matching

In the standard bilingual case, choosing the best TM match amounts to selecting the sentence pair (s, t) from the coarse candidate set $\text{LSH}(q_i)$ that achieves the highest fuzzy match score FMS of the (source) query q_i against the source side $s_{i,j}$ of the TM pair, and returning its target side $t_{i,j}$.

$$(s,t)_{i,best} = \operatorname*{argmax}_{(s,t)_{i,j} \in \text{LSH}(q_i)} \text{FMS}(q_i, s_{i,j}).$$

For the target-language scenario, however, this step is not straightforward. We want to select a target sentence t from a set of target-only candidates given a query q_i in the source language, however, in order to do this, we require a cross-language similarity score CLIR. To generate a target candidate set with coarse retrieval we use the 1-best translation $Tr(q_i)$ by an SMT decoder trained on bilingual data as a query[2].

$$t_{i,best} = \operatorname*{argmax}_{t_{i,j} \in \text{LSH}(Tr(q_i))} \text{CLIR}(q_i, t_{i,j}).$$

To determine the best match among the candidates in a fine-grained way, we investigate three different cross-language techniques.

1-best FMS. This model uses as a selection criterion the fuzzy match score of the candidate $t_{i,j}$ given the most likely translation hypothesis produced for the query q_i by an SMT model, $Tr(q_i)$.

$$\text{CLIR}(q_i, t_{i,j}) = \text{FMS}(Tr(q_i), t_{i,j})$$

This corresponds to a direct translation baseline in cross-language information retrieval.

In addition to this simple model, we explore two methods that operate on the full translation hypergraph of the query. Both techniques are similar to the translation retrieval technique presented by Dong et al. (2014). They perform Viterbi search on a translation lattice of the input sentence that is enriched, besides the default SMT features, with n-gram features that indicate the overlap status between the current state in the lattice and a given TM match. We adopt this approach for the hypergraph built by the `cdec` decoder (Dyer et al., 2010). As a cross-lingual similarity measure we then compute the Viterbi score on the query hypergraph $Hg(q_i)$ for each match candidate $t_{i,j}$, i.e.

$$\text{CLIR}(q_i, t_{i,j}) = \max_{p \in Hg(q_i)} \sum_{e \in p} w_{\text{SMT}} \cdot \phi_{\text{SMT}}(e(q_i)) + w_{\text{n-gr}} \cdot \phi_{\text{n-gr}}(e(q_i), t_{i,j}))$$

where p is a path through the hypergraph, e the set of edges on the path, ϕ are feature values of an edge, w the corresponding weights, and $\cdot$ denotes the vector dot product. We explore two different ways to incorporate n-gram features $\phi_{\text{n-gr}}$ in addition to the SMT feature set ϕ_{SMT}.

Unigram oracle. Since n-gram features are non-local and the size of the hypergraph grows when adding n-gram features for orders higher than $n = 1$ (Chiang, 2007), we restrict our first model to unigram precision and a brevity penalty feature; the latter is only active at goal state. In this way, two additional features are inserted into the log-linear model, using the TM match candidate as an oracle.

[2] We also tested query constructions involving a larger set of possible translations, but found that using the 1-best translation prediction of the baseline system yielded superior results.

Additional language model. To be able to include higher-order n-gram matches, we add the match candidates as an additional language model to the decoder.This approach makes use of the fact that `cdec` handles the extension of the hypergraph to accommodate for the non-local higher order n-grams. Cube pruning (Chiang, 2007) is used to make the search feasible.

In both cases, we keep the weights of the SMT features fixed, which have been optimized for translation performance on a development set, and only adjust the additional weights in relation. This is done by pairwise ranking (Hopkins and May, 2011). The gold standard ranking of the TM candidates is given by $\text{FMS}(t_{i,j}, r_i)$ with respect to the reference r_i for q_i. The learning goal is to adjust the weights of the n-gram features so as to rank the TM match highest that has the smallest distance to the reference. Note, that we do not optimize the translation performance of the derivation, which corresponds to the Viterbi path. This could potentially replace the re-ranking step and we plan to explore this option in the future.

3.3 Re-ranking SMT output

To incorporate the retrieved TM match into the SMT pipeline we use a simple re-ranking model on the n-best list output by the baseline SMT system and select the best hypothesis $\hat{h}$ under this model. We balance information from the SMT model and the TM by computing a linear interpolation of SMT model score SMT and fuzzy match score FMS between hypothesis h and best TM target match $t_{i,best}$. We also add a confidence-weighted version of the FMS score using the retrieval score (CL)IR between TM match and original query q_i as confidence measure:

$$\begin{aligned}\hat{h} = \operatorname*{argmax}_{h \in H(q_i)} w_1 \times \text{SMT}(h) \\ + w_2 \times \text{FMS}(h, t_{i,best}) \\ + w_3 \times ((\text{CL})\text{IR}(q_i, t_{i,best}) \times \text{FMS}(h, t_{i,best})).\end{aligned}$$

We experimented with more features, including n-gram overlap and a brevity penalty, but found that they did not add any information that was not already present in the model. We learn weights for the different components of the score by pairwise ranking using PRO (Hopkins and May, 2011). This time the gold-standard ranking is induced on the n-best list of SMT outputs by TER match against the reference.

domain	sentences	vocabulary size	
		src	tgt
acquis (en-fr)	1M	121K	140K
oo3 (en-zh)	50K	6K	8K
ntcir (jp-en)	1.6M	96K	185K
pattr (en-de)	10.1M	728K	679K

Table 1: Statistics for experimental data.

	acquis	oo3	ntcir	pattr
RR	16.85	5.98	16.9	5.85
SL	27.27	6.48	33.91	33.55

Table 2: Test set repetition rates (RR) and average sentence length (SL) in tokens.

4 Experiments

Since translation memories are most effective on text that has a certain amount of repetition, we evaluate our approach on typical localization data, from the IT, legal and intellectual property domains[3] (Table 1). All corpora are freely available for research purposes. We report repetition rate (Cettolo et al., 2014) and average sentence length in Table 2 and show the number of matches for each fuzzy match interval in Table 3. Among the freely available corpora, only the JRC-Acquis corpus has been used previously in combinations of TM and SMT (Koehn and Senellart, 2010; Li et al., 2014). Most works in this area report results on TM data from industrial partners that are not publicly available. Usually, these datasets feature a large proportion of fuzzy matches in high ranges, e.g. between 80% and 100%, which makes it possible for the combined systems to achieve a large boost in score. Our reported results are in a smaller range, but achieved on data with much less high-percentage matches. We manage to gain improvements in performance from matches with an associated fuzzy match score between 10% and 80%.

[3]Europarl has been used as a dataset by (Koehn and Senellart, 2010), but performance of the enriched SMT system actually dropped below the baseline, showing that less repetitive corpora are badly suited for the TM adaptation methods.

We prepared an English-Chinese corpus of IT manuals from the OPUS[4] corpus (Tiedemann, 2012), the OpenOffice 3 (OO3) data. We only kept pairs that contained at least one Chinese character[5]. The Chinese side was segmented using the Stanford Word Segmenter (Tseng et al., 2005) with the Penn Treebank standard. Development and test sets were created by randomly sampling 1,000 sentence pairs each and remaining pairs used for training. We used English-French legal data from the JRC-Acquis corpus[6] (Steinberger et al., 2006) and sampled dev, devtest and test set from documents published in 2000. The remaining years were used for training. We evaluated our approach on two patent data sets; English-German data from the PatTR[7] corpus (Wäschle and Riezler, 2012) and Japanese-English data from the NTCIR[8] challenge (Utiyama and Isahara, 2007). We used NTCIR-10 dev, test[9] and training set. Held-out data sets for PatTR were sampled from documents from 2006, the remaining data formed the training set.

	acquis	oo3	ntcir	pattr
0-10%	5	0	15	17
10-20%	68	4	118	121
20-30%	89	3	200	205
30-40%	56	10	167	187
40-50%	51	3	95	88
50-60%	70	13	58	56
60-70%	52	14	28	19
70-80%	59	15	17	28
80-90%	109	29	8	18
90-99%	136	21	1	8
100%	292	500	6	19

Table 3: Number of test sentences with source side fuzzy match score in a certain range.

We trained a baseline SMT system using the `cdec` decoder (Dyer et al., 2010) and the accompanying tools, i.e. `fast align` (Dyer et al., 2013) on each data set. A 6-gram language model was trained with SRILM (Stolcke, 2002) on the target side of the training data. The weights of the log-linear model were optimized with MIRA (Watanabe et al., 2007) on a held-out development set reserved for this purpose (dev). We employed the baseline model to produce query translations and hypergraphs for the cross-lingual retrieval of target matches as well as to produce 500-best lists, which we re-ranked according to our model given the best match found after fine-grained retrieval. Retrieval and re-ranking parameters were optimized on an additional held-out (devtest) set. All presented results were obtained on a third (test) data set. To compare source and different target retrieval methods in a fair setting, we used the bilingual data from training the SMT model as translation memory, restricted to the target side for target retrieval. To evaluate our target retrieval approach in more a realistic setting, we furthermore set up an experiment for the English-German patent task, where SMT training data and monolingual TM deviate. We assume that we have parallel data from patent claims and the task is to translate text from a different genre, patent descriptions, for which only data in the target language available as well as a small amount of bitext to tune parameters on – a typical domain adaptation scenario. The available monolingual data is used to extend both the language model as well as the target-language TM (Table 4).

	genre	size (sent.)
parallel train (en-de)	cl.	6M
dev/devtest/test (en-de)	desc.	1K (each)
LM-train (de)	cl.+descr.	16.2M
TM (de)	cl.+desc.	16.2M

Table 4: Data for domain adaptation scenario.

We report BLEU (Papineni et al., 2002) and TER (Snover et al., 2006) evaluation scores. Statistical significance of all results was assessed following the method described in Clark et al. (2011) using the source code provided by the authors[10].

4.1 Results

Results in Table 5 show that adding the TM information always improves over the baseline, up to 1.23 BLEU and -3.77 TER. Improvements in TER (the optimized metric) are always significant at $p < 0.05$. Both source and target-side match re-

[4]http://datahub.io/de/dataset/opus

[5]We tested for Chinese characters by checking if they were in the Unicode range `[0x4E00, 0x9FFF]`.

[6]`https://ec.europa.eu/jrc/en/language-technologies/jrc-acquis`

[7]`http://www.cl.uni-heidelberg.de/statnlpgroup/pattr/`

[8]`http://research.nii.ac.jp/ntcir/ntcir-10/`

[9]We merged, shuffled and again split up the data into three sets, to generate a devtest set.

[10]`https://github.com/jhclark/multeval`

	acquis		oo3		ntcir		pattr	
	BLEU	TER	BLEU	TER	BLEU	TER	BLEU	TER
baseline	61.43%	28.16%	36.04%	50.83%	24.52%	66.52%	26.89%	57.51%
+src-rr	62.62%	**26.63%**	**36.65%**	**50.01%**	**25.51%**	**62.75%**	27.11%	57.04%
	+1.19%	**-1.57%**	**+0.61%**	**-0.82%**	**+0.99%**	**-3.77%**	+0.22%	-0.47%
+tgt-FMS-rr	**62.92%**	26.79%	36.26%	50.13%	25.23%	63.59%	**27.31%**	**56.78%**
	+1.48%	-1.37%	+0.22%*	-0.70%	+0.71%	-2.93%	**+0.42%**	**-0.73%**
+tgt-Oracle-rr	62.23%	27.56%	36.16%	50.17%	24.55%	66.20%	27.03%	57.25%
	+0.80%	-0.60%	+0.12%	-0.66%	+0.03%*	-0.31%	+0.13%*	-0.26%
+tgt-LM-rr	62.29%	27.45%	36.09%	50.15%	24.63%	66.11%	26.98%	57.29%
	+0.85%	-0.71%	+0.05%*	-0.67%	+0.11%*	-0.41%	+0.09%*	-0.21%

Table 5: BLEU and TER difference to baseline for TM integration on by source-side matching and re-ranking (+src-rr) and variants of target-side matching and re-ranking (+tgt-*-rr). All improvements, except marked with *, are significant w.r.t the baseline at $p < 0.05$. Best results in **bold face**.

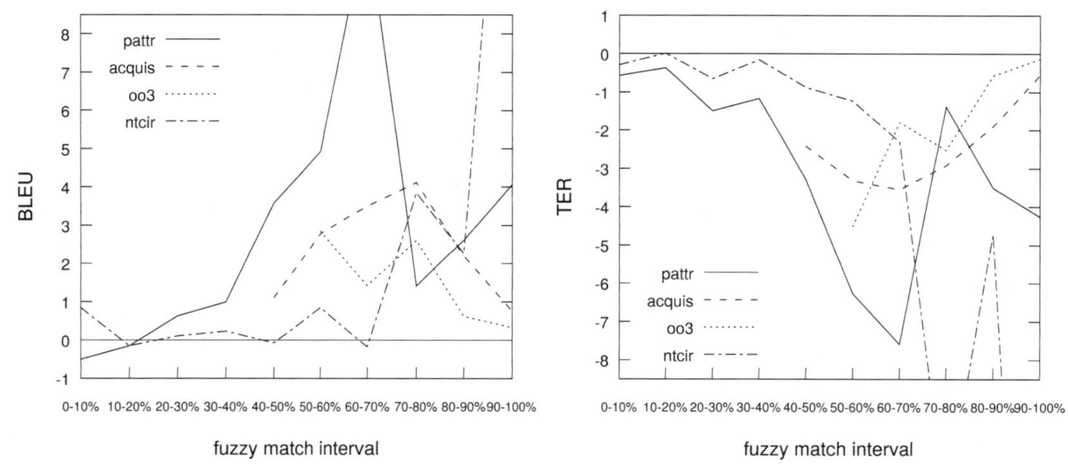

Figure 1: Δ BLEU and Δ TER between baseline and system output on different fuzzy match intervals

trieval beat the baseline. Re-ranking using target-side only matches beats source-side retrieval on two datasets. n-gram based models for choosing the best target match always perform worse than the fuzzy-match-score based models.

Figure 1 shows detailed results on the different fuzzy match intervals, in particular the difference between +tgt-FMS-rr system and the baseline. It is interesting to note that the highest gains are achieved in the 70-80% range, while previous research reports highest gains in the 95-100% range. This is apparently dependent on the data set, but it also suggests, that the baseline SMT system is already very good in the high match range, at least for short sentences. For ntcir we achieve extremely high numbers in the 90-100% range and for pattr in the 60-70% but these scores are achieved on very few examples (7 and 14, respectively) and therefore cannot be expected to be stable. The difference between the datasets is probably due to the average sentence length – shorter sentences with a perfect match in the TM are easier to reproduce for the SMT system than longer ones, due to the smaller number of translation options. It is also remarkable, that for ntcir and pattr datasets even extremely low-range matches are beneficial. While there are some drops in terms of BLEU, TER always goes down, even on 0-10% matches. Having established that target-side retrieval performs comparably to source retrieval, we evaluate our approach in the domain adaptation setting, where additional monolingual data for the TM is available. Results are given in Table 6. We find significant improvements over the competitive baseline with an adapted language model without adding any bilingual data.

	BLEU	TER
baseline	21.58%	62.54%
+tgt-FMS-rr	**21.81%**	**62.18%**
	+0.23%	**-0.36%**

Table 6: Results for domain adaptation scenario.

Figure 2 compares translation output between baseline and the +tgt-FMS-rr extension, showing that the system is able to correct syntactical errors, but also, that some changes consist only of swapping translations for a term, where both translations would be correct choices. In this case, the translation both gains and loses from this phenomenon with regard to the reference. We assume that this holds for the whole test set: in some cases out system will randomly pick the right (used by the reference) translation; sometimes adding a match will change a correct translation. Since overall our system improves significantly over the baseline, meaningful changes are made frequently.

5 Conclusion

We present an approach to integrate large corpora as translation memories into an SMT system, which yields consistent and significant improvements over baseline results on IT, legal and patent data. In contrast to previous approaches, the discriminative model is light-weight and needs no phrase-segmentation or alignment between TM source and target, allowing for the integration of partial matches found in the target language. Results with target-language matches are comparable to using a target reference of source-side matches.

In future work, we would like to extend our approach to multiple fuzzy matches for one source sentence that cover different spans of the input, as proposed in Li et al. (2014). Furthermore, we would like to conduct experiments on a translation memory gained from real-world industrial data with post-editing feedback.

References

Biçici, E. and Dymetman, M. (2008). Dynamic translation memory: Using statistical machine translation to improve translation memory fuzzy matches. In *Computational Linguistics and Intelligent Text Processing*, pages 454–465.

Bloodgood, M. and Strauss, B. (2014). Translation memory retrieval methods. In *EACL*.

Broder, A. Z. (1997). On the resemblance and containment of documents. In *Compression and Complexity of Sequences*, pages 21–29.

Cettolo, M., Bertoldi, N., and Federico, M. (2014). The repetition rate of text as a predictor of the effectiveness of machine translation adaptation. In *AMTA*.

Chiang, D. (2007). Hierarchical phrase-based translation. *Computational Linguistics*, 33(2):201–228.

Clark, J. H., Dyer, C., Lavie, A., and Smith, N. A. (2011). Better hypothesis testing for statistical machine translation: Controlling for optimizer instability. In *ACL-HLT*.

Dong, M., Cheng, Y., Liu, Y., Xu, J., Sun, M., Izuha, T., and Hao, J. (2014). Query lattice for translation retrieval. In *COLING*.

Dyer, C., Chahuneau, V., and Smith, N. A. (2013). A simple, fast, and effective reparameterization of IBM model 2. In *NAACL-HLT*.

Dyer, C., Lopez, A., Ganitkevitch, J., Weese, J., Ture, F., Blunsom, P., Setiawan, H., Eidelman, V., and Resnik, P. (2010). cdec: A decoder, alignment, and learning framework for finite-state and context-free translation models. In *ACL*.

He, Y., Ma, Y., van Genabith, J., and Way, A. (2010a). Bridging SMT and TM with translation recommendation. In *ACL*.

He, Y., Ma, Y., Way, A., and Van Genabith, J. (2010b). Integrating n-best SMT outputs into a TM system. In *COLING*.

Hopkins, M. and May, J. (2011). Tuning as ranking. In *EMNLP*.

Koehn, P. and Senellart, J. (2010). Convergence of translation memory and statistical machine translation. In *AMTA*.

Li, L., Way, A., and Liu, Q. (2014). A discriminative framework of integrating translation memory features into SMT. In *AMTA*.

Ma, Y., He, Y., Way, A., and van Genabith, J. (2011). Consistent translation using discriminative learning: A translation memory-inspired approach. In *ACL*.

source	*in one particular embodiment , the aliphatic hydroxy carboxylic acids bear the hydroxyl group and the carboxyl group on the same carbon atom .*
baseline	*in einer besonderen ausführungsform die aliphatischen hydroxycarbonsäuren , die die hydroxylgruppe und die carboxylgruppe an ein und demselben kohlenstoffatom tragen .*
+tgt-FMS-rr	*in einer besonderen ausführungsform* ***tragen*** *die aliphatischen hydroxycarbonsäuren die hydroxygruppe und die carbonsäuregruppe* ***am gleichen c - atom*** *.*
tm match	*in einer besonderen ausführungsform des erfindungsgemäßen verfahrens tragen die aliphatischen hydroxycarbonsäuren die hydroxy - und carbonsäuregruppe am selben c - atom .*
reference	*in einer besonderen ausführungsform tragen die aliphatischen hydroxycarbonsäuren die hydroxy - und carboxyl gruppe am gleichen c - atom .*

Figure 2: Example system output on patent test set: With the TM match, the syntax of the output has been corrected: the subordinate clause has been removed and the verb *tragen* placed correctly in the main clause. *kohlenstoffatom* became *c - atom*, which is both correct, but the latter is the term used in the reference; on the other hand, *carboxylgruppe* was correctly output by the baseline, but changed to *carbonsäuregruppe* – correct, but not the term used in the reference.

Papineni, K., Roukos, S., Ward, T., and Zhu, W.-J. (2002). BLEU: a method for automatic evaluation of machine translation. In *ACL*.

Pedregosa, F., Varoquaux, G., Gramfort, A., Michel, V., Thirion, B., Grisel, O., Blondel, M., Prettenhofer, P., Weiss, R., Dubourg, V., et al. (2011). Scikit-learn: Machine learning in Python. *The Journal of Machine Learning Research*, 12:2825–2830.

Rajaraman, A. and Ullman, J. D. (2012). *Mining of massive datasets*. Cambridge University Press.

Sikes, R. (2007). Fuzzy matching in theory and practice. *MultiLingual*, 18(6):39–43.

Simard, M. and Isabelle, P. (2009). Phrase-based machine translation in a computer-assisted translation environment. *MT Summit XII*.

Smith, J. and Clark, S. (2009). Ebmt for SMT: A new EBMT-SMT hybrid. In *EBMT*.

Snover, M., Dorr, B., Schwartz, R., Micciulla, L., and Makhoul, J. (2006). A study of translation edit rate with targeted human annotation. In *AMTA*.

Steinberger, R., Pouliquen, B., Widiger, A., Ignat, C., Erjavec, T., Tufis, D., and Varga, D. (2006). The JRC-Acquis: A multilingual aligned parallel corpus with 20+ languages. In *LREC*.

Stolcke, A. (2002). SRILM – an extensible language modeling toolkit. In *ICSLP*.

Tiedemann, J. (2012). Parallel data, tools and interfaces in OPUS. In *LREC*.

Tseng, H., Chang, P., Andrew, G., Jurafsky, D., and Manning, C. (2005). A conditional random field word segmenter for SIGHAN bakeoff 2005. In *SIGHAN*.

Ture, F., Elsayed, T., and Lin, J. (2011). No free lunch: brute force vs. locality-sensitive hashing for cross-lingual pairwise similarity. In *SIGIR*.

Utiyama, M. and Isahara, H. (2007). A japanese-english patent parallel corpus. *MT Summit XI*.

Wang, K., Zong, C., and Su, K.-Y. (2013). Integrating translation memory into phrase-based machine translation during decoding. In *ACL*.

Wang, K., Zong, C., and Su, K.-Y. (2014). Dynamically integrating cross-domain translation memory into phrase-based machine translation during decoding. In *COLING*.

Wäschle, K. and Riezler, S. (2012). Analyzing parallelism and domain similarities in the MAREC patent corpus. In *IRFC*.

Watanabe, T., Suzuki, J., Tsukada, H., and Isozaki, H. (2007). Online large-margin training for statistical machine translation. In *EMNLP*.

Zhechev, V. and van Genabith, J. (2010). Seeding statistical machine translation with translation memory output through tree-based structural alignment. In *SSST*.

Target-side Generation of Prepositions for SMT

Marion Weller[1,2], **Alexander Fraser**[2], **Sabine Schulte im Walde**[1]

[1] IMS, University of Stuttgart – (wellermn|schulte)@ims.uni-stuttgart.de
[2] CIS, Ludwig-Maximilian University of Munich – fraser@cis.uni-muenchen.de

Abstract

We present a translation system that models the selection of prepositions in a target-side generation component. This novel approach allows the modeling of all subcategorized elements of a verb as either NPs or PPs according to target-side requirements relying on source and target side features. The BLEU scores are encouraging, but fail to surpass the baseline. We additionally evaluate the preposition accuracy for a carefully selected subset and discuss how typical problems of translating prepositions can be modeled with our method.

1 Introduction

The translation of prepositions is a difficult task for machine translation; a preposition must convey the source-side meaning while also meeting target-side constraints. This requires information that is not always directly accessible in an SMT system. Prepositions are typically determined by governors, such as verbs (*to believe in sth.*) or nouns (*interest in sth.*). Functional prepositions tend to convey little meaning and mostly depend on target-side restrictions, whereas content-bearing prepositions are largely determined by the source-side, but may also be subject to target-side requirements, as in the following example: *go to the cinema/to the beach* → *ins Kino/an den Strand gehen.*

In this paper, we treat prepositions as a target-side generation problem and move the selection of prepositions out of the translation system into a post-processing component. During translation, we use an abstract representation of prepositions as a place-holder that serves as a basis for the generation of prepositions in the post-processing step. In this step, all subcategorized elements of a verb are considered and allotted to their respective functions – as PPs with an overt preposition, but also as NPs with an "empty" preposition, e.g. *to call for sth.* → *∅ etw. erfordern.* In a standard SMT system, subcategorization is difficult to capture in the language model or by the translation rules if the verb and its subcategorized elements are not adjacent.

In the following, we outline a method to handle prepositions with a target-side generation model in an English-German morphology-aware SMT system. We study two aspects: (i) features for a meaningful abstract representation of prepositions and (ii) how to predict prepositions in the translation output using a combination of source and target-side information. In addition, we compare prepositions in the machine translation output with those in the reference translation for a selected subset. Finally, we discuss examples illustrating typical problems of translating prepositions.

2 Related Work

Most research on translating prepositions has been reported for rule-based systems. Naskar and Bandyopadhyay (2006) outline a method to handle prepositions in an English-Bengali MT system using WordNet and an example base for idiomatic PPs. Gustavii (2005) uses bilingual features and selectional constraints to correct translations in a Swedish-English system. Agirre et al. (2009) model Basque prepositions and grammatical case using syntactic-semantic features such as subcategorization triples for a rule-based system which leads to an improved translation quality for prepositions. Shilon et al. (2012) extend this approach

input	lemmatized SMT output	prep	morph. feat.	inflected	gloss
$\emptyset$ $\longrightarrow$	PREP	$\emptyset$-Acc	–		
what	welch<PWAT>	Acc	Acc.Fem.Sg.Wk	welche	which
role	Rolle<+NN><Fem><Sg>	Acc	Acc.Fem.Sg.Wk	Rolle	role
$\emptyset$ $\longrightarrow$	PREP	$\emptyset$-Nom	–		
the	die<+ART><Def>	Nom	Nom.Masc.Sg.St	der	the
giant	riesig<ADJ>	Nom	Nom.Masc.Sg.Wk	riesige	giant
planet	Planet<+NN><Masc><Sg>	Nom	Nom.Masc.Sg.Wk	Planet	planet
has	gespielt<VVPP>	–	–	gespielt	played
played	hat<VAFIN>	–	–	hat	has
in $\longrightarrow$	PREP	bei-Dat	–	bei	for
the	die<+ART><Def>	Dat	Dat.Fem.Sg.St	der	the
development	Entwicklung<+NN><Fem><Sg>	Dat	Dat.Fem.Sg.Wk	Entwicklung	development
of $\longrightarrow$	PREP	$\emptyset$-Gen	–		
the	die<+ART><Def>	Gen	Gen.Neut.Sg.St	des	of-the
solar system	Sonnensystem<+NN><Neut><Sg>	Gen	Gen.Neut.Sg.Wk	Sonnensystems	solar system

Figure 1: Prediction of prepositions, morphological features and generation of inflected forms for the lemmatized SMT output. German cases: Acc-Accusative, Nom-Nominative, Dat-Dative, Gen-Genitive.

with a statistical component for ranking translations. Weller et al. (2014) use noun class information as tree labels in syntactic SMT to model selectional preferences of prepositions. The presented work is similar to that of Agirre et al. (2009), but is applied to a fully statistical MT system. The main difference is that Agirre et al. (2009) use linguistic information to select appropriate translation rules, whereas we generate prepositions in a post-processing step.

A related task to generating prepositions is the generation of determiners, which are problematic when translating from languages without definiteness morphemes, e.g. Czech or Russian. Tsvetkov et al. (2013) create synthetic translation options to augment a standard phrase-table. They use a classifier trained on local contextual features to predict whether to generate or remove determiners for the target-side of translation rules. Another related task is error correction of second language learners, e.g. Rozovskaya and Roth (2013), which also comprises the correction of prepositions.

In addition to the standard evaluation metric BLEU, we evaluate the accuracy of prepositions in cases where the governing verb and governed noun in the translation output match with the reference translation. Conceptually, this is loosely related to semantically focused metrics (e.g. MEANT, Lo and Wu (2011)), as we go beyond a "flat" n-gram matching but evaluate a meaningful entity, in our case a preposition-noun-verb triple.

3 Methodology

Our approach is integrated into an English-German morphology-aware SMT system which first translates into a lemmatized representation with a component to generate fully inflected forms in a second step, an approach similar to the work by Toutanova et al. (2008) and Fraser et al. (2012). The inflection requires the modeling of the grammatical *case* of noun phrases (among other features), which corresponds to determining the syntactic function[1]. Weller et al. (2013) describe modeling *case* in SMT; we want to treat all subcategorized elements of a verb in one step and extend their setup to cover the prediction of prepositions in both PP and NPs (i.e., the "empty" preposition).

3.1 Translation and Prediction Steps

To build the translation model, we use an abstract target-language representation in which nouns, adjectives and articles are lemmatized and prepositions are substituted with place-holders. Additionally, "empty" place-holder prepositions are inserted at the beginning of noun phrases. To obtain a symmetric data structure, place-holders for "empty" prepositions are also added to source NPs.

When generating surface forms for the translation output, a phrase containing a place-holder can be realized as a noun phrase (with an "empty" preposition) or as an overt prepositional phrase (by generating the preposition's surface form).

Figure 1 illustrates the process: for the English input with extra null-prepositions (column 1), the SMT system outputs a lemmatized representation with place-holder prepositions (column 2). In a first step, prepositions and *case* for the SMT output are predicted (column 3). Then, the three remaining inflection-relevant morphological features *number*, *gender* and *strong/weak* are predicted on "regular" sentences without place-holders, given

[1]The subject usually is in *nominative* case and direct/indirect objects are *accusative/dative*.

the prepositions from the previous step (column 4). In the last step, fully inflected forms[2] are produced based on features and lemmas (column 5). As the inflected forms are generated at the end of the pipeline, portmanteau prepositions, i.e. prepositions merged with an article in certain conditions, such as *zu+dem=zum* (*to+the*), are easily handled.

Due to the lemmatized representation, all subcategorized elements of a verb are available in an abstract form and can be allotted to their respective functions (subject, object, PPs) and be inflected accordingly. Furthermore, the generation of (functional) prepositions is independent of structural mismatches of source and target side: for example, as translation of *to pay attention to sth.*, both *auf etw. achten* and *∅ etw. beachten* are possible, but require a different realization of the place-holder (∅ vs. overt preposition).

For the prediction of prepositions, we combine source and target-side features into a first-order linear chain CRF which provides a flexible framework to make use of different knowledge sources. We use distributional information about subcategorization preferences to model functional prepositions, whereas source-side features (such as the aligned word) tend to be more important for predicting prepositions conveying content. These features address both functional and content-bearing prepositions, but are designed to not require an explicit distinction between the two categories because the model is optimized on the relevant features for each context during training.

During the generation step, the relevant information (such as governing verb/noun and subcategorization preferences) is presented in a refined form, as opposed to the limited information available in a standard SMT system (such as immediate context in a translation rule or language model). It is thus able to bridge large distances between the verb and its subcategorized elements.

4 Abstract Representation of Prepositions

In addition to providing a means to handle subcategorized elements by target-side generation, one objective of the reduced representation of prepositions is to obtain a more general SMT system with a generally improved translation performance. Our experiments will show, however, that replacing prepositions by simple place-holders decreases the translation quality. The effect that a simplified SMT system loses discriminative power has also been observed by e.g. Toutanova et al. (2008) who found that keeping morphological information during translation can be preferable to removing it from the system despite the problem of increased data sparseness. We will thus evaluate systems with varying levels of information annotated to the place-holders (cf. section 6.2).

As an extension to the basic approach with plain place-holders, we experiment with enriching the place-holders such that they contain more relevant information and represent the content of a preposition while still being abstract. To this end, we enrich the place-holders with syntactically motivated features. For example, the representation can be enriched by annotating the place-holder with the grammatical case of the preposition it represents: for overt prepositions, case is often an indicator of the content (such as direction/location), whereas for empty prepositions (NPs), case indicates the syntactic function. As extension, we mark whether a place-holder is governed by a noun or a verb.

Furthermore, we take into account whether a preposition is functional or conveys content: based on a subcategorization lexicon (Eckle, 1999), we decide whether a place-holder in a given context is subcategorized or not. This idea is extended to a system containing both place-holder and normal prepositions: assuming that merely functional prepositions contribute less in terms of meaning, these are replaced by an abstract representation (case and type of governor), whereas for all non-functional prepositions, the actual preposition with annotation (case and type of governor) are kept.

5 Predicting Prepositions

In this section, we explain the features used to predict the values of the place-holder prepositions and evaluate the prediction quality on clean data.

5.1 Features for Predicting Prepositions

Table 1 illustrates the features for predicting prepositions: in addition to target-side context in the form of adjacent lemmas and POS-tags (5 words left/right), we combine three types of features: (1) source-side features, (2) projected source-side information and (3) target-side subcategorization frames. The source-side information consists of

- the word aligned to the place-holder preposition: a source-side overt or empty preposition

[2]We only generate inflected forms for NPs/PPs (nouns, adjectives, determiners); verbs are inflected throughout the system.

lemma	gloss	source-side			projected source-side		target-side	label
		prp	func,noun	g.verb	noun	g.verb	subcat	
aber	*but*	–	–	–	–	–	–	-
PRP	*PRP*	∅	subj, we	endure	wir	leiden	∅-Nom:5 ∅-Acc:0 *unter-Dat*:4	∅-Nom
wir	*we*	–	–	–	–	–	–	Nom
leiden	*suffer*	–	–	–	–	–	–	-
...	...	...	...	...	...	...	...	...
auch	*too*	–	–	–	–	–	–	-
PRP	*PRP*	∅	obj, effect	endure	Treibhauseffekt	leiden	∅-Nom:5 ∅-Acc:0 *unter-Dat*:4	unter-Dat
die	*the*	–	–	–	–	–	–	Dat
Treibhaus effekt	*greenhouse effect*	–	–	–	–	–	–	Dat

Table 1: Prediction features in the training data. Source-sentence with inserted empty prepositions: "*..., ∅ we too are having to endure ∅ the greenhouse effects*".

("prp" in column "source-side" in table 1)

- its governing verb or noun (column "g.verb")
- the governed noun and its syntactic function in relation to its governor (col. "func,noun")

These source-side features, extracted from dependency parses (Choi and Palmer, 2012), are then projected to the target-side based on the word alignment (column "projected source-side"). Using source-side projections to identify the governor on the target-side eliminates the need to parse the disfluent MT output.

Finally, we use distributional subcategorization information as our third feature type (column "target-side subcat"). Relying on distributional subcategorization information (cf. section 6.1), we provide subcategorizational preferences for the observed verb in the form of *verb-preposition-case* tuples. The grammatical case indicates whether the noun is predominantly used as subject or direct/indirect object with an empty preposition. From the tuples, the system can learn, for example, that *unter etwas leiden* is a lot more plausible than *∅ etwas leiden*, even though the English sentence contains no preposition (*to endure sth.*). For each preposition, including ∅, we list how often the verb occurred with the respective preposition-case combination, with values ranging from 0 (no evidence) to 5 (high amount of observations); table 1 only shows three of these pairs.

From this training example, the model can learn that the second place-holder, even though aligned to an empty preposition governing an object on the English side, is not likely to be realized as a direct object as there is no evidence of the verb *leiden* (*to suffer*) with an accusative object, but a strong preference for the preposition *unter+Dat*. The projected noun (*Treibhauseffekt*) should rule out the possibility of ∅-Nom, as it is an unlikely subject of *leiden*. On the other hand, for the first place-holder preposition, all features point to a realization as ∅-Nom (subject). This example illustrates how the features can bridge the gap between the verb *leiden* and the place-holder to be realized as *unter* (middle part of the sentence omitted in the table).

In addition to tuples of the form *verb-preposition-case*, we also use *noun-noun*$_{genitive}$ tuples (not shown in table 1) to help the system decide whether two adjacent nouns headed with a place-holder should be realized as a *noun-noun*$_{genitive}$ construction (equivalent with English *noun-of-noun*), a *noun-prep-noun* construction or as two adjacent (subcategorized) NPs, for example NP_{Acc} NP_{Dat} (direct/indirect object).

5.2 Evaluation of Prediction Accuracy

The success of generating-prepositions in SMT depends to a large extent on the quality of the prediction component. Before beginning with the MT experiments, we thus evaluate the quality of predicting prepositions on clean data, the tuning-set.

We use the Wapiti toolkit (see section 6.1) to train a CRF to predict prepositions. We opted for a sequence model to take into account decisions from previous positions. Even though it only looks at previous decisions on bigram-level, the annotation of *case* on all elements of noun phrases should prevent that two adjacent noun phrases be assigned the same value for *case*.

Table 2 shows the performance of predicting prepositions on clean data. In the column "prep+case", we evaluate the accuracy of the prediction of both the preposition and its grammatical case, whereas the column "prep" gives the accuracy when only looking at the predicted preposition. We compare a model using source-side and projected source-side features (1) and a model with additional subcategorization information (2). Source-side information and its target-side pro-

	Features	prep+case	prep
1	basic + source	73.58	85.76
2	basic + source + subcat	73.42	85.78

Table 2: Results on clean data (3000 sentences).

prep	acc.	top-3 predicted (freq)
∅	95.17	∅ (10235), in (134), von (95)
in	79.19	in (1123), ∅ (170), von (21)
vor	77.14	vor (81), ∅ (10), bei (3)
nach	68.70	nach (90), ∅ (22), in (4)
zu	64.67	zu (238), ∅ (60), in (21)
an	61.09	an (179), ∅ (47), in (22)
unter	60.71	unter (34), ∅ (12), von (4)
auf	59.56	auf (215), ∅ (59), in (32)
aus	55.38	aus (72), ∅ (25), von (19)
wegen	22.22	wegen (4), für (4), ∅ (3)

Table 3: Individual prediction results.

jection are crucial – without source-information, content-conveying prepositions would need to be guessed – the addition of subcategorization information does not lead to further gains, though.

Table 3 lists the prediction results for some of the prepositions to be modeled, ranging from 95% to 22%. The realization as empty preposition constitutes by far the majority. In the list of the top-3 predicted prepositions, it becomes obvious that the realization as ∅ instead of an overt preposition is also the most frequent error; similarly, the prepositions *von/in* (*of/in*), all high-frequency prepositions, are often output instead of the correct preposition.

6 Experiments and Evaluation

Here, we present the setup and results of our experiments. In addition to the traditional metric BLEU, we assess the quality of the translated prepositions for a subset where relevant elements (verb, noun) match with the reference. Finally, we discuss some examples before concluding the paper.

6.1 Data and Experimental Setup

We trained a standard phrase-based Moses system on 4.3M lines of EN–DE data (WMT'14) with a 10.3M sentence language model. For the lemmatized representation of the morphology-aware SMT system, the German part was parsed with BitPar (Schmid, 2004) and analyzed with the morphological tool SMOR (Schmid et al., 2004). The models for predicting inflectional features and prepositions were built with the Wapiti toolkit (Lavergne et al., 2010). The inflectional models (*case, number, gender strong/weak*) were trained on lemma and tag information of the German part of the parallel data. The models to predict prepositions were trained on half of the parallel data due to the considerably larger amount of labels that can be predicted. The subcategorization tuples were extracted from German web data (Scheible et al. (2013), Faaß and Eckart (2013)) and Europarl. We used WMT'13 as tuning and WMT'14 as test sets[3].

6.2 Evaluation with BLEU

Table 4 shows the results of experiments with the baseline system (a), a morphology-aware SMT system with no special treatment for prepositions[4]. As a variant of the baseline system (b), we removed all prepositions from the translation output to be re-predicted. This does not lead to much change in BLEU, illustrating that the prediction step itself is not harmful. However, only changing existing prepositions is not sufficient and it is not possible to model empty vs. overt prepositions.

Table 5 shows results for the variants of the place-holder systems. Using a basic place-holder (□) representation (S1) leads to a considerably drop in relation to the baseline in table 4. Annotating the place-holder with *case* (S2) leads to an improvement of ca. 0.4, indicating that the abstract representation of the place-holders plays a significant role here.

In (S3), we mark whether the preposition is governed by a verb or a noun, to no avail. As an extension, we annotate the status of the place-holder: subcategorized or non-subcategorized in (S4), which seems to slightly help, even though the observed differences are very small. Assuming that functional prepositions contribute only little in terms of meaning, only subcategorized prepositions are represented by place-holders, whereas non-functional prepositions are kept. Again, we show two variants: in (S5a), all prepositions are re-predicted, while in (S5b), the forms of non-functional prepositions in the MT output are kept and only those for functional prepositions are predicted – this last result reaches the baseline level.

While none of the variants outperforms the baseline, we consider the results encouraging as they illustrate (i) that the representation of prepositions during the translation step considerably influences the MT quality (S2) and (ii) that applying the prediction step to a carefully selected subset of prepo-

[3]In the current version, we only work with the 1-best output of the MT system, and do not consider the n-best list.

[4]For comparison, Baseline$_{surface}$ shows the score for a non-morphology-aware system operating on surface forms.

System	Prepositions	BLEU	CRF
Baseline$_{surface}$	–	16.84	–
Baseline (a)	–	17.38	–
Baseline (b)	re-predict	17.36 17.31	src src+subcat

Table 4: Baseline variants (3003 sentences).

	Representation of place-holders	BLEU source	BLEU src+sub
S1	□	16.81	16.77
S2	□+Case	17.23	17.23
S3	□+Case+(V|N)	16.91	16.89
S4	□+Case+(V|N)+subcat	17.09	17.08
S5a	□+Case+(V|N): functional prp +Case+(V|N): non-func.	17.12	17.06
S5b	□+Case+(V|N): functional prp +Case+(V|N): non-func.	17.29	17.29

Table 5: Results for place-holder systems.

sitions improves the results (S5a vs. S5b).

6.3 Evaluation of Prepositions

BLEU is known to not capture subtle differences between two translation systems very well. Thus, we present a second evaluation in which we analyze the translation accuracy of prepositions.

It is difficult to automatically assess the quality of the translation of prepositions as the choice of a preposition depends on its context, mainly the verbs and/or nouns it occurs with. It is not sufficient to compare the prepositions occurring in the reference translation with those in the translation output, as the used verbs/nouns or even the entire structure of the sentence might differ. We will thus restrict the evaluation to cases where the relevant parts, namely the governing verb and the noun governed by the preposition are the same in the reference sentence and in the translation output[5]: in such cases, an automatic comparison of the preposition in the MT output with the preposition in the reference sentence is possible.

To obtain the set for which to evaluate the prepositions, we took each preposition in the reference sentence[6] governing a proper noun or named entity. The governing verb is identified relying on dependency parses of the reference translation. For extracting the equivalents of the relevant parts (preposition, noun, verb) in the translation output, we made use of the alignments with the English source sentence as pivot. The matching is made on lemma-level.

[5]We ignore PPs governed by nouns (such as *N von/an N* (*N of N*)) as they are often equivalent with genitive structures.

[6]The preposition needs to be in the group of the 17 prepositions which are subject of modeling in this work.

	BL	S2	S5
verb$_{MT}$ = verb$_{REF}$	502	469	503
verb$_{MT}$ = verb$_{REF}$, noun$_{MT}$ = noun$_{REF}$	270	260	271

Table 6: Subsets where governing verb/governed noun are the same in MT output and reference.

	BL	S2	S5a	S5b
verb$_{MT}$ = verb$_{REF}$	245 48.8%	233 49.7%	261 51.9%	250 49.7%
verb$_{MT}$ = verb$_{REF}$, noun$_{MT}$ = noun$_{REF}$	179 66.3%	174 66.9%	188 69.4%	178 65.7%

Table 7: Percentage of correct prepositions for the subsets from table 6.

Table 6 gives an overview of the amount of cases where the reference contains a preposition and its noun and governing verb are the same in the MT output; in the set of 3003 sentences, this is the case for a subset of 270 (baseline), 260 (S2, the best place-holder-only system) and 271 (S5). Note that the slightly less prep-noun-verb triples of S2 that match the reference compared to the baseline are not per-se a sign for inferior translation quality as we did not consider the possibility of synonymous translations.

Table 7 shows the amount of prepositions for the respective subsets that were considered correct, i.e. match with the reference. While the difference is very small, the percentage of correct prepositions is slightly higher for the systems S2/5a. Systems 5a/b are based on the same MT output; however, 5a fares better in this evaluation even though 5b had a higher BLEU score. We thus assume that BLEU did not improve based on the examined subset.

This analysis also shows that the translation quality of prepositions is a problem in need of more attention[7]. It has to be noted, though, that this evaluation only gives partial insights into the performance of the systems. The main problem is that the evaluation is centered around prepositions in the reference translation, which often is (structurally) different from the source sentence and consequently also the translation output. Thus, sentences with prepositions in the translation, but not in the reference, are not considered. Nevertheless, we regard this evaluation as suitable to evaluate the correctness of prepositions in an automatic way.

6.4 Examples

Here, we discuss outputs from the baseline and system 2 (cf. table 5) that cover the different syn-

[7]In some cases however, prepositions in the MT output are acceptable even if they do not match with the reference.

1	SRC	... malmon 's team will have to improve **on** recent performances .
	BL	... malmon das Team wird **über** die jüngsten Leistungen zu verbessern. *... malmon the team will* **over** *the recent performances improve.*
	NEW	... malmon das Team hat ∅ die jüngsten Leistungen zu verbessern . *... malmon the team has-to ∅ the recent performances improve*
	REF	... muss sich das Malmon-Team im Vergleich zu den vergangenen Auftritten auf jeden Fall steigern . *... must -refl- the malmon-team in comparison to the past performances in any case improve.*
2	SRC	outer space offers many possibilities for studying ∅ substances under extreme conditions ...
	BL	in den Weltraum bietet viele Möglichkeiten für das Studium ∅ Stoffe unter extremen Bedingungen ... *in the space offers many possibilities* $study_{noun}$ *∅ substances under extreme conditions ...*
	NEW	der Raum bietet viele Möglichkeiten zum Studium **von** Stoffen unter extremen Bedingungen ... *in the space offers many possibilities for* $study_{noun}$ **of** *substances under extreme conditions ...*
	REF	Das Weltall bietet viele Möglichkeiten, Materie unter extremen Bedingungen zu studieren ... *the universe offers many possibilities , substances under extreme conditions to study ...*
3	SRC	nowadays there are specialists **in** renovation to suit the needs of the elderly.
	BL	heutzutage gibt es Spezialisten **in** der Renovierung der Bedürfnisse der älteren Menschen. *nowadays there are specialists* **in** *the renovation of the needs of the elderly.*
	NEW	heutzutage gibt es Spezialisten **für** Renovierung , die die Bedürfnisse der älteren Menschen. *nowadays there are specialists* **for** *renovation, that the needs of the elderly.*
	REF	heute gibt es auch **für** den altersgerechten Umbau Spezialisten . *tody there are also for the age-appropriate renovation specialists.*
4	SRC	... what role the giant planet has played **in** the development of the solar system.
	BL	... welche Rolle der riesige Planet gespielt hat, **in** der Entwicklung des Sonnensystems. *... which role the giant planet played has,* **in** *the development of-the solar system.*
	NEW	... welche Rolle der riesige Planet gespielt hat **bei** der Entwicklung des Sonnensystems. *... which role the giant planet played has* **in** *the development of-the solar system.*
	REF	... welche Rolle der Riesenplanet bei der Entwicklung des Sonnensystems gespielt hat . *... which role the giant-planet in the development of the solar-system played has.*

Table 8: Example sentences.

tactic phenomena, namely different types of structural differences in source and target language, referred to in the introductory sections.

In (1), the preposition *on* should not be translated, as the verb *verbessern* (*to improve*) subcategorizes a direct object (*Leistungen/performances*). While there is a preposition (*über*) in the baseline, no preposition is produced by the new system, leading to a correct translation. As the reference does not match with the MT output, this sentence is not counted in the evaluation from the previous section or given credit from BLEU, even though it improved over the baseline.

In (2), the constellation is opposite: with no preposition in the English sentence, the baseline output is missing a preposition, marked with ∅. Here, the German structure is different as the verb *studying* is expressed by a noun (*Studium*). In this construction, the phrase containing *Stoffe* (*substances*) needs to be expressed as the PP *von Stoffen* (*of substances*). Alternatively, a *noun*-$noun_{genitive}$ structure is possible – our system is able to produce both versions.

In (3), the literal translation of *in* in the baseline is not grammatical and the translation does not express the meaning of the source sentence. The new translation contains the appropriate preposition *für* and also correctly reproduces the source sentence.

Similarly, the preposition *bei* in (4) is a better choice than *in* in the baseline, even though the baseline sentence is understandable. This sentence pair is counted in the evaluation from the previous section, as the verb (*gespielt*) and noun (*Sonnensystem*) each match with the reference translation.

7 Conclusion and Future Work

We presented a novel system with an abstract representation for prepositions during translation and a post-processing component for generating target-side prepositions. In this setup, we effectively combine relevant source-side and target-side features. By making use of an abstract representation and then assigning all subcategorized elements to their respective functions to be inflected accordingly, our method can explicitly handle structural differences in source and target language. We thus believe that this is a sound strategy to handle the translation of prepositions.

While the systems fail to improve over the baseline, our experiments show that a meaningful representation of prepositions is crucial for translation quality. In particular, the annotation of *case* resulted in the best of all placeholder-only systems –

this information can be considered as a "light" semantic annotation. Consequently, a more semantically motivated annotation representing the semantic class of a preposition (e.g. temporal, local) might lead to a more meaningful representation and remains an interesting idea for future work. Alternatively, integrating the generation step of the prepositions into the decoding process, e.g. following (Tsvetkov et al., 2013), might be another promising strategy.

In our evaluation we discussed typical problems arising when translating prepositions. Furthermore, we addressed the problem of automatically evaluating the quality of prepositions in sentences that are often structured differently than the reference sentence by considering only the respective relevant elements. As the translation of prepositions remains a difficult problem in machine translation, an automatic method that takes into account both the morpho-syntactic as well as the semantic aspects of the realization of prepositions in their respective contexts is needed. In our evaluation, we take first steps into this direction.

Acknowledgments

This project has received funding from the European Union's Horizon 2020 research and innovation programme under grant agreement No 644402, the DFG grants *Distributional Approaches to Semantic Relatedness* and *Models of Morphosyntax for Statistical Machine Translation* and a DFG Heisenberg Fellowship.

References

Agirre, Eneko, Aitziber Atutxa, Gorka Labaka, Mikel Lersundi, Aingeru Mayor, and Kepa Sarasola. 2009. Use of Rich Linguistic Information to Translate Prepositions and Grammatical Cases to Basque. In *Proceedings of EAMT*.

Choi, Jinho D. and Martha Palmer. 2012. Getting the Most out of Transition-Based Dependency Parsing. In *Proceedings of ACL*.

Eckle, Judith. 1999. *Linguistisches Wissen zur automatischen Lexikon-Akquisition aus deutschen Textcorpora*. Ph.D. thesis, Universität Stuttgart.

Faaß, Gertrud and Kerstin Eckart. 2013. SdeWaC – a Corpus of Parsable Sentences from the Web. In *Proceedings of GSCL*.

Fraser, Alexander, Marion Weller, Aoife Cahill, and Fabienne Cap. 2012. Modeling Inflection and Word-Formation in SMT. In *Proceedings of EACL*.

Gustavii, Ebba. 2005. Target-Language Preposition Selection - an Experiment with Transformation-Based Learning and Aligned Bilingual Data. In *Proceedings of EAMT*.

Lavergne, Thomas, Olivier Cappé, and François Yvon. 2010. Practical very large scale CRFs. In *Proceedings of ACL*.

Lo, Chi-kiu and Dekai Wu. 2011. MEANT: An inexpensive, high-accuracy, semi-automatic Metric for Evaluating Translation Utility via Semantic Frames. In *Proceedings of ACL*.

Naskar, Sudip Kumar and Sivaji Bandyopadhyay. 2006. Handling of Prepositions in English to Bengali Machine Translation. In *Proceedings of ACL-SIGSEM*.

Rozovskaya, Alla and Dan Roth. 2013. Joint Learning and Inference for Grammatical Error Correction. In *Proceedings of EMNLP*.

Scheible, Silke, Sabine Schulte im Walde, Marion Weller, and Max Kisselew. 2013. A Compact but Linguistically Detailed Database for German Verb Subcategorisation relying on Dependency Parses from a Web Corpus. In *Proceedings of WaC*.

Schmid, Helmut, Arne Fitschen, and Ulrich Heid. 2004. SMOR: a German Computational Morphology Covering Derivation, Composition, and Inflection. In *Proceedings LREC 2004*.

Schmid, Helmut. 2004. Efficient Parsing of Highly Ambiguous Context-Free Grammars with Bit Vectors. In *Proceedings of COLING*.

Shilon, Reshef, Hanna Fadida, and Shuly Wintner. 2012. Incorporating Linguistic Knowledge in Statistical Machine Translation: Translating Prepositions. In *Proceedings of the Workshop on Innovative Hybrid Approaches to the Processing of Textual Data*.

Toutanova, Kristina, Hisami Suzuki, and Achim Ruopp. 2008. Applying Morphology Generation Models to Machine Translation. In *Proceedings of ACL*.

Tsvetkov, Yulia, Chris Dyer, Lori Levin, and Archna Bhatia. 2013. Generating English Determiners in Phrase-Based Translation with Synthetic Translation Options. In *Proceedings of WMT*.

Weller, Marion, Alexander Fraser, and Sabine Schulte im Walde. 2013. Using Subcategorization Knowledge to Improve Case Prediction for Translation to German. In *Proceedings of ACL*.

Weller, Marion, Sabine Schulte im Walde, and Alexander Fraser. 2014. Using Noun Class Information to Model Selectional Preferences for Translating Prepositions in SMT. In *Proceedings of AMTA*.

Word Alignment Based Parallel Corpora Evaluation and Cleaning Using Machine Learning Techniques

Ieva Zariņa
University of Latvia

Pēteris Ņikiforovs
Tilde

Raivis Skadiņš
Tilde

{lu-ieva.zarina,peteris.nikiforovs,raivis.skadins}@tilde.lv

Abstract

This paper presents a method for cleaning and evaluating parallel corpora using word alignments and machine learning algorithms. It is based on the assumption that parallel sentences have many word alignments while non-parallel sentences have few or none. We show that it is possible to build an automatic classifier, which identifies most of non-parallel sentences in a parallel corpus. This method allows us to do (1) automatic quality evaluation of parallel corpus, and (2) automatic parallel corpus cleaning. The method allows us to get cleaner parallel corpora, smaller statistical models, and faster MT training, but this does not always guarantee higher BLEU scores.

An open-source implementation of the tool described in this paper is available from https://github.com/tilde-nlp/c-eval.

1 Introduction

In statistical machine translation, translation quality is largely dependent on the amount of parallel data available. In practice, a large chunk of data considered parallel might not be so, and it can interfere with good data and reduce translation quality.

The problem of low quality parallel corpora is getting more and more important because it is becoming popular to build parallel corpora from web data using fully automatic methods. The quality of such corpora often is very low, especially in case of multilingual corpora, which are built by people who do not know the languages they are working with. As a result, we get corpora with broken encoding, many alignment errors and even texts in different languages.

The problem can be mitigated by removing blatantly obvious non-parallel text that can be detected with handwritten rules. But that does not help in cases where there are alignment errors or two sentences are kind-of parallel but the translation is wrong or incomplete. The cleaning of such parallel text would require human involvement since devising rules for catching such errors would be nearly impossible.

The idea presented in this work is to compare word alignments in a parallel text with those found in a non-parallel text. The intuition being that truly parallel text should have many alignments on word level while unrelated non-parallel text should have few to no alignments.

Since word alignment computation is already a step in the training process of many phrase-based statistical machine translation systems, it can be used as input data for the corpus evaluation and cleaning method that we propose.

Another benefit of cleaning a corpus is a reduced size, which leads to smaller storage and computational costs of statistical machine translation systems.

2 Related Work

This paper is about evaluation and cleaning of parallel corpora, which has been researched from different aspects before. Typically corpus evaluation and cleaning are separate steps in the corpus development process, and corpus development goes through several cycles of evaluation and cleaning while corpus quality reaches acceptable level.

Corpus quality is evaluated by both calculating quantitative measurements and assessing its suitability for the purpose. One of the most important quality aspects of a parallel corpus is sentence alignment quality, which shows how accurately a corpus is broken into sentences and whether aligned sentences are translations of each other. It is common to use the same metrics for corpus quality evaluation as for sentence alignment evaluation. The sentence alignment evaluation has been well established in ARCADE project/shared task (Langlais et al., 1998), where quality is assessed calculating precision, recall and F-measure both in segment and sub-segment levels. In the same way precision is also used for corpora evaluation. To calculate the precision we need an annotated subset of the corpus where each sentence alignment is marked as correct or not. There are different ways how to get such annotations, Smith et al. (2013), Skadiņš et al. (2014) and Seljan et al. (2010) use a human annotated random subset of corpus, while Kaalep and Veskis (2007) obtain annotations from two different but similar versions of the corpus. Another approach in corpora quality assessment has been used by Steinberger et al. (2012), they tested alignment in a production setting where translators were confronted with the automatically aligned translations and were encouraged to notify any alignment errors.

Although many parallel corpora have been declared to be suitable for different purposes, many of them have not been formally evaluated (Steinberger et al., 2012; Tiedemann, 2012; Callison-Burch, 2009, Chapter 2.2.) and many have been just partially evaluated only for suitability for MT (Koehn, 2005; Eisele & Chen, 2010; Smith et al., 2013; Skadiņš et al., 2014), i.e., authors build MT systems to illustrate that corpus is useful for MT.

Corpus cleaning in practice has often been limited to applying a set of handwritten rules (regular expressions) to detect blatantly obvious cases where two sentences are not parallel (Rueppel et al., 2011; Ruopp, 2010; etc.). More advanced corpora cleaning includes filters that check text language (Lui & Baldwin, 2012) and spelling, and filter out machine translated content (Rarrick et al., 2011). And there are corpora cleaning methods that automatically identifies sentences that are not in conformity with the rest of the corpus; Okita (2009) removes outliers by the literalness score between a pair of sentences, Jiang et al. (2010) introduce lattice score-based data cleaning method, and Taghipour et al. (2011) use density estimators to detect the outliers. These methods allow to identify potentially non-parallel sentences and to filter out sentences with conformity level below a certain threshold; these methods filter out specified amount of data, but they do not estimate how much data should be filtered out. The method proposed in this paper deals with both issues: (1) automatic quality evaluation of parallel corpus and (2) automatic parallel corpus cleaning. Similar word alignment based corpus cleaning method is used by Stymne et al. (2013), but unlike this work they use alignment based heuristics to filter out bad sentence pairs.

3 Proposed Method

3.1 Intuition

Word alignment is a task in natural language processing of identifying translation relationships among the words in a parallel text. It is commonly used in phrase-based statistical machine translation (Koehn et al., 2003) where word alignments are used to extract phrases. One of the commonly used phrase extraction algorithms is to take sequential word alignments in a sentence and expand them as much as possible. The better the word alignments, the better the phrases.

Alignments in a parallel text can be computed with the Expectation Maximization algorithm which means that alignments in a sentence are dependent on similar alignments elsewhere in the corpus. These are called IBM Models 1-5 (Brown et al., 1993).

We can presume that if a corpus is good then there should be many word alignments in sentences. If there are mostly correct sentences in a parallel corpus then the sentences where there are few or no alignments might not be parallel. While comparing good alignments with bad alignments for large data is a daunting task for a human, it is perfectly suited for machine learning, which we explore in this paper.

The idea is to develop a model with machine learning for classifying a pair of sentences as either parallel or not. As such, it is necessary to train such a model with positive and negative examples. Positive examples can be an approved parallel corpus while negative examples can be generated from a good corpus by shuffling translations or artificially generating bad translations.

For machine learning algorithms to do their job it is necessary to convert text into set of features (numbers), each feature representing a clue for the algorithm how to classify the input data.

3.2 Features

Fast Align word aligner (Dyer et al, 2013) which implements modified IBM Model 2 was used. It provides us with the alignments and the statistical likelihood of each token-to-token translation. From this data we obtain the features that are used for machine learning.

We generated various probable features. For example, we calculate the Threshold score by dividing the count of alignments that are present in both alignment directions (intersection of alignment count) with the total count of alignments in the respective line (for each language direction). Further features were calculated from the alignment probability scores for each token that are provided by Fast Align in the alignment process.

From the list of probable features the most relevant ones were chosen that provide statistical significance for the machine learning.

We used WEKA (Hall et al., 2009) for 10-fold cross validation with a constant seed to evaluate all the features. Correlation-based Feature Subset Selection for Machine Learning by M. A. Hall (1999) with the best first search method was used to evaluate the significance of all features in the DGT-TM 2007 (Steinberger et al., 2012) English to Latvian corpus of 100,000 correct and 100,000 incorrect lines.

The most significant alignment feature proved to be the fourth dealing with the nth root of the multiplication of the probabilities of n tokens (geometric mean). The formulae of the selected features can be seen below (n represents the number of tokens in a line).

1) $Threshold\ score = \frac{intersection\ of\ alignment\ count}{total\ line\ alignment\ count}$
2) $\frac{Summed\ prob.\ score}{n}$
3) $lg(\frac{|Summed\ prob.\ score|}{n})$
4) $\sqrt[n]{|Multiplied\ prob.score|}$
5) $lg(\sqrt[n]{|Multiplied\ prob.score|})$

In addition to word alignments, we explored the possibility to enhance the accuracy by including features that are derived from the text itself. For example, the ratio of source sentence token count and target sentence token count, division of common number count and all unique number count in source and target sentences, etc. We calculate features from tokens, numbers, symbols, words and symbols in both source and target sentences – total 43 textual features.

The computation of textual features for a large amount of input data was about two times slower that the computation of alignment features. More importantly, the result quality including textual features together with alignment features increased the precision only by 0.2%. For these reasons, text features were discarded.

3.3 Machine Learning

Once we finalized a list of possible features and selected the most relevant ones, we moved on to the next step of putting them to use with the help of machine learning algorithms.

In order to employ machine learning algorithms and to train a model, we had to provide good (correctly aligned parallel corpora) and bad (aligned corpora with shuffled lines) data. The algorithms then go through each good and bad features and produce a statistical model against which another corpus can be benchmarked.

We evaluated several machine learning algorithms and set out to find those that achieved the highest precision with acceptable performance time as well as a high rate of true positives – an important point when evaluating machine learning algorithms (Flach, 2012).

According to Hill et al. (1998) decision-tree based algorithms would be very suited for working with large data and finding the distinguishing line between data from good and bad corpus. As a result, a data model would be obtained that could be used in filtering each line of a given corpus.

Accuracy as well as training and classification run times of several machine learning algorithms were evaluated on the first 100,000 lines of the DGT-TM 2007 EN-LV corpus. The results are summarized in Table 1.

As can be seen, the algorithms perform rather similarly, though the performance time greatly varies from 15.8 seconds up to 7.5 minutes for a corpus containing 100,000 lines. The REPTree algorithm was chosen because of its high precision paired with relatively good speed.

Algorithm	Precision	Time, s
J48	98.01%	340
J48graft	98.04%	450
RandomForest	98.16%	358
RandomTree	97.43%	58
ExtraTrees	97.17%	26
REPTree	98.03%	130
NaiveBayes	95.72%	16

Table 1. Machine learning algorithm performance comparison for Fast Align features.

4 Evaluation

Firstly, we evaluated the tool by looking at the BLEU score (Papineni et al., 2002) changes, qualitative changes and the quality score of EUBokshop (OPUS edition) corpus, which is known to be cluttered with bad data. It has been automatically extracted from web data (PDF files), containing parallel corpora for 24 official European Union languages (Skadiņš et al., 2014). For testing we chose the Latvian, English and French language pairs.

We evaluated several well-known corpora with the Corpus Cleaner tool as well as whether the results were consistent with qualitative evaluation. The chosen corpora consisted of: EN-FR 10^9 parallel corpus (Callison-Burch, 2009, Chapter 2.2.), EN-DE and EN-FR versions of CommonCrawl (Smith et al., 2013), DGT-TM 2012 (Steinberger et al., 2012), EMEA (Tiedemann, 2012), Europarl (Koehn, 2005), JRC-Aquis (Steinberger et al., 2006), WIT3 (Cettolo et al., 2012).

A number of different models were built and used to test if models were language independent.

4.1 Evaluation in MT

Since the main use for this cleaning method is machine translation, we evaluated how the cleaning method affects the BLEU score.

For the MT evaluation we trained an SMT system with the original EU Bookshop corpus and noted the BLEU score.

We applied the same procedure to the cleaned version of the corpus. Table 2 summarizes the BLEU scores and the amount of good lines after cleaning for the explored language pairs can be seen.

The BLEU score for both the original and cleaned MT systems was nearly identical with the cleaned corpus having a slightly lower BLEU score than the original. However, this does not necessarily mean no improvement.

Generally, in MT systems the less data you have, the less likely you are to have correct translations, and as it has been shown by Goutte et al. (2012), phrase-based SMT is quite robust to noise. Therefore bigger corpus despite containing more corrupt lines is not that detrimental to machine translation since it gets lost in translation anyway.

Language	**BLEU score, baseline**	**BLEU score, cleaned**	***Good* lines**
LV-EN	32.54	32.50	67.19%
LV-FR	24.31	23.47	39.63%

Table 2. BLEU score for original and cleaned EU Bookshop corpora (OPUS), *good* line amount after cleaning.

While the BLEU score nearly did not change for the cleaned corpora, the corpus size, however, did. The cleaned corpora was respectively about 70% and 40% the size of the original. This means that training and memory costs were much lower than the original corpus required. Moreover, the huge difference in cleaned corpus size in comparison with the original producing the same BLEU score indicates that indeed the corrupt lines that the MT system also had deemed unfit were filtered out.

4.2 Qualitative Evaluation

To qualitatively evaluate the cleaning method, we randomly took 200 lines from the original as well as the cleaned corpora for Latvian-English and Latvian-French language pairs. We manually evaluated them for incorrect or erroneous alignment. The results are shown in Table 3. The manual evaluation was done by one evaluator.

	LV-EN	LV-FR
Sentences from the original corpus that were classified as *good* by the human evaluator	78%	72%
Sentences that were classified as *good* by the human evaluator from sentences that were classified as *good* by the corpus cleaner.	90%	95%
Sentences that were classified as *good* by the human evaluator from sentences that were classified as *bad* by the corpus cleaner.	11%	10%

Table 3. The amount of good lines in EU Bookshop corpora

The qualitative results clearly show the improvement in corpus quality. Taking into account that the size of corpora was approximately 30% smaller after cleaning and performance rate of about 90%, it can be concluded that a significant part of bad data was removed.

4.3 Corpora Evaluation with Different Models

As a part of the corpora cleaning process, we implemented a corpus evaluation solution. The percentage score of a corpus shows the amount of good lines in the text.

As models for cleaning could be constructed from any corpora that is recognized of good quality, we set to determine if the models are language independent. That is, if different models (made from approximately equal quality corpora) would produce the same results for a given parallel corpus.

The models were trained on the DGT-TM 2007 corpus consisting of EN-LV, EN-FR, EN-LT, and FR-LV language pairs. The graph lines represent the score of each corpus using the corresponding model (along the X axis). Models themselves were evaluated using WEKA tool. The results are shown below in Figure 1.

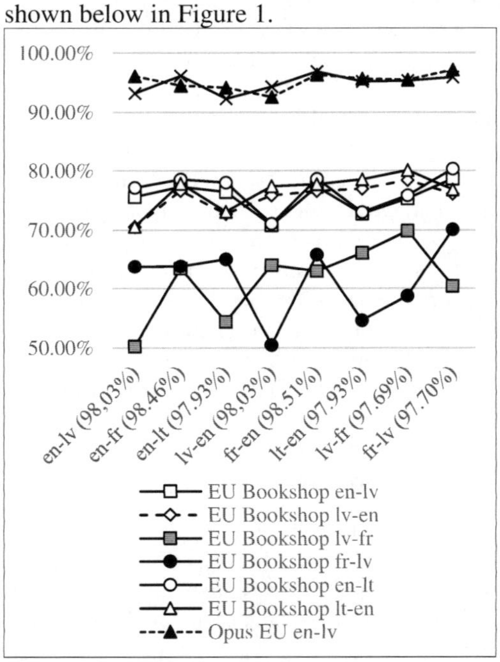

Figure 1. Corpora evaluation with different models.

The results show, overall, that the lower the quality of corpus, the more varied the cleaning results from different models will be.

It can be concluded that while there is a difference in the performance of the models (worst case up to 20%), it evens out with the increase of the quality of the corpora (approx. 5% variation). To sum up, for precise corpus evaluation, it would be best to use a model that has been built for the particular language pair.

To see how the method fares with already good data, we evaluated the DGT-TM English-Lithuanian corpus with the DGT-TM English-Latvian model as well as the DGT-TM French-English corpus with the DGT-TM Latvian-English model. It removed approximately 3% of good sentences, which we think is acceptable. Similarly OPUS EU Constitution corpus, which is considered fairly accurate, saw about 5% cut and showed considerably more stable results across all models than EU Bookshop corpora signaling reliable performance in case of high quality corpora.

4.4 Evaluated Corpora Comparison

Initially we started our evaluations using well known good quality corpora. As can be seen in Table 4, all of the evaluated corpora are of high quality (around 98%) corresponding with previous evaluations and qualitative evaluations of 100 sentences randomly taken from the English to Latvian language pair. The quality of the above corpora was measured with corresponding models built from the first 100,000 lines of the DGT-TM-2007 corpus.

	DGT-TM 2012	EMEA	Europarl	JRC Acquis	WIT[3]
EN-DE	98.91%	95.54%	99.01%	99.30%	97.65%
EN-ES	98.24%	96.74%	99.36%	99.18%	98.46%
EN-FR	98.84%	96.39%	99.58%	98.89%	99.30%
EN-IT	98.01%	95.65%	98.94%	99.02%	97.74%
EN-LV	97.75%	94.26%	99.67%	98.36%	98.34%
EN-LV QE	99%	91%	99%	98%	97%

Table 4. Corpora quality evaluation by Corpus Cleaner and qualitative evaluation (QE)

We also evaluated less credible corpora (See Table 5). Significant differences can be seen between EUBookshop Tilde and OPUS editions with approximately 20% increase in quality. This result is understandable as Tilde has considerably improved the quality of EUBookshop by filtering and manually editing it (Skadiņš et al., 2014).

In order to compare the results of the CommonCrawl EN-DE corpus quality with the work done by Stymne et al. (2013), it was additionally cleaned by removing sentence pairs with larger than three ratio, sentences with more than 60 tokens as well as the corpus was lowercased. This reduced the corpus by 4.28%. Consequently filtering the original CommonCrawl reduced the amount by 16%, while 13% was removed from the cleaned version of the CommonCrawl corpus.

Corpus	Language pair	Corpus Cleaner Quality	QE
EN-FR 10[9]	EN-FR	84.20%	89%
CommonCrawl	EN-FR	80.02%	70%
CommonCrawl (original)	EN-DE	83.94%	55%
CommonCrawl (filtered)	EN-DE	87.25%	59%
EUBookshop (TILDE)	EN-LV	96.19%	93%
	EN-FR		77%
EUBookshop (OPUS)	EN-LV	76.45%	67%
	FR-LV	71.52%	73%

Table 5. Corpora quality evaluation by Corpus Cleaner and qualitative evaluation (QE)

Stymne's et al. research shows a considerably larger corpus reduction (27%) based on alignment evaluation, 5.3% reduction by cleaning the text and in addition 8.8% by removing sentences with wrong detected language. The approach taken by Stymne et al. looks at a manually annotated gold corpus of 100 lines, and extrapolates from that good calculated values from alignment intersection against sentence length, similarly as Threshold score described previously. This manual method generates more strict results and consequently marks more lines as bad. However, the qualitative evaluation of CommonCrawl both original and cleaned versions correspond to that in Stymne's et al. work signaling that the used methods should be looked into more thoroughly.

Language detection as employed by Stymne et al. produced high quality results. While, wrong language use shows up in the alignment quality up to a certain level producing a small intersection set, it could, nevertheless, be considered as an additional feature in the corpus cleaner tool.

English-French10[9] and CommonCrawl EN-FR corpora show a moderate level of accuracy as well as the qualitative evaluation confirms this result deviating by 5% and 10% respectively.

5 Conclusion and Future Work

We have shown that by using word alignment features we can build an automatic classifier, which identifies most non-parallel sentences in a parallel corpus. This method allows us to do (1) automatic quality evaluation of a parallel corpus, and (2) automatic parallel corpus cleaning. The method allows us to get cleaner parallel corpora, smaller statistical models, and faster MT training, but unfortunately this does not always guarantee higher BLEU scores.

In this paper, we are reporting our first results. It is still necessary, however, to test the method for a much wider range of languages and corpora to verify that the method is applicable for other language pairs and to see whether the automatic corpora quality evaluation correlates with human judgment.

We used Fast Align, which is based on IBM Model 2; but IBM Model 1, which requires less computation power, may prove just as effective. Similarly, it would be useful to evaluate higher IBM Models to see how much the results are improved at the cost of longer running time.

We discarded text features for use as the input data for the classifier, but that does not mean that they are not useful. They might as well be used with handwritten rules as an additional step in the cleaning pipeline, either before this method is applied or afterwards. We are planning to revise textual features. In this research, we focused on identifying alignment errors, but textual features can be useful to identify broken encoding, texts in wrong language and other corpora quality issues.

More consistent results across language models could be achieved improving bad training data generation. It is possible that during the shuffling process some lines are aligned in a way that produces a somewhat valid translation, therefore yielding inconsistent data for the machine-learning algorithm.

Acknowledgements

The research leading to these results has received funding from the research project "Optimization methods of large scale statistical models for innovative machine translation technologies", project financed by The State Education Development Agency (Latvia) and European Regional Development Fund, contract nr. 2013/0038/2DP/2.1.1.1.0/13/APIA/VIAA/029. We would like to thank Valdis Girgždis and Maija Kāle for their contribution to this research.

References

Brown, P. F., Pietra, V. J. D., Pietra, S. A. D., & Mercer, R. L. (1993). The mathematics of statistical machine translation: Parameter estimation. Computational linguistics, 19(2), 263-311.

Callison-Burch, C., Koehn, P., Monz, C., & Schroeder, J. (2009). Findings of the 2009 Workshop on Statistical Machine Translation. In Proceedings of the Fourth Workshop on Statistical Machine Translation (pp. 1–28). Athens, Greece: Association for Computational Linguistics. Retrieved from http://www.aclweb.org/anthology/W/W09/W09-0401

Cettolo, M., Girardi, C., & Federico, M. (2012, May). WIT3: Web inventory of transcribed and translated talks. In Proceedings of the 16th Conference of the European Association for Machine Translation (EAMT) (pp. 261-268).

Dyer, C., Chahuneau, V., & Smith, N. A. (2013). A Simple, Fast, and Effective Reparameterization of IBM Model 2. In HLT-NAACL (pp. 644-648).

Eisele, A., & Chen, Y. (2010). MultiUN: A Multilingual Corpus from United Nation Documents. In D. Tapias, M. Rosner, S. Piperidis, J. Odjik, J. Mariani, B. Maegaard, ... N. C. (Conference Chair) (Eds.), Proceedings of the Seventh conference on International Language Resources and Evaluation (pp. 2868–2872). European Language Resources Association (ELRA).

Flach, P. (2012). The Art and Science of Algorithms that Make Sense of Data (pp. 55). New York, USA: Cambridge University Press.

Goutte, C., Carpuat, M., & Foster, G. (2012). The impact of sentence alignment errors on phrase-based machine translation performance. In Conference of the Association for Machine Translation in the Americas (AMTA). San Diego, CA.

Hall, M. A. (1999). Correlation-based feature selection for machine learning (Doctoral dissertation, The University of Waikato).

Hall, M., Frank, E., Holmes, G., Pfahringer, B., Reutemann, P., & Witten, I. H. (2009). The WEKA Data Mining Software: An Update. SIGKDD Explor. Newsl., 11(1), 10–18. doi:10.1145/1656274.1656278

Hill, L. O., Chawla, N., Bowyer, K. W. (1998) Decision Tree Learning on Very Large Data Sets. Department of Computer Science and Engineering, University of South Florida. Retrieved from https://www3.nd.edu/~dial/papers/SMC98.pdf

Jiang, J., Way, A., & Carson-Berndsen, J. (2010). Lattice Score Based Data Cleaning For Phrase-Based Statistical Machine Translation.

Kaalep, H. J., & Veskis, K. (2007). Comparing parallel corpora and evaluating their quality. Proceedings of MT Summit XI, 275-279.

Koehn, P., Och, F. J., Marcu, D. (2003). Statistical phrase based translation. Proceedings of the Joint Conference on Human Language Technologies and the Annual Meeting of the North American Chapter of the Association of Computational Linguistics (HLT/NAACL).

Koehn, P. (2005). Europarl : A Parallel Corpus for Statistical Machine Translation. MT Summit, 11, 79–86. Retrieved from http://mt-archive.info/MTS-2005-Koehn.pdf

Langlais, P., Simard, M., Veronis, J., Armstrong, S., Bonhomme, P., Debili, F., ... & Theron, P. (1998). Arcade: A cooperative research project on parallel text alignment evaluation.

Lui, M., & Baldwin, T. (2012). Langid.Py: An Off-the-shelf Language Identification Tool. In Proceedings of the ACL 2012 System Demonstrations (pp. 25–30). Stroudsburg, PA, USA: Association for Computational Linguistics.

Och, F. J., & Ney, H. (2003). A systematic comparison of various statistical alignment models. Computational Linguistics, 29(1):19-51, March.

Okita, T. (2009). Data Cleaning for Word Alignment. In Proceedings of the ACL-IJCNLP 2009 Student Research Workshop (pp. 72–80). Stroudsburg, PA, USA: Association for Computational Linguistics.

Papineni, K., Roukos, S., Ward, T., Zhu, W. (2002). BLEU: a method for automatic evaluation of machine translation. Proceedings of the 40th Annual Meeting of the Association of Computational Linguistics.: ACL

Rarrick, S., Quirk, C., & Lewis, W. (2011). MT Detection in Web-Scraped Parallel Corpora. In Proceedings of MT Summit XIII. Asia-Pacific Association for Machine Translation.

Rueppel, J., Jiang, L., Yu, G., and Flournoy, R. (2011). AIR-based light clients for supporting Moses engine training. In Proceedings of the 13th Machine Translation Summit (pp. 503–506). Xiamen.

Ruopp, A. (2010). How to implement open source machine translation solutions (TAUS report): TAUS BV.

Seljan, S., Tadić, M., Agić, Ž., Šnajder, J., Bašić, B. D., & Osmann, V. (2010). Corpus Aligner (CorAl) Evaluation on English-Croatian Parallel Corpora. In N. C. (Conference Chair), K. Choukri, B. Maegaard, J. Mariani, J. Odijk, S. Piperidis, … D. Tapias (Eds.), Proceedings of the Seventh International Conference on Language Resources and Evaluation (LREC'10). Valletta, Malta: European Language Resources Association (ELRA).

Skadiņš, R., Tiedemann, J., Rozis, R., & Deksne, D. (2014). Billions of Parallel Words for Free: Building and Using the EU Bookshop Corpus. In N. C. (Conference Chair), K. Choukri, T. Declerck, H. Loftsson, B. Maegaard, J. Mariani, … S. Piperidis (Eds.), Proceedings of the Ninth International Conference on Language Resources and Evaluation (LREC'14) (pp. 1850–1855). Reykjavik, Iceland: European Language Resources Association (ELRA).

Smith, R. J., Saint-Amand, H., Plamada, M., Koehn, P., Callison-Burch, C., & Lopez, A. (2013). Dirt Cheap Web-Scale Parallel Text from the Common Crawl. In Proceedings of the 51st Annual Meeting of the Association for Computational Linguistics (Volume 1: Long Papers) (pp. 1374–1383). Association for Computational Linguistics. Retrieved from http://aclweb.org/anthology/P13-1135

Steinberger, R., Pouliquen, B., Widiger, A., Ignat, C., Erjavec, T., Tufis, D., & Varga, D. (2006). The JRC-Acquis: A multilingual aligned parallel corpus with 20+ languages. In Proceedings of the 5th International Conference on Language Resources and Evaluation (LREC'2006), (pp. 24-26). Genoa, Italy

Steinberger, R., Eisele, A., Klocek, S., Pilos, S., & Schlüter, P. (2012). DGT-TM: A freely available Translation Memory in 22 languages. In N. C. (Conference Chair), K. Choukri, T. Declerck, M. U. Doğan, B. Maegaard, J. Mariani, … S. Piperidis (Eds.), Proceedings of the Eight International Conference on Language Resources and Evaluation (LREC'12). Istanbul, Turkey: European Language Resources Association (ELRA).

Stymne, S., Hardmeier, C., Tiedemann, J., & Nivre, J. (2013). Tunable distortion limits and corpus cleaning for SMT. In WMT 2013; 8-9 August; Sofia, Bulgaria (pp. 225-231). Association for Computational Linguistics.

Taghipour, K., Khadivi, S., & Xu, J. (2011). Parallel Corpus Refinement as an Outlier Detection Algorithm. MT Summit XIII. Machine Translation Summit (MT-Summit-11), 13. September 19-23, Xiamen, China. NA, Xiamen.

Tiedemann, J. (2012). Parallel Data, Tools and Interfaces in OPUS. In N. C. (Conference Chair), K. Choukri, T. Declerck, M. U. Doğan, B. Maegaard, J. Mariani, … S. Piperidis (Eds.), Proceedings of the Eight International Conference on Language Resources and Evaluation (LREC'12). Istanbul, Turkey: European Language Resources Association (ELRA).

User Papers

Content Translation: Computer-assisted translation tool for Wikipedia articles

Niklas Laxström
University of Helsinki
Dept. of Modern Languages
and
Wikimedia Foundation
nlaxstrom@wikimedia.org

Pau Giner
Wikimedia Foundation
pginer@wikimedia.org

Santhosh Thottingal
Wikimedia Foundation
sthottingal@wikimedia.org

Abstract

The quality and quantity of articles in each Wikipedia language varies greatly. Translating from another Wikipedia is a natural way to add more content, but the translation process is not properly supported in the software used by Wikipedia. Past computer-assisted translation tools built for Wikipedia are not commonly used. We created a tool that adapts to the specific needs of an open community and to the kind of content in Wikipedia. Qualitative and quantitative data indicates that the new tool helps users translate articles easier and faster.

1 Introduction

Wikipedia is the most multilingual encyclopedic knowledge archive, with over 280 languages with varying amount of content. Knowledge available for a user is limited by the languages used to access it. Translation has been a common way to expand knowledge across languages in Wikipedia. The editing activity of the top 46 language editions of Wikipedia shows that 25% of edits by multilingual users are for the same article in different languages (Hale, 2013).

It is not necessary to use any tool to translate Wikipedia articles. However, it is a complicated process and mainly done by experienced Wikipedia editors.

There were many attempts to build tools to support translation of articles. None has seen widespread use: in our research only few users reported using those tools when translating Wikipedia articles.

In this paper we present a new approach to support translation which has been designed taking into account the unique needs of Wikipedia content and their community. Content Translation (CX) is a new tool that automates many steps of the translation process and validates the approach in practice. It was first enabled on 8 Wikipedias as an opt-in feature to create new articles in January 2015. Selected language pairs have machine translation (MT) support.

2 Previous work

MediaWiki, the software powering Wikipedia, is translated to hundreds of languages using the Translate extension. No such solution was available for translating Wikipedia articles, leaving a gap in the translation support.

There were at least ten instances of translation tools built for Wikipedia[1]. Those tools can be divided into two groups based on whether the tool creators already possessed MT software. The first group is composed of companies such as Google and Microsoft, but also smaller companies and researchers. The other group of tools has been created just for Wikipedia article translation, mostly by volunteers.

Among the earliest tools were GTT by Google and WikiBhasha by Microsoft, using their own MT services (García and Stevenson, 2009; Kumarana et al., 2011). Later, Casmacat for professionals and researchers (Alabau et al., 2013) and CoSyne for multilingual MediaWikis (Bronner et al., 2012), unlike Wikipedias which are monolingual.

Common to all such tools is that they are not integrated into Wikipedia. To use them one needs to go to another website or install software. CX

[1]Details collected at https://meta.wikimedia.org/wiki/Machine_translation

is integrated into Wikipedia and provides a WYSIWYG editor (what you see is what you get).

3 Designing the translation experience

The design of CX was aimed at improving the existing process users followed when translating. Following the principles of User-Centered Design (Norman and Draper, 1986), we organised periodic user research sessions to (a) better understand the user needs during the existing translation process, and (b) validate new ideas on how to improve this process.

3.1 User research

We recruited 106 participants using a survey[2]. From their responses we identified dictionaries (76% of participants used them), and Wikipedia (60%) as their most used tools when translating. MT (53%), spell checkers (48%) and glossaries (42%) were also common. Less than 6% of the participants mentioned tools specifically aimed at Wikipedia article translation, such as those described in Section 2, and no tool was mentioned by more than one participant.

We organised 16 research sessions. Sessions were organised in two parts. In the first part, contextual inquiry techniques (Beyer and Holtzblatt, 1998) were applied to observe user behaviour while translating, and identify their needs. The second part was a usability testing study (Nielsen, 1994) to evaluate different design ideas in the form of prototypes.

3.2 Design principles

The research sessions were instrumental to guide the design of the translation experience[3]. The following design principles summarise the approach we followed when designing the tool.

Freedom of translation

There is a significant diversity in Wikipedia content across languages. On average, two articles from different languages on the same topic have just 41% of common content (Hecht and Gergle, 2010). In contrast to other kinds of content, such as software user interface strings or documentation, Wikipedia articles are not intended to be exact translations that are always kept in sync. In order to support that content diversity, CX does not force users to translate the full article. As illustrated in Figure 1, users add content to the translation one paragraph at a time. When a paragraph is added, an initial translation based on MT is provided for the user to edit. MT is used if available, but the user can also start with the source text or an empty paragraph if that is preferred.

Unlike other tools that define a strong boundary to translate on a per sentence basis, working at a paragraph level allows users to reorganise sentences and accommodate different editing patterns.

Provide context information

In CX the original article and the translation are shown side-by-side. Each paragraph is dynamically aligned vertically with the corresponding translated paragraph, regardless of the difference in length. This allows users to quickly have an overview of what has already been translated and what has not.

Contextual information reduces the need for the user to navigate and reorient. When translating a sentence, the corresponding sentence in the original document is highlighted. In addition, when manipulating the content, options are provided anticipating the user's next steps. In Figure 1, based on the user's text selection, the user can explore the article related to the selected text (in the source or target languages), or turn the selected text into a link. Dictionary can be accessed inside the tool by selecting a word or by using the search box in the tools column.

Focus on the translation

We identified many steps in the translation process that could be automated. Users spend time making sure each link they translated points to the correct article in the target Wikipedia, and recreating the text formatting that was lost when using an external translation service. They also look for categories available in the target Wikipedia to classify the translated article, and save constantly during the process to avoid losing their work.

CX deals with those aspects automatically. When adding a paragraph, the initial translation preserves the text format. Modifications to the translated content are saved automatically. Links point to the right articles if they exist and existing categories are added to the article thanks to Wikidata[4], a structured data knowledge repository, that maps corresponding concepts across lan-

[2] https://goo.gl/iKQIDh

[3] A detailed design specification is available at https://www.mediawiki.org/wiki/CX

[4] https://www.wikidata.org

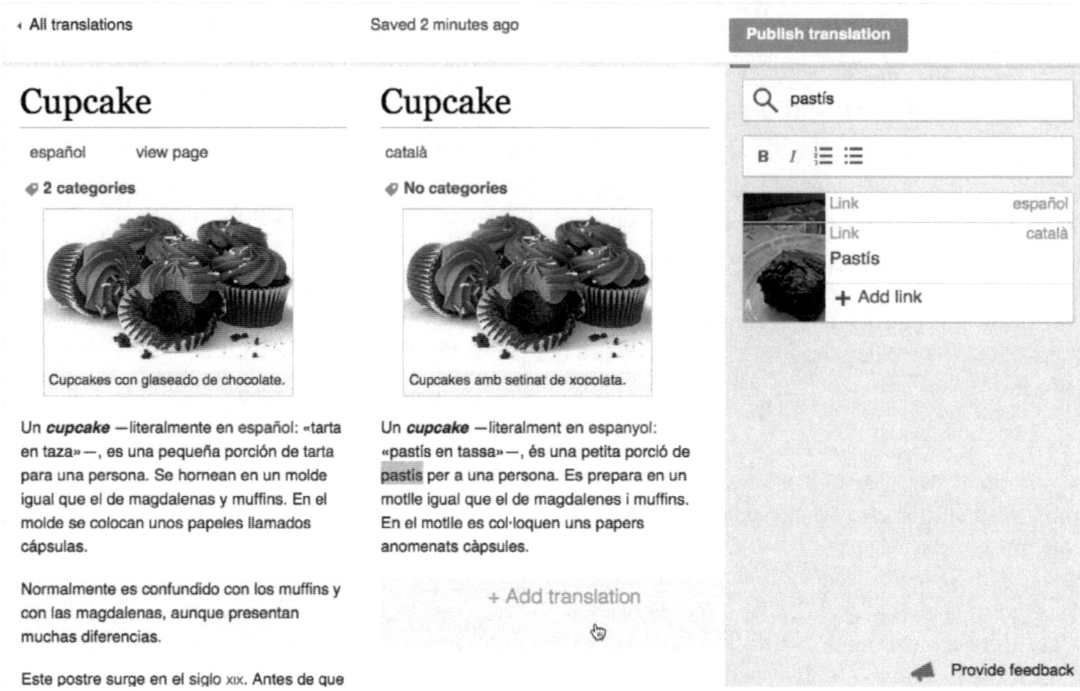

Figure 1: The source and translated content side-by-side and additional tools on the right.

guages. As those aspects are automated, users can focus on adapting content for the initial version of the article rather than on technical and formatting tasks.

Quality is key

One of the concerns raised early by the participants was about MT quality. Users were concerned about the potential proliferation of low quality content in Wikipedia articles.

In order to respond to that concern, CX keeps track of the amount of text that is added from MT without further modification by the users. When a given threshold is exceeded, a warning is shown to users encouraging them to focus on quality more than quantity.

4 WYSIWYG implementation

MediaWiki's wikitext is not standardised. For a long time, the only way to use wikitext was to render it to HTML with MediaWiki. Parsoid[5] is a Wikimedia project that implements a second parser for wikitext. To follow the principle *focus on translation* principle we only provide limited editing and formatting options and side-step a lot of complexity of Wikipedia article structure without negatively affecting the translation process. CX is the first translation tool that provides a WYSIWYG editor using the annotated HTML provided by Parsoid.

Some MT services neither support HTML input nor provide reordering information. Preserving markup is an essential requirement for CX because wikitext adaptation and WYSIWYG editing are based on the markup. We devised an algorithm that can reconstruct the reordering information by making the MT service do some additional work.

5 MT evaluation

We use the subjective evaluations of MT quality for a given language pair to decide whether we will include a MT service for a language pair in the tool. To evaluate a MT for a given language pair, we ask the potential future users of the tool to translate articles using it and tell whether it was useful for them or not.

We run a MT service on our servers using the open-source Apertium project (Forcada et al., 2011), but we support other MT providers as well.

[5]`https://www.mediawiki.org/wiki/Parsoid`

6 Evaluation

Currently the tool is only available to self-selected users (most of them experienced editors), hence the results cannot be generalised to the whole community. Further studies on the resulting quality over a long term will help.

The low deletion ratio for articles created using CX suggests that there are no major problems in terms of quality. In three months of exposing the tool as an opt-in feature, 900 articles were published using CX with an overall deletion ratio lower than 1% across all languages, which is lower than the deletion rate for all new articles.

We noticed that there is a significant difference between the number of created articles in different target language Wikipedias, which cannot be explained by the number of active users, number of available articles to translate nor the availability of MT. For example in three months the Catalan Wikipedia saw 455 articles created by translating from Spanish with CX, but in the Portuguese Wikipedia only 25. Both language pairs have MT provided by Apertium. Statistics about the tool are collected publicly[6].

We have not yet made precise measurements on translation time saving, but we got positive reports from our users. In a roundtable[7] organised with editors of the Catalan Wikipedia, an experienced editor reported a 70% time saving.

We found that English is the most used source language, consistent with Hale's findings on multilingual user behaviour (2013).

7 Conclusions

We developed a tool that addresses the specific needs of an open community and the specifics of the kind of content in Wikipedia. CX is a computer-assisted translation tool with a WYSIWYG editor and automatic link adaptation. CX supports multiple different MT providers, but by integrating the open source Apertium project we were able to quickly provide MT for multiple language pair We developed MT education and tracking features to address community concerns about proliferation of poor quality translations.

User feedback for CX is supportive and data also shows that quality of the published translations is good, alleviating the community concerns. The low translation activity in multiple languages where the tool is already available needs further research. Close integration in Wikipedia allows CX to recruit users and suggest articles to translate in ways not possible with the previous tools.

[6] `https://www.mediawiki.org/wiki/Content_translation/analytics`

[7] `https://blog.wikimedia.org/2014/09/29/round-table-with-editors-from-the-catalan-wikipedia/`

References

Alabau, Vicent, Ragnar Bonk, Christian Buck, Michael Carl, Francisco Casacuberta, Mercedes García-Martínez, Jesús González, Philipp Koehn, Luis Leiva, Bartolomé Mesa-Lao, et al. 2013. Casmacat: An open source workbench for advanced computer aided translation. *The Prague Bulletin of Mathematical Linguistics*, 100:101–112.

Beyer, H. and K. Holtzblatt. 1998. *Contextual Design: Defining Customer-centered Systems*. Interactive Technologies Series. Morgan Kaufmann.

Bronner, Amit, Matteo Negri, Yashar Mehdad, Angela Fahrni, and Christof Monz. 2012. Cosyne: Synchronizing multilingual wiki content. In *Proceedings of the Eighth Annual International Symposium on Wikis and Open Collaboration*, WikiSym '12, pages 33:1–33:4, New York, NY, USA. ACM.

Forcada, Mikel L, Mireia Ginestí-Rosell, Jacob Nordfalk, Jim ORegan, Sergio Ortiz-Rojas, Juan Antonio Pérez-Ortiz, Felipe Sánchez-Martínez, Gema Ramírez-Sánchez, and Francis M Tyers. 2011. Apertium: a free/open-source platform for rule-based machine translation. *Machine translation*, 25(2):127–144.

García, Ignacio and Vivian Stevenson. 2009. Reviews-google translator toolkit. *Multilingual computing & technology*, 20(6):16.

Hale, Scott A. 2013. Multilinguals and wikipedia editing. *CoRR*, abs/1312.0976.

Hecht, Brent and Darren Gergle. 2010. The tower of babel meets web 2.0: User-generated content and its applications in a multilingual context. In *Proceedings of the SIGCHI Conference on Human Factors in Computing Systems*, CHI '10, pages 291–300, New York, NY, USA. ACM.

Kumarana, Narend, S Ashwani, and D Vikram. 2011. Wikibhasha: Our experiences with multilingual content creation tool for wikipedia. In *Proceedings of Wikipedia Conference India, Wikimedia Foundation*.

Nielsen, Jakob. 1994. *Usability Engineering*. Interactive technologies. AP Professional.

Norman, D.A. and S.W. Draper. 1986. *User centered system design: new perspectives on human-computer interaction*. New Perspectives on Human-Computer Interaction Series. Lawrence Erlbaum Associates.

Pre-reordering for Statistical Machine Translation of Non-fictional Subtitles

Magdalena Plamadă[1] **Gion Linder**[2] **Phillip Ströbel**[1] **Martin Volk**[1]

[1]Institute of Computational Linguistics
University of Zurich
Binzmühlestrasse 14
CH-8050 Zurich
{plamada, volk}@cl.uzh.ch
phillip.stroebel@uzh.ch

[2]SWISS TXT
Schweizerische Teletext AG
Alexander-Schöni-Strasse 40
CH-2501 Biel
gion.linder@swisstxt.ch

Abstract

This paper describes the challenges of building a Statistical Machine Translation (SMT) system for non-fictional subtitles. Since our experiments focus on a "difficult" translation direction (i.e. French-German), we investigate several methods to improve the translation performance. We also compare our in-house SMT systems (including domain adaptation and pre-reordering techniques) to other SMT services and show that pre-reordering alone significantly improves the baseline systems.

1 Introduction

The recent advances in Statistical Machine Translation (SMT) have drawn the interest of the language industry towards it. The main advantages of integrating automatic translations are both cost and time savings, since the translation efforts can be reduced to post-editing activities. Experiments for different topical domains (such as software localization, film subtitling or automobile marketing texts) reported time savings between 20% and 30% (Volk, 2008; Plitt and Masselot, 2010; Läubli et al., 2013). These success stories strengthen our motivation to build a SMT system specialized on non-fictional content (e.g. documentaries, informative broadcasts).

The challenge of this task lies in the desired translation direction, namely from French into German. As the target language is morphologically richer than the source language, we expect difficulties in generating grammatically correct output. This drawback can be overcome by means of hierarchical models (Huck et al., 2013), improved morphological processing (Cap et al., 2014) or models enriched with part-of-speech (POS) information (Stüker et al., 2011). Another known issue with translations into German is the word order (e.g. the long-range disposal of separable prefix verbs or composed tenses), which can result in missing verbs or verb particles in the translated output. A general solution when translating between languages with different word order is to reorder the source texts according to the word order in the target language, as suggested by Niehues and Kolls (2009).

In this paper we investigate how well these techniques can be applied for subtitles and we particularly focus on the problem of missing verbs. We show that handling this aspect alone improves the SMT performance. We furthermore discuss whether the SMT performance is good enough to be incorporated in the translation workflow of a subtitling company.

2 The proposed solution

2.1 Domain description

SWISS TXT provides multimedia solutions for the Swiss National Radio and Television association. The company includes a subtitling division, which is responsible for producing subtitles for the broadcasted TV shows in the Swiss national languages: German, French, Italian and Rumansh. The subtitles are localized for the region where the TV show is broadcast (e.g. in the German-speaking part of Switzerland subtitles are only displayed in German). In order to ensure the desired quality, this work is done manually.

In a small cooperation project, we investigated whether SMT can facilitate the translation process, with a special focus on translating the subtitles of a French TV news magazine (called TP[1]) into German. The magazine covers a variety of topics, such as politics, society, economy or history with both Swiss and international foci.

2.2 Reordering approach

Although the standard SMT training includes by default a reordering step, the model cannot handle long-distance verb components. Therefore we apply an additional reordering step on the French input during pre-processing (also called pre-reordering), in which we focus on verb "dependencies". Our approach is rule-based and makes the distinction between main and subordinate clauses, since the position of the German verbs differs from clause to clause. For example, in declarative main clauses the finite verb is in the second position, whereas in some interrogative and exclamatory sentences it is in initial position (verb first). And in some subordinate clauses it can take a clause-final position.

Our reordering rules are mostly based on POS tags, but sometimes they also include word lemmas. They are learned from a subset of the French treebank consisting of 12,500 sentences from the LeMonde newspaper (Abeillé and Barrier, 2004). We first tag and parse the French sentences[2] and identify the main and subordinate clauses. Subsequently we extract the POS sequences corresponding to main and subordinate clauses respectively, and calculate their frequency. The most frequent patterns are then manually analyzed and corresponding reordering rules are generated.

As an example, consider the French sentence *FR orig* (English: I hope that this will level off.) and the extracted reordering rule. In this case, the auxiliary verb *va* has to be placed in the end of the subordinate clause, in order to comply with the German word order (as in *FR reordered*).

FR orig J'*/CLS* espère*/V* que*/CS* ça*/PRO* va*/V* se*/CLR* stabiliser*/VINF* .*/PONCT*

PRO V CLR VINF → PRO CLR VINF V

FR reordered J'espère que ça se stabiliser va.

[1] Full name suppressed due to privacy concerns

[2] `http://alpage.inria.fr/statgram/frdep/fr_stat_dep_malt.html`

A frequency distribution of these patterns shows that there are a couple of reoccurring patterns and many tag sequences which are rare (in agreement with Zipf's law). The rule set in these experiments consists of 30 rules, which cover approximately 70% of the sentences in need for reordering.

3 SMT experiments

3.1 Data description

It is known that good SMT performance can be obtained with considerable amounts of similar training data. In our case, only 40 subtitle files of the TP magazine were available in both languages, since the TV show has only recently been broadcast in the German-speaking part. Therefore we had to make use of other parallel resources, as similar as possible to the texts we intend to translate. A brief description of the data sets follows:

In-domain data The dataset consists of the 40 comparable files[3] of the informative broadcast *TP*.

"Similar in-domain" data I [4] The dataset consists of TED talks transcriptions in German and French from the WIT3 corpus[5].

"Similar in-domain" data II [4] The dataset consists of subtitles of informative broadcasts with the same profile (called TV)[1].

Out-of-domain data The dataset consists of freely available subtitles from the OPUS OpenSubtitles corpus[6].

The size of the parallel data sets used for our SMT experiments is detailed in table 1. We report the number of sentences because we decided to train the system on whole sentences, since the bigger corpora (OPUS and TED) were already available in this format. For this purpose, TV and TP subtitles have also been merged into sentences. The development and the test data have been withheld from the in-domain corpus.

3.2 System description

The SMT systems are trained with the Moses toolkit, according to the guidelines on the official

[3] We call them comparable because not every German subtitle/sentence has a corresponding French one and vice versa.

[4] Non-fictional texts, written in a different style than the one to translate

[5] `https://wit3.fbk.eu/`

[6] `http://opus.lingfil.uu.se/`

Data set	Sentences	DE Words	FR Words
OPUS	3,326,000	20,635,000	20,853,000
TV	641,000	5,905,000	8,760,000
TED	137,000	2,166,000	2,881,000
TP	11,000	113,000	144,000
Dev set	1350	14,000	14,800
Test set	300	3,000	3,200

Table 1: The size of the German-French data sets

website, with the difference that we lowercase the data instead of truecasing it[7]. The model combinations (phrase table combination, language model interpolation) are generated with the tools available in the Moses distribution. The parameters of the global models are optimized through Minimum Error Rate Training (MERT) on an in-domain development set (Och, 2003). The translation performance is measured in terms of several evaluation metrics on a single reference translation using `multeval`[8].

Since the collected data sets are very heterogeneous, training a system on concatenated data did not make any sense because we would risk that bigger corpora overpower the small in-domain one. To avoid this, we make use of a common domain adaptation technique, namely mixture-modeling (Sennrich, 2012), and we apply it to both the translation and the language models. The components of the combined translation models have been trained independently on the corresponding parallel corpora (OPUS, TED etc.), whereas the language models are trained on the target side of these corpora.

The *Hierarchical* system is trained by the same principles, but uses hierarchical models instead of plain phrase-based models. Such models learn translation rules from parallel data by means of probabilistic synchronous context-free grammars and are able to handle languages with different word order. The *Improved* system uses mixed phrase-based models, but unlike the baseline system, the models are trained on reordered sentences. Reordering is performed during preprocessing and has been applied to training, development and test data alike. However, reordering only makes sense if the main clause and the subordinate ones are in the same translation unit. Since a common practice in subtitling is to separate subordinate clauses from the main clause (due to length restrictions), we had to join the subtitles in order for the reordering to be effective.

3.3 Results

The results of the SMT experiments are summarized in table 2. As expected, both the hierarchical and the improved systems outperform the baseline in the automatic evaluation, as reflected by all reported scores (BLEU, METEOR and TER).

System	BLEU ↑	METEOR ↑	TER ↓
Baseline	16.4	34.9	64.5
Hierarchical	17.1	35.3	64.2
Improved	17.4	35.9	63.9
Google Translate	14.3	30.3	68.7

Table 2: SMT results for French-German

However, the system trained on reordered sentences is slightly better than the hierarchical one, as the following example shows. We also compared our in-house systems against Google Translate (a large scale SMT system)[9] and we systematically score better. However, this effect can partially be attributed to the lexical choices, which are different from the reference, as the following example shows.

FR orig: -Rémy est loin d'imaginer ce qui va lui arriver .
Baseline: -Rémy ist nicht, was geschehen wird .
Hierarchical: Es ist nicht, was geschehen wird .
Improved: -Rémy ist weit weg, sich vorzustellen, was ihm geschieht .
Google: -Rémy hat keine Ahnung, was mit ihm geschehen wird .
DE ref: Rémy hat keine Vorstellung, was ihm bevorsteht .

The same happens with the *Improved* system, which generates an almost correct German sentence following the syntax from the original sentence (which is different from the reference). We also note that this output is better than what the rest of our in-house systems generate because the verbs are no longer missing and they are correctly placed according to the type of clause (main/subordinate). However, a better option would have been to translate the phrase *être loin d'imaginer* (EN: to be far from imagining) as a multiword unit, but our systems do not specifically handle these kind of phrases.

[7] `http://www.statmt.org/moses/?n=Moses.Baseline`

[8] `https://github.com/jhclark/multeval`

[9] `http://translate.google.com`

In order to assess the improvements from a translator's perspective, we conducted a small human evaluation experiment with one potential user. The purpose of the experiment was to judge the usefulness of the MT output in general, with respect to post-editing efforts. The test data consisted of a real subtitle file with no additional preprocessing (e.g. merging into sentences). According to his judgment, 33.5% of the subtitles can be used directly or with small corrections, 48.5% of the subtitles need improvements, but post-editing would still be faster than translating from scratch, whereas 18% of the subtitles require a retranslation. We consider these findings more insightful than the automatic scores, as they can be used to further improve our SMT system.

4 Conclusion

In this paper we have described our efforts of building a SMT system for translating French subtitles into German. This was particularly challenging since only a small in-domain corpus was available and thus different corpora (with different styles) had to be combined into a single system. We addressed this issue by applying mixture modeling, thus ensuring that Swiss-specific terms were preferred over alternative translations. For example, the French verb *évincer* (EN: to expel sb.) was consistently translated as *ausschaffen* (as learned from our in-domain corpus), instead of *ausschliessen* (as found in other corpora).

We have also shown how the translation quality can be improved by pre-reordering the input sentences. This preprocessing step used a set of POS-based rules extracted from a parsed French corpus. Although our approach focused on the correct placement of verbs depending on the clause type (main vs. subordinate), the system trained with reordered sentences gained 1 BLEU point on top of the baseline. This finding suggests that a more refined set of reordering rules will contribute to further improving translations. It is also conceivable to include morphological information (as suggested by other approaches) for the purpose of generating correct word forms.

We cannot help noticing that the obtained BLEU scores were still in a low range. We think that this was partially due to our test set, which often contained paraphrases instead of literal translations. On the other hand, the human evaluation showed a high acceptance rate of the MT output, since only 18% was assessed as unusable. This kind of output could be easily suppressed in a quality estimation post-processing step. This way we would only deliver translations in which our system is confident, allowing post-editors to save both time and efforts.

References

Abeillé, Anne and Nicolas Barrier. 2004. Enriching a French Treebank. *Proceedings of the Fourth Conference on Language Resources and Evaluation.*

Cap, Fabienne, Alexander Fraser, Marion Weller, and Aoife Cahill. 2014. How to Produce Unseen Teddy Bears: Improved Morphological Processing of Compounds in SMT. *Proceedings of the 14th Conference of the European Chapter of the Association for Computational Linguistics.* 579–587.

Huck, Matthias, Joern Wuebker, Felix Rietig, and Hermann Ney. 2013. A Phrase Orientation Model for Hierarchical Machine Translation. *Proceedings of the Eighth Workshop on Statistical Machine Translation.* 452–463.

Läubli, Samuel, Mark Fishel, Manuela Weibel, and Martin Volk. 2013. Statistical Machine Translation for Automobile Marketing Texts. *Proceedings of the Machine Translation Summit XIV.* 265–272.

Niehues, Jan and Muntsin Kolss. 2009. A POS-Based Model for Long-Range Reorderings in SMT. *Proceedings of the Fourth Workshop on Statistical Machine Translation.* 206–214.

Och, Franz Josef. 2003. Minimum Error Rate Training in Statistical Machine Translation. *Proceedings of the 41st Annual Meeting on Association for Computational Linguistics - Volume 1.* 160–167.

Plitt, Mirko and François Masselot. 2010. A Productivity Test of Statistical Machine Translation Post-editing in a Typical Localisation Context. *Prague Bulletin of Mathematical Linguistics*, 93:7–16.

Sennrich, Rico. 2012. Perplexity Minimization for Translation Model Domain Adaptation in Statistical Machine Translation. *Proceedings of the 13th Conference of the European Chapter of the Association for Computational Linguistics.* 539–549

Stüker, Sebastian, Kevin Kilgour, and Jan Niehues. 2011. Quaero Speech-to-Text and Text Translation Evaluation Systems. *High Performance Computing in Science and Engineering '10.* 529–542.

Volk, Martin. 2008. The Automatic Translation of Film Subtitles. A Machine Translation Success Story? *Resourceful Language Technology: Festschrift in Honor of Anna Sågvall Hein.* 202–214.

SMT at the International Maritime Organization: Experiences with Combining In-house Corpora with Out-of-domain Corpora

Bruno Pouliquen
World Intellectual Property Organization
34, chemin des Colombettes
CH-1211 Geneva, Switzerland
bruno.pouliquen@wipo.int

Marcin Junczys-Dowmunt
Adam Mickiewicz University
ul. Umultowska 87
61-614 Poznań, Poland
junczys@amu.edu.pl

Blanca Pinero
International Maritime Organization
4 Albert Embankment
London SE17SR, United Kingdom
bpinero@imo.org

Michał Ziemski
United Nations
8-14, Avenue de la Paix
CH-1211 Geneva, Switzerland
mziemski@unog.ch

Abstract

This paper presents a machine translation tool – based on Moses – developed for the International Maritime Organization (IMO) for the automatic translation of documents from Spanish, French, Russian and Arabic to/from English. The main challenge lies in the insufficient size of inhouse corpora (especially for Russian and Arabic). The United Nations (UN) granted IMO the right to use UN resources and we describe experiments and results we obtained with different translation model combination techniques. While BLEU results remain inconclusive for combinations, we also analyze user preferences for certain models (when choosing betweeen IMO only or combined with UN). The combined models are perceived by translators as being much better for general texts while IMO only models seem better for technical texts.

1 Introduction

This paper describes the installation and training of TAPTA, an MT tool, for the automatic translation of IMO documents. TAPTA has been previously installed at other international organizations (Pouliquen et. al 2013). IMO is a specialized agency of the United Nations system dealing with safe and secure seas and the protection of the marine environment. It has three working languages (English, French and Spanish) with parallel corpora of ca. 60 million words each. A much smaller number of documents (conventions and reports totaling ca. 6 million words per language) are translated into the other official languages of the United Nations (Arabic, Chinese[1], Russian). IMO felt that the introduction of MT would help translators in their daily work, given similar experiences in other UN agencies and repetitive nature of their documentation due to periodic reporting. While building the SMT corpora, the specific terminology used in the maritime domain and the "house style" were also important considerations. The large imbalance in the number of parallel documents between language poses a problem which we try to solve by integrating larger parallel corpora which "complete" the IMO models (especially for Russian and Arabic)[2]. The corpora provided by the United Nations Secretariat were thought to be ideal for this purpose as the language pairs are the same and working practices in both translation services are very similar. Authorization was granted to merge the corpora.

2 Data and preprocessing

The International Maritime Organization has 6 official languages (Arabic, English, Spanish, French,

[1]Work on Chinese data has been postponed and is not described in this paper.

[2]Documents were provided by the Documentation Division (New York) of the Department for General Assembly and Conference Management, the main entity of the United Nations Secretariat charged with the production of parliamentary documentation.

Russian and Chinese), which means that, if such an organization wanted a translation tool for all language pair combinations, it would require 42 translation engines. A rule-based translation system would be extremely costly to build and maintain. A data-driven approach is usually more suitable when a big parallel corpus exists, therefore we focused on SMT.

Moses (Koehn et al. 2007) has been trained with a parallel corpora extracted consisting of IMO documents translated between January 2000 and October 2014 (ca. 20,000 documents for English, French and Spanish, about 400 documents for Russian/Arabic, see Table 1). The provided corpora have been extracted from original Word or PDF documents, identical IDs between languages allow to align documents for each language pair. We use an in-house (WIPO) sentence aligner. The tool processes each parallel text document and produces a set of aligned sentences after applying the following steps:

- Sentence splitting
- Tokenization
- Sentence alignment with our sentences aligned (based on Champollion (Ma 2006)) — produces an "aligned-segment-matching-score"
- filtering out whole documents with an average-segment-matching-score below a given threshold
- filtering out sets of consecutive segments having a low scores
- filtering out sets of consecutive segments that are sorted by alphabetical order[3]
- filtering out sentences having only one word or more than 80 words, or a source/target word ratio more than 9

3 SMT system

3.1 Baseline system

The baseline SMT system consists of an extended Moses (Koehn et al. 2007) configuration. Durrani et al. (2013) report on improvements for various language pairs when an Operation Sequence Model (OSM) is added to the phrase-based decoder. Class-based language models seem to be a good compromise between increased n-gram length and total model size. We use automatically calculated word cluster ids as classes. We had good experience with word2vec (Mikolov et al. 2012) in the context of larger SMT models and use this tool to compute 200 word classes from the target language data. The target language corpora are mapped to sequences of classes and 9-gram language model are estimated. The final phrase-tables of the larger models (English-French, English-Spanish) have been significance pruned (Johnson et al. 2007) for size reduction. In our experiments significance pruning results in no quality loss while reducing translation model size by a factor of 5. The standard 5-gram language models and the 9-gram word-class models are estimated with Modified Kneser-Ney smoothing (Chen and Goodman 1996, Heafield et al. 2013). To reduce size requirements, we use heavily quantized binary models with no noticeable quality reduction. Pruning is applied to all singleton n-grams with n equal to or greater than 3.

Lang.	IMO corpus			UN
pair	Docs	Words	Segments	Words
en-fr	17132	53.8 M	2.60 M	316 M
en-es	16213	54.0 M	2.50 M	295 M
en-ru	318	5.6 M	0.30 M	296 M
en-ar	296	4.1 M	0.23 M	304 M
en-zh	[not available yet]			280 M

Table 1: Size of the parallel corpora used for training. The fourth and fifth columns show the training size (in millions of English words) for IMO and UN corpus.

3.2 Attempts at domain adaptation

We explore two model combination methods for both, translation models and language models: linear and log-linear interpolation. Log-linear model interpolation is natively supported in Moses via its feature function framework. Translation models and language models can be log-linearly interpolated just by adding them to the Moses configuration files. Parameter tuning then chooses the appropriate interpolation weights which are actually feature weights. Linear interpolation, though a standard method for language models, is more involved. In the case of language models, we

[3] In both IMO and UN, it is very common to sort enumerations of countries, persons, organizations, etc. by alphabetical order, which will of course often be different between languages and results in very noisy sentence alignment.

compute a new static linearly interpolated language model from IMO and UN data target language data. Interpolation weights are optimized on the dev set. In the case of translation models we use a new feature function available in Moses that allows for setting up virtual phrase tables that are in fact linearly interpolated translation models (Sennrich 2012). We use the same interpolation weights as previously determined for linear language model interpolation. The two interpolated translation models are the original IMO and UN translation models as used in stand-alone translators. Results are mixed, we report the best results for our experiments (see Table 2, Section 5.1). Log-linear interpolation is downright harmful (and therefore omitted), for the larger language pairs (en-fr and en-es) any of the interpolation methods seem to be unhelpful, improvements for en-es are within the range of optimizer instability. For the smaller models (en-ar, en-ru) we observe quite significant improvements that stem mainly from linear translation model interpolation.

4 Translating

4.1 Server configuration

The server has been installed on a virtual machine running Ubuntu, the same machine is being used for training and decoding. Server specifications are: 12 cores, 64 GB RAM and 1 TB of disk space.

The server runs several Moses decoders (one decoder is a Moses single-thread executable). Each decoder is encapsulated in a Java RMI interface server which allows to operate several concurrent decoders. Each sentence submitted is queued and sent to the next free decoder. Since both, the phrase table as well as all the language models, rely on memory mapping and shared memory, having several independent workers instead of a multithreaded architecture does not represent much of a memory problem. Common data is shared automatically between processes. Thanks to our experience in installing the tool, we were able to install and configure the server in 2 days (not including research model parameters and specific experiments with model combinations). Training one IMO model takes ca. 20 hours.

4.2 User interface

4.2.1 Web interface: gist translation

A web interface allows users to submit short texts and access the corresponding automatic translation (with highlighting of parallel segments or words).

Figure 1: Translating with the "auto hotkey"

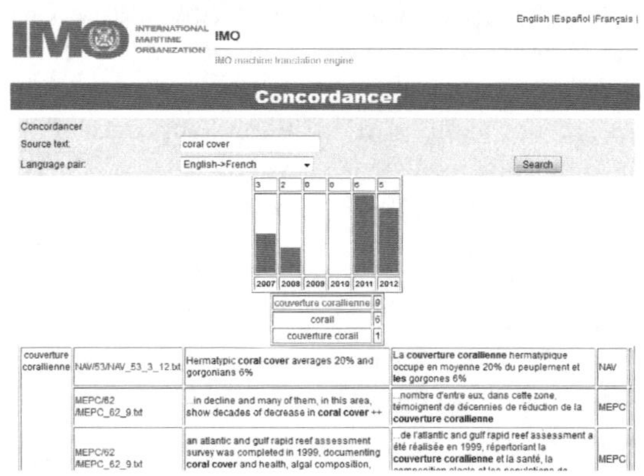

Figure 2: Concordancer for term "coral cover", the graph shows the term usage over years, next the most used translations are display, then the full parallel segments with links to original documents.

4.2.2 "Auto hotkey" access

Translators in IMO use specific software (MultiTrans Prism) and do not wish to copy-paste texts in order to use the tool. So we decided to use the "auto hotkey" open source software (`http://www.autohotkey.com`), which allows users to call the tool with a keystroke, translations are then copied to the clipboard and users can paste it into the translation in-progress (see Figure 1 for an example screen shot).

4.2.3 Concordancer

Users can access the concordancer using a Web interface or through a different "hotkey". The concordancer is based on a Lucene index containing the word aligned corpus. This concordancer displays segments containing the search term and the corresponding aligned words. A first window dis-

	IMO only	Combined	Google
en-fr	54.24	54.03	32.58
en-es	52.68	52.99	35.18
en-ru	58.77	60.20	20.56
en-ar	41.20	44.18	16.58
en-zh		[not available]	

Table 2: BLEU scores for each language pair, compared with a combined model and with Google translate.

plays the usage of the term by year, a second window displays the aligned words by order of frequency, the user can immediately see which translation is the most common (see Figure 2 for an example).

5 Results/Evaluation

5.1 Automatic evaluation

BLEU scores (Papineni et al. 2002) were used to compare human translations with automatic translations (one reference) on a set slightly more than 2000 sentences which have been set apart before model training.

5.2 Human perception

It is always difficult to measure user acceptance, especially at this early stage. However we can now observe that, on average, more than 1500 words are translated every day using our tool. Some users "jump" between various models (eg. users prefer IMO-only models for English-to-Spanish, but nevertheless use the combined model in more than 10% of the cases). Even though the automatic evaluation scores do not show significant improvement with combined models, translators judged combined models to be better for general texts while IMO-only models work better for more technical texts. Additional functionality such as the concordancer are readily embraced and found useful alongside the pure translation function.

6 Conclusion and future work

During our experiments, we had to face both, a scarcity problem (small IMO corpora for some languages) and a scalability problem (large UN corpora). However, our experience shows that open source solutions can sometimes provide better results than generic commercial products. Moreover, sharing the tool between these organizations facilitates sharing of corpora and the spread of MT in international organizations. User comments include that the Web interface is intuitive and the "auto-hotkey" is an easy and fast way of accessing translations; integration like this requires very little training and this training can be done internally. Future work includes: better integration into the users' environment and a biannual retraining of all the models. We believe the model combination technique can still be improved. An area to explore would be to "automatically" choose the best model to translate a given document/sentence.

Acknowledgements

The authors wish to thank Mrs Olga O'Neil, Director, Conference Division, IMO, for making this collaboration possible, and Ms Cecilia Elizalde, UNHQ, for her invaluable assistance in obtaining the UN corpora.

References

Pouliquen B., C. Elizalde, M. Junczys-Dowmunt, C. Mazenc, and J. Garca-Verdugo. 2013. Large-scale Multiple Language Translation Accelerator at the United Nations, *Proc. of MT Summit 2013*.

Chen S. F. and J. Goodman. 1996. An Empirical Study of Smoothing Techniques for Language Modeling, in *Proc. of ACL 1996*.

Durrani, N., A. Fraser, H. Schmid, H. Hoang, and P. Koehn. 2013. Can Markov Models over Minimal Translation Units Help Phrase-based SMT? in *ACL*.

Heafield, K, I. Pouzyrevsky, J. H. Clark, and P. Koehn. 2013. Scalable Modified Kneser-Ney Language Model Estimation, in *Proc. of ACL 2013*.

Johnson, H., J. D. Martin, G. F. Foster, and R. Kuhn. 2007. Improving Translation Quality by Discarding Most of the Phrasetable, *Proc. of EMNLP 2007*.

Koehn, Philipp, Hieu Hoang, Alexandra Birch, Chris C. Burch, Marcello Federico, Nicola Bertoldi, Brooke Cowan, Wade Shen, Christine Moran, Richard Zens, Chris Dyer, Ondej Bojar, Alexandra Constantin, Evan Herbst. 2007. Moses: Open Source Toolkit for Statistical Machine Translation. *Proc. of ACL 2007*.

Koehn, Phillip. 2010. *Statistical Machine Translation*. Textbook, Cambridge University Press.

Ma, Xiaoyi. 2006. Champollion: A Robust Parallel Text Sentence Aligner. *Proc. of LREC-2006*.

Mikolov, T., K. Chen, G. Corrado, and J. Dean. 2013. Efficient Estimation of Word Representations in Vector Space, *CoRR, vol. abs/1301.3781*.

Papineni, K., S. Roukos, T. Ward, and WJ Zhu. 2002. BLEU: a Method for Automatic Evaluation of Machine Translation, *Proc. of ACL 2002*.

Sennrich R. 2012, Perplexity Minimization for Translation Model Domain Adaptation in Statistical Machine Translation. *Proc. of EACL 2012*.

Evaluation of the domain adaptation of MT systems in ACCURAT

Gregor Thurmair
Linguatec,
Gottfried-Keller-Str. 12, 81375 Munich, Germany
gregor.thurmair@gmx.de

Abstract[1]

The contribution reports on an evaluation of efforts to improve MT quality by domain adaptation, for both rule-based and statistical MT, as done in the ACCURAT project (Skadiņa et al. 2012). Comparative evaluation shows an increase of about 5% for both MT paradigms after system adaptation; absolute evaluation shows an increase in adequacy and fluency for SMT. While the RMT solution is superior in quality in both comparative and absolute evaluation, the gain by domain adaptation is higher for the SMT paradigm.

1 Introduction

The objective of this contribution is to evaluate improvements achieved by adapting Machine Translation systems to narrow domains, using data from comparable corpora.

Language direction chosen was German to English; the automotive domain, subdomain of transmission / gearbox technology, was selected as an example for a narrow domain. In order to assess the effect of domain adaptation on MT systems with different architecture, both a data driven (SMT) and a knowledge-driven (RMT) system were evaluated.

2 Evaluation Objects: MT systems adapted to narrow domains

The evaluation object are two versions of an MT system: A baseline version, *without* domain tuning, and an adapted version, *with* domain tuning. Their comparison shows to which extent the domain adaptation can improve MT quality.

The evaluation objects were created as follows:

For the **baseline** systems, on the RMT side, an out-of-the-box system of Linguatec's 'Personal Translator' PT (V.14) was used, which is a rule-based MT system, based on the IBM slot-filler grammar technology (Aleksić & Thurmair 2011) and a bilingual lexicon of about 200K transfers. On the SMT side, a baseline Moses system was trained with standard parallel data (Europarl, JRC etc.), plus some initial comparable corpus data as collected in the first phase of ACCURAT.

For the **adaptation** of the baseline systems, data were collected from the automotive domain. These data were obtained by crawling sites of automotive companies being active in the transmission field (like ZF, BASF, Volkswagen and others), using the focused crawler described in (Papavassiliou et al. 2013). They were then aligned and cleaned manually. Some sentence pairs were set aside for testing, the rest was given to the two systems as development and test sets. The resulting narrow-domain automotive corpus has about 42.000 sentences for German-to-English.

For the SMT system, domain adaptation was done by adding these sentences to the training and development sets, and building a new SMT system.

In case of rule-based technology, domain adaptation involves terminology creation, as the main means of adaptation. The following steps were taken: (1) extraction of the phrase table from the just described domain-adap6ted SMT system; (2) extraction of bilingual terminology candidates from this phrase table, resulting in a list of about 25.000 term candidates; (3) preparation of these candidates for dictionary import; creation of linguistic annotations, removal of already existing entries etc.; the final list of imported entries was about 7100 entries; (4) crea-

[1] This research was funded in the context of the FP7-ICT project ACCURAT (248347),

tion of a special 'automotive' user dictionary, to be used additionally for automotive translations.
This procedure is described in detail in (Thurmair & Aleksić 2012).
Result of these efforts were four test systems, for German-to-English, and tuned for automotive domain with the same adaptation data:
SMT-base: Moses with just baseline data
SMT-adapted: Moses baseline plus in-domain data
RMT-base: PT-baseline out-of-the-box
RMT-adapted: PT with an automotive dictionary.

3 Evaluation Data

In total about 1500 sentences were taken from the collected strongly comparable automotive corpora for tests, with one reference translation each. The sentences represent 'real-life' data; they were not cleaned or corrected..

4 Evaluation methodology

4.1 General options

Several methods can be applied for the evaluation of MT results, cf. Figure 1.

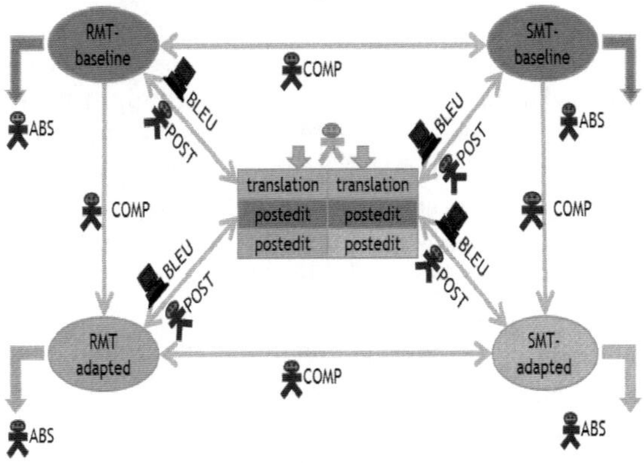

Fig. 1: Evaluation graph

1. Automatic comparison (called BLEU in Fig. 1) is the predominant paradigm in SMT. BLEU (Papineni et al. 2002) and/or NIST (NIST 2002) scores can be computed for different versions of MT system output. Because of their known shortcomings (Callison-Burch et al. 2009) evaluations ask for human judgment in addition.
2. Comparative evaluation (called COMP in Fig. 1) compares two systems, or two versions of the same system. It asks whether or not one translation is better / equal / worse than the other.

While this approach can find which of two systems has an overall better score, it cannot answer the question what the real quality of the two systems is: 'Equal' can mean that both sentences are perfect, but also that both are unusable.
3. Absolute evaluation (called ABS in Fig. 1) therefore is required to determine the quality of a given translation. It looks at one translation of a sentence at a time, and determines its accuracy and fluency on a n-point scale.
4. Postediting evaluation (called POST in Fig. 1) reflects the task-oriented aspect of evaluation (Popescu-Belis 2008). It measures the distance of an MT output to a human (MT-postedited) output, either in terms of time, or of the keystrokes needed to produce a corrected translation from a raw translation (Tatsumi 2009; HTER: Snover et al. 2009).

Postediting evaluation adds reference translations to the evaluation process.

The evaluation graph as shown in Fig. 1 combines these evaluation methods, avoids biased results as produced by a single method, and gives a complete picture of the evaluation efforts.

4.2 Evaluation in ACCURAT

In the ACCURAT narrow domain task, the following evaluation methods were used:
Automatic evaluation of the four systems (SMT and RMT, baseline and adapted) using BLEU.
Comparative evaluation of the pairs SMT-baseline vs. SMT-adapted, and RMT-baseline vs. RMT-adapted; this produces the core information how much the systems can improve.
Absolute evaluation of the systems SMT-adapted and RMT-adapted, to gain insight into translation quality, and consequently the acceptance of such systems for real-world use.

Other forms of evaluation were not included, esp. postediting evaluation was done in other tasks in the ACCURAT project (cf. Skadiņš et al. 2011). But to have a complete picture, other ABS and COMP directions were evaluated, but with 1 tester only.

For the evaluation, a special tool was created called 'Sisyphus II', to be used offline by freelancers, randomly proposing evaluation data, and creating an XML file for later evaluation.

5 Evaluation Results

5.1 Automatic Evaluation

The automatic evaluation for the four test systems was done using BLEU scores. The results are shown in Table 1.
For both system types there is an increase in BLEU; more moderate for the RMT than for the SMT system. Also, the SMT system performs

better in this evaluation method. However it is known that BLEU is biased towards SMT systems (Hamon et al. 2006, Culy & Riehemann 2003).

	SMT	RMT
baseline	17.36	16.08
adapted	22.21	17.51
improvement	4.85	1.43

Table 1: BLEU scores for SMT and RMT

5.2 Comparative Evaluation

Three testers were used, all of them good speakers of English with translation background. They inspected randomly selected subsets of the 1500 test sentences. Results are given in Tab. 2.

	total inspected	base better	both equal	adapted better	improvement
Total SMT	2060	447	1061	552	5.10%
Total RMT	2505	158	2072	275	4.67%

Table 2: Comparative Evaluation: baseline vs. adapted, for SMT and RMT[2]

Both types of systems show an improvement of about 5% after domain adaptation. It is a bit more for the SMT than for the RMT, due to a strong RMT baseline system.

The result is consistent among the testers: All of them see a higher improvement for the SMT than for the RMT.

It may be worthwhile noticing that in the RMT evaluation, a large proportion of the test sentences (nearly 60%) came out identical in both versions. In the SMT system, nearly no sentence came out unchanged; this fact increases the postediting effort for consecutive versions of SMT output.

In a sideline evaluation, a comparison was made between the RMT and SMT systems, for both baseline and adaptations, cf. Tab. 3.

	total inspected	SMT better	both equal	RMT better	in %
baseline	501	47	170	284	47.3%
adapted	489	38	203	260	44.3%

Table 3: Comparative Evaluation SMT vs. RMT, for baseline and adapted

The result shows that the RMT quality is considered significantly better than the SMT quality. The main reason for this seems to be that the SMT German-English frequently eliminates verbs in sentences, which makes the output much less understandable.

It should be noted, however, that the distance between the system types is smaller in the adapted than in the baseline versions (by 3%).

5.3 Absolute Evaluation

Absolute evaluation assesses how usable the resulting translation would be after the system was adapted. A total of 1100 sentences, randomly selected from the 1500 sentence test base, were inspected by three testers for adequacy and fluency. Table 4 gives the result.

	inspected	1: fully	2: mostly	3: partially	4: none	average	% of 1+2
		SMT adapted					
adequacy	1103	200	204	517	182	2.62	36,63
fluency	1103	300	285	362	156	2.34	53,04
		RMT adapted					
adequacy	1103	300	285	362	156	2.02	53,04
fluency	1103	300	285	362	156	1.80	53,04

Table 4: Absolute evaluation for SMT-adapted and RMT-adapted systems[3]

It can be seen that testers evaluate the SMT somewhat between 'mostly' and 'partially' fluent / comprehensible, and the RMT close to 'mostly' fluent / comprehensible. If the percentage of level 1/2 evaluations is taken, both adequacy and fluency rates are significantly higher for RMT output. All testers agree in this evaluation, with similar average results.

It could be worthwhile to mention that the opinion often heard that the SMT produces more fluent output that the RMT cannot be corroborated with the evaluation data here: The RMT output is clearly considered to be more fluent than the SMT output (1.80 vs. 2.34).

As far as the interrater agreement is concerned, the test setup made it difficult to compute it: All testers used the same test set but tested only a random subset of it. So there are only few data points common to all testers (only 20 in many cases). For those, only weak agreement could be found (with values below 0.4 in Cohen's kappa). However, all testers show consistent behaviour in the evaluation, and came to similar conclusions overall, as has been explained above.

[2] Computed as: (#-better MINUS #-worse) DIV #-sentences

[3] Computed as: (SUM (#-sentences TIMES rank)) DIV #-sentences. Lower scores are better.

6 Conclusion

Figure 5 gives all evaluation results. All evaluation methods indicate an improvement of the adapted versions over the baseline versions.

Automatic evaluation: For SMT, the BLEU score increases from 17.36 to 22.21; for RMT, it increases from 16.08 to 17.51.

Comparative evaluation: For SMT, an improvement of 5.1% was found; for RMT, and improvement of 4.67% was found.

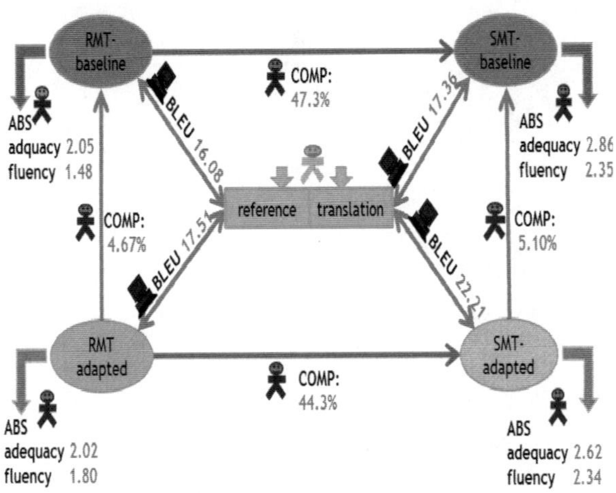

Fig. 5: Evaluation graph for ACCURAT task

Absolute evaluation: For SMT, adequacy improved from 2.86 to 2.62, fluency slightly from 2.35 to 2.34; for RMT, adequacy improved from 2.05 to 2.02, fluency decreased from 1.48 to 1.8.

The improvement is more significant for the SMT system than for the RMT; this may be due to the fact that the RMT baseline system was stronger than the SMT baseline.

For SMT improvement, (Pecina et al. 2012) report improvements between 8.6 and 16.8 BLEU (relative) for domain adaptation; results here are in line with these findings.

Comparing the evaluation methods, the findings corroborate statements (cf. Hamon et al. 2006) that the 'human-based' methods (COMP and ABS) differ from the automatic ones (BLEU) if different types of MT systems are to be compared.

Overall, the 'human-based' evaluation methods (COMP, ABS) have shown that a trained RMT system still outperforms a trained SMT system; however the SMT system profits more from adaptation.

References

Aleksić, V., Thurmair, Gr., 2011: Personal Translator at WMT 2011. Proc. WMT Edinburgh, UK.

Callison-Burch, Chr., Koehn, Ph., Monz, Ch., Schroeder, J., 2009: Findings of the 2009 Workshop on Statistical Machine Translation. Proc 4th Workshop on SMT, Athens

Culy, Chr., Riehemann, S.,2003: The Limits of N-Gram Translation Evaluation Metrics. Proc. MT Summit New Orleans

Hamon, O., Popescu-Belis, A., Choukri, K., Dabbadie, M., Hartley, A., W. Mustafa El Hadi, W., Rajman, M., and Timimi, I., 2006. CESTA: First Conclusions of the Technolangue MT Evaluation Campaign. Proc. LREC Genova, Italy.

NIST (2002). Automatic Evaluation of Machine Translation Quality Using n-gram Co-occurrences Statistics (http://www.nist.gov/speech/tests/mt/)

Papavassiliou, V., Prokopidis, P., Thurmair, Gr., 2013: A modular open-source focused crawler for mining monolingual and bilingual corpora from the web. Proc. 6th Workshop BUCC, Sofia, Bulgaria

Papineni, K., Roukos, S., Ward, T., Zhu, W., 2002: BLEU: a Method for Automatic Evaluation of Machine Translation. Proc. ACL, Philadelphia

Pecina, P., Toral, A., Papavassiliou, V., Prokopidis, P., van Genabith, J., 2012: Domain Adaptation of Statistical machine Translation using Web-Crawled Resources: A Case Study // Proceedings of the EAMT 2012, Trento, Italy.

Popescu-Belis, A., 2008: Reference-based vs. task-based evaluation of human language technology. Proc. LREC

Skadiņa, I., Aker, A., Mastropavlos, N., Su, F., Tufis, D., Verlic, M., Vasiļjevs, A., Babych, B., Clough, P., Gaizauskas, R., Glaros, N., Paramita, M.L., Pinnis, M., 2012: Collecting and Using Comparable Corpora for Statistical Machine Translation. Proc. 8th LREC Istanbul

Skadiņš, R., Puriņš, M., Skadiņa, I., Vasiļjevs, A., 2011: Evaluation of SMT in localization to under-resourced inflected language. Proc. EAMT Leuven

Snover, M., Madnani, N., Dorr, B., Schwartz, R., 2009. Fluency, Adequacy, or HTER? Exploring Different Human Judgments with a Tunable MT Metric. In Proc. of WMT09

Tatsumi, M., 2009: Correlation Between Automatic Evaluation Metric Scores, Post-Editing Speed, and Some Other Factors. Proc. MT Summit XII Ottawa

Thurmair, Gr., Aleksić, V., 2012: Creating Term and Lexicon Entries from Phrase Tables. Proc. EAMT 2012 Trento, Italy.

Project/Product Descriptions

MixedEmotions: Social Semantic Emotion Analysis for Innovative Multilingual Big Data Analytics Markets

ICT-15-2014 Big data and Open Data Innovation and take-up - Innovation Action

Industry Partners	Academic Partners
Expert System, Italy	Insight Centre for Data Analytics, National University of Ireland, Galway (coordinator)
Millward Brown, Czech Republic	
Paradigma Tecnológico, Spain	Universidad Politécnica de Madrid, Spain
Phonexia, Czech Republic	University of Passau, Germany
SindiceTech, Ireland	Brno University of Technology, Czech Republic
Deutsche Welle, Germany	

Project duration: April 2015 - March 2017

Summary

Emotion analysis is central to tracking customer and user behaviour and satisfaction, which can be observed from user interaction in the form of explicit feedback through email, call centre interaction, social media comments, etc., as well as implicit acknowledgment of approval or rejection through facial expressions, speech or other non-verbal feedback. In Europe specifically, but increasingly also globally, an added factor here is that user feedback can be in multiple languages, in text as well as in speech and audio-visual content. This implies different cultural backgrounds and thus different ways to produce and perceive emotions in everyday interactions, beyond the fact of having specific rules for encoding and decoding emotions in each language.

Making sense of accumulated user interaction from different ('mixed') data sources, modalities and languages is challenging and has not yet been explored in fullness in an industrial context. Commercial solutions exist but do not address the multilingual aspect in a robust and large-scale setting and do not scale up to huge data volumes that need to be processed, or the integration of emotion analysis observations across data sources and/or modalities on a meaningful level, i.e. keeping track of entities involved as well the connections between them (who said what? to whom? in the context of which event, product, service?)

The MixedEmotions project will implement an integrated Big Linked Data platform for emotion analysis across heterogeneous data sources, languages and modalities, building on existing state-of-the-art tools, services and approaches that will enable the tracking of emotional aspects of user interaction and feedback on an entity level. The platform will provide an integrated solution for:

- Large-scale emotion analysis and fusion on heterogeneous, multilingual, text, speech, video and social media data streams, leveraging open access and proprietary data sources, exploiting also social context by leveraging social network graphs
- Semantic-level emotion information aggregation and integration through robust extraction of social semantic knowledge graphs for emotion analysis along multidimensional clusters

The platform will be developed and evaluated in the context of three cross-domain pilot projects that are representative of a variety of data analytics markets: Social TV, Brand Reputation Management, Call Centre Operations.

The ACCEPT Academic Portal: Bringing Together Pre-editing, MT and Post-editing into a Learning Environment

Pierrette Bouillon, Johanna Gerlach, Asheesh Gulati, Victoria Porro, Violeta Seretan
Université de Genève FTI/TIM, accept@unige.ch
www.accept-portal.unige.ch

Description

The ACCEPT Academic Portal is a user-centred online platform specifically designed to offer a complete machine translation workflow including pre-editing and post-editing steps for teaching purposes. The platform leverages technology developed in the ACCEPT[1] European Project (2012-2014) devoted to improving the translatability of user-generated content. Originally available as a series of plug-ins and demonstrators on the ACCEPT portal[2], the various software components have been interconnected into an easy-to-use platform reproducing all phases of a real MT workflow. The platform provides a unique environment to study the interaction between MT-related processes and to assess the contribution of new technologies to translation. It will be useful for research and teaching purposes alike.

The platform allows a user to select existing data (or supply their own data, in plain text format) and to subject it to a sequence of processes, until the desired output is reached. Source and target content reformulation can be performed automatically or interactively, the interface allowing experimentation with specific editing rules, visual comparison, on-the-fly translation, XLIFF-based recording of post-editing actions, and one-click export of results. The steps can be executed in a flexible manner according to the desired scenario; users may, for instance, upload their own machine-translated texts and perform post-editing only. Users can stop at any step in the workflow and download their results. In-context documentation (tool tips, user guide) is available at all steps. The platform has a minimalistic app-like look-and-feel for optimised user experience. It is designed for the non-expert, and can therefore bring the MT benefits to a larger community of users.

The platform's main modules and functionalities are briefly described below.

- Start page: Selection of data (existing; own data entered in text area; own data uploaded as text file); selection of language pairs (en–fr, fr–en and en–de are currently supported); selection of processing scenario (different combinations of pre-editing, MT and post-editing).
- Pre-editing module: Automatic or interactive checking using the ACCEPT rules developed for user-generated content using the Acrolinx technology (www.acrolinx.com).
- MT module: Translation using the ACCEPT phrase-based Moses system adapted to user-generated content.
- Post-editing module: Free post-editing; interactive checking using ACCEPT post-editing rules for user-generated content; final check with pre-editing rules; XLIFF report.
- Statistics page: Final summary; editing statistics; XLIFF-based report (keystrokes, time); results download.

The ACCEPT Academic Portal can be freely accessed at: www.accept-portal.unige.ch.

---

[1] *ACCEPT: Automated Community Content Editing PorTal*, FP7 grant agreement 288769 (www.accept-project.eu; accessed: March, 2015).
[2] www.accept-portal.com (Accessed: March, 2015).

Russian-Chinese Sentence-level Aligned News Corpus

Wenjun Du
Luoyang University of Foreign Languages
471003 Luoyang, Henan, China
13014792136@163.com

Wuying Liu*
School of Foreign Language, Linyi University
276005 Linyi, Shandong, China
wyliu@lyu.edu.cn

Junting Yu
Luoyang University of Foreign Languages
471003 Luoyang, Henan, China
junting_yu@163.com

Mianzhu Yi
Luoyang University of Foreign Languages
471003 Luoyang, Henan, China
mianzhuyi@gmail.com

Summary

With the continuous development of Sino-Russian cooperation in the political, economic, diplomatic, and security, Russian-Chinese and Chinese-Russian translations are becoming more and more important. The Russian-Chinese Sentence-level Aligned News (RCSAN) corpus is a list of bilingual sentence pairs and is checked by linguists and domain experts. The RCSAN corpus contains total 59,332 pairs of Russian-Chinese sentences, which are extracted manually from raw Russian-Chinese news documents on the Internet websites in various domains, for instance, political, economic, social, cultural, diplomatic, security, and sports. The RCSAN corpus is stored as UTF-8 code plain text, which can be used in computer-aided Translation, Tran lingual Information Processing, Statistical Machine Translation, and Natural Language Processing. Supported by the RCSAN corpus, we try to investigate sentence alignment methods, computer-aided translation methods, and machine translation evaluation methods in Russian to Chinese. The RCSAN corpus will be used as a translation memory in our Russia-Chinese news computer-aided translation system.

Figure 1. Snapshot of RCSAN Corpus.

* Corresponding Author.

HimL (Health in my Language)

Funding agency: European Union
Funding call identification: H2020-ICT-2014-1
Type of project: Innovation Action
Project ID number: 644402
http://www.himl.eu

List of partners
University of Edinburgh, United Kingdom (coordinator)
Charles University, Prague, Czech Republic
LMU Munich, Germany
Lingea, Czech Republic
NHS 24, United Kingdom
Cochrane, United Kingdom

Project duration: February 2015 — January 2018

Summary

To an ever-increasing extent, web-based services are providing a frontline for healthcare information in Europe. They help citizens find answers to their questions and help them understand and find the local services they need. However, due to the number of languages spoken in Europe, and the mobility of its population, there is a high demand for these services to be available in many languages. In order to satisfy this demand, we need to rely on automatic translation, as it is infeasible to manually translate into all languages requested. The aim of HimL is to use recent advances in machine translation to create and deploy a system for the automatic translation of public health information, with a special focus on meaning preservation. In particular, we will include recent work on domain adaptation, translation into morphologically rich languages, terminology management, and semantically enhanced machine translation to build reliable machine translation for the health domain. The aim will be to create usable, reliable, fully automatic translation of public health information, initially testing with translation from English into Czech, Polish, Romanian and German. In the HimL project we will iterate cycles of incorporating improvements into the MT systems, with careful evaluation and user acceptance testing.

MT-enhanced fuzzy matching with Transit NXT and STAR Moses

Nadira Hofmann
nadira.hofmann@star-group.net
www.star-group.net

Description

The STAR Group developed the translation memory system (TMS) Transit NXT and an SMT system based on Moses. It made sense to combine these two technologies in order to provide translators with assistance from both sources.

The first step was integration at a project-handling level: As with standard TMS, the text is first pretranslated using validated translations from the translation memory. The remaining "deltas" (new or changed segments) are sent to the MT engine for translation. This means that the translator is offered two types of suggestion for "deltas": Fuzzy matches from the translation memory and machine translations from the MT engine. The translator checks the suggestions, selects the one which is most suitable and, if necessary, makes any linguistic amendments: A fuzzy match must, by definition, always be amended, though an MT translation may not need to be.

In practice, it quickly became apparent that the MT quality is especially high for those segments for which there is also a very good fuzzy match. The reason for this was obvious: MT engines are typically trained using a customer-specific translation memory and therefore provide results which are linguistically very similar to any human translations that are available. In this quality range, it is viewing, reading and comparing the suggestions that cost translators the most time: Once the best suggestion is selected, amendments are negligible.

Therefore, the second step was to make it easier for the translator to make their selection: Fuzzy match and MT suggestion were combined into a single, joint translation suggestion. This makes the number of suggestions clearer and simplifies both checking and decision-making.

The third step addressed the question of how a combined suggestion from fuzzy match and MT suggestion should be displayed. For "classic" fuzzy matches, the translator needs to be able to compare the "old" and "new" segments, which therefore requires the corresponding additional information. In conjunction with MT suggestions, this is superfluous: It simply needs to be clear to the translator which part of the segment comes from the translation memory and which part from the MT engine.

The result is a compact translation suggestion that combines the advantages of a fuzzy match from a validated translation memory with the efficiency of an MT engine. With this "MT-enhanced fuzzy matching", the translator can focus on post-editing and minimise the time spent viewing, selecting and adapting translation suggestions from these two sources.

HandyCAT

Chris Hokamp and Qun Liu
{chokamp, qliu}@computing.dcu.ie

CNGL/ADAPT/Dublin City University
Project Website: http://handycat.github.io
Github: https://github.com/chrishokamp/handycat

Project Description

We present HandyCAT, a new open-source Computer Aided Translation (CAT) tool, designed specifically for conducting research on Computer-Aided Translation. The User Interface (UI) itself, as well as the backend services, such as the Translation Memory engine, the MT system interface, the concordancer, and the glossary engine, are completely open-source.

The HandyCAT UI is implemented as a web application which runs in any modern browser. HandyCAT uses the XLIFF standard, and supports the core elements from both the XLIFF 1.2 and XLIFF 2.0 standards. GraphTM, the graph-based translation memory component, supports the TMX format, as well as several text input formats.

We introduce a factorization of the core interface components which allows a CAT tool to be viewed as a collection of standalone components connected by consistent APIs, facilitating research on new user interactions such as multi-modal input and interface control, and on new components created specifically for the post-editing task. Because the tool is designed primarily for CAT research, we have also designed a logging API which allows component creators to design logging customizable logging behavior for their components.

Although several open-source CAT tools have already been developed, no web-based tool provides a full CAT ecosystem as an open-source platform, including all user interface components and data services. Because the backend data services are prerequisites for a modern CAT interface, it can be difficult to design and conduct new user studies using existing open-source interfaces.

HandyCAT is built around the concepts of *containers* and *interactive areas*. Any CAT tool has some standard components which can be presented to users in various ways. Both the visual presentation and the interaction design will have an impact on the translator's experience. Therefore, HandyCAT is designed to allow researchers to create parameterized components which are easy to test and modify.

Several translation services provide free and/or paid APIs to proprietary services such as translation memories, machine translation, and glossaries. Connecting these APIs with HandyCAT is straightforward, allowing users and researchers to quickly integrate new services, or existing services which may have designed for other purposes.

All components of HandyCAT are completely open-source, meaning that the tool can easily be extended and improved. Because modern CAT tools are complex applications, developing a baseline tool with standard features requires significant effort. By using HandyCAT, researchers can implement only the components relevant to their work, while relying on the platform to provide the core CAT tool functionality, and to provide the statistics and logging necessary for analysis.

TraMOOC: Translation for Massive Open Online Courses

Funding agency: The European Commission
Funding call identification: H2020-ICT-2014-1 - ICT-17-2014
Type of project: Innovation Action
Project ID number: 644333
http://www.tramooc.eu

List of partners
Humboldt Universität zu Berlin (UBER), Germany (coordinator)
Dublin City University (DCU), Ireland
The University of Edinburgh (UEDIN), UK
Ionian University (IURC), Greece
Stichting Katholieke Universiteit (Radboud University & Radboud UMC), The Netherlands
EASN Technology Innovation Services BVBA (EASN TIS), Belgium
Deluxe Media Europe Ltd (Deluxe Media Europe Ltd), UK
Stichting Katholieke Universiteit Brabant Universiteit van Tilburg, The Netherlands
IVERSITY GMBH (iversity.org), Germany
KNOWLEDGE 4 ALL FOUNDATION (K4A), UK

Project duration: February 2015 — January 2018

Summary

Massive open online courses have been growing rapidly in size and impact. TraMOOC aims at developing high-quality translation of all types of text genre included in MOOCs from English into eleven European and BRIC languages (DE, IT, PT, EL, DU, CS, BG, CR, PL, RU, ZH) that are hard to translate into and have weak MT support. Phrase-based and syntax-based SMT models will be developed for addressing language diversity and supporting the language-independent nature of the methodology. For a high quality, automatic translation approach and for adding value to existing infrastructure, extensive and advanced bootstrapping of new resources will be performed. An innovative multi-modal automatic and human evaluation schema will further ensure translation quality. For human evaluation, an innovative, strict-access control, time- and cost-efficient crowdsourcing setup will be used. Translation experts, domain experts and end users will also be involved. Separate task mining applications will be employed for implicit translation evaluation: (i) topic detection will be applied to source and translated texts and the resulting entity lists will be compared, leading to further qualitative and quantitative translation evaluation results; (ii) sentiment analysis performed on MOOC users' blog posts will reveal end user opinion/evaluation regarding translation quality. Results will be combined into a feedback vector and used to refine parallel data and retrain translation models towards a more accurate second phase translation output. The project results will be showcased and tested on the Iversity MOOC platform and on the VideoLectures.net digital video lecture library.

Streamlining Translation Workflows with StyleScorer

David Landan, Olga Beregovaya
<first.last>@welocalize.com
Welocalize, Inc.

Description

The need for quick-turnaround, high-volume machine translation (MT) projects continues to grow in the localization industry. There is a wide range of quality requirements not only across different clients, but often within a single client across different content types (sales & marketing materials, user-generated content, website content, user manuals, etc.). Most clients have style guides or manuals which translators and post-editors are instructed to adhere to, and there may be different styles for the different content types. To help balance the increase in project complexity with clients' needs for faster turnaround times, we created the StyelScorer tool.

StyleScorer compares a new (candidate) document against two or more other documents (the training set); it assigns the candidate document a score between 0 and 4 (higher scores indicate greater stylistic similarity between the candidate document and the training set). StyleScorer generates this score via a weighted combination of several components, including document dissimilarity, perplexity, and unary classification using both neural networks and support vector machines. The candidate document and training set must be written in the same language (for best results, they should be the same locale as well), and the documents in the training set should have internal consistency of style.

We have found StyleScorer to be useful in various stages of the translation workflow by using it on both source- and target-language documents. Many clients wishing to start a new MT program don't have sufficient bilingual assets to train a targeted MT system. By looking for open-source bilingual data where the source-language text is a close stylistic match to the client's training set, we increase the amount of bilingual training data available to build relevant in-domain MT engines.

Once an MT system is deployed, we can use StyleScorer on source-language documents to obtain an estimate of MT output quality by scoring candidate documents against a training set created from the MT engine training set. We can then use StyleScorer on a target-language training set to estimate the amount of post-editing effort required to bring the MT output in line with the desired target-language style. The benefits here are two-fold: documents above a given threshold can be automatically marked as passing, and post-editors can focus their attention on the lower-scoring documents.

We are now also experimenting with using StyleScorer as part of the linguistic QA process. Randomly selected post-edited documents are checked against the target-language test set. Low scoring documents are given a second round of review, with two possible outcomes: further post-edits are required before the document is given a passing grade, or the low-scoring document is deemed acceptable. In the latter case, we update the training set with new target-language documents to accurately capture the acceptable style patterns.

Sõjakooli Sõnastik
Estonian-English Reversible Smart Phone Dictionary
of Military Terms and Relevant Vocabulary

Epp Leete, MA, Translator, Head of Translation and Editing Group
Estonian National Defence College
https://play.google.com/store/apps/details?id=mobi.lab.wardict

Description

The smart phone dictionary for Android phones and tablets is being developed by a team that includes a translator, terminologist, English teachers, native speakers of English (a linguist and a person with a military background), and servicemen as needed. As of April 2015 there are about 1200 entries.

Entries come from two main sources: translations and curricula of the ENDC. All entries are harmonized with language and subject matter experts before entering them in the dictionary, e.g. firearm parts were synchronized with a firing instructor, terminologist and English native speaker before teaching the subject in English classes. In this way, in addition to making specialised vocabulary available, a more harmonized use of specialised language is ensured both in English and Estonian.

Features:

- Military terms and relevant general vocabulary (environment, medicine), phrases;
- Fields: education, structure of the ENDC and EDF, weaponry, equipment, R&D, administration and services, general military (flexible, can be added or deleted anytime);
- Entry fields in L1 and L2: word/term, abbreviation, definition, field, source (for definition), note;
- Works offline and renews every two weeks;
- Can be linked to MemoQ and other translation environments.

Word or Term?

Although the difference between a term and a word is very clear in theory, it is less clear in reality. As a general rule, a word becomes a term when defined or explained.

In order to decide whether a linguistic unit is a term or not, the needs of potential users (servicemen, students, employees) are taken into account. For example, *densely forested* does not have to be defined in a military setting, although it should probably be clearly defined in a dictionary of forestry in order to distinguish it from other types of forested areas.

Points of Discussion

Considering the hard work that definition compilation entails, very often notes are added instead of definitions, e.g. *trigger* (*in a pistol, assault rifle*); *trigger bar* (in a pistol): here a note indicates which weapons have a particular part instead of defining it.

The terms that signify basic military concepts (e.g. *ammunition, pistol, assault rifle*) are not defined, as potential users are expected to know the meaning (compared with civilians who might not be able to distinguish between *pistol* and *assault rifle* (calling them both *weapon*), or *armoured personnel carrier*, *infantry fighting vehicle*, and even *main battle tank* (calling them all *tank*)).

One issue to be settled with regard to linking the dictionary to a translation environment is how to handle single/multiple L1 entries with multiple L2 equivalents, e.g. *branch*, *arm* and *service arm* for *relvaliik;* or *loomevargus, plagiaat* for *intellectual property theft, plagiarism,* without creating separate entries for one and the same concept.

FALCON: Federated Active Linguistic data CuratiON

Building the Localization Web

EU FP7
SME STREP
ICT SME-DCA Call 2013, FP7-ICT-2013-SME-DCA
No. 610875
http://www.falcon-project.eu

List of partners
Trinity College Dublin, Ireland
XTM International, UK
Interverbum Technology, Sweden
Dublin City University, Ireland
SKAWA Innovation, Hungary

Project duration: Oct 2013 — Sept 2015

Summary

FALCON assembles a state of the art online translation tool chain that combines web site translation, translation management, computer aided translation and terminology management products. This tool chain tool chain has been enhanced with open-source automatic term extraction and machine translation technology. Iterative quality improvement in this language technology is delivered by using linked data to actively manage the curation and reuse of language resources within customer projects. The work demonstrates the integration the management of iterative SMT training with active curation of MT corrections and target term capture by post-editors in a live localisation workflow using this commercial tool chain. Key capabilities offered are:

- Targeting of translator effort to rapidly bootstrap automation quality; Translator judgements are the source of all resources used in machine translation and multilingual text analytics. Active curation targets available translator skills to optimise the improvement of language technology quality through incremental training. Specifically, the order of segment post-editing it optimised to harvest and integrate corrections to poor MT and translation of important terms as early as possible in a project.
- Building MT-ready terminology: Morphologically-rich multilingual terminology resources can dramatically improve MT quality through forced decoding of terms in source segments to their known translations
- Open Data for the analysis and reuse of translations and terms; Analysis of how available language resources can be applied to streams of new content will benefit from open data, provenance and licensing information formats to facilitate the discovery, selection, negotiation and reuse of resources, including those continuously generated by new translation projects and released through the public sector.

Tapadóir

The Department of Arts, Heritage and the Gaeltacht, Govt. of Ireland
MT development for translation workflow

List of partners
CNGL/ADAPT, Ireland
National Centre for Language Technology, Ireland
Dublin City University, Ireland
Department of Arts, Heritage and the Gaeltacht, Government of Ireland

Project duration: July 2014 — January 2016

Summary

Tapadóir (from the Irish “tapa” – fast) is a statistical machine translation project which has just completed its pilot phase. The heart of the project is the development of an English–Irish translation system, intended for integration into the workflow of a professional translator at an Irish government department. In practice, this means statistical machine translation from a highly-resourced majority language (English) to an under-resourced minority language (Irish) with significant linguistic differences. A secondary aim is the production of English–Irish parallel corpora suitable for future translation tool and NLP developers.

There is high demand for Irish-language translated texts within Irish government departments, and this MT integration aims to increase the speed of translation to meet this demand. Tapadóir currently out-performs (based on BLEU score) Google Translate on data from our use case domain (official government documents and reports). The official European Commission machine translation service, MT@EC, rate their English-to-Irish MT system as suitable for gist translation, but below useful editable quality, the standard required by the client. While MT@EC also build custom pilot projects based on existing user data, the client’s data is limited. Therefore, further data collection constitutes a large proportion this project’s remit.

English-to-Irish translation holds a number of challenges. From an NLP perspective, Irish is very much under-resourced, and much of the project so far has focused on corpus development. The target language is also morphologically much richer than the source (e.g. initial mutations, synthetic verb forms, case), and the resulting data sparsity further compounds the these translation challenges. Linguistically, the language pair word order is divergent (Subject-Verb-Object vs. Verb-Subject-Object), with other word order differences at lower levels, such as adjectives following nouns, and the genitive noun following its possessed object in Irish.

To cope with this, we are currently developing source-side reordering rules to address word-order divergence, and we are exploring ways to overcome the morphological discrepancies. Our aim is to use various methods to provide useful machine translation output for an unusual and challenging language pair. Rather than aiming to investigate the general effectiveness of particular methods, we are attempting to find the best practical combination for this resource-poor and linguistically challenging use-case. We expect that our work will be of use to developers of MT systems for other under-resourced languages.

The Tapadóir MT engine will be deployed for in-house use by the Irish Department of Arts, Heritage and the Gaeltacht. However, we hope to make freely available the resources gathered/created over the course of its development, for the sake of future Irish-language projects.

Okapi+QuEst: Translation Quality Estimation within Okapi

Gustavo Henrique Paetzold, University of Sheffield, ghpaetzold1@sheffield.ac.uk
Lucia Specia, University of Sheffield, l.specia@sheffield.ac.uk
Yves Savourel, ENLASO, ysavourel@enlaso.com
https://bitbucket.org/okapiframework/quest

Description

Due to the ever growing applicability of machine translation, estimating the quality of translations automatically has become a necessary task in various scenarios, for example, when deciding whether a machine translation is good enough for human post-editing. This demonstration presents the outcome of a collaborative project between the University of Sheffield and ENLASO, funded by EAMT, the European Association for Machine Translation. The project aimed to integrate a lightweight and user-friendly version of QuEst (http://www.quest.dcs.shef.ac.uk/) – a quality estimation toolkit, into Okapi (http://www.opentag.com/okapi/) – a framework with various components and applications designed to help create and improve translation and localisation processes. As result, Okapi users are now offered a software plugin to build and apply quality estimation models for translations produced within the framework. In addition to the standard functionalities of QuEst, the project involved the creation of new methods to facilitate the generation of the linguistic resources necessary for building quality estimation models.

When installed in the Okapi Framework, the QuEst plugin introduces three "steps" to the Okapi Pipeline, which includes 75 other steps (for example, a Moses translation step). Users can create translation quality estimation tasks by adding the relevant QuEst steps to their pipeline. The three steps provided by the QuEst plugin in Okapi are:

- **SVM Model Builder step**: Provides an easy way for users to extract features from texts and train translation quality estimation models using the LibSVM tool. These models can then be used by the Quality Estimation step.

- **Quality Estimation step**: Allows users to apply an existing quality estimation model or a model created by the SVM Model Builder step to produce quality estimation scores for new translations.

- **Properties Setting step**: Gathers the quality estimation scores produced by the Quality Estimation step and place them into an XLIFF which can be interpreted by annotation tools such as Ocelot (http://open.vistatec.com/) and used in annotation tasks, such as quality inspection by humans.

The Okapi version with QuEst can be downloaded from https://code.google.com/p/okapi-quest/. The tool is free, open-source and cross-platform (Java). It is easy to install and is provided with clear documentation through wikipages with step-by-step tutorials. Different from the standalone version of QuEst, it produces most necessary linguistic resources automatically to help inexperienced users. Following Okapi's tradition, the tool offers a graphical interface, making it easier to use.

CRACKER: Cracking the Language Barrier

EC, Horizon 2020, ICT17, Coordination and Support Action, GA No. 645357

http://www.cracker-project.eu

List of partners
Deutsches Forschungszentrum für Künstliche Intelligenz GmbH, Germany (Coordinator: Georg Rehm)
Charles University in Prague, Czech Republic
Evaluations and Language Resources Distribution Agency SA, France
Fondazione Bruno Kessler, Italy
Athena Research and Innovation Center in Information, Communication and Knowledge Technologies, Greece
University of Edinburgh, UK
University of Sheffield, UK

Project duration: January 2015 – December 2017

Summary

The European machine translation (MT) research community is experiencing increased pressure for rapid success – from the legal and political frameworks and schedules of the EU, such as the Digital Single Market, but also from the globalising business world. At the same time, the research community has to cope with a striking disproportion between the scope of the challenges and the available resources, especially for translation to and from languages that have only fragmentary or no technological support at all.

CRACKER pushes towards an improvement of MT research in terms of efficiency and effectiveness by implementing the successful example of other disciplines where massively collaborative research on shared resources – guided by interoperability, standardisation, agreed major challenges and comprehensive success metrics – has led to breakthroughs that would have been impossible otherwise. The nucleus of this new research, development, and innovation strategy towards high-quality MT is the group of projects funded through Horizon 2020 Call ICT-17a/b (QT21, HiML, TraMOOC, MMT, partly extending to relevant FP7 actions such as QTLeap, LIDER and MLi), that will be supported by CRACKER (ICT-17c) in coordination, evaluation and resources.

In order to achieve its challenging goals efficiently, CRACKER will build upon, consolidate and extend initiatives for collaborative MT research supported by earlier EU-funded actions. These include evaluation campaigns such as the Workshop on Statistical Machine Translation (WMT) and the International Workshop on Spoken Language Translation (IWSLT), the META-SHARE open infrastructure for sharing language resources and technologies with extensions for MT assembled by QTLaunchPad, and open-source tool building and training (MT Marathons). Coordination, communication and outreach to user communities will build upon existing networks and communication infrastructures such as the META-FORUM event series and strong involvement of industrial associations.

LTCKnowHow: Empowering the Social Enterprise in the Language Industry

Dr Adriane Rinsche
The Language Technology Centre
www.ltcinnovates.com

Description

The "KnowHow" project, partly funded by the EU Research Executive Agency project scaled up the existing OrganiK Knowledge Management platform (http://www.organik-project.eu) from the research prototype it was into an industrial-grade *knowledge management platform as a service* (KM-PaaS) that supports social business applications. LTC's role as a project partner was to produce a final product, which will support the social enterprise in the language industry (LI) and produced LTCKnowHow

LTCKnowHow is a standalone platform as a service which captures knowledge assets, such as user guides, process manuals, product descriptions as well as discussion comments and other informal contributions company-wide and uses intelligent information processing components to improve the collaboration among customers, internal staff and external LSPs. Using the content analyzer, recommender, and semantic search components, knowledge assets from customers and external LSPs can be intelligently captured, filtered, stored, and reused.

Users access a flexible structure of workspaces for a particular topic such as a project, client, internal company procedures, R&D problem or support query amongst the many other possible sources of information that can be stored in the system. Using this platform, users can discuss and share knowledge in a user friendly environment. All posted content is searchable using groundbreaking semantic features and a content recommender system, which suggest useful content based on the users' browsing activities.

LTC has implemented the system across its entire business functions and is engaging in trials to evaluate and quantify the outcome of the initial project objectives in order to deliver a unique product tailored to the LI market. By using LTC KnowHow companies in the Language Industry can expect:

- Faster and even more reliable average project quality and delivery times. Question-answering functionality is improved for stakeholders in the production process. Easily accessible knowledge assets can help resolve problems such as subject context and specific terminology, while bottlenecks in project management can also be identified and removed. Furthermore, the smooth operations resulting from social collaboration within the enterprise will reduce the risk of severe project delays, while keeping project managers and stakeholders better informed to support other service benefits.
- Increased customer satisfaction. Customer support issues are both managed clearly and solved quicker. Through efficient problem solving, the information that is made available is both presented quickly and is relevant. The visibility of the process and collaboration also increases value.
- Increased intelligence for R&D and new product development. By interacting more closely with customers, suppliers and partners, all stakeholders will be able to contribute interactively to product enhancements and new product development.

- Improved operations management. Information discovery and retrieval will help boost operational efficiency. General operational policies and guidelines are at users' fingertips and changes and updates can be communicated clearly whilst operational uncertainties are discussed and resolved centrally.

Multi-Dialect Machine Translation (MuDMaT)

Natural Science and Engineering Research Council of Canada (NSERC) Research Project NSERC 356097-2008

List of partners

Fatiha Sadat, University of Quebec in Montreal, QC, Canada (coordinator)

Project duration: January 2014 — December 2017

Summary

The Multi-Dialect Machine Translation (MuDMaT) project aims to encourage research and development of Machine Translation (MT) systems for less resourced languages and their variants or dialects. More specifically, the MuDMaT project deals with three Maghrebi (North African) Arabic dialects for machine translation with very scarce resources: the Tunisian, the Algerian and the Moroccan. Many ideas of this project can be applied to any less-resourced language variant or dialect.

In this project, an Arabic dialect can play a role as a source dialect in machine translation system when translating into French with considering the Modern Standard Arabic (MSA) as pivot language. Moreover, this dialect can play a role as a target dialect when translating from French and/or MSA. A third translation module focuses on translations from a dialect into another dialect using MSA as pivot language.

At the current stage, MuDMaT targets building hybrid statistical and rule-based machine translation systems from multiple Arabic dialects into MSA and French and vice versa. Statistical machine translation based on parallel corpora has been very successful and widely used in major translation systems' engines. Our interest in this project focuses on comparable corpora, which are defined as monolingual corpora covering roughly the same subject area or author's name or dates in different languages but without being exact translations of each other. In our project, comparable corpora are built by mining the World Wide Web and more specifically the social media such as blogs. Other linguistic resources such as lexicons (and grammar) that are automatically extracted from the Web or collaboratively built (through crowdsourcing) are exploited in this multi-dialect translation system.

The project has already been running for a year and a demonstration using the Tunisian dialect in a rule-based translation system for translating texts into MSA and French was achieved. We are working towards the construction of more linguistic resources such as comparable and parallel corpora for the Tunisian dialect and MSA that will help enhance the hybrid statistical and rule-based MT system. The other North African Arabic dialects will be included in the rule-based translation system during this research project.

The availability of the multi-dialect machine translation system will be through the years 2015, 2016 and 2017.

АБУМАТРАН
ABUMATRAN

Abu-MaTran: Automatic building of Machine Translation

FP7-PEOPLE-2012-IAPP
http://www.abumatran.eu

List of partners	
DCU	Dublin City University, Ireland (coordinator)
prompsit	Prompsit Language Engineering SL, Spain
Universitat d'Alacant Universidad de Alicante	Universitat d'Alacant, Spain
	University of Zagreb, Faculty of Humanities and Social Sciences, Croatia
IEA ILSP	Athena Research and Innovation Center in Information Communication & Knowledge Technologies, Greece

Project duration: January 2013 — December 2016

Summary

Abu-MaTran seeks to enhance industry–academia cooperation as a key aspect to tackle one of Europe's biggest challenges: multilingualism. We aim to increase the hitherto low industrial adoption of machine translation by identifying crucial cutting-edge research techniques (automatic acquisition of corpora and linguistic resources, pivot-language techniques, linguistically augmented statistical translation and diagnostic evaluation), making them suitable for commercial exploitation. We also aim to transfer back to academia the know-how of industry to make research results more robust. We work on a case study of strategic interest for Europe: machine translation for the language of a new member state (Croatian) and related languages. All the resources produced will be released as free/open-source software, resulting in effective knowledge transfer beyond the consortium. The project has a strong emphasis on dissemination, through the organisation of workshops that focus on inter-sectoral knowledge transfer. Finally, we have a comprehensive outreach plan, including the establishment of a Linguistic Olympiad in Spain, open-day activities and the participation in the Google Summer of Code.

At EAMT 2015 we will present the results of the second milestone of the project (December 2014). To mention just a few: (i) MT systems for English–Croatian based on free/open-source software and web crawled and publicly available data, both generic and specific for the tourism domain, (ii) tools developed in the project (e.g. web crawling of parallel data and paradigm guessing) and (iii) outcomes of the project's dissemination activities (e.g. software management for researchers, data creation for RBMT systems and establishment of a linguistics Olympiad).

MNH-TT: A Platform to Support Collaborative Translator Training

Masao Utiyama, Kyo Kageura, Martin Thomas, Anthony Hartley
NICT/University of Tokyo/University of Leeds/Rikkyo University
https://edu.ecom.trans-aid.jp (currently with basic authentication)

Description

Recent research in translator training has shown the importance of bringing the actual translation situation into the teaching setup (Kiraly, 2000). As most real-world translations are carried out not on a personal basis but on a project basis, this implies that trainees need to gain competence not only in translation in its narrower sense but also in how to play a role in, carry out, and manage translation projects (cf. CEN, 2006).

Against this backdrop, we are developing the web-based system MNH-TT (Minna no Hon'yaku[1] for Translator Training), which assists and promotes collaborative translator training that emulates real-world translation situations[2]. The system has the following features:

(1) Facilitating project-based translator training: Translation training in MNH-TT is carried out on the basis of a translation project. Learners take part in the project with different roles and carry out different tasks such as project management, making a brief, translation, revision, terminology management, etc.

(2) Supporting learners by providing standard action categories in important aspects of translation: Project participants are guided to communicate with other participants in a certain way, in the process learning the essential elements of project-based collaborative translation. The translation editor guides revisers and reviewers to use pre-defined error categories (Secară, 2005), through which learners become conscious of error types.

(3) Accumulating logs of activities and promoting reflective learning: MNH-TT takes (a) revision logs, (b) reference lookup logs, and (c) dialogue act logs. These logs can be looked up in summary format by individual project participants or by instructors. They not only promote reflective self-learning but also enable instructors to diagnose learners' weak and strong points. In addition, once a sufficient number of logs have been accumulated, they can be used as the basis for developing methods for automatically guiding trainee translators.

The essential parts of the system are fully operational as of now, with interfaces in English, Japanese, German, Chinese and Korean, and is being tested by trial users, which include University of Granada, Kobe College, Tokyo University of Foreign Studies, University of Leeds, Univeresity of Tübingen, Rikkyo University, and University of Tokyo.

References:

CEN (2006) *EN 15038: European Quality Standard for Translation Services*. European Committee for Standardization.

Kilary, D. (2000) *A Social Constructivist Approach to Translator Education*. Manchester: St. Jerome Press.

Secară, A. (2005) "Translation evaluation: a state of the art survey," *Proceedings of the eCoLoRe/MeLLANGE Workshop*.

[1] Minna no Hon'yaku means "translation by/of/for all".

[2] This work is partly supported by JSPS Grant-in-Aid (A) 25240051 "Archiving and using translation knowledge to construct collaborative translation training aid system."

Smart Computer Aided Translation Environment – SCATE

IWT – Agentschap voor Innovatie door Wetenschap en Technologie
Strategic basic research
Project Nr. 130041
http://www.ccl.kuleuven.be/scate

University of Leuven (CCL - ESAT/PSI - LIIR – Fac. Arts Antwerp), Belgium
University of Ghent (LT3), Belgium
Hasselt University (tUL - iMinds, Expertise Centre for Digital Media), Belgium

Project duration: March 2014 – February 2018

Summary

We aim at improving the translators' efficiency through five different **scientific objectives**.
Concerning **improvements in translation technology**, we are investigating syntax-based fuzzy matching in which we estimate similarity based on syntactic edit distance or similar measures. We are working on syntax-based MT using synchronous tree substitution grammars induced from parallel node-aligned treebanks, and are building a decoder to use these grammars in translation.
Concerning **improvements in evaluation of computer-aided translation**, we have developed a taxonomy of typical MT errors and are constructing a manually annotated corpus of 3000 segments of Google Translate MT errors. Post-editing behaviour of translators is being monitored.
Concerning **improvements in automated terminology extraction from comparable corpora**, we have developed C-BiLDA, a multilingual topic model. It does not assume linked documents to have identical topic distributions. On the task of cross-lingual document categorization, we trained it on a comparable corpus of Wikipedia documents, and inferred cross-lingual document representations on a dataset for document categorization. The document representations and category labels are fed to an SVM classifier: we train on the source language and predict the labels for the target language documents. C-BiLDA outperforms the state-of-the-art in multilingual topic modeling.
Concerning **improvements in speech recognition accuracy,** we clustered words by their translations in multiple languages. If words share a translation in many languages, they are considered synonyms. By adding context and by filtering out those that do not belong to the same part of speech, we find meaningful word clusters to incorporate into a language model. We found no improvements, and attribute this in part to errors made by the MT system and to the incorporation technique (hard clustered class-based n-grams). We will take context into account during evaluation and/or further improve the word clusters by using the translations as features in vector space modeling techniques.
Concerning **improvements in work flows and personalised user interfaces**, we *reviewed existing translation systems*, and created an inventory of the various features and configuration options of the systems. Six Flemish companies are *interviewed* regarding their practices and their vision for future CAT tools. A *worldwide survey* has been conducted with more than 135 responses. Detailed analyses of translators' practices have been conducted by observing more than 7 translators by conducting a *contextual inquiry*.
In the upcoming period, the results of the different studies will be analysed in order to obtain a model of how CAT tools can support workflows for specific translators. This model will be used as a base for the personalised visualisations as part of interfaces for translation work. In contrast with traditional engineering approaches, this model will also be usable by translators as part of the configuration of their personal CAT tool.